Practical Artificial Intelligence

Machine Learning, Bots, and Agent Solutions Using C#

Arnaldo Pérez Castaño

Apress®

Practical Artificial Intelligence

Arnaldo Pérez Castaño
Havana, Cuba

ISBN-13 (pbk): 978-1-4842-3356-6   ISBN-13 (electronic): 978-1-4842-3357-3
https://doi.org/10.1007/978-1-4842-3357-3

Library of Congress Control Number: 2018943123

Managing Director, Apress Media LLC: Welmoed Spahr
Acquisitions Editor: Natalie Pao
Development Editor: James Markham
Coordinating Editor: Jessica Vakili

Cover designed by eStudioCalamar

Cover image designed by Freepik (www.freepik.com)

Distributed to the book trade worldwide by Springer Science+Business Media New York, 233 Spring Street, 6th Floor, New York, NY 10013. Phone 1-800-SPRINGER, fax (201) 348-4505, email orders-ny@springer-sbm.com, or visit www.springeronline.com. Apress Media, LLC is a California LLC and the sole member (owner) is Springer Science + Business Media Finance Inc (SSBM Finance Inc). SSBM Finance Inc is a **Delaware** corporation.

For information on translations, please email rights@apress.com, or visit http://www.apress.com/rights-permissions.

Apress titles may be purchased in bulk for academic, corporate, or promotional use. eBook versions and licenses are also available for most titles. For more information, reference our Print and eBook Bulk Sales web page at http://www.apress.com/bulk-sales.

Any source code or other supplementary material referenced by the author in this book is available to readers on GitHub via the book's product page, located at www.apress.com/9781484233566. For more detailed information, please visit http://www.apress.com/source-code.

Printed on acid-free paper

To ML, thanks for the theater and the lovely moments

*To my mother, my father, my brother, my grandma,
and my entire family, thanks for your immense support*

Table of Contents

About the Author

Arnaldo Pérez Castaño is a computer scientist based in Havana, Cuba. He's the author of *PrestaShop Recipes* (Apress, 2017) and a series of programming books—*JavaScript Fácil, HTML y CSS Fácil*, and *Python Fácil* (Marcombo S.A.)—and writes AI-related articles for *MSDN* Magazine, VisualStudio Magazine.com, and *Smashing* Magazine. He is one of the co-founders of Cuba Mania Tour (`http://www.cubamaniatour.com`).

His expertise includes Java, VB, Python, algorithms, optimization, Matlab, C#, .NET Framework, and artificial intelligence. Arnaldo offers his services through `freelancer.com` and served as reviewer for the *Journal of Mathematical Modelling and Algorithms in Operations Research*. Cinema and music are some of his passions. Many of his colleagues around the world call him "Scientist of the Caribbean." He can be reached at `arnaldo.skywalker@gmail.com`.

About the Technical Reviewer

James McCaffrey works in the Machine Learning Group at Microsoft Research in Redmond, WA. James has a Ph.D. in cognitive psychology and computational statistics from the University of Southern California, a BA in psychology, a BA in applied mathematics, and an MS in computer science. James is a frequent speaker at developer conferences. James learned to speak to the public while working at Disneyland as a college student, and he can still recite the entire Jungle Cruise ride narration from memory.

Acknowledgments

First of all, a big thank you to Dr. James McCaffrey from Microsoft Research in Redmond, WA, who kindly accepted the role of technical reviewer of this book. I e-met James when writing articles for *MSDN* Magazine. His comments at that time were always very useful, and they continued to be extremely useful throughout the review process of this book. I must also thank James for his patience because what it was supposed to be a nine-chapter book eventually became a seventeen-chapter book, and he stood up with us along the way.

Another thank you must go to my editors, Pao Natalie and Jessica Vakili, who were also very patient and understanding during the writing process.

Finally, I would like to acknowledge all researchers on AI/machine learning out there who day after day try to push this very important field of science forward with new advancements, techniques, and ideas. Thank you, all!

Introduction

Practical Artificial Intelligence (PAI) is a book that proposes a new model for learning. Most AI books deeply focus on theory and abandon practical problems that demonstrate the theory introduced throughout the book. In PAI we propose a model that follows Benjamin Franklin's (Founding Father of the United States of America) ideas: *"Tell me and I forget. Teach me and I remember. Involve me and I learn."* Therefore, PAI includes theoretical knowledge but guarantees that at least one fully coded (C#) practical problem is included in every chapter as a way to allow readers to better understand and as a way to get them involved with the theoretical concepts and ideas introduced during the chapter. These practical problems can be executed by readers using the code associated with this book and should give them a better insight into the concepts herein described.

Explanations and definitions included in PAI are intended to be as simple as they can be (not putting aside the fact that they belong to a mathematical, scientific environment) so readers from different backgrounds can engage with the content and understand it using minimal mathematical or programming knowledge.

Chapters 1 and 2 explore logic as a fundamental founding block of many sciences, like mathematics or computer science. In these chapters, we will describe propositional logic, first-order logic, and automated theorem proving; related practical problems coded in C# will be presented.

Throughout chapters 3–7, we will focus on agents and multi-agent systems. We'll dive into the different types of agents and their architectures, then we'll present a big practical problem where we'll code a Mars Rover whose task is to find water on Mars. We'll include another practical problem where we set up a group of agents to communicate using Windows Communication Foundation (WCF), and finally, we'll end this part of the book by presenting another practical problem (Chapter 7) where a group of agents forming a multi-agent system will collaborate and communicate to clean a room of its dirt.

Chapter 8 will describe a sub-field of AI known as simulation, where by using statistical, probabilistic tools we simulate a scenario of real life. In this case, we'll simulate the functioning of an airport, with airplanes arriving at and departing from the airport during a certain period of time.

Chapters 9–12 will be dedicated to supervised learning, a very important paradigm of machine learning where we basically teach a machine (program) to do something (usually classify data) by presenting it with many samples of pairs `<data, classification>`, where `data` could be anything; it could be animals, houses, people, and so on. For instance, a sample set could be `<elephant, big>`, `<cat, small>`, and so forth. Clearly, for the machine to be able to understand and process any data we must input numerical values instead of text. Throughout these chapters we will explore support vector machines, decision trees, neural networks, and handwritten digit recognition.

Chapter 13 will explain another very important paradigm of machine learning, namely unsupervised learning. In unsupervised learning we learn the structure of the data received as input, and there are no labels (classifications) as occurred in supervised learning; in other words, samples are simply `<data>`, and no classification is included. Thus, an unsupervised learning program learns without any external help and by looking only at the information provided by the data itself. In this chapter, we will describe clustering, a classic unsupervised learning technique. We will also describe multi-objetive clustering and multi-objective optimization. A method for constructing the Pareto Frontier, namely Pareto Frontier Builder, proposed by the author, will be included in this chapter.

Chapter 14 will focus on heuristics and metaheuristics, a topic we will be mentioning in previous chapters and will finally be studied here. We will describe mainly two metaheuristics: genetic algorithms and tabu search, which are two of the main representatives of the broadest classes of metaheuristics, which are population-based metaheuristics and single solution–based metaheuristics.

Chapter 15 will explore the world of game programming, specifically games where executing a search is necessary. Many of the popular search algorithms will be detailed and implemented. A practical problem where we design and code a sliding tiles puzzle agent will also be included.

Chapter 16 will dive into game theory, in particular a sub-field of it known as adversarial search. In this field, we will study the Minimax algorithm and implement an Othello agent that plays using this strategy (Minimax).

Chapter 17 will describe a machine-learning paradigm that nowadays is considered the future of artificial intelligence; this paradigm is reinforcement learning. In reinforcement learning, agents learn through rewards and punishment; they learn over time like humans do, and when the learning process is long enough they can achieve highly competitive levels in a game, up to the point of beating a human world champion (as occurred with backgammon and Go).

CHAPTER 1

Logic & AI

In this chapter, we'll introduce a topic that is vital not only to the world of artificial intelligence (AI) but also to many other areas of knowledge, such as mathematics, physics, medicine, philosophy, and so on. It has been deeply studied and formalized since ancient times by great philosophers like Aristotle, Euclid, and Plato and by some of the greatest mathematicians of all time. Born in the early ages of mankind, it represents a basic tool that allowed science to flourish up to the point where it is today. It clarifies and straightens our complicated human minds and brings order to our sometimes disordered thoughts.

Logic, this matter to which we have been referring thus far, will be the main focus of this chapter. We'll be explaining some of its fundamental notions, concepts, and branches, as well as its relation to computer science and AI. This subject is fundamental to understanding many of the concepts that will be addressed throughout this book. Furthermore, how can we create a decent artificial intelligence without logic? Logic directs rationality in our mind; therefore, how can we create an artificial version of our mind if we bypass that extremely important element (logic) that is present in our "natural" intelligence and dictates decisions in many cases—or, to be precise, rational decisions.

Propositional logic; first-order logic; practical problems where we'll learn how to create a logic framework, how to solve the SAT (satisfiability) problem using an outstanding algorithm called DPLL, and how to code a first, simple, naive cleaning robot using first-order logic components—these topics will get us started in this book.

© Arnaldo Pérez Castaño 2018
A. Pérez Castaño, *Practical Artificial Intelligence*,
https://doi.org/10.1007/978-1-4842-3357-3_1

Note   Logic can be branched into mathematical logic, philosophical logic, computational logic, Boolean logic, fuzzy logic, quantum logic, and so forth. In this book, we will be dealing with computational logic, the field related to those areas of computer science and logic that necessarily overlap.

What Is Logic?

Intuitively we all have a notion of what logic is and how useful it can be in our daily lives. Despite this common sense or cultural concept of logic, surprisingly there is, in the scientific community, no formal or global definition (as of today) of what logic is.

In seeking a definition from its founding fathers, we could go back in time to its roots and discover that the word *logic* actually derives from the Ancient Greek *logike*, which translates as "concept, idea, or thought."

Some theorists have defined logic as "the science of thought." Even though this definition appears to be a decent approximation of what we typically associate with logic, it's not a very accurate definition because logic is not the only science related to the study of thoughts and reasoning. The reality is that this subject is so deeply ingrained at the foundation of all other sciences that it's hard to provide a formal definition for it.

In this book, we'll think of logic as a way to formalize human reasoning.

Since computational logic is the branch of logic that relates to computer science, we'll be describing some important notions on this subject. Ultimately, the concepts described here will be useful throughout this book and in every practical problem to be presented.

Note   Logic is used extensively in computer science: at the processor level by means of logical gates, in hardware and software verification such as floating-point arithmetic, in high-level programming like constraint programming, and in artificial intelligence for problems such as planning, scheduling, agents control, and so forth.

Propositional Logic

In daily life and during our human communication process, we constantly listen to expressions of the language that possess a certain meaning; among these we can find the propositions.

Propositions are statements that can be classified according to their veracity (True or 1, False or 0, etc.) or according to their modality (probable, impossible, necessary, etc.). Every proposition expresses a certain thought that represents its meaning and content. Because of the wide variety of expressions in our language, they can be classified as narratives, exclamatory, questioning, and so forth. In this book, we'll focus on the first type of proposition, narratives, which are expressions of judgment, and we'll simply call them propositions from this point on.

The following list presents a few examples of propositions:

1. "Smoking damages your health."

2. "Michael Jordan is the greatest basketball player of all time."

3. "Jazz is the coolest musical genre in the world."

4. "100 is greater than 1."

5. "There are wonderful beaches in Havana."

6. "World War II ended in 1945."

7. "I listen to Sting's music."

8. "I will read poems from Spanish poet Rafael Alberti."

These are **simple** or **atomic propositions** that we can use in any ordinary day during any ordinary conversation. In order to add complexity and transform them into something a bit more meaningful we can rely on **compound propositions**, which are obtained by means of logical connectors linking simple propositions like the ones previously listed.

Hence, from the propositions just listed we could obtain the following (not necessarily correct or meaningful) compound propositions.

1. "There are NOT wonderful beaches in Havana."

2. "Smoking damages your health AND 100 is greater than 1."

3. "Michael Jordan is the greatest basketball player of all time OR World War II ended in 1945."

4. "IF Jazz is the coolest musical genre in the world THEN I listen to Sting's music."

5. "I will read poems from Spanish poet Rafael Alberti IF AND ONLY IF 100 is greater than 1."

Logical connectives in these cases are shown in capital letters and are represented by the words or phrases "**NOT**", "**AND**", "**OR**", "**IF …THEN**" and "**IF AND ONLY IF**".

Simple or atomic propositions are denoted using letters (p, q, r, etc.) known as **propositional variables**. We could name some of the preceding propositions as follows:

1. **p** = "Smoking damages your health."

2. **q** = "Michael Jordan is the greatest basketball player of all time."

3. **r** = "Jazz is the coolest musical genre in the world."

4. **s** = "100 is greater than 1."

A proposition that can be either True (1) or False (0) depending on the truth value of the propositions that compose it is known as a **formula**. Note that a formula can be simple; in other words, it can be composed of a single proposition. Consequently, every proposition is considered a formula.

The syntax of propositional logic is governed by the following rules:

1. All variables and propositional constants (True, False) are formulas.

2. If F is a formula then NOT F is also a formula.

3. If F, G are formulas then F AND G, F OR G, F => G, F <=> G also represent formulas.

An **interpretation** of a formula F is an assignation of truth values for every propositional variable that occurs in F and determines a truth value for F. Since every variable always has two possible values (True, False or 1, 0) then the total number of interpretations for F is 2^n where *n* is the total number of variables occurring in F.

A proposition that is True for every interpretation is said to be a **tautology** or **logic law**.

A proposition that is False for every interpretation is said to be a **contradiction** or **unsatisfiable**.

We'll be interested in studying the truth values of combined propositions and how to compute them. In the Satisfiability problem, we receive as input a formula, usually in a special, standardized form known as Conjunctive Normal Form (soon to be detailed), and we'll try to assign truth values for its atomic propositions so the formula becomes True (1); if such assignment exists, we say that the formula is **Satisfiable**. This is a classic problem in computer science and will be addressed throughout this chapter.

In the next section, we'll take a closer look at logical connectives, as they are determinant in establishing the final truth value of a formula.

Logical Connectives

Commonly, logical connectives are represented using the following symbols:

- $\neg$ denotes **negation ("NOT")**

- $\wedge$ denotes **conjunction ("AND")**

- $\vee$ denotes **disjunction ("OR")**

- => denotes **implication ("IF ... THEN")**

- <=> denotes **double implication or equivalence ("IF AND ONLY IF")**

Logical connectives act as unary or binary (receive one or two arguments) functions that provide an output that can be either 1 (True) or 0 (False). In order to better understand what the output would be for every connective and every possible input, we rely on **truth tables**.

Note   The tilde symbol (~) is also used to indicate negation.

In a truth table, columns correspond to variables and outputs and rows correspond to every possible combination of values for each propositional variable. We'll see detailed truth tables for every connective in the following subsections.

Negation

If we have a proposition *p* then its negation is denoted ¬*p* (read Not *p*). This is a unary logical connective because it requires a single proposition as input.

Let's try to negate some of the propositions previously presented:

1. "Smoking DOES NOT damage your health."

2. "Michael Jordan is NOT the greatest basketball player of all time."

3. "Jazz is NOT the coolest musical genre in the world."

4. "100 is NOT greater than 1."

5. "There are NOT wonderful beaches in Havana."

6. "World War II DID NOT end in 1945."

The truth table for the negation connective is the following (Table 1-1).

Table 1-1. *Truth Table for Negation Logical Connective*

p	¬p
1	0
0	1

From Table 1-1 we can see that if a proposition p is True (1) then its negation (¬p) is False (0), and vice versa if the proposition is False.

Conjunction

If we have propositions p, q then their conjunction is denoted $p \wedge q$ (read p AND q). This is a binary logical connective; it requires two propositions as input.

The conjunction of the previous propositions can be obtained by simply using the AND word, as follows:

1. "Smoking damages your health AND I will read poems from Spanish poet Rafael Alberti."

2. "Michael Jordan is the greatest basketball player of all time AND jazz is the coolest musical genre in the world."

3. "100 is greater than 1 AND there are wonderful beaches in Havana."

The truth table for the conjunction connective is shown in Table 1-2.

Table 1-2. *Truth Table for the Conjunction Logical Connective*

p	q	p ∧ q
1	0	0
0	1	0
0	0	0
1	1	1

Table 1-2 permits us to see that $p \wedge q$ is True only when both p and q are True simultaneously.

Disjunction

If we have propositions *p, q* then their disjunction is denoted $p \vee q$ (read *p OR q*). This is a binary logical connective; it requires two propositions as input.

The disjunction of the previous propositions can be obtained by simply using the OR word, as follows:

1. "I will read poems from Spanish poet Rafael Alberti OR I listen to Sting's music."

2. "Michael Jordan is the greatest basketball player of all time OR jazz is the coolest musical genre in the world."

3. "World War II ended in 1945 OR there are wonderful beaches in Havana."

The truth table for the conjunction connective is as follows (Table 1-3).

Table 1-3. *Truth Table for the Disjunction Logical Connective*

p	q	p ∨ q
1	0	1
0	1	1
0	0	0
1	1	1

From Table 1-3 we can see that $p \vee q$ is True when either *p* or *q* are True.

Implication

Countless expressions in mathematics are stated as an implication; i.e., in the manner "if . . . then." If we have propositions p, q then their implication is denoted $p => q$ (read p *IMPLIES* q). This is a binary logical connective; it requires two propositions as input and indicates that from p veracity we deduce q veracity.

We say that q is a **necessary condition** for p to be True and p is a **sufficient condition** for q to be True.

The implication connector is similar to the conditional statement (if) that we find in many imperative programming languages like C#, Java, or Python. To understand the outputs produced by the connective let us consider the following propositions:

- p = John is intelligent.

- q = John goes to the theater.

An implication $p => q$ would be written as "If John is intelligent then he goes to the theater." Let's analyze each possible combination of values for p, q and the result obtained from the connective.

Case 1, where $p = 1$, $q = 1$. In this case, John is intelligent and he goes to the theater; therefore, $p => q$ is True.

Case 2, where $p = 1$, $q = 0$. In this case, John is intelligent but does not go to the theater; therefore, $p => q$ is False.

Case 3, where $p = 0$, $q = 1$. In this case, John is not intelligent even though he goes to the theater. Since p is False and $p => q$ only indicates what happens when $p = $ John is intelligent, then proposition $p => q$ is not negated; hence, it's True.

Case 4, where $p = 0$, $q = 0$. In this case, John is not intelligent and does not go to the theater. Since p is False and $p => q$ only indicates what happens when p is True, then $p => q$ is True.

In general, proposition $p => q$ is True whenever $p = 0$ because if condition p does not hold (John's being intelligent) then the consequence (John goes to the theater) could be anything. It could be interpreted as "If John is intelligent then he goes to the theater"; otherwise, "If John is not intelligent then anything could happen," which is True.

The truth table for the implication connective is shown in Table 1-4.

Table 1-4. *Truth Table for the Implication Logical Connective*

p	q	p => q
1	0	0
0	1	1
0	0	1
1	1	1

Proposition $p => q$ is True when p is False or both p and q are True.

Equivalence

Propositions p, q are said to be equivalent, denoted $p <=> q$ (read *p Is Equivalent to q* or *p If and Only If q*), if it occurs that $p => q$ and $q => p$ both have the same value.

The double implication or equivalence connective will output True only when propositions p, q have the same value.

The truth table for the equivalence connective can be seen in Table 1-5.

Table 1-5. *Truth Table for the Equivalence Logical Connective*

p	q	p <=> q
1	0	0
0	1	0
0	0	1
1	1	1

Considering propositions p, q, r, the equivalence connective satisfies the following properties:

- Reflexivity: $p <=> p$

- Transitivity: if $p <=> r$ and $r <=> q$ then

  $p <=> q$

- Symmetry: if $p <=> q$ then $q <=> p$

Both the implication and equivalence connectives have great importance in mathematical, computational logic, and they represent fundamental logical structures for presenting mathematical theorems. The relationship between artificial intelligence, logical connectives, and logic in general will seem more evident as we move forward in this book.

Laws of Propositional Logic

Now that we have gotten acquainted with all logical connectors, let's introduce a list of logic equivalences and implications that, because of their significance, are considered *Laws of Propositional Logic*. In this case, *p*, *q*, and *r* are all formulas, and we will use the ≡ symbol to denote that *p* <=> *q* is a tautology; i.e., it's True under any set of values for *p*, *q* (any interpretation). In such cases we say that *p* and *q* are *logically equivalent*. This symbol resembles the equal sign used in arithmetic because its meaning is similar but at a logical level. Having *p* ≡ *q* basically means that *p* and *q* will always have the same output when receiving the same input (truth values for each variable).

Logical equivalences:

1. $p \lor p \equiv p$ (idempotent law)

2. $p \land p \equiv p$ (idempotent law)

3. $[p \lor q] \lor r \equiv p \lor [q \lor r]$ (associative law)

4. $[p \land q] \land r \equiv p \land [q \land r]$ (associative law)

5. $p \lor q \equiv q \lor p$ (commutative law)

6. $p \land q \equiv q \land p$ (commutative law)

7. $p \land [q \lor r] \equiv [p \land q] \lor [p \land r]$ (distributive law over ^)

8. $p \lor [q \land r] \equiv [p \lor q] \land [p \lor r]$ (distributive law over ˅)

9. $p \lor [p \land q] \equiv p$

10. $p \land [p \lor q] \equiv p$

11. $p \lor 0 \equiv p$

12. $p \land 1 \equiv p$

13. $p \lor 1 \equiv 1$

14. $p \land 0 \equiv 0$

15. $p \lor \lnot p \equiv 1$

16. $p \land \lnot p \equiv 0$ (contradiction)

17. $\lnot[\lnot p] \equiv p$ (double negation)

18. $\neg 1 \equiv 0$

19. $\neg 0 \equiv 1$

20. $\neg[p \lor q] \equiv \neg p \land \neg q$ (De Morgan's law)

21. $\neg[p \land q] \equiv \neg p \lor \neg q$ (De Morgan's law)

22. $p \Rightarrow q \equiv \neg p \lor q$ (definition =>)

23. $[p \Leftrightarrow q] \equiv [p \Rightarrow q] \land [q \Rightarrow p]$ (definition <=>)

Note the use of brackets in some of the previous formulas. As occurs in math, brackets can be used to group variables and their connectives all together to denote order relevance, association with logical connectives, and so forth. For instance, having a formula like $p \lor [q \land r]$ indicates the result of subformula $q \land r$ is to be connected with the disjunction logical connective and variable p.

In the same way as we introduced the $\equiv$ symbol for stating that p, q were logically equivalent we now introduce the $\approx$ symbol for denoting that p, q are *logically implied*, written $p \approx q$. If they are logically implied then $p \Rightarrow q$ must be a tautology.

Logical implications:

1. $p \approx q \Rightarrow [p \land q]$

2. $[p \Rightarrow q] \land [q \Rightarrow r] \approx p \Rightarrow q$

3. $\neg q \Rightarrow \neg p \approx p \Rightarrow q$

4. $[p \Rightarrow q] \land [\neg p \Rightarrow q] \approx q$

5. $[p \Rightarrow r] \land [q \Rightarrow r] \approx [p \lor q] \Rightarrow r$

6. $\neg p \Rightarrow [q \land \neg q] \approx p$

7. $p \Rightarrow [q \land \neg q] \approx \neg p$

8. $\neg p \Rightarrow p \approx p$

9. $p \Rightarrow \neg p \approx \neg p$

10. $p => [\neg q => [r \wedge \neg r]] \approx p => q$

11. $[p \wedge \neg q] => q \approx p => q$

12. $[p \wedge \neg q] => \neg p \approx p => q$

13. $[p => q] \wedge [\neg p => r] \approx q \vee r$

14. $\neg p => q \approx p \vee q$

15. $p => q \approx q \vee \neg p$

16. $p \approx p \vee q$

17. $p \wedge q \approx p$

18. $p \approx q => p$

Many of these laws are very intuitive and can be easily proven by finding all possible values of the variables involved and the final outcome of every formula. For instance, equivalence $\neg[p \vee q] \equiv \neg p \wedge \neg q$, which is known as De Morgan's law, can be proven by considering every possible value for p, q in a Truth table, as shown in Table 1-6.

Table 1-6. *Truth Table Verifying* $\neg[p \vee q] \equiv \neg p \wedge \neg q$

p	q	¬[p ∨ q]	¬p ∧ ¬q
0	0	1	1
0	1	0	0
1	0	0	0
1	1	0	0

So far we have presented some of the basic topics of computational logic. At this point, the reader might wonder what the relationship between propositional logic and artificial intelligence may be. First of all, propositional logic and logic in general are the founding fields of many areas related to AI. Our brain is crowded with logical decisions, On (1) / Off (0) definitions that we make every step of the way, and that on multiple occasions are justified by our "built-in" logic. Thus, because AI tries to emulate our human brain at some level, we must understand logic and how to operate with it in order to create solid, logical AIs in the future. In the following sections we'll continue our studies of propositional logic, and we'll finally get a glimpse of a practical problem.

Normal Forms

When checking satisfiability, certain types of formulas are easier to work with than others. Among these formulas we can find the normal forms.

- Negation Normal Form (NNF)

- Conjunctive Normal Form (CNF)

- Disjunctive Normal Form (DNF)

We will assume that all formulas are implication free; i.e., every implication $p => q$ is transformed into the equivalent $\neg p \lor q$.

A formula is said to be in *negation normal form* if its variables are the only subformulas negated. Every formula can be transformed into an equivalent NNF using logical equivalences 17, 20, and 21 presented in the previous section.

Note   Normal forms are useful in automated theorem proving (also known as automated deduction or ATP), a subfield of automated reasoning, which at the same time is a subfield of AI. ATP is dedicated to proving mathematical theorems by means of computer programs.

A formula is said to be in *conjunctive normal form* if it's of the form $(p1 \land p2 \dots \lor pn) \land (q1 \lor q2 \dots \lor qm)$ where each pi, qj is either a propositional variable or the negation of a propositional variable. A CNF is a conjunction of disjunctions of variables, and every NNF can be transformed into a CNF using the Laws of Propositional logic.

A formula is said to be in *disjunctive normal form* if it's of the form $(p1 \land p2 \dots \land pn) \lor (q1 \land q2 \dots \lor qm)$ where each pi, qj is either a propositional variable or the negation of a propositional variable. A DNF is a disjunction of conjunctions of variables, and every NNF can also be transformed into a CNF using the Laws of Propositional Logic.

At the end of this chapter, we'll examine several practical problems where we'll describe algorithms for computing NNF and CNF; we'll also look at the relationship between normal forms and ATP.

Note   A canonical or normal form of a mathematical object is a standard manner of representing it. A canonical form indicates that there's a unique way of representing every object; a normal form does not involve a uniqueness feature.

Logic Circuits

The topics presented thus far regarding propositional logic find applications in design problems and, more importantly, in digital logic circuits. These circuits, which execute logical bivalent functions, are used in the processing of digital information.

Furthermore, the most important logical machine ever created by mankind (the computer) operates at a basic level using logical circuits.

The computer, the most basic, classical example of an AI container, receives input data (as binary streams of ones and zeroes). It processes that information using logic and arithmetic (as our brain does), and finally it provides an output or action. The core of the computer is the *CPU (central processing unit),* which is composed of the *ALU (arithmetic-logic unit)* and the *CU (control unit).* The ALU—and therefore the entire computer—processes information in digital form using a binary language with the symbols 1 and 0. These symbols are known as *bits,* the elemental unit of information in a computer.

Logical circuits represent one of the major technological components of our current computers, and every logical connective described so far in this chapter is known in the electronics world as a *logical gate.*

A logical gate is a structure of switches used to calculate in digital circuits. It's capable of producing predictable output based on the input. Generally, the input is one of two selected voltages represented as zeroes and ones. The 0 has low voltage and the 1 has higher voltage. The range is between 0.7 volts in emitter-coupled logic and approximately 28 volts in relay logic.

Note   Nerve cells known as neurons function in a more complex yet similar way to logical gates. Neurons have a structure of dendrites and axons for transmitting signals. A neuron receives a set of inputs from its dendrites, relates them in a weighted sum, and produces an output in the axon depending on the frequency type of the input signal. Unlike logical gates, neurons are adaptables.

Every piece of information that we input into the computer (characters from the keyboard, images, and so on) are eventually transformed into zeroes and ones. This information is then carried on and transported via logic circuits in a discontinuous or discreet manner. Information flows as successive signals commonly made by electronic impulses constituted by high (1) and low (0) voltage levels, as illustrated in Figure 1-1.

Figure 1-1. *Digital information flow*

Logic circuits in the ALU transform the information received by executing the proper logical gates (AND, OR, and so on). As a result, any transformation endured by the incoming information is describable using propositional logic. Circuits are built that connect various elementary electronic components. We will abstract each electronic component and the operation it represents into one of the diagrams shown in Figures 1-2, 1-3, and 1-4.

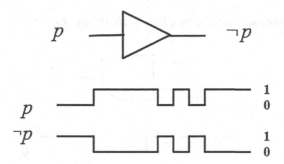

Figure 1-2. *Representation of negation component (NOT)*

In Figure 1-5 we can see, as a first example of a logic circuit, a *binary comparer*. This circuit receives two inputs p, q (bits) and outputs 0 if p and q are equal; otherwise, it outputs 1. To verify that the output of the diagram illustrated in Figure 1-5 is correct and actually represents a binary comparer, we could go over all possible values of input bits p, q and check the corresponding results.

A simple analysis of the circuit will show us that whenever inputs p, q have different values then each will follow a path in which it is negated, with the other bit left intact. This will activate one of the conjunction gates, outputting 1 for it; thus, the final disjunction gate will output 1 as well, and the bits will not be considered equals. In short, when the two inputs are equal, the output will be 1, and if the inputs are not equal the output will be 0.

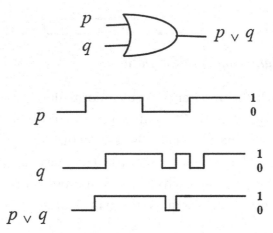

Figure 1-3. *Representation of disjunction component (OR)*

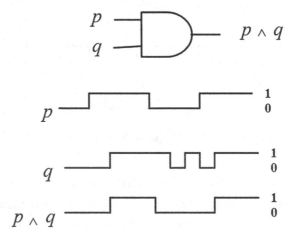

Figure 1-4. *Representation of conjunction component (AND)*

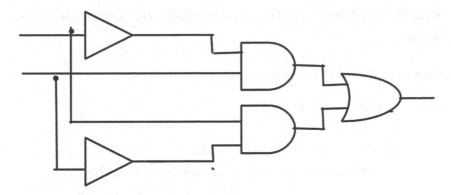

Figure 1-5. *Binary comparer circuit*

Now that we have studied various topics related to propositional logic, it's time to introduce a first practical problem. In the following section we'll present a way to represent logic formulas in C# using the facilities provided by this powerful language. We'll also see how to find all possible outputs of a formula using binary decision trees.

Practical Problem: Using Inheritance and C# Operators to Evaluate Logic Formulas

Thus far, we have studied the basics of propositional logic, and in this section we'll present a first practical problem. We'll create a set of classes, all related by inheritance, that will allow us to obtain the output of any formula from inputs defined a priori. These classes will use *structural recursion*.

In structural recursion the structure exhibited by the class—and therefore the object—is recursive itself. In this case, recursion will be present in methods from the Formula class as well as its descendants. Using recursion, we'll be calling methods all the way through the hierarchy tree. Inheritance in C# will aid recursion by calling the proper version of the method (the one that corresponds to the logical gate that the class represents).

In Listing 1-1 the parent of every other class in our formula design is presented.

Listing 1-1. Abstract Class Formula

```
public abstract class Formula
{
    public abstract bool Evaluate();
    public abstract IEnumerable<Variable> Variables();
}
```

The abstract Formula class states that all its descendants must implement a Boolean method Evaluate() and an IEnumerable<Variable> method Variables(). The first will return the evaluation of the formula and the latter the variables contained within it. The Variable class will be presented shortly.

Because binary logic gates share some features we'll create an abstract class to group these features and create a more concise, logical inheritance design. The BinaryGate class, which can be seen in Listing 1-2, will contain the similarities that every binary gate shares.

Listing 1-2. Abstract Class BinaryGate

```
public abstract class BinaryGate : Formula
{
    public Formula P { get; set; }
    public Formula Q { get; set; }

    public BinaryGate(Formula p, Formula q)
    {
        P = p;
        Q = q;
    }
```

```
    public override IEnumerable<Variable> Variables()
    {
        return P.Variables().Concat(Q.Variables());
    }
}
```

In Listing 1-3 the first logic gate, the AND gate, is illustrated.

Listing 1-3. And Class

```
public class And: BinaryGate
    {
        public And(Formula p, Formula q): base(p, q)
        { }

        public override bool Evaluate()
        {
            return P.Evaluate() &&Q.Evaluate();
}
    }
```

The implementation of the And class is pretty simple. It receives two arguments that it passes to its parent constructor, and the Evaluate method merely returns the logic AND that is built in to C#. Very similar are the Or, Not, and Variable classes, which are shown in Listing 1-4.

Listing 1-4. Or, Not, Variable Classes

```
public class Or : BinaryGate
    {
        public Or(Formula p, Formula q): base(p, q)
        { }

        public override bool Evaluate()
```

```csharp
        {
            return P.Evaluate() || Q.Evaluate();
        }
    }

    public class Not : Formula
    {
        public Formula P { get; set; }

        public Not(Formula p)
        {
            P = p;
        }

        public override bool Evaluate()
        {
            return !P.Evaluate();
        }

        public override IEnumerable<Variable> Variables()
        {
            return new List<Variable>(P.Variables());
        }
    }

    public class Variable : Formula
    {
        public bool Value { get; set; }

        public Variable(bool value)
        {
            Value = value;
}
```

```
    public override bool Evaluate()
    {
        return Value;
    }

    public override IEnumerable<Variable> Variables()
    {
        return new List<Variable>() { this };
    }
}

}
```

Notice the Variable class is the one we use for representing variables in formulas. It includes a Value field, which is the value given to the variable (true, false), and when the Variables() method is called it returns a List<Variable> whose single element is itself. The recursive inheritance design that we have come up with then moves this value upward in the inheritance to output the IEnumerable<Variable> with the correct objects of type Variable when requested.

Now, let's try to create a formula and find its output from some defined inputs, as illustrated in Listing 1-5.

Listing 1-5. Creating and Evaluating Formula ¬p ∨ q

```
var p = new Variable(false);
var q = new Variable(false);

var formula = new Or(new Not(p), q);

Console.WriteLine(formula.Evaluate());

p.Value = true;
Console.WriteLine(formula.Evaluate());

Console.Read();
```

The result obtained after executing the previous code is illustrated in Figure 1-6.

Figure 1-6. *Result after executing code in Listing 1-5*

Since every implication can be transformed into a free implication formula using the OR and NOT expressions (according to the laws of propositional logic) and every double implication can be set free of implications' transforming it into a conjunction of implications, then having the preceding logic gates is enough to represent any formula.

Practical Problem: Representing Logic Formulas as Binary Decision Trees

A *binary decision tree (BDT)* is a labelled binary tree satisfying the following conditions:

- The leaves are labelled with either 0 (False) or 1 (True).

- Non-leaf nodes are labelled with positive integers.

- Every non-leaf node labelled i has two child nodes, both labelled $i + 1$.

- Every branch leading to a left child has a low value (0), and every branch leading to a right child has a high value (1).

Note   A binary decision tree is just another way of representing or writing the truth table of a formula.

In Figure 1-7 we can see a binary decision tree with leaf nodes represented as squares and non-leaf nodes represented as circles.

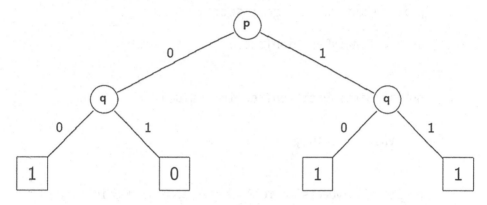

Figure 1-7. *Binary decision tree for p $\lor$ ¬q*

In a BDT, every level of the tree matches a variable, and its two branches correspond to its possible values (1, 0). A path from the root to a leaf node represents an assignment for all variables of the formula. The value found at a leaf node represents an interpretation of the formula; i.e., the result of an assignation from the root.

Now that we have studied some topics related to propositional logic, it's time to create our first AI data structure. As we'll see, by using the Formula class introduced in the last practical problem we will be able to create our binary decision tree in just a few lines of code. Three constructors, for different uses, will be included in the class, as shown in Listing 1-6.

Listing 1-6. Constructors and Properties of BinaryDecisionTree Class

```
public class BinaryDecisionTree
    {
        private BinaryDecisionTreeLeftChild { get; set; }
        private BinaryDecisionTreeRightChild { get; set; }
        private int Value { get; set; }

        public BinaryDecisionTree()
        { }

        public BinaryDecisionTree(int value)
{
            Value = value;
        }

        public BinaryDecisionTree(int value, BinaryDecisionTreelft,
        BinaryDecisionTreergt)
        {
            Value = value;
LeftChild = lft;
RightChild = rgt;
}
    ...
}
```

A binary decision tree is a recursive structure; as a result, its template or class will include two properties, LeftChild and RightChild, that are of type BinaryDecisionTree. The Value property is an integer that identifies the variable as provided in the order given by the Variables() method in the Formula class; this order is equivalent to the height of the tree; i.e., in the first level the root node will have value 0, then at level (height) 1 every node (all representing the same variable) will have value 1 and so on.

Note   In a binary decision tree every level represents a variable in the formula. The left branch leaving a node (variable) corresponds to the decision where that variable will have value 0 (false), and the right branch indicates that the variable will have value 1 (true).

The static methods shown in Listing 1-7 will take care of building the binary decision tree.

Listing 1-7. Methods to Build Binary Decision Tree from Formula

```
public static BinaryDecisionTreeFromFormula(Formula f)
    {
        return TreeBuilder(f, f.Variables(), 0, "");
    }

    private static BinaryDecisionTreeTreeBuilder(Formula f,
    IEnumerable<Variable> variables, intvarIndex, string path)
    {
        if (!string.IsNullOrEmpty(path))
variables.ElementAt(varIndex - 1).Value = path[path.Length - 1]
!= '0';

        if (varIndex == variables.Count())
            return new BinaryDecisionTree(f.Evaluate() ?
            1 : 0);

        return new BinaryDecisionTree(varIndex,
        TreeBuilder(f, variables, varIndex + 1, path + "0"),
TreeBuilder(f, variables, varIndex + 1, path + "1"));
    }
```

The public method FromFormula uses an auxiliary private method that relies on recursion to create the tree.

The `varIndex` variable defines the height of the tree or, equivalently, the index of the variable representing that tree level.

`Path` stores the evaluation of every variable as a binary string; e.g., "010" denotes the path where the root variable *r* is evaluated false, then its left child *lft* is evaluated true, and finally *lft*'s right child is evaluated false. Once we have reached a depth that equals the number of variables of the formula, we evaluate the formula with the assignment matching the path built so far and leave the final result in a leaf node.

By traversing the decision tree we can obtain the output of the formula under a predefined set of values (path from root to leaf node) for its variables. This feature can be very useful during decision-making processes because the tree structure is very intuitive and easy to interpret and understand. Decision trees will be covered deeply in Chapter 4; for now we should know that they provide several advantages or benefits. Among these, it's worth mentioning that they create a visual representation of all possible outputs and follow-up decisions in one view. Each subsequent decision resulting from the original choice is also depicted on the tree so we can see the overall effect of any one decision. As we go through the tree and make choices, we'll see a specific path from one node to another and the impact a decision made now could have down the road.

As mentioned before, we will describe in the next section various practical problems related to normal forms. We'll learn how to transform a formula in its regular state to negation normal form (NNF) and from there to conjunctive normal form (CNF). This transformation will come in handy when manipulating formulas and especially for developing logic-related algorithms like DPLL.

Practical Problem: Transforming a Formula into Negation Normal Form (NNF)

In this problem, we'll finally study an algorithm that transforms any formula into negation normal form. Remember, normal forms are useful because

- they reduce logic operators (implication, etc.);

- they reduce syntactical structure (nesting of subformulas); and

- they can be taken advantage of to seek efficient data structures.

The NNF transformation algorithm is determined by the following recursive ideas; assuming F is the input formula, this is a pseudocode.

Function NNF(F):

If F is a variable or negated variable Then return F

If F is ¬(¬p) Then return NNF(p)

If F is p ∧ q Then return NNF(p) ∧ NNF(q)

If F is p ∨ q Then return NNF(p) ∨ NNF(q)

If F is ¬(p ∨ q) Then return NNF(¬p) ∧ NNF(¬q)

If F is ¬(p ∧ q) Then return NNF(¬p) ∨ NNF(¬q)

We will assume that all formulas are implication free and take advantage of the Formula hierarchy to implement the pseudocode described.

Note   The formulas $\neg p \wedge q$, $p \vee q$, $(p \wedge (\neg q \vee r))$ are all in negation normal form. The formulas $\neg(q \vee \neg r)$, $\neg(p \wedge q)$ on the other hand are not in negation normal form as some of these formulas include Or, And formulas that are being negated. To be in NNF only variables can be negated.

We'll start by modifying the `Formula` abstract class as shown in Listing 1-8.

Listing 1-8. Abstract Method ToNnf() Added to Abstract Class Formula

```
public abstract class Formula
    {
        public abstract bool Evaluate();
        public abstract IEnumerable<Variable> Variables();
public abstract Formula ToNnf();
}
```

The And, Or classes require a little modification, including an override to the newly created ToNnf() abstract method (Listing 1-9).

Listing 1-9. And, Or Classes with ToNnf() Method Override

```
public class And: BinaryGate
    {

        public And(Formula p, Formula q): base(p, q)
        { }

        public override bool Evaluate()
        {
            return P.Evaluate() &&Q.Evaluate();
        }
```

```
public override Formula ToNnf()
        {
return new And(P.ToNnf(), Q.ToNnf());
        }
}

    public class Or : BinaryGate
    {
        public Or(Formula p, Formula q): base(p, q)
        { }

        public override bool Evaluate()
        {
            return P.Evaluate() || Q.Evaluate();
        }

public override Formula ToNnf()
        {
return new Or(P.ToNnf(), Q.ToNnf());
        }
    }
```

The Not class incorporates most of the steps (if statements) from the NNF pseudocode; its final implementation can be seen in Listing 1-10.

Listing 1-10. Not Class with Nnf() Override

```
public class Not : Formula
    {
        public Formula P { get; set; }
        public Not(Formula p)
        {
            P = p;
        }
```

```
    public override bool Evaluate()
    {
        return !P.Evaluate();
}

    public override IEnumerable<Variable> Variables()
    {
        return new List<Variable>(P.Variables());
    }
      Public override Formula ToNnf()
     {
if (P is And)
            return new Or(new Not((P as And).P), new Not((P
            as And).Q));
        if (P is Or)
            return new And(new Not((P as Or).P), new Not((P
            as Or).Q));
       if (P is Not)
            return new Not((P as Not).P);
          return this;
     }
  }
```

Finally, the Variable class includes a simple override of the Nnf()
abstract method inherited from its parent; the entire class is shown in
Listing 1-11.

Listing 1-11. Variable Class with Nnf() Override

```
public class Variable : Formula
    {
        public bool Value { get; set; }
        public Variable(bool value)
        {
            Value = value;
        }

        public override bool Evaluate()
        {
            return Value;
        }

        public override IEnumerable<Variable> Variables()
        {
            return new List<Variable>() { this };
}

public override Formula ToNnf()
        {
            return this;
        }
    }
```

To obtain an NNF out of a formula we can simply call the Nnf() method in some instance of the Formula class.

Practical Problem: Transforming a Formula into Conjunctive Normal Form (CNF)

A conjunctive normal form (CNF) is basically an AND of ORs; i.e., groups of variables or negated variables all connected using disjunction connectives where all groups are related among themselves by conjunctive connectives; e.g., $(p \lor q) \land (r \lor \neg q)$. Because of the multiple reasons detailed earlier, we are interested in taking a formula to CNF. A pseudocode of the CNF transformation algorithm is presented in the next lines.

Function CNF(F):

If F is a variable or negated variable Then return F

If F is p ∧ q Then return CNF(p) ∧ CNF(q)

If F is p ∨ q Then return DISTRIBUTE-CNF (CNF(p),CNF(q))

Function DISTRIBUTE-CNF(P, Q):

If P is R ∧ S Then return DISTRIBUTE-CNF (R, Q) ∧ DISTRIBUTE-CNF (R, Q)

If Q is T ∨ U Then return DISTRIBUTE-CNF (P, T) ∧ DISTRIBUTE-CNF (P, U)

return P ∨ Q

The CNF algorithm relies on an auxiliary method called DISTRIBUTE-CNF that uses the distributive laws of propositional logic to decompose a formula in order to get it closer to the excepted form of a CNF.

Note   The CNF algorithm assumes the input formula is already in NNF. Every NNF formula can be transformed into an equivalent CNF formula using the distributive laws of propositional logic.

As we did with the NNF algorithm, we'll insert the CNF algorithm into the `Formula` hierarchy that we have been enhancing in the previous practical problems. Necessary edits to the `Formula` abstract class are shown in Listing 1-12.

Listing 1-12. Adding ToCnf() and DistributeCnf() Methods to the Formula Class

```
public abstract class Formula
{
        public abstract bool Evaluate();
        public abstract IEnumerable<Variable> Variables();
        public abstract Formula ToNnf();
        public abstract Formula ToCnf();

public Formula DistributeCnf(Formula p, Formula q)
        {
if (p is And)
return new And(DistributeCnf((p as And).P, q), DistributeCnf
((p as And).Q, q));
if(q is And)
                return new And(DistributeCnf(p, (q as And).P),
                DistributeCnf(p, (q as And).Q));

return new Or(p, q);
}
    }
```

Now that we have added the abstract method to the parent class we can include the corresponding overrides in the child classes `And`, `Or` as shown in Listings 1-13 and 1-14.

Listing 1-13. And Class with ToCnf() Method Override

```
public class And: BinaryGate
{

        public And(Formula p, Formula q): base(p, q)
        { }

        public override bool Evaluate()
        {
            return P.Evaluate() &&Q.Evaluate();
        }

        public override Formula ToNnf()
        {
            return new And(P.ToNnf(), Q.ToNnf());
        }

public override Formula ToCnf()
{
return new And(P.ToNnf(), Q.ToNnf());
}
    }
}
```

The override implementation of the ToCnf() methods in the Or and And classes represents a direct result drawn from the pseudocode of the CNF function (Listing 1-14).

Listing 1-14. Or Class with ToCnf() Method Override

```
public class Or : BinaryGate
    {
        public Or(Formula p, Formula q): base(p, q)
        { }

        public override bool Evaluate()
```

```
    {
        return P.Evaluate() || Q.Evaluate();
    }

    public override Formula ToNnf()
    {
        return new Or(P.ToNnf(), Q.ToNnf());
}
```

```
public override Formula ToCnf()
{
return DistributeCnf(P.ToCnf(), Q.ToCnf());
}
    }
```

The Not and Variable classes will simply return a reference to themselves on their ToCnf() override as shown in Listing 1-15.

Listing 1-15. ToCnf() Method Override in Not, Variable Classes

```
public override Formula ToCnf()
{
    return this;
}
```

Remember: The CNF algorithm expects as input a formula in NNF; therefore, before executing this algorithm we need to call the ToNnf() method and then the ToCnf() on the Formula object created. In the following chapter, we'll start diving into an application of AI and logic that's directly related to all the practical problems we have seen thus far: automated theorem proving.

Summary

In this chapter, we analyzed the relationship between AI and logic. We introduced a basic logic—propositional logic. We described various codes that included a hierarchy for representing formulas (variables, logical connectives, and so on), and we complemented this hierarchy with different methods. Among these methods were the negation normal form transformation algorithm and the conjunctive normal form transformation algorithm (relies on the distributive laws previously introduced). We also described a binary decision tree for representing formulas and their possible evaluations.

In the next chapter, we'll begin studying a very important logic that extends propositional logic: first-order logic. At the same time, we'll dive into the world of automated theorem proving (ATP) and present a very important method for determining satisfiability of a formula, the DPLL algorithm:

(x)IsFriend(x, Arnaldo)(x)IsFriend(x, Arnaldo) (y) IsWorkingWith(y, Arnaldo)

CHAPTER 2

Automated Theorem Proving & First-Order Logic

Following the line of thought begun in Chapter 1, we'll start this chapter by introducing a topic related to AI and logic: *automated theorem proving*. This is a field of AI that serves mathematicians in their research and assists them in proving theorems, corollaries, and so forth. In this chapter, we'll also devote some pages to *first-order logic*, a logic that extends propositional logic by allowing or including quantifiers (universal and existential) and providing a more complete framework for easily representing different types of logical scenarios that could arise in our regular life.

At the same time, we'll keep extending the Formula hierarchy introduced in Chapter 1 by inserting clauses and CNF C# classes and describing a very important method for solving the SAT (satisfiability) problem: the DPLL algorithm. Practical problems will help us to better understand every concept hereafter described. We will end the chapter by presenting a simple cleaning robot that will use some of the terms of first-order logic and show how they can be applied in a real-life problem.

© Arnaldo Pérez Castaño 2018
A. Pérez Castaño, *Practical Artificial Intelligence*,
https://doi.org/10.1007/978-1-4842-3357-3_2

Automated Theorem Proving

An *automated theorem Prover (ATP)* is a computer program that can generate and check mathematical theorems and search for a proof of the theorem's veracity; i.e., its statement is always true. Theorems are expressed using some mathematical logic, such as propositional logic, first-order logic, and so on. In this case, we'll only consider an ATP that uses propositional logic as its language. We can think of an ATP's workflow as illustrated in the diagram in Figure 2-1.

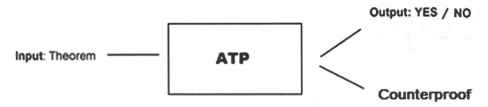

Figure 2-1. *ATP workflow diagram*

ATPs were originally created for mathematical computation but recently have gained notice in the scientific community as a wide range of potential applications have been associated with them. One of the several applications of ATPs is adding intelligence to databases of mathematical theorems; in other words, using automated theorem provers to astutely query for equivalent theorems within a database of mathematical theorems. An ATP would be used to verify whether a theorem within the database was mathematically equivalent to another entered by the user. String-matching algorithms or similar techniques wouldn't be good enough for such an application since the user may have phrased the theorem in a different way than how it was stored in the database, or the searched-for theorem could be a logical consequence rather than a direct clone of existing theorems.

Another application of theorem provers and formal methods can be found in the verification of hardware and software designs. Hardware verification happens to be an extremely important task. The commercial cost of an error in the design of a modern microprocessor, for instance, is potentially so large that verification of designs is essential.

Software verification is similarly crucial as mistakes can be very costly in this area. Examples of the catastrophic consequences of such mistakes are the destruction of the Ariane 5 rocket (caused by a simple integer overow problem that could have been detected by a formal verification procedure) or the error in the floating-point unit of the Pentium II processor.

The classical application of ATPs of course is that for which it was created—as a tool to aid mathematicians in their research. One could say ATPs are mathematicians' favorite robots.

Note   Some logics are more powerful and can express and prove more theorems than others. Propositional logic is usually the weakest and simplest of them all.

Theorem provers vary depending on the amount of human guidance that is required in the proof search and the sophistication of the logical language that may be used to express the theorem that is to be proven. A tradeoff between the automation degree and the sophistication of the logical language must be taken into account.

A high degree of automation is only possible if the language is constrained. Proofs for flexible, high-order languages generally require human guidance, and the associated theorem prover is referred to as a *proof assistant*.

This human assistance can be provided by the programmer's giving hints a priori or interacting with the ATP during the proof process through a prompt.

The simplest type of ATP is the SAT (SATisfiability) solver, which relies on propositional logic as theorem language. SAT solvers are very useful, but the expressive power of propositional logic is limited, and Boolean expressions can become quite large. Additionally, the SAT problem was the first to be proved NP(Non-Polynomial)-complete in complexity (S.A. Cook, "The Complexity of Theorem-proving Procedures"). There is a large amount of research done in finding heuristics for efficient SAT solving.

In pure mathematics, proofs are somewhat informal; they are "validated" by peer review and are intended to convince and convey an intuitive, clear idea of how the proof works, and the theorem statement should be always true. ATPs provide formal proofs where the output could be, as shown in Figure 1-8, the Boolean values Yes, No (True, False), or maybe a counterexample if the statement is found to be False.

Note   Software and hardware verification using the approach of model checking works well with propositional logic. Expressions are obtained after considering a state machine description of the problem and are manipulated in the form of binary decision trees.

An Automated Theorem Proving (ATP) can usually handle two types of tasks: they can check theorems in their logic or they can automatically generate proofs.

When *proof checking*, the ATP receives as input a formal proof, which consists of a list (steps) of formulas, each justified either by an axiom or inference rule applied to previous formulas:

```
Formulas                Justification
F1                      Axiom
F2                      Rule X and F1
...                     ...
Theorem
```

These types of proofs are very easy to check mechanically; we just need to make sure that every justification is valid or is applied correctly.

However, *proof generation* is much harder. We need to generate a list of formulas, each with a valid justification and guaranteeing that the last formula is the theorem to be proven. For simple problems, proof generation is very useful; for example, type inference (C#, Java), safety of web applications, and so forth.

So far we have described a SAT solver—the binary decision tree, which is suitable for small problems. However, its size is exponential, and to check satisfiability we would need to explore the entire tree in the worst-case scenario. Hence, in future sections we'll detail more on this topic and on how to obtain better results using other methods.

Note   In 1976 Kenneth Appel and Wolfgang Haken proved the four-color theorem using a program that performed a gigantic case analysis of billions of cases. The four-color theorem states that it's possible to paint a world map using only four colors and guaranteeing that there will not be two neighboring countries that share the same color.

Practical Problem: Clauses and CNFs Classes in C#

In this section, we'll enhance the logic framework we have been developing throughout this chapter with the addition of the Clause and Cnf classes. We'll make use of these classes when coding the DPLL algorithm, probably the most ingenious algorithm for determining the satisfiability of a logic formula and a basic tool for automated theorem proving.

Before we start developing this new enhancement, let's take a brief look at some definitions that will come in handy for understanding the classes that we'll be developing soon.

A *literal* is either a variable or the negation of a variable (e.g., p, $\neg p$, q, $\neg q$).

A *clause* is a disjunction of literals $p1 \lor p2 \lor ... \lor pm$, and every CNF is a set of clauses. From now on we'll denote a clause as $\{p1, p2, ... pm\}$ where every $pi(i = 1, 2, ... , m)$ is a literal.

In Listing 2-1 we illustrate the proposed `Clause` class.

Listing 2-1. Clause Class

```
public class Clause
    {
        public List<Formula> Literals { get; set; }

        public Clause()
        {
            Literals = new List<Formula>();
        }

        public bool Contains(Formula literal)
        {
if (!IsLiteral(literal))
                throw new ArgumentException("Specified formula
                is not a literal");

foreach (var formula in Literals)
            {
                if (LiteralEquals(formula, literal))
                    return true;
            }

            return false;
        }
```

```
        public Clause RemoveLiteral(Formula literal)
        {
if (!IsLiteral(literal))
                throw new ArgumentException("Specified formula
                is not a literal");
var result = new Clause();

            for (vari = 0; i<Literals.Count; i++)
            {
                if (!LiteralEquals(literal, Literals[i]))
result.Literals.Add(Literals[i]);
            }

            return result;
        }

        public bool LiteralEquals(Formula p, Formula q)
        {
            if (p is Variable && q is Variable)
                return (p as Variable).Name == (q as
                Variable).Name;
            if (p is Not && q is Not)
                return LiteralEquals((p as Not).P, (q as Not).P);

            return false;
        }

    public bool IsLiteral(Formula p)
    {
            return p is Variable || (p is Not && (p as Not).P
            is Variable);
    }
}
```

The Clause class contains the following methods:

- public bool Contains(Formula literal):
  determines whether a given literal belongs to the clause

- public Clause RemoveLiteral(Formula literal):
  returns a new Clause that does not contain the literal
  passed as argument

- public bool LiteralEquals(Formula p, Formula
  q): determines whether literals *p*, *q* are equal

- public bool IsLiteral(Formula p): determines
  whether a given formula is a literal

The Cnf class, which represents a conjunctive normal form, is illustrated in Listing 2-2.

Listing 2-2. Cnf Class

```
public class Cnf
    {
        public List<Clause> Clauses { get; set; }

        public Cnf()
        {
            Clauses = new List<Clause>();
        }

        public Cnf(And and)
        {
            Clauses = new List<Clause>();
RemoveParenthesis(and);
        }
```

```
public void SimplifyCnf()
{
Clauses.RemoveAll(TautologyClauses);
}

private bool TautologyClauses(Clause clause)
{
    for (vari = 0; i<clause.Literals.Count; i++)
    {
        for (var j = i + 1;
        j <clause.Literals.Count - 1; j++)
        {
            // Checking that literal i and literal
            j are not of the same type; i.e., both
            variables or negated literals.
            if (!(clause.Literals[i] is Variable
            &&clause.Literals[j] is Variable) &&
                !(clause.Literals[i] is Not &&clause.
                Literals[j] is Not))
            {
var not = clause.Literals[i] is Not ? clause.Literals[i] as
Not : clause.Literals[j] as Not;
var @var = clause.Literals[i] is Variable ? clause.Literals[i]
as Variable : clause.Literals[j] as Variable;
                if (IsNegation(not, @var))
                    return true;
            }
        }
    }

    return false;
}
```

```
        private bool IsNegation(Not f1, Variable f2)
        {
            return (f1.P as Variable).Name == f2.Name;
        }

private void Join(IEnumerable<Clause> others)
        {
Clauses.AddRange(others);
        }

        private voidRemoveParenthesis(And and)
        {
varcurrentAnd = and;

            while (true)
            {
                // If P is OR or literal and Q is OR or literal.
                if ((currentAnd.P is Or || currentAnd.P is
                Variable || currentAnd.P is Not) &&
                    (currentAnd.Q is Or || currentAnd.Q is
                    Variable || currentAnd.Q is Not))
                {
Clauses.Add(new Clause { Literals = new List<Formula>(currentAnd.
P.Literals()) });
Clauses.Add(new Clause { Literals = new List<Formula>(currentAnd.
Q.Literals()) });
                    break;
                }
                // If P is AND and Q is OR or literal.
                if (currentAnd.P is And && (currentAnd.Q is Or ||
                currentAnd.Q is Variable || currentAnd.Q is Not))
                {
```

```
Clauses.Add(new Clause { Literals = new List<Formula>(currentAnd.
Q.Literals()) });
currentAnd = currentAnd.P as And;
                }
                // If P is OR or literal and Q is AND.
                if ((currentAnd.P is Or || currentAnd.P is
                Variable || currentAnd.P is Not) &&currentAnd.
                Q is And)
                {
Clauses.Add(new Clause { Literals = new List<Formula>(currentAnd.
P.Literals()) });
currentAnd = currentAnd.Q as And;
                }
                // If both P and Q are ANDs.
                if (currentAnd.P is And &&currentAnd.Q is And)
                {
RemoveParenthesis(currentAnd.P as And);
RemoveParenthesis(currentAnd.Q as And);
                    break;
                }
            }
        }
```

The Cnf class contains the following methods:

- public void SimplifyCnf(): simplifies the formula by deleting every clause containing both p and $\neg p$. Since $p \lor \neg p$ is always true, the entire clause becomes true, and its analysis is unnecessary.

- public bool TautologyClauses(Clause clause): determines whether the given clause contains p and $\neg p$

- `private bool IsNegation(Not f1, Variable f2)`: determines whether $f1$ is the negation of variable $f2$

- `private void Join(IEnumerable<Clause> others)`: concatenates the `IEnumerable<Clause>` others to Cnf's clauses

- `private voidRemoveParenthesis(And and)`: changes Cnf to a list of clauses

The method `RemoveParenthesis(And and)` is in charge of executing a very important task. This method transforms the CNF formula that we have as a series of concatenated AND connectives, `And(p1, And(p2, And( ... ) ))`, into a list of clauses.

The `Formula` hierarchy we have been using thus far has saved us from having to implement a parser for logic formulas, but it cost us just a little bit on clarity. We aim to recover it by executing this method and transforming the `And` formula representing CNFs into a list of clauses. This new representation will come in handy for any CNF-related algorithm that we may need to develop; it will certainly be useful for the DPLL algorithm that we will introduce shortly.

Note   If you would like to develop a parser for logic formulas, you can use ANTLR (Another Tool for Language Recognition), a very useful tool that helps developers in the grammar-writing process and the creation of parsers. ANTLR generates and outputs parsers as Java or C# classes (.cs files), allowing you to include them later in your projects and use them at will.

The `RemoveParenthesis(And and)` method consists basically of a `while` loop with several conditions contained within. These conditions might mark the end of the loop, and each of them matches a different

scenario that could arise as we consider the types of formulas *P* and *Q*
from the argument And. These scenarios are as follows:

- P, Q are ORs or literals.

- (P is OR or literal) and Q is And.

- P is And and (Q is OR or literal).

- P, Q are both And.

Notice in the body of RemoveParenthesis(And and) that there exist
several calls to a Literals() method. This method must be created and
inserted all across the Formula hierarchy as we did before with the ToNnf()
and ToCnf() methods. We start from the top, the Formula abstract class, as
shown in Listing 2-3.

Listing 2-3. Adding Literals() Abstract Method to Formula Abstract
Class

```
public abstract class Formula
    {
        public abstract bool Evaluate();
        public abstract IEnumerable<Variable> Variables();
        public abstract Formula ToNnf();
        public abstract Formula ToCnf();
        public abstract IEnumerable<Formula> Literals();
...
}
```

Now, we need to spread concrete implementations of the Literals()
method throughout the hierarchy. In Listing 2-4 we present the concrete
implementation for the remaining classes.

Listing 2-4. Adding the Literals() Method to the Remaining Classes of the Hierarchy

```
public abstract class BinaryGate : Formula
    {
...

public override IEnumerable<Formula> Literals()
        {
return P.Literals().Concat(Q.Literals());
}
    }

public class Not : Formula
{
...

public override IEnumerable<Formula> Literals()
        {
return P is Variable ? new List<Formula>() { this }:
P.Literals();
}
}

public class Variable : Formula
{
        ...

public override IEnumerable<Formula> Literals()
        {
                returnnew List<Formula>() { this };
            }
}
```

Up to this point we have built a framework for logic in C#; now, it's time to examine one of the simplest yet most efficient and ingenious algorithms for determining the satisfiability of a formula: the DPLL algorithm.

DPLL Algorithm

The *Davis-Putnam-Logemann-Loveland (DPLL)* algorithm is a decision-making procedure that uses backtracking to search for an assignment that makes a formula in CNF satisfiable. It was introduced in two articles in 1960 (by Davis, Putnam) and 1962 (by Davis, Logemann, Loveland) and even today still forms the basis for most efficient SAT solvers; it has even been extended for small pieces of more complex logic, like first-order logic.

The SAT problem was the first problem to be proven to be NP-Complete; as a result, it's essential to find efficient procedures that solve it. Furthermore, this problem has applications in automated theorem proving, planning, scheduling, and many other areas of artificial intelligence, so throughout the years it has inspired great interest in the scientific community.

DPLL receives as input a CNF formula and tries to build an assignment that verifies the formula using backtracking and applying certain rules that simplify and reduce the complexity of the current formula. The set of possible assignments is represented using a binary tree very much like the binary decision tree we presented in Chapter 1.

A pseudocode of the algorithm is illustrated in the following lines:

```
DPLL(cnf):
        TERMINATION-CONDITIONS(cnf)

cnf' = Rule_OneLiteral(cnf)

cnf'' = Rule_PureLiteral(cnf')
```

```
    // Splits the decision tree into branches p and ¬p
    splitted = Rule_Split(cnf'')
    return DPLL(splitted[p]) || DPLL(splitted[¬p])

TERMINATION-CONDITIONS(cnf):
    If cnf.Clauses is Empty:
        return True
    If cnf.Clauses contains Empty_Clause:
        return False
```

DPLL builds a tree that is shaped using three rules: OneLiteral, PureLiteral, and Split. The first two determine the formula that is contained in every node while the latter creates new branches in the tree. Let us examine them one by one:

- OneLiteral: If there is a unit clause—i.e., a clause containing only one literal p—then delete that clause as well as every clause containing p. Then, delete the negation of p (¬p) from every clause of CNF. If a formula is to be satisfiable then this literal necessarily must be 1 since it determines the truth value of its clause.

- PureLiteral: If there is a literal p such that ¬p does not belong to any clause of CNF then delete every clause containing p. In this case, we can assign value 1 to p since its negation does not exist in CNF.

- Split: After applying the Pure Literal rule we know that if there's a literal p then its negation must also be there. Thus, we select a literal p and divide the set of clauses into Cp, C¬p, and R. The set of clauses Cp contains all clauses including literal p. C¬p every clause containing ¬p and R the set of clauses that do not contain p or ¬p.

Finally we obtain the sets Cp + R and C¬p + R, where
Cp + R is the set obtained after adding every clause
in R to Cp; C¬p + R is the set obtained after adding
every clause in R to C¬p. These two sets will be the
new CNFs root nodes for the left and right branches
of the tree that we are forming under the DPLL
procedure.

An example of these rules can be seen in the following lines; in each
case an initial CNF formula is presented and then each rule is applied to it.

One Literal Example
```
CNF = {{p, q, ¬r},{p, ¬q}, {¬p}, {r}, {u}}
-Apply OneLiteral rule with L = ¬p
CNF' = {{p, q, ¬r},{p, ¬q}, {r}, {u}}
-Removing ¬L = p from clauses in Cnf'
CNF'' = {{q, ¬r},{¬q}, {r}, {u}}
```

Pure Literal Example
```
CNF = {{p, q},{p, ¬q}, {r, q}, {r, ¬q}}
-Apply PureLiteral rule with L = p
CNF' = {{r, q}, {r, ¬q}}
```

Split Example
```
CNF = {{p, ¬q, r},{¬p, q}, {¬r, q}, {¬r, ¬q}}
-Apply Split rule with L = p
CNF' = {{¬q, r}, {¬r, q}, {¬r, ¬q}}
CNF'' = {{q}, {¬r, q}, {¬r, ¬q}}
```

The DPLL algorithm as well as all its auxiliary methods will be
included in the Cnf class. The public Dpll() method will rely on an
auxiliary private Dpll method that will receive as argument a copy of the
Cnf class as shown in Listing 2-5.

Listing 2-5. Dpll() Method and Its Auxiliary Method Dpll(Cnf cnf)

```
public bool Dpll()
{
    return Dpll(new Cnf {Clauses = new
    List<Clause>(Clauses)});
}

private bool Dpll(Cnfcnf)
{
    // The CNF with no clauses is assumed to be True
    if (cnf.Clauses.Count == 0)
        return true;

    // Rule One Literal: if there exists a clause with
    a single literal
    // we assign it True and remove every clause
    containing it.
varcnfAfterOneLit = OneLiteral(cnf);

    if (cnfAfterOneLit.Item2 == 0)
        return true;

    if (cnfAfterOneLit.Item2 < 0)
        return false;

cnf = cnfAfterOneLit.Item1;

    // Rule Pure Literal: if there exists a literal and
    its negation does not exist in any clause of Cnf
varcnfPureLit = PureLiteralRule(cnf);

    // Rule Split: splitting occurs over a literal and
    creates 2 branches of the tree
var split = Split(cnfPureLit);

    return Dpll(split.Item1) || Dpll(split.Item2);
}
```

From Listing 2-5 we can see that the Dpll(Cnfcnf) method is pretty close to matching exactly the DPLL pseudocode previously presented. First, we check that there are some clauses in the current Cnf class, and then we execute the first simplification rule, which is the One Literal rule. As illustrated in Listing 2-6, the OneLiteral(Cnfcnf) method returns a Tuple<Cnf, int> where the resulting Cnf class in the tuple will be the one obtained after executing the simplification and the resulting integer can be either -1, 0, or 1. If its value is 0 then the Cnf formula has no more clauses to check, and therefore it must be true (satisfiable); if its value is -1 then an empty clause was found in the Cnf and it must be false (unsatisfiable). Finally, in cases where it has value 1 the procedure must continue as no conclusive result of Cnf's satisfiability has been found.

A description of the two auxiliary methods used by OneLiteral(Cnfcnf) are detailed here:

- Negate Literal(Formula literal): receives as argument a Formula assumed to be a literal and returns its negation. In any other case returns null.

- UnitClause(Cnfcnf): finds a clause with a single literal and returns this literal. In cases where there's not such a clause it returns null.

The code of this rule would be as in Listing 2-6.

Listing 2-6. OneLiteral() Rule and Its Auxiliary Methods

```
private Tuple<Cnf, int>OneLiteral(Cnfcnf)
        {
varunitLiteral = UnitClause(cnf);
        if (unitLiteral == null)
            return new Tuple<Cnf, int>(cnf, 1);

varnewCnf = new Cnf();
```

```
            while (unitLiteral != null)
            {
varclausesToRemove = new List<int>();
vari = 0;

            // 1st Loop - Finding clauses where the
            // unit literal is, these clauses will not be
            // considered in the new Cnf
foreach (var clause in cnf.Clauses)
            {
                if (clause.Literals.Any(literal =>clause.
                LiteralEquals(literal, unitLiteral)))
clausesToRemove.Add(i);
i++;
            }

            // New Cnf after removing every clause where
            // unit literal is
newCnf = new Cnf();

            // 2nd Loop - Leave clause that do not include
            // the unit literal
            for (var j = 0; j <cnf.Clauses.Count; j++)
            {
                if (!clausesToRemove.Contains(j))
newCnf.Clauses.Add(cnf.Clauses[j]);
            }
            // No clauses, which implies SAT
            if (newCnf.Clauses.Count == 0)
                return new Tuple<Cnf, int>(newCnf, 0);
```

```
                // Remove negation of unit literal from
                remaining clauses
varunitNegated = NegateLiteral(unitLiteral);
varclausesNoLitNeg = new List<Clause>();

foreach (var clause in newCnf.Clauses)
                {
varnewClause = new Clause();

                    // Leaving every literal except the unit
                    literal negated
foreach (var literal in clause.Literals)
                        if (!clause.LiteralEquals(literal,
                        unitNegated))
newClause.Literals.Add(literal);

clausesNoLitNeg.Add(newClause);
                }

newCnf.Clauses = new List<Clause>(clausesNoLitNeg);
                // Resetting variables for next stage
cnf = newCnf;
unitLiteral = UnitClause(cnf);
                // Empty clause found
                if (cnf.Clauses.Any(c =>c.Literals.Count == 0))
                    return new Tuple<Cnf, int>(newCnf, -1);
            }

        return new Tuple<Cnf, int>(newCnf, 1);
    }
```

```
public Formula NegateLiteral(Formula literal)
{
    if (literal is Variable)
        return new Not(literal);
    if (literal is Not)
        return (literal as Not).P;
    return null;
}

private Formula UnitClause(Cnfcnf)
{
foreach (var clause in cnf.Clauses)
        if (clause.Literals.Count == 1)
            return clause.Literals.First();
    return null;
}
```

The OneLiteral method consists of a while loop that ends when either
there are no more clauses of a single literal in the current Cnf class or one
of the termination conditions (no clauses in Cnf or empty clause found) is
reached. Inside this while loop there's a first loop that stores the positions
of unit clauses in every clause, including the current unit literal. There is
a second loop that builds up a new Cnf class by skipping those clauses
whose positions were stored in the first loop. A third and final loop within
the while does an analogous job to the first two loops but in this case
makes sure the negation of the unit literal is removed from every clause in
the new Cnf obtained after the execution of the first two loops.

In Listing 2-7 we can see the code of the Pure Literal rule, which is
typically applied after the One Literal rule.

Listing 2-7. PureLiteral() Rule and Its Auxiliary Methods

```
private CnfPureLiteralRule(Cnfcnf)
        {
varpureLiterals = PureLiterals(cnf);
            if (pureLiterals.Count() == 0)
                return cnf;

varnewCnf = new Cnf();
varclausesRemoved = new SortedSet<int>();

            // Checking what clauses contain pure literals
foreach (varpureLiteral in pureLiterals)
            {
                for (vari = 0; i<cnf.Clauses.Count; i++)
                {
                    if (cnf.Clauses[i].Contains(pureLiteral))
clausesRemoved.Add(i);
                }
            }

            // Creating the new set of clauses
            for (vari = 0; i<cnf.Clauses.Count; i++)
            {
                if (!clausesRemoved.Contains(i))
newCnf.Clauses.Add(cnf.Clauses[i]);
            }

            return newCnf;
        }

        private IEnumerable<Formula>PureLiterals(Cnfcnf)
            {
var result = new List<Formula>();
```

```
foreach (var clause in cnf.Clauses)
foreach (var literal in clause.Literals)
                {
                        if (PureLiteral(cnf, literal))
result.Add(literal);
                }

            return result;
        }

        private bool PureLiteral(Cnfcnf, Formula literal)
        {
var negation = NegateLiteral(literal);

foreach (var clause in cnf.Clauses)
            {
foreach (var l in clause.Literals)
                        if (clause.LiteralEquals(l, negation))
                            return false;
            }

            return true;
        }
```

The PureLiteralRule method takes care of executing the Pure Literal rule over the new Cnf class returned by the One Literal rule. It relies on the following auxiliary methods:

- PureLiterals(Cnf cnf): returns a list of pure literals found in Cnf class

- PureLiteral(Cnf cnf, Formula literal): determines whether a given literal is a pure literal; i.e., it return false if its negation exists in Cnf class; true otherwise.

The PureLiteralRule() method finds all pure literals in the Cnf class and removes them from every clause in the CNF formula; a new Cnf with the resulting clauses is returned.

As a final point, the Split() method is shown in Listing 2-8.

Listing 2-8. Split() Rule and Its Auxiliary Methods

```
        private Tuple<Cnf, Cnf> Split(Cnfcnf)
        {
var literal = Heuristics.ChooseLiteral(cnf);
var tuple = SplittingOnLiteral(cnf, literal);

            return new Tuple<Cnf, Cnf>(RemoveLiteral(tuple.Item1,
            literal), RemoveLiteral(tuple.Item2,
            NegateLiteral(literal)));
        }

        private CnfRemoveLiteral(Cnfcnf, Formula literal)
        {
var result = new Cnf();

foreach (var clause in cnf.Clauses)
result.Clauses.Add(clause.RemoveLiteral(literal));

            return result;
        }

        private Tuple<Cnf, Cnf>SplittingOnLiteral(Cnfcnf,
        Formula literal)
        {
            // List of clauses containing literal
var @in = new List<Clause>();
            // List of clauses containing Not(literal)
varinNegated = new List<Clause>();
```

```
            // List of clauses not containing literal nor
            Not(literal)
var @out = new List<Clause>();
var negated = NegateLiteral(literal);

foreach (var clause in cnf.Clauses)
            {
                if (clause.Contains(literal))
                    @in.Add(clause);
                else if (clause.Contains(negated))
inNegated.Add(clause);
                else
                    @out.Add(clause);
            }

varinCnf = new Cnf { Clauses = @in };
varoutCnf = new Cnf { Clauses = @inNegated };
inCnf.Join(@out);
outCnf.Join(@out);

            return new Tuple<Cnf, Cnf>(inCnf, outCnf);
        }
```

This method uses the following auxiliary methods:

- `RemoveLiteral(Cnf cnf, Formula literal)`: returns a new Cnf class where each clause will not contain the literal received as argument

- `SplittingOnLiteral(Cnf cnf, Formula literal)`: returns a tuple containing two CNFs according to the Split rule previously described

In the Split() method we make a call to a static method ChooseLiteral() from a class named Heuristics; this method outputs the first literal from the CNF formula and takes it as the *branching literal*.

Heuristics and metaheuristics are topics that we'll analyze deeply in Chapter 7. For the time being, let us think of a heuristic as a procedure that, drawn from experience, helps us in attaching human, empiric knowledge to the process of solving a certain problem.

Note   In the SplittingOnLiteral() method we declared variables @in, inNegated, and @out with the purpose of storing clauses that contain the literal selected for splitting or branching, its negation, and any other clause respectively. We use the @ prefix because *in* and *out* are keywords in C#.

In DPLLs, tree construction is extremely important for efficiency reasons in order to properly select the literal that will be used for branching; i.e., the literal that will be used to split the current node and create new branches of the tree. We'll content ourselves with the naïve, simple method that we have for branching, and later in this book we will dive into better ways to select and branch.

Practical Problem: Modeling the Pigeonhole Principle in Propositional Logic

The Pigeonhole Principle, also known as Dirichlet's Box Principle, is a simple yet fundamental idea in mathematics. It was formulated back in the 1800s by the German mathematician Peter Gustav Lejeune Dirichlet, the scientist who defined the concept of *function* as we know it today—one of his multiple contributions in many fields.

The principle states that if you have n pigeonholes and m pigeons where $m > n$ (# pigeons > # pigeonholes) then there's at least one pigeonhole containing two pigeons.

To formulate the principle in propositional logic, let us consider variable p_ij, which will indicate that pigeon i is mapped to pigeonhole j. We'll try to create a CNF formula that models this problem and then find out about its satisfiability.

The following constraints will determine the clauses of the resulting CNF formula.

- **$p\_i1 \lor p\_i2 \lor ... \lor p\_in$, for each i <= m**

- **$\neg p\_ik \lor \neg p\_jk$, for each i, j <= m and k <= n, i ≠ j**

The first rule guarantees that every clause (pigeonhole) contains at least one pigeon. The second rule or constraint is applied to every distinct pair of variables and guarantees that there are not two pigeons in the same pigeonhole. In the following practical problem, we'll see an example of how to test the Pigeonhole Principle in our program.

Practical Problem: Finding Whether a Propositional Logic Formula is SAT

In this practical problem we'll use the hierarchy and the DPLL algorithm previously described to determine whether a given propositional logic formula is satisfiable. To provide better visualization of results we'll implement a Name property in the Variable class as well as ToString() overrides in classes Not, And, Or, Variable, and Cnf (Listing 2-9).

Listing 2-9. Adding Name Property to Variable Class and ToString()
Overrides for Variable, Not, And, Or, and Cnf Classes

```
public class Variable : Formula
    {
        public bool Value { get; set; }
        public string Name { get; set; }

        ...

        public override string ToString()
        {
            return Name;
        }
    }
public class Not : Formula
    {
        ...

        public override string ToString()
        {
            return "!" + p;
        }
    }
public class Or : BinaryGate
    {
        ...

        public override string ToString()
        {
            return  "(" + P + " | " + Q + ")";
        }
    }
```

```
public class And : BinaryGate
    {
        ...
        public override string ToString()
        {
            return  "(" + P + " & " + Q + ")";
        }
    }

public class Cnf : BinaryGate
    {
        ...
        public override string ToString()
        {
            if (Clauses.Count > 0)
            {
                var result = "";
                foreach (var clausule in Clauses)
                {
                    var c = "";
                    foreach (var literal in clausule.Literals)
                        c += literal + ",";

                    result += "(" + c + ")";
                }
                return result;
            }

            return "Empty CNF";
        }
    }
```

Let's start by trying to input the next formula into our program:

$(p \lor q) \land (p \lor \neg q) \land (\neg p \lor q) \land (\neg p \lor \neg r)$

We'll use the And, Or, Variable, and Not classes to create this formula, as illustrated in Listing 2-10.

Listing 2-10. Creating Formula $(p \lor q) \land (p \lor \neg q) \land (\neg p \lor q) \land (\neg p \lor \neg r)$ and Finding Out If It's Satisfiable Using the DPLL Algorithm

```
var p = new Variable(true) { Name = "p" };
var q = new Variable(true) { Name = "q" };
var r = new Variable(true) { Name = "r" };

var f1 = new And(new Or(p, q), new Or(p, new Not(q)));
var f2 = new And(new Or(new Not(p), q), new Or(new Not(p),
new Not(r)));
var formula = new And(f1, f2);
varnnf = formula.ToNnf();
Console.WriteLine("NNF: " + nnf);

nnf = nnf.ToCnf();
varcnf = new Cnf(nnf as And);
cnf.SimplifyCnf();

Console.WriteLine("CNF: " + cnf);
Console.WriteLine("SAT: " + cnf.Dpll());
```

The result obtained after executing this code is shown in Figure 2-2.

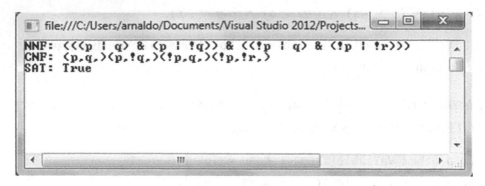

Figure 2-2. *Results after executing the previous code*

Now, let's try a different formula (Listing 2-11; Figure 2-3):

(p ∨ q ∨ ¬r) ∨ (p ∨ q ∨ r) ∧ (p ∨ ¬q) ∧ ¬p

Listing 2-11. Creating Formula (p ∨ q ∨ ¬r) ∨ (p ∨ q ∨ r) ∨ (p ∨ ¬q) ∨ ¬p
and Finding Out If It's Satisfiable Using the DPLL Algorithm

```
var f1 = new Or(p, new Or(q, new Not(r)));
var f2 = new Or(p, new Or(q, r));
var f3 = new Or(p, new Not(q));
var formula = new And(f1, new And(f2, new And(f3, new Not(p))));
```

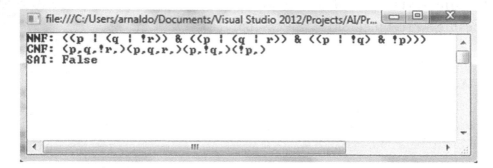

Figure 2-3. *Results after executing the DPLL algorithm on the
previous formula*

We will use one final formula to test the algorithm and the `Formula` hierarchy introduced in this chapter (Listing 2-12; Figure 2-4).

(p ˅ q ˅ r) ^ (p ˅ q ˅ ¬r) ^ (p ˅ ¬q ˅ r) ^ (p ˅ ¬q ˅ ¬r) ^ (¬p ˅ q ˅ r) ^ (¬p ˅ q ˅ ¬r) ^ (¬p ˅ ¬q ˅ r)

Listing 2-12. Creating Formula (p ˅ q ˅ r) ^ (p ˅ q ˅ ¬r) ^ (p ˅ ¬q ˅ r) ^ (p ˅ ¬q ˅ ¬r) ^ (¬p ˅ q ˅ r) ^ (¬p ˅ q ˅ ¬r) ^ (¬p ˅ ¬q ˅ r) and Finding Out If It's Satisfiable Using the DPLL Algorithm

```
var f1 = new Or(p, new Or(q, r));
var f2 = new Or(p, new Or(q, new Not(r)));
var f3 = new Or(p, new Or(new Not(q), r));
var f4 = new Or(p, new Or(new Not(q), new Not(r)));
var f5 = new Or(new Not(p), new Or(q, r));
var f6 = new Or(new Not(p), new Or(q, new Not(r)));
var f7 = new Or(new Not(p), new Or(new Not(q), r));
var formula = new And(f1, new And(f2, new And(f3, new And(f4,
new And(f5, new And(f6, f7))))));
```

```
file:///C:/Users/arnaldo/Documents/Visual Studio 2012/Projects/AI/Practical.AI/bin/Debug/Practica...
NNF: ((p | (q | r)) & ((p | (q | !r)) & ((p | (!q | r)) & ((p | (!q | !r)) & ((!
p | (q | r)) & ((!p | (q | !r)) & ((!p | (!q | r)))))))
CNF: (p,q,r,)(p,q,!r,)(p,!q,r,)(p,!q,!r,)(!p,q,r,)(!p,q,!r,)(!p,!q,r,)
SAT: True
```

Figure 2-4. *Results after executing the DPLL algorithm on the previous formula*

Recalling now the Pigeonhole Principle (described in the last practical problem), let's consider the case where $m = 3$, $n = 2$. This case would be encoded in our program as shown in Listing 2-13.

Listing 2-13. Pigeonhole Principle Modeled in Our Program for the Case Where m = 3, n = 2; i.e., *m* pigeons, *n* pigeonholes

```
// Pigeonhole Principle m = 3, n = 2
var p11 = new Variable(true) { Name = "p11" };
var p12 = new Variable(true) { Name = "p12" };

var p21 = new Variable(true) { Name = "p21" };
var p22 = new Variable(true) { Name = "p22" };

var p31 = new Variable(true) { Name = "p31" };
var p32 = new Variable(true) { Name = "p32" };

var f1 = new Or(p11, p12);
var f2 = new Or(p21, p22);
var f3 = new Or(p31, p32);

var f4 = new Or(new Not(p11), new Not(p21));
var f5 = new Or(new Not(p11),  new Not(p31));
var f6 = new Or(new Not(p21), new Not(p31));

var f7 = new Or(new Not(p12), new Not(p22));
var f8 = new Or(new Not(p12), new Not(p32));
var f9 = new Or(new Not(p22), new Not(p32));

var formula = new And(f1, new And(f2, new And(f3, new And(f4,
new And(f5, new And(f6, new And(f7, new And(f8, f9)))))))));
```

The result for this case, as expected, would be False since we cannot occupy every pigeonhole with a single pigeon.

In the last few sections we have been studying propositional logic and some of the algorithms and methods related to it. We also analyzed the relationship between logic and AI and described what ATP stands for, as well as some of its uses and advantages. Let's remember that ATP is an area that attempts to automate mathematicians' work and that SAT solvers are very useful tools in this area. In the following sections we'll start looking at a more complex logic than propositional logic, first-order logic, which is an extension of propositional logic, and we'll get a glimpse of some of the benefits it provides over the simpler propositional logic.

First-Order Logic

Propositions that we have studied thus far consist of a subject (object or individual) and a predicate.

Given a set of objects or subjects, the relations and properties defined among these objects are known as *predicates.*

Examples of predicates are the following:

1. $x > x$

2. $5 + y - x = 1$

3. $x > 2$

After considering the previous examples, we may ask ourselves, what would be the difference between propositions and predicates?

In the latest predicate examples we have constants (1, 2, 5), relations (>, =), and functions (+, -), and they all have a fixed interpretation, but the same doesn't occur with numerical variables (x, y). The indetermination that these variables introduce in regards to the value that they can take causes the expression to not be logically considered as a proposition. Depending on the value that variables x, y may take, the previous expressions could become True or False—hence, become propositions.

In logic, expressions 1, 2, 3 are referred to as *nth predicates*; i.e., a predicate with *n* variables. Considering examples 1, 2, and 3, we can say that the first expression is a unary predicate and the second a binary predicate. A *property* is a unary predicate, a particular type of relationship with the subject itself; thus, it's thought of as a special case of predicate.

Note   Predicates represent relations between subjects, objects, and individuals. They lack veritative value; i.e., they don't have True or False values like propositions do.

First-order logic (FOL) extends propositional logic by allowing certain forms of reasoning about objects in logical statements.

In propositional logic we have variables that stand for facts or statements that might be true or not, like "World War II ended in 1952" or "*Star Wars* was directed by George Lucas," but you can't have variables that represent things like cars, pencils, or the temperature. In FOL, variables refer to things of the world like pencils or the temperature, and we can quantify them, allowing us to express in one sentence what in propositional logic would probably take several.

In general, some of the reasons why we need FOL are as follows:

- We need a way of saying that an individual or subject has a certain property or that certain individuals are related in a particular way (e.g., that Zofia is single, or that she is married to Albert, or that Johnny is Ben's dog).

- We need a way of saying that all subjects (of a certain type) have a certain property (e.g., that all birds have wings or there exists a man taller than 7 feet).

- We need a way of referring to entities that are functionally determined by other entities (e.g., the *height* of a person; the *weight* of an object; the *sum* of two numbers).

The simplified representation that propositional logic provides makes it very complicated to model numerous problems that typically arise in our ordinary life. As a result, we must rely on a more complex logic like FOL.

The reasons described earlier motivate the syntax of FOL. Its syntax allows us to form (using a formal language) formulas similar to English sentences, such as IsDog("Johnny") (Is Johnny a dog?), Misses("Katty", "John") (Katty misses John) or ∀x (IsDog(x) => ¬CanFly(x)) (For all object *x*, if *x* is a dog then *x* cannot fly).

The components of FOL are the *connectives* of propositional logic; *terms*, which can be *constants* (a, b, John, Lucas, etc.), *variables* (x, y, etc.), or *functions* (F, G, H, etc.) applied to other terms; *propositional constants* (True, False), *predicates* (IsDog, CanFly, etc.), which represent the properties of a single object or relationships among two or more objects, and *quantifiers* ('for all ...' denoted as ∀, 'there exists ...' denoted as ∃ and 'there exists only one ...' denoted as ∃!). The big novelty in FOL is without a doubt the appearance of quantifier operators.

A *formula* can be a predicate applied to one or more terms, the equality of two terms (i.e., t1 = t2; ∀(v)F'(v), ∃(v)F'(v) if v is a variable and F' is a formula), or anything deriving from the application of logic connectives of propositional logic to other formulas.

In the following lines we detail a bit more the FOL syntax:

```
constant ::= a | A | b | B | c | C | John | Block1 | Block2 | ...
variable ::= x | y | z | x1| x2 | block1 | ...
function::= f | g | h | weight | sum | mother-of | ...
term ::= constant | variable | function (term , ..., term)
predicate::= A | B | C |IsDog| Loves |IsBrother ...
binary connective ::=^ | ˅ | => | <=>
formula ::= predicate (term , ..., term) | (term = term)
| ¬formula | ((formula) binary connective (formula)) |
∀(variable) formula | ∃(variable) formula
```

In propositional logic we interpreted a formula as the assignment of truth values to its propositional variables. In FOL the introduction of predicates and quantifiers gives us formulas whose evaluation depends on the interpretation given in some domain (integers, real numbers, cars, pencils . . . anything we can think of) or universe of objects; the concept of interpretation in this case is a bit more complicated.

Note   An interpretation of a formula is a pair (D, A) where D is the domain and A an assignment for each constant, function, predicate, and so on.

In order to define the interpretation I of a formula in a domain or set of objects D we must consider the following *rules of interpretation*:

1. If c is a constant then c has domain D. This mapping indicates how names (constants are basically names) are connected to objects of the universe. We may have a constant Johnny, and the interpretation of Johnny in the world of dogs could be a particular dog.

2. If P is a predicate then P has D x D x ... D domain; i.e., there's a mapping from predicates to relations in D.

3. If f is a function then f has domain D, an image also in D; i.e., there's a mapping from functions to functions in D.

Given an interpretation *I* of a formula *F* under domain *D*, *I* follows the following *rules of evaluation*:

1. If P(v1, v2, ... ,vn) is a predicate then P is True if (v1, v2, ... , vn) is a relation in D; i.e., (v1, v2, ... , vn)∈ D x D x ... x D. Recall that an n-ary relation is a set of n-tuples.

2. If F, F' are formulas of FOL then F ∧ F', F ∨ F', F => F', F <=> F', ¬F have the same veritative value in domain D as they would have using the same operators in propositional logic; i.e., these operators have the same truth tables in both logics.

3. The formula ∀(v)F(v) is True if F(v) is True for all values of v in D.

4. The formula ∃(v)F(v) is True if F(v) is True for at least one value of v in D.

Let's examine an example that will clarify how interpretation and evaluation works in FOL; consider the following interpretation *I* of a formula under domain *D*:

```
∃(x)IsFriend(x, Arnaldo)∧∃(y)IsWorkingWith(y, Arnaldo)
```

```
D = {John, Arnaldo, Mark, Louis, Duke, Sting, Jordan, Miles,
Lucas, Thomas, Chuck, Floyd, Hemingway}
Constants = {Arnaldo}
Predicates = {IsFriend, IsWorkingWith}
I(Arnaldo) = Arnaldo
I(IsFriend) = {(John, Arnaldo), (Mark, Louis), (Duke, Sting),
(Jordan, Miles)}
I(IsWorkingWith) = {(Lucas, Arnaldo), (Thomas, Chuck), (Floyd,
Hemingway)}
```

For determining the truth value of the previous interpretation we have that

∃(x)IsFriend(x, Arnaldo)

for *x* = John is True because tuple or relation (John, Arnaldo) belongs to IsFriend; therefore, ∃(x)IsFriend(x, Arnaldo) is also True.

∃(y)IsWorkingWith(y, Arnaldo)

for *y* = Lucas is True because tuple or relation (Lucas, Arnaldo) belongs to IsWorkingWith; therefore, ∃(y)IsWorkingWith(y, Arnaldo) is also True.

Since both ∃(x)IsFriend(x, Arnaldo) and ∃(y)IsWorkingWith(y, Arnaldo) are True, their conjunction is True, and the interpretation is also True.

Predicates in C#

Since we are exploring the world of FOL and its most notable components (predicates, quantifiers, and so forth) it would be worth mentioning that in C# we can make use of the Predicate<T> delegate, a construct that allows us to test whether an object of type T fulfills a given condition. For example, we could have the Dog class as follows (Listing 2-14).

Listing 2-14. Dog Class

```
public class Dog
  {
        public string Name { get; set; }
        public double Weight { get; set; }
        public Gender Sex { get; set; }

        public Dog(string name, double weight, Gender sex)
        {
            Name = name;
```

```
                Weight = weight;
                Sex = sex;
}
    }

    public enum Gender {
        Male, Female
    }
```

Then, we can use a predicate to filter and get objects that satisfy certain properties, as illustrated in Listing 2-15, where we create a list of dogs and then use the Find() method, which expects a predicate as argument, to "find" all objects (dogs) satisfying the given predicates.

Listing 2-15. Using a Predicate in C# to Filter and Get Objects (Dogs in This Case) That Are Males and Dogs Whose Weight Exceeds 22 Pounds

```
varjohnny = new Dog("Johnny", 17.5, Gender.Male);
var jack = new Dog("Jack", 23.5, Gender.Male);
varjordan = new Dog("Jack", 21.2, Gender.Male);
varmelissa = new Dog("Melissa", 19.7, Gender.Female);
var dogs = new List<Dog> { johnny, jack, jordan, melissa };
Predicate<Dog>maleFinder = (Dog d) => { return d.Sex == Gender.
Male; };
Predicate<Dog>heavyDogsFinder = (Dog d) => { return d.Weight>=
22; };

varmaleDogs = dogs.Find(maleFinder);
varheavyDogs = dogs.Find(heavyDogsFinder);
```

At this point, we have gotten ourselves into the world of propositional logic and FOL. In the next section we will present a practical problem where we'll see some FOL in action.

Practical Problem: Cleaning Robot

In this section we'll see many of the concepts described earlier (functions, predicates, and so forth) being applied in the creation of a cleaning robot, whose world is illustrated in Figure 2-5.

Figure 2-5. *Cleaning robot in the grid. Dirt is marked as orange balls and logically represented on the grid as integers. Following this idea, the cell on the upper-left corner (first one) has value 5.*

This cleaning robot tries to get rid of the dirt in a grid of n x m (n rows, m columns). Each cell in the grid is an integer d, where d indicates the count of dirt in that cell. When $d = 0$ that cell is considered clean.

The robot will have the following features:

- It moves one step at a time in four possible directions (left, up, right, down).

- It does not abandon a cell until is completely clean, and it picks dirt up one step at a time; i.e., if on a dirty cell it will clean a unit of dirt at a time (leaving -1 dirt) and then continue to its next decision stage.

- It stops when everything is clean or its task has exceeded a given time in milliseconds.

Our cleaning robot will rely on the following predicates and functions:

- `IsDirty()` is a predicate that determines if the cell where the robot is happens to be dirty.

- `IsTerrainClean()` is a predicate that determines if every cell on the terrain is clean.

- `MoveAvailable(int x, int y)` is a predicate that determines whether a move to (x, y) in the terrain is legal.

- `SelectMove()` is a function that randomly selects a move.

- `Clean()` is a function that simply cleans (-1) a dirt from current cell; i.e., the cell where the robot is at that moment.

- `Move(Direction m)` is a function that moves the robot in direction m.

- `Print()` is a function that prints the terrain.

- `Start(intmilliseconds)` is a function that commands the robot to start cleaning up. The code of this method matches the robot behavior explained earlier. The integer argument `milliseconds` represents the maximum time the robot will be cleaning, in milliseconds.

The robot is encoded in a `CleaningRobot` C# class that goes as shown in Listing 2-16.

Listing 2-16. CleaningRobot Class

```
public class CleaningRobot
    {
        private readonlyint[,] _terrain;
        private static Stopwatch _stopwatch;
        public int X { get; set; }
        public int Y { get; set; }
        private static Random _random;

public CleaningRobot(int [,] terrain, int x, int y)
        {
            X = x;
            Y = y;
_terrain = new int[terrain.GetLength(0), terrain.GetLength(1)];
Array.Copy(terrain, _terrain, terrain.GetLength(0) * terrain.
GetLength(1));
            _stopwatch = new Stopwatch();
            _random = new Random();
        }

        public void Start(intmilliseconds)
        {
        _stopwatch.Start();

        do
        {
            if (IsDirty())
                Clean();
            else
                Move(SelectMove());

        } while (!IsTerrainClean() && !(_stopwatch.Elapsed
        Milliseconds>milliseconds));
        }
```

```
        // Function
        private Direction SelectMove()
        {
var list = new List<Direction> { Direction.Down, Direction.Up,
Direction.Right, Direction.Left };
            return list[_random.Next(0, list.Count)];
        }

        // Function
        public void Clean()
        {
            _terrain[X, Y] -= 1;
        }

        // Predicate
        public bool IsDirty()
        {
            return _terrain[X, Y] > 0;
        }

        // Function
        private void Move(Direction m)
        {
            switch (m)
            {
                case Direction.Up:
                    if (MoveAvailable(X - 1, Y))
                        X -= 1;
                        break;
                case Direction.Down:
                    if (MoveAvailable(X + 1, Y))
                        X += 1;
                        break;
```

```
                case Direction.Left:
                        if (MoveAvailable(X, Y - 1))
                            Y -= 1;
                        break;
                case Direction.Right:
                        if (MoveAvailable(X, Y + 1))
                            Y += 1;
                        break;
            }
        }

        // Predicate
        public bool MoveAvailable(int x, int y)
        {
            return x >= 0 && y >= 0 && x < _terrain.
            GetLength(0) && y < _terrain.GetLength(1);
        }

        // Predicate
        public bool IsTerrainClean()
        {
            // For all cells in terrain; cell equals 0
foreach (var c in _terrain)
                if (c > 0)
                    return false;

            return true;
        }

        public void Print()
        {
var col = _terrain.GetLength(1);
vari = 0;
var line = "";
```

```
Console.WriteLine("--------------");
foreach (var c in _terrain)
            {
                line += string.Format(" {0} ", c);
i++;
                if (col == i)
                {
Console.WriteLine(line);
line = "";
i = 0;
                }
            }
        }
    }

    public enumDirection
    {
        Up, Down, Left, Right
}
```

The constructor of the class receives as arguments the terrain and two integers x, y that represent the initial position of the robot on the terrain.

The print() method was included for testing purposes. Let's suppose we have the terrain as shown in the following code and then we execute the robot, i.e., call the Start() method on it, as seen in Listing 2-17.

Listing 2-17. Starting the Cleaning Robot

```
var terrain = new [,]
                {
                    {0, 0, 0},
                    {1, 1, 1},
                    {2, 2, 2}
};
```

```
varcleaningRobot = new CleaningRobot(terrain, 0, 0);
cleaningRobot.Print();
cleaningRobot.Start(50000);
cleaningRobot.Print();
```

The terrain contains dirt on the second (1 on each column) and
third rows (2 on each column), and after the robot has finished his task,
according to one of the termination conditions (everything's clean or
time's up) stated before, we obtain the result seen in Figure 2-6.

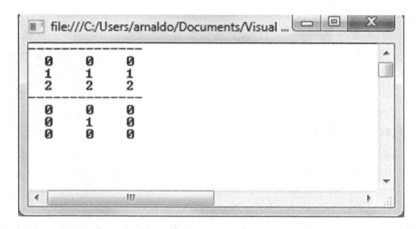

Figure 2-6. *Terrain before and after the cleaning of the robot*

As occurred before when developing the DPLL algorithm, we need a
heuristic for selecting the next move of the agent. We'll get into the field of
heuristics and metaheuristics in Chapter 7.

This cleaning robot is a very naïve, simple agent; the topic of agents in
AI will be addressed in the next chapter. For the moment, we have created
the necessary basis to start diving into more complicated and interesting
subjects and branches of AI. In any case, future topics to be studied will be
related to logic as it's the basis of many sciences and areas of knowledge.

Summary

In the last two chapters we analyzed the relationship between AI and logic. We introduced two fundamental types of logic: propositional logic and first-order logic. We examined various codes that included a hierarchy for representing formulas (variables, logical connectives, and so on), and we complemented this hierarchy with different methods. Among these methods we presented the negation normal form transformation algorithm, the conjunctive normal form transformation algorithm (relies on the distributive laws previously introduced), and the DPLL algorithm, which is a classic algorithm for determining the satisfiability of a formula. Additionally, we described a binary decision tree for representing formulas and their possible evaluations and a practical problem where a simple, naïve cleaning robot uses first-order logic concepts to formulate its simple intelligence.

In the next chapter, we'll begin explaining agents and many of the concepts around these (proactive, reactive) that we may have heard of before from video-game fans, AI fans, friends, or colleagues.

CHAPTER 3

Agents

In this chapter, we'll begin describing a very important field of study in the world of AI: agents. Nowadays, agents represent an area of strong interest for many subfields of computer science and AI. They are being used in a great number of applications, ranging from comparatively small systems such as email filters to complex, colossal systems such as air traffic control.

In the next pages we'll address agents as fundamental AI entities; we will start by getting acquainted with a possible agent definition (as there's no global agreement regarding this concept). We'll examine different agents' properties and architectures and analyze a practical problem that will help us understand how to develop agents in C#. Practical problems examined in this and the following chapter will set the concepts presented throughout this chapter on firm ground, and many of them will be connected to classical problems of AI.

We'll give meaning and definition to many of the words that we typically hear today from videogamers, AI hobbyists, or programmers associated with AI—words such as *reactive, proactive, perceptions, actions, intentions*, or *deliberation*. Typical examples of agents that we might know are a robot (like the cleaning robot from last chapter), a web-based shopping program, a traffic-control system, software daemons, and so on.

© Arnaldo Pérez Castaño 2018
A. Pérez Castaño, *Practical Artificial Intelligence*,
https://doi.org/10.1007/978-1-4842-3357-3_3

Note   Agents are colloquially known as *bots*, which derives from the word *robot*. They could use metallic bodies similar to the ones we see in science fiction films or just consist of computer software installed on our phone, like Siri. They may possess human abilities like speech and speech recognition and be able to act on their own.

What's an Agent?

As mentioned earlier, there's no agreement on a global concept of the term *agent*. Let's remember that the same thing occurred with the concept of logic (recall that we analyzed it in Chapter 2).

To provide a definition of the term *agent* we will consider different definitions from various authors and take the most generic features from all of them, attaching some self-logic to it.

Since *agent* is a term drawn from AI, we must bear in mind that, as happens with everything in the field of AI, it relates to creating an artificial entity, something that emulates and enhances, if possible, the making of a set of human tasks in a certain way and environment.

Hence, an *agent* is an entity (human, computer program) that, using a set of sensors (to sense maybe heat, pressure, and so on, kind of like humans do), is capable of obtaining a set of percepts or inputs (warm, high pressure, and so forth) and has the ability to act (turn on AC, move to different location) upon that environment through actuators.

Actuators for the human case can be their legs, arms, or mouth, and in the robot case it can be their robotic arms, wheels, or similar.

Percepts or inputs are every piece of data that the agent receives through its sensors.

In the human case *sensors* can be eyes, nose, ears, or anything that we actually have for pulling information out of the world, our daily environment. In the robot case, sensors can be their cameras, microphone, or anything that they can use to obtain inputs from the environment. In both cases the input received is transformed into percepts, which represent pieces of information with some logic attached. For instance, using our ears we could notice that, when entering a room, the music in it is too loud. How does the process of noticing and receiving this perception work? Our ears sense the loud sounds in the room, and that information is passed on to our brain, which processes it and creates a percept labelled "loud music," and then we know. Optionally, we could act upon that percept and use our arms and hands (actuators) to lower the volume on the music. The same occurs with nonhuman agents, but at a software level and maybe using some robotic parts (arms, wheels, and so on).

From a mathematical point of view, the definition of *agent* can be viewed as a function that uses a set of tuples or relations from a set of percepts as the domain and has a set of actions (Figure 3-1); i.e., assuming F is the agent's function, P the set of percepts, and A the set of actions, F: P^* → A. Now that we have provided a definition for the very important term of *agent*, it's time to define what we will refer to as an *intelligent agent*.

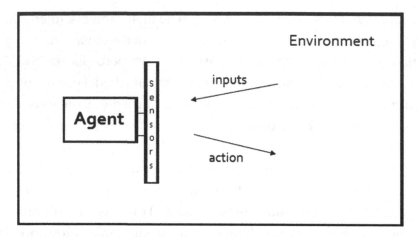

Figure 3-1. An agent in its environment. The agent uses its sensory components to receive inputs from the environment. It processes these inputs and eventually outputs an action that affects the environment. This will be a continuous interaction as long as the agent remains active.

An *intelligent agent* is an autonomous agent capable of executing its actions while considering several agent properties, such as reactivity, proactiveness, and social ability. The main difference between an agent and an intelligent agent are the words *intelligent* and *autonomous*, the latter of which is associated with the independence that is expected in its behavior, while the first relates to the properties just mentioned. These properties and others will be the main topic of the following sections.

Note   An agent does not necessarily need to be an intelligent agent since that feature involves a set of more human or advanced attributes (reactivity, proactiveness, social ability, and so on) that a simple agent such as a movement detector may not need. Thus, to be as general as possible, we begin with the more generic agent definition and then discuss the intelligent agent definition.

Agent Properties

Now that we have gotten acquainted with the agent and intelligent agent concepts, it's time to describe those properties mentioned that make an agent intelligent.

Autonomy refers to the ability of agents to act without the direct intervention of humans or other agents and have control over their own actions and internal state.

Reactivity refers to the ability of agents to perceive their environment and respond in a timely fashion (response must be useful) to the percepts received in it so as to meet the agent's designated goals.

Proactiveness refers to the ability of agents to exhibit goal-directed behavior and take the initiative by creating plans or similar strategies that would lead them to satisfy their designated goals.

Social ability refers to the capability of an agent to interact with other agents (possible humans) in a multi-agent system to achieve its designated goals. Since this property relates to multi-agents' environments, we'll address it further in the next chapter.

Another very important property is that of *rationality*. We say that an agent is rational if it acts in order to achieve its goals and will never act in such a way as to prevent its goals from being achieved.

Purely reactive agents decide what to do without looking at their percepts history. Their decision-making process is based solely on the current percept without looking at their past; hence, they have no memory or do not consider it. Mathematically speaking the agent function of a purely reactive agent is F: $P \rightarrow A$. As we can see, an agent that only exhibits the reactive property will only need the current percept in order to provide an action.

> **Note**   The agent's function for a generic agent is F: $P^* \rightarrow A$. The asterisk on top of the P denotes a relation of zero or more percepts; i.e., a set of tuples of length n where $n >= 0$; this is the number that replaces the asterisk. In the purely reactive agent case, $n = 1$.

The decision-making process in a reactive agent is implemented as a direct mapping from state to action. Agents incorporating this property react to the environment without reasoning about it. The cleaning robot described in the last chapter is an example of a reactive agent; remember we had rules like the ones shown in Listing 3-1.

Listing 3-1. Simple Rule of the Cleaning Robot from Last Chapter, a Reactive Agent

```
if (IsDirty())
Clean();
      else
Move(SelectMove());
```

These were simply rules that made our robot react to the environment without any reasoning whatsoever. The SelectMove() method returned a random move to be executed by the agent, so no heuristic (to be seen in Chapter 14) or any other type of goal-directed analysis or behavior was incorporated into this agent. As happens with the cleaning robot, every reactive agent is basically hardwired as a set of if ... then rules.

What advantages do we get from developing reactive agents?

1. It is really easy to code them, and they allow us to obtain an elegant, legible code.

2. They are easy to track and understand.

3. They provide robustness against failures.

What would be the disadvantages or limitations of a purely reactive agent?

1. Since they make decisions based on local information—in other words, information about the agent's current state—it's difficult to see how such decision making could take into account non-local information; hence, they have a "short horizon" view.

2. It is difficult to make them learn from experience and improve their performance over time.

3. It's hard to code reactive agents that must incorporate a large number of behaviors (too many situations -> action rules).

4. They don't have any proactive behavior; therefore, they do not make plans or care about the future, just about the present or immediate action to execute.

Reacting to an environment is quite easy, but we regularly need more from our agents; we need them to act on our behalf and do things for us. In order to accomplish these tasks, they must have goal-directed behavior—they must be proactive.

Proactive agents will be looking to create and achieve secondary goals that will eventually lead them to fulfill their primary goals. As part of their operation, such agents should be able to anticipate needs, opportunities, and problems, and act on their own initiative to address them. They should also be able to recognize opportunities on the fly; for example, available resources, pattern anomalies, chances of cooperation, and so forth.

A common example of a proactive agent is a personal assistant agent, like those likely installed on one of our devices. This agent can be running constantly on our phone, keeping track of our location and preferences and proactively suggesting places to visit according to those preferences (cultural activities in the area, restaurant offering our type of food, and so on).

In general we'll want our agents to be reactive; that is, respond to the changing conditions of the environment in a timely fashion or equivalently respond to short-term goals. We also want them to be proactive and systematically work toward meeting long-term goals. Having an agent that *balances* these two properties is an open research problem.

In this chapter, we'll analyze a practical problem in which we'll add proactive features to the cleaning robot presented in Chapter 1.

Other properties of agents that, although not considered basic properties like the ones previously mentioned, still are relevant are shown in Table 3-1.

Table 3-1. *Other Agent Properties*

Property	Description
Coordination	It means the agent is capable of executing some activity in a shared environment with other agents. It answers the question, How do you divide a task between a group of agents? Coordination occurs through plans, workflows, or any other management tool.
Cooperation	It means the agent is able to cooperate with other agents so as to fulfill their common goal (share resources, results, distributed problem solving). They either succeed or fail all together, as a team.
Adaptability	Also referred to as learning, it means the agent is reactive, proactive, and capable of learning from its own experiences, the environment, and its interactions with others.
Mobility	It means the agent is able to transport itself from one shell to another and use different platforms.
Temporal continuity	It means the agent is continuously running.

(continued)

Table 3-1. (*continued*)

Property	Description
Personality	It means the agent has a well-defined personality and a sense of emotional state.
Reusability	It means successive agent instances can require keeping instances of the agent class for information reuse or to check and analyze previously generated information.
Resource limitation	It means the agent can act only as long as it has resources at its disposal. These resources are modified by its actions and also by delegating.
Veracity	It means the agent will not knowingly communicate false information.
Benevolence	It means the agent will run under the assumption it does not have conflicting goals, and it will always try to do what is asked of it.
Knowledge-level communication	It means the agent will have the ability to communicate with human agents and maybe other nonhuman agents using a humanlike language (English, Spanish, etc.).

Now that we have detailed some significant agent properties, let's examine some of the different types of environment in which our agent can be interacting; eventually, we'll also introduce various agent architectures that we could implement for our agent.

Types of Environments

Depending on the type of environment, an agent may or may not need a set of properties. Hence, the decision-making process of the agent is affected by the features exposed by the environment in which it runs. These features make up the typos of onvironment that will be described in this section.

In a *deterministic* environment every action taken by the agent will have a single possible outcome; i.e., there is no uncertainty about the resulting state or percept after executing an action (Figure 3-2).

Action A

S ———— S1

Figure 3-2. *Deterministic environment; an agent is in state S and can only move to state or percept S1 after executing an action A. Every state is linked to just one state; i.e., there's a single possible outcome for every action executed by the agent.*

On the other hand, a *non-deterministic* environment is one in which actions executed by agents do not have a well-determined state and rather than just being a single state it could be a set of states; for instance, executing action A could lead to states S1, S2, or S3. This is non-deterministic, as illustrated in Figure 3-3. Non-deterministic environments are the most complicated environments for agent design. Board games using dice are usually non-deterministic, as the roll of the dice could bring the agent to any state, and it depends on the values displayed on the dice.

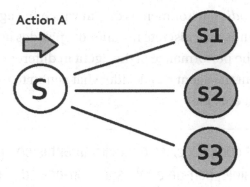

Figure 3-3. *Non-deterministic environment; an agent is in state S and after executing action A it could move to states S1, S2, or S3. Every state is linked to a set of states; i.e., there are multiple possible outcomes for every action executed by the agent.*

In a *static* environment only actions executed by the agent will affect the environment and cause it to alter. In *dynamic* environments there are multiple processes operating, many of which are not related in any way to the agent, yet they still affect the environment and change it. The physical world is a highly dynamic environment.

A *discrete* environment is one in which there are a fixed, finite number of actions and percepts. Alternatively, a *continuous* environment is one in which both actions and percepts are not determined by a finite number. Board games like Chess, Sliding Tiles Puzzle, Othello, or Backgammon represent discrete environments. However, an environment consisting of an actual city represents a continuous environment as there's no way to limit to a fixed, finite number the percepts that the agent may perceive in such an environment.

An *accessible* environment is one in which the agent can obtain accurate, complete, and updated information about the environment's state. An *inaccessible* environment is the opposite—it's one in which the agent cannot obtain accurate, complete, updated information. The more accessible an environment is the easier it will be to design an agent for it.

Finally, an *episodic* environment is one in which the agent's performance depends on a discrete number of episodes and there's no relation between the performance of the agent in different episodes. In this type of environment the agent can decide what action to execute based only on the current episode.

Note   The most complex class of environment is composed of those that are inaccessible, non-deterministic, non-episodic, dynamic, and continuous.

Agents with State

Thus far we have considered agents that map a percept or sequence of percepts to an action. Because agents (not reactive ones) are capable of mapping from a sequence of percepts, they are aware of their history. In this section, we'll go further and examine agents that also maintain state.

The state of an agent will be maintained by means of an *internal data structure*, which will be used to store information about the environment while the agent is being executed. As a result, the decision-making process could be based on the information stored in this data structure.

The agent function then slightly changes to incorporate this new feature.

$F: I \times P^* \rightarrow A$

where I is the set of internal environmental states stored by the agent, P the set of percepts, and A the actions set.

Hence, with stateless agents we just had F: $P^* \rightarrow$ A; now in this case we added the necessary consideration of the internal data structure by making the agent function receive as arguments an internal state and a percept or sequence of percepts; i.e.,

$F(I, P_1, P_2 \ldots P_N) = A.$

It is worth noting that state-based agents like the ones defined in this section are actually vastly more powerful than an agent without state.

In the next practical problem, we'll enhance the cleaning robot described in Chapter 1 by adding state to it.

Practical Problem: Modeling the Cleaning Robot as an Agent and Adding State to It

In this practical problem, we'll modify the CleaningRobot class that we described in the last chapter to adapt it to the agent paradigm (percepts, actions, and so on), specifically to the agent's function. We'll also add state to this agent in the form of a List<Tuple<int, int>> that will store cells already visited and cleaned. We'll see the benefits of having such state and compare it with the CleaningRobot class that is stateless.

We shall name this class CleaningAgent, and its constructor will be very much like the constructor of the CleaningRobot, as seen in Listing 3-2. For this new class, we'll add the Boolean TaskFinished field, which will indicate when the task of the agent is finished, and the List<Tuple<int, int>> __cellsVisited, which will determine the set of cells that have been already visited.

Listing 3-2. Constructor and Fields of the Cleaning Agent

```
public class CleaningAgent
    {
        private readonly int[,] _terrain;
        private static Stopwatch _stopwatch;
        public int X { get; set; }
        public int Y { get; set; }
        public bool TaskFinished { get; set; }
        // Internal data structure for keeping state
```

```
    private readonly List<Tuple<int, int>> __cellsVisited;
    private static Random _random;

    public CleaningAgent(int [,] terrain, int x, int y)
    {
        X = x;
        Y = y;
        _terrain = new int[terrain.GetLength(0), terrain.
        GetLength(1)];
        Array.Copy(terrain, _terrain, terrain.GetLength(0)
        * terrain.GetLength(1));
        _stopwatch = new Stopwatch();
        _cellsVisited= new List<Tuple<int, int>>();
        _random = new Random();
    }
}
```

The working loop of the agent is now related to the agent function; i.e., it executes an action based on the set of perceptions it gets from the environment. The loop ends when the task is finished or the maximum execution time (in milliseconds) is reached, as shown in Listing 3-3.

Listing 3-3. Loop of the Agent Matching the Agent's Function Definition

```
    public void Start(int miliseconds)
    {
        _stopwatch.Start();

        do
        {
            AgentAction(Perceived());
        }
```

```
    while (!TaskFinished && !(_stopwatch.
    ElapsedMilliseconds > miliseconds));
}
```

The methods `Clean()`, `IsDirty()`, `MoveAvailable(int x, int y)`, and `Print()` will remain as they were in the `CleaningRobot` class; these are illustrated in Listing 3-4.

Listing 3-4. Methods Clean(), IsDirty(), MoveAvailable(int x, int y), and Print() as They Were in the CleaningRobot Class

```
public void Clean()
{
    _terrain[X, Y] -= 1;
}

public bool IsDirty()
{
    return _terrain[X, Y] > 0;
}

public bool MoveAvailable(int x, int y)
{
    return x >= 0 && y >= 0 && x < _terrain.
    GetLength(0) && y < _terrain.GetLength(1);
}

public void Print()
{
    var col = _terrain.GetLength(1);
    var i = 0;
    var line = "";
    Console.WriteLine("--------------");
    foreach (var c in _terrain)
```

```
            {
                line += string.Format("  {0}  ", c);
                i++;
                if (col == i)
                {
                    Console.WriteLine(line);
line = "";
                    i = 0;
                }
            }
        }
```

The set of perceptions will be obtained by a method shown in Listing 3-5, which returns a list of percepts that will be represented by an enum (declared outside of the CleaningAgent class) that defines every possible perception in the CleaningAgent environment; this enum can also be seen in Listing 3-5.

Listing 3-5. Percepts enum and the Perceived() Method That Returns a List<Percepts> Containing Every Perception the Agent Has Obtained from the Environment

```
public enum Percepts
    {
        Dirty, Clean, Finished, MoveUp, MoveDown, MoveLeft,
        MoveRight
}

private List<Percepts> Perceived()
    {
            var result = new List<Percepts>();

            if (IsDirty())
                result.Add(Percepts.Dirty);
```

```
    else
        result.Add(Percepts.Clean);
    if (_cellsVisited.Count == _terrain.GetLength(0) *
    _terrain.GetLength(1))
        result.Add(Percepts.Finished);

    if (MoveAvailable(X - 1, Y))
        result.Add(Percepts.MoveUp);

    if (MoveAvailable(X + 1, Y))
        result.Add(Percepts.MoveDown);

    if (MoveAvailable(X, Y - 1))
        result.Add(Percepts.MoveLeft);

    if (MoveAvailable(X, Y + 1))
        result.Add(Percepts.MoveRight);

    return result;
}
```

As mentioned before, this agent will maintain a state corresponding to the history of cells visited. For that purpose we implement the UpdateState() method seen in Listing 3-6.

Listing 3-6. Method for Updating the State of the Agent; i.e., Cells Visited

```
private void UpdateState()
    {
        if (!_cellsVisited.Contains(new Tuple<int, int>(X, Y)))
            _cellsVisited.Add(new Tuple<int, int>(X, Y));
    }
```

The method that puts it all together is AgentAction(List<Percepts> percepts) shown in Listing 3-7. In this method, we go through every percept obtained from the environment and act accordingly. For instance, if the current cell is clean we update the state (internal data structure) of the agent by adding that cell to the _cellsVisited list; if we perceive that the current cell is dirty we clean it and so on for each situation or percept and its consequence or action. Additionally, Listing 3-7 also illustrates the methods RandomAction(List<Percepts> percepts) and Move(Percepts p). The first selects a random movement percept (MoveUp, MoveDown, etc.) to be executed, and the latter executes the movement percept supplied as argument.

Note that this agent will always check its state and percept (recall I x P is the domain of agents with state) before moving, and it will always try to move to an adjacent cell not previously visited.

Listing 3-7. Method for Updating the State of the Agent; i.e., Cells Visited

```
public void AgentAction(List<Percepts> percepts)
{
    if (percepts.Contains(Percepts.Clean))
        UpdateState();
    if (percepts.Contains(Percepts.Dirty))
        Clean();
    else if (percepts.Contains(Percepts.Finished))
        TaskFinished = true;
    else if (percepts.Contains(Percepts.MoveUp) && !_
cellsVisited.Contains(new Tuple<int, int>(X - 1, Y)))
            Move(Percepts.MoveUp);
```

```
            else if (percepts.Contains(Percepts.MoveDown) &&
!_cellsVisited.Contains(new Tuple<int, int>(X + 1, Y)))
                Move(Percepts.MoveDown);
            else if (percepts.Contains(Percepts.MoveLeft) &&
!_cellsVisited.Contains(new Tuple<int, int>(X, Y - 1)))
                Move(Percepts.MoveLeft);
            else if (percepts.Contains(Percepts.MoveRight) &&
!_cellsVisited.Contains(new Tuple<int, int>(X, Y + 1)))
                Move(Percepts.MoveRight);
            else
                RandomAction(percepts);
        }

        private void RandomAction(List<Percepts> percepts)
        {
            var p = percepts[_random.Next(1, percepts.Count)];
Move(p);
}

        private void Move(Percepts p)
        {
            switch (p)
            {
                case Percepts.MoveUp:
                    X -= 1;
                    break;
                case Percepts.MoveDown:
                    X += 1;
                    break;
                case Percepts.MoveLeft:
                    Y -= 1;
                    break;
```

```
        case Percepts.MoveRight:
            Y += 1;
            break;
    }
}
```

What advantages does the cleaning agent provide us over the stateless cleaning robot? In order to answer this question, let's first note that the strategy (recording of its environment history by saving visited cell coordinates) we are using with the cleaning agent is very intuitive. Imagine you need to find some product X in a big city where there exist over 100 stores; how would you accomplish such a task? Intuitively, you would visit a store once and then record in your mind that you already visited that store and the product was not there, thus saving the time of having to revisit it. You would then move from one store to the next until you found the product, always keeping in mind that stores already visited are a waste of time. That's basically what our cleaning agent tries to do this with the exception that there might be times when already-visited cells will have to be revisited because the agent can only move to adjacent cells and they all may have been visited at some point. In Figure 3-4 we can see a basic comparison between the cleaning agent and the cleaning robot.

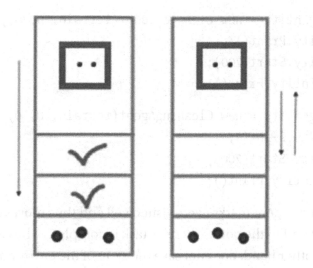

Figure 3-4. *The cleaning agent (in blue) searches the environment, saving coordinates of visited cells, while the cleaning robot (in red) does not save the state of the environment or its history; therefore, it simply makes random moves that could take it up or down and even going in circles, thus consuming more time to clean the dirt on the last cell.*

In Listing 3-8 we have an environment of 1000 x 1 cells, i.e., 1000 rows and one column, and dirt is located just in the last row.

Listing 3-8. Method for Updating the State of the Agent; i.e., Cells Visited

```
var terrain = new int[1000, 1];

  for (int i = 0; i < terrain.GetLength(0); i++)
 {
        for (int j = 0; j < terrain.GetLength(1); j++)
 {
                if (i == terrain.GetLength(0) - 1)
                    terrain[i, j] = 1;
 }
   }
```

```
var cleaningEntity = new CleaningRobot(terrain, 0, 0);
cleaningEntity.Print();
cleaningEntity.Start(200);
    cleaningEntity.Print();

var cleaningEntity = new CleaningAgent(terrain, 0, 0);
cleaningEntity.Print();
cleaningEntity.Start(200);
    cleaningEntity.Print();
```

The cleaning agent marks every visited cell and thus moves faster to the last cell and to the point where its task is complete. The cleaning robot, on the other hand, does not save the state of the environment, so it doesn't have any internal structure that may help it decide what move should be the correct one and can basically move up and down randomly several times and even in circles. The cleaning agent has a data structure with information on the environment to aid it in applying some logic and making rational decisions, and the cleaning robot does not. As a result of the code shown in Listing 3-8, the random robot is incapable of cleaning the dirt on the last cell, whereas the agent is able to do it in the time given (Figure 3-5).

Figure 3-5. *On the left, the result obtained after executing CleaningRobot; on the right, the result after executing CleaningAgent. The first leaves dirt on the last row, while the latter is able to clean it.*

Thus far in this chapter we have examined agents' properties and environments and described a practical problem where we could see an agent with state overrunning the cleaning robot presented in the last chapter. In future sections, we'll study some of the most popular agent architectures.

Agent Architectures

Agent architectures represent predefined designs that consider different agent properties, like the ones studied earlier, to provide a scheme or blueprint for building agents.

One can think of the different concepts presented so far in an analogy where agents are buildings; their properties are similar to building properties (color, height, material used, etc.); their architecture is what it would be in a building, i.e., the infrastructure supporting it and defining its functionality; and agent types (soon to be detailed) would be as the types of buildings that we have (commercial, governmental, military, etc.).

113

Agent architecture as the basis of the agent's functionality indicates how the agent will function. Up to this moment we have seen the agent's function as an abstract one; architecture's being a functionality-defining component will give us a model to implement such a function.

Reactive Architectures: Subsumption Architecture

In the same way we could have an illuminated property and luminous architecture—in other words, one that is focused on offering the greatest lightness—we could also have a reactive agent and reactive-based architecture, one that is focused on reactivity above all. This is the case with agent-reactive architectures.

In a *reactive architecture* as it occurs in a reactive agent, each behavior is a mapping from percepts or environment states to actions. In Figure 3-6 we can see a diagram showing a reactive architecture.

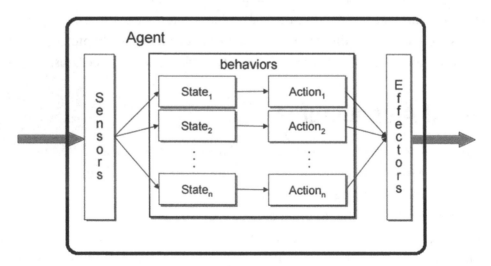

Figure 3-6. *Reactive architecture diagram*

The cleaning agent developed in previous sections is a clear example of reactive architecture. We already know from the agent's properties section that being purely reactive involves some setbacks: there's no learning in this type of architecture; it's usually handcrafted, which makes it very difficult to create large systems; it can be used only for its original purpose, and so on.

One of the most popular—and arguably the best known—reactive architectures is the *Subsumption architecture*, developed by Rodney Brooks in the mid-1980s. His architecture is said to be a *behavior-based* architecture; it rejected the idea of logic-based agents—i.e., those that rely fully on logic to represent the world, its interactions, and its relations—in an attempt to set a new approach apart from the traditional AI of his time.

Note   Behavior-based agents use biological systems as building blocks and rely on adaptability. They tend to show more biological features than their AI counterparts and can repeat actions, make mistakes, demonstrate tenacity, and so forth, sort of like ants do.

The main ideas behind Brooks' architecture are the following:

1. Intelligent behavior can be generated without explicit representations like the ones proposed by symbolic AI.

2. Intelligent behavior can be generated without explicit abstract reasoning of the kind that symbolic AI proposes.

3. Intelligence is an emergent property of certain complex systems.

The Subsumption architecture possesses two fundamental characteristics:

1. An agent's decision-making process is executed through a set of *task-accomplishing behaviors* where each *behavior module* can be seen as an individual agent function. Because this is a reactive architecture every agent function is a mapping from a percept or state to an action.

2. Behavior modules are intended to achieve a particular task, and each behavior "competes" with others to exercise control over the agent.

3. Many behaviors can fire simultaneously, and the multiple actions proposed by these behaviors are executed according to a *subsumption hierarchy*, with the behaviors arranged into layers.

4. Lower layers in the hierarchy are able to inhibit higher layers: the lower a layer is the higher is its priority.

The principle of the subsumption hierarchy is that higher layers will indicate more abstract behaviors. For instance, considering our cleaning agent, one would like to give a high priority to the "clean" behavior; thus, it'd be encoded in the lower layers where it has a higher priority.

Note   Symbolic AI is sometimes called Old Fashioned AI or Good Old Fashioned AI. It was popular in the 1950s and 1960s and was based on the idea of representing knowledge through symbols (logic formulas, graphs, rules, etc.). Hence, methods of Symbolic AI are developed on the basis of logic, theory of formal languages, various areas of discrete mathematics, and so forth.

Looking again at the cleaning agent, we can see that it follows the Subsumption architecture (Listing 3-9).

Listing 3-9. Cleaning Agent Action Function Follows the Subsumption Architecture

```
public void AgentAction(List<Percepts> percepts)
{
            if (percepts.Contains(Percepts.Clean))
                UpdateState();
            if (percepts.Contains(Percepts.Dirty))
                Clean();
            else if (percepts.Contains(Percepts.Finished))
                TaskFinished = true;
            else if (percepts.Contains(Percepts.MoveUp) && !_
            cellsVisited.Contains(new Tuple<int, int>(X - 1, Y)))
                Move(Percepts.MoveUp);
            else if (percepts.Contains(Percepts.MoveDown) && !_
            cellsVisited.Contains(new Tuple<int, int>(X + 1, Y)))
                Move(Percepts.MoveDown);
            else if (percepts.Contains(Percepts.MoveLeft) && !_
            cellsVisited.Contains(new Tuple<int, int>(X, Y - 1)))
                Move(Percepts.MoveLeft);
            else if (percepts.Contains(Percepts.MoveRight) && !_
            cellsVisited.Contains(new Tuple<int, int>(X, Y + 1)))
                Move(Percepts.MoveRight);
            else
                RandomAction(percepts);
        }
```

The cleaning agent establishes an order for the behaviors exhibited; this order corresponds to the subsumption hierarchy illustrated in Figure 3-7.

Dirty - > Clean	1
Finished -> Stop	2
MoveUp Available ^ NoVisited(Up) -> MoveUp	3
MoveDown Available ^ NoVisited(Down) -> MoveDown	4
MoveLeft Available ^ NoVisited(Left) -> MoveLeft	5
MoveRight Available ^ NoVisited(Right) -> MoveRight	6
Anything Else -> Move Randomly	7

Figure 3-7. *Subsumption hierarchy for cleaning agent*

The order of priority established by the subsumption hierarchy in the cleaning agent is 1, 2, 3, 4, 5, 6, and 7, with 7 being the behavior with the highest priority.

This architecture inherits the problems of reactive architectures (no learning, hardwired rules, and so on). Beyond that, modeling complex systems requires many behaviors to be included in the hierarchy, making it too extensive and unfeasible. Up to this point we have described agent properties and the reactive architecture, providing an example of one of these (probably the best-known example), the Subsumption architecture. In the next sections, we'll look at other agent architectures, like the BDI (Belief Desire Intention) and Hybrid architectures.

Deliberative Architectures: BDI Architecture

In a purely *deliberative* architecture agents follow a goal-based behavior where they are able to reason and plan ahead. Deliberative architectures usually incorporate some sort of symbolic representation of the world via logic, graphs, discreet math, and so forth, and decisions (for example, about what actions to perform) are typically made via logical reasoning using pattern matching and symbolic manipulation. Readers familiar with logical or functional programming languages like Prolog, Haskell, or FSharp may be able to understand the meaning of *symbolic* a lot easier. Deliberative architectures usually face two problems that need to be solved:

1. Translating the real world into an appropriate, accurate symbolic version of it that is efficient and useful for the purpose of the agent. This problem is usually time-consuming, especially if the environment is too dynamic and changing from time to time.

2. Symbolically representing information about real-world entities, relations, processes, and so forth and how to reason and make decisions with this information.

Problem number 1 guided work on face recognition, speech recognition, learning, and so on, and Problem number 2 inspired the work on knowledge representation, automated scheduling, automated reasoning, automatic planning, and so forth. Regardless of the immense volume of scientific material that these problems generated, most researchers accepted the fact that they weren't even near solved. Even apparently trivial problems, such as essential reasoning, turned out to be exceptionally difficult. The underlying problem seems to be the difficulty of thoorem proving in even very simple logics, and the complexity of

119

symbol manipulation in general; recall that first-order logic (FOL) is not even *decidable*, and modal extensions attached to it (including representations of belief, desire, time, and so on) tend to be highly undecidable.

Note   The term *decidable* or *decidability* relates to the decision problem; i.e., the problem that can be defined as outputting Yes (1) or No (0) to a question on the input values. The satisfiability problem (SAT) is a particular case of decision problem. Thus, we say that a theory (set of formulas) is decidable if there is a method or algorithm for deciding whether a given randomly chosen formula belongs to that theory.

The generic deliberative architecture is illustrated in Figure 3-8.

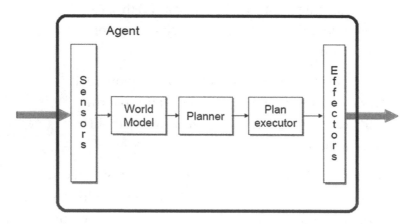

Figure 3-8. *Deliberative architecture*

Multiple deliberative architectures like BDI (soon to be detailed) find their roots in the philosophical tradition of understanding *practical reasoning*, the process of deciding moment by moment which action to execute when seeking to fulfill our goals. Human practical reasoning consists of two activities:

1. Deciding what state of affairs we want to achieve (deliberation).

2. Deciding how to achieve these states of affairs (means-end reasoning or planning).

From the preceding activities we can conclude that deliberations output intentions and means-end reasoning outputs plans.

Note   There is a difference between practical reasoning and theoretical reasoning. The former is directed toward actions, while the latter is directed toward beliefs.

Means-end reasoning is the process of deciding how to achieve an end using means available; in the AI world this is known as *planning*. For the agent to generate a plan it typically requires a representation or goal intention to achieve, a representation of actions it can perform, and a representation of its environment (Figure 3-9).

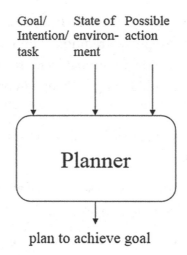

Goal/   State of Possible
Intention/ environ- action
task   ment

Planner

plan to achieve goal

Figure 3-9. *Inputs and output flow of the planning component of an agent*

How does deliberation occur? In the deliberation process there's a first step called *alternatives generation* in which the agent generates a set of alternatives (goals, desires) for consideration. In a second step called *filtering* the agent chooses between available options and commits to some of them. These chosen options or alternatives are its intentions.

The key question in deliberative architectures is "How can the agent deliberate on its (probably conflicting) goals to decide which ones it will pursue?" The answer to this question is provided by the goal-deliberation strategy that is particular to every deliberative architecture; the most popular of these is the BDI architecture created by Michael E. Bratman in his book *Intentions, Plans and Practical Reason* (1987).

Note   Considering their interaction with time, a reactive architecture exists in the present (with short duration), while a deliberative architecture reasons about the past and projects (plans, etc.) into the future.

The *Beliefs, Desires, and Intentions (BDI)* architecture contains explicit representations of an agent's beliefs, desires, and intentions. Beliefs (what it thinks) are generally regarded as the information an agent has about its environment; we could say *knowledge* instead of *belief*, but we would rather use the more general term *belief* because what the agent believes may be false sometimes. Desires (what it wants) are those things the agent would like to see achieved, we don't expect an agent to act on all its desires. Intentions (what it is doing) are those things the agent is committed to doing, and they are basically the result of filtering desires; the BDI architecture is illustrated in Figure 3-10.

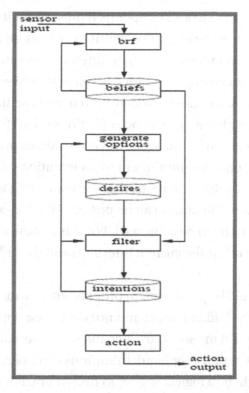

Figure 3-10. *BDI architecture*

Beliefs are usually described by predicates outputting True or False values (for example, IsDirty(x,y)) and represent the internal knowledge the agent has of the world.

Desires are fulfilled when they are present in the belief base (or manually removed by the agent). Like the belief base, the desire base is updated during the execution of the agent. Desires can be related by hierarchical links (sub/super desires) when a desire is created as an intermediary goal (for example, to clean dirt on a terrain one could have two subdesires or subgoals: move to every dirty cell and clean it). Desires have a priority value that can change dynamically and is used to select a new intention from among the set of desires when necessary.

Once the agent considers all its options it must commit to some of them, in this case and as an example it will commit to just one, to its only available option, which later becomes its intention. Intentions eventually lead to actions, and the agent is supposed to act by trying to achieve its intentions. The agent is supposed to make reasonable attempts to achieve its intentions, and it may follow a sequence of actions (plan) for this purpose.

The intention chosen by the agent will constrain its practical reasoning from that point on; once a commitment to an intention exists the agent will not contemplate other intentions that are conflicting with the ones already set in motion. Intentions can be put on hold (for example, when they require a subdesire to be achieved). For this reason, there is a stack of intentions; the last one is the current intention and the only one that is not on hold.

Intentions should be persistent; in other words, we must devote every available resource to fulfilling them and not drop them immediately if they aren't achieved in the short run, because then we will be achieving none all the time. On the other hand, intentions can't persist for too long, because there might be a logical reason to drop them. For example, there may come a time when the cleaning agent has nothing else to do (clean), maybe because it inhabits a multi-agent environment and other agents have finished the cleaning task.

Intentions make up a set of important roles associated with practical reasoning:

- *Intentions motivate planning*: Once an agent has decided to achieve an intention it must plan a course of action to accomplish that intention.

- *Intentions constrain future deliberation*: Once an agent commits to an intention it will not contemplate other intentions that are conflicting with the chosen intention.

- *Intentions persist*: The agent will not renounce its intentions without any rational cause; it will persist typically until either the agent believes it has successfully achieved them or it believes it cannot achieve them, or because the purpose for the intention is no longer present.

- *Intentions influence beliefs upon the future*: Once the agent adopts certain intentions, some planning for the future under the assumption that those intentions chosen will be achieved is necessary and logical.

From time to time it is important for the agent to stop and reconsider its intentions, as some could have become irrational or impossible. This reconsideration stage implies a cost at both spatial and temporal lines, and it also presents us with a problem:

- A *bold agent* that doesn't stop enough to reconsider its intentions might be trying to achieve an intention that is no longer possible.

- A *cautious agent* that stops too frequently to reconsider its intentions might be spending too many resources on the reconsideration stage and not enough on achieving its intentions.

A balance or tradeoff between the event-driven and goal-directed behaviors of the agent is the solution for this dilemma.

Note   Experiments have demonstrated that bold agents do better than cautious agents in environments that don't change too often. In the other scenario (environment changes frequently), cautious agents outperform bold agents.

The process of practical reasoning in a BDI agent relies on the following components. In the next points B is assumed to be the set of beliefs, D the set of desires, and I the set of intentions:

- A set of current *beliefs* representing information the agent has about its environment

- A *belief revision function (brf)* that receives percepts and the agent's beliefs as inputs and determines a new set of beliefs:

  brf: $P \times B \to B$

- An *option-generation function (options)* that receives beliefs about its environment and intentions (if any) as inputs and determines the options (desires) of the agent:

  options: $B \times I \to D$

- A set of current *options* representing probable courses of action for the agent to follow

- A *filter function (filter)* representing the deliberation process of the agent and using beliefs, desires, and intentions as inputs to determine the agent's intentions:

  filter: $B \times D \times I \to I$

- A set of current *intentions* representing the agent's commitments

- An *action-selection function* that uses current intentions as inputs to determine an action to perform

It comes as no surprise that the state of a BDI agent at any moment is a triple (B, D, I). The BDI agent's action function seems pretty simple when we don't get into details; it's shown in the next pseudocode here:

```
function AgentAction(P):
        B = brf(P, B)
        D = options(D, I)
        I = filter(B, D, I)
end
```

In the next chapter we'll present a practical problem where we'll develop an AI for a Mars Rover whose architecture will be BDI; this problem will help us set firm ground for many of the concepts introduced during this section.

Hybrid Architectures

Multiple researchers have argued that neither a purely deliberative agent nor a purely reactive agent is a good strategy when we design an agent. *Hybrid architectures* in which the agent possesses both a goal-based component where they are able to reason and plan ahead and a reactive component that allows them to react immediately to situations of the environment are usually preferred over the alternative of a purely deliberative or purely reactive agent.

In general, hybrid architecture agents are composed of the following subsystems or components:

- *Deliberative component*: contains a representation of the world that can be at some level symbolic; it builds plans and makes decisions as in the deliberative architecture

- *Reactive component*: capable of reacting to certain situations without complex reasoning (situation -> consequence rules)

Thus, hybrid agents have reactive and proactive properties, and the reactive component is usually given some precedence over the deliberative one.

The divided and somewhat hierarchical structure where reactive and deliberative components coexist has lead to the natural idea of layering architectures, which represents the hybrid agents' design. In this type of architecture, an agent's control components are arranged into a hierarchy, with higher layers dealing with information at higher levels of abstraction.

Typically, we will have at least two layers in a layered architecture: one to deal with the reactive behavior and one to deal with the proactive behavior. In practice, there is no reason why there couldn't be more layers. Generally speaking, we can count two types of layered architectures:

- *Horizontal layering*: In horizontally layered architectures, the agent's layers are each directly connected to the sensory input and action output. As a result, each layer acts like an agent, producing suggestions as to what action to perform.

- *Vertical layering*: In vertically layered architectures, sensory input and action output are each processed through every layer in one or possibly various directions.

Both horizontal and vertical layering are illustrated in Figure 3-11.

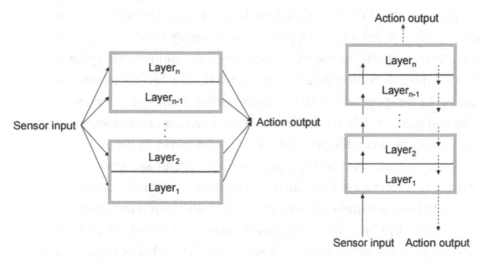

Figure 3-11. *Horizontally layered architecture (on the left) and vertically layered architecture (on the right). Note that in vertically layered architectures there could be more than just one pass through every layer.*

Horizontally layered architectures are very simple in their conceptual design; agents exhibiting *n* behaviors will require *n* layers, one for each behavior. Despite this positive point, the fact that each layer is actually competing with others to suggest an action could cause the agent to show incoherent behavior. In order to provide consistency, a *mediator function* is usually required to act as "middle man" and decide which layer controls the agent at any given moment.

The mediator function involves high complexity, as all possible interactions between all layers must be considered to finally output an action. Creating such a control mechanism is extremely difficult from a designer's point of view.

In vertically layered architectures these problems are diminished because there's an order between layers, and the last layer is the one outputting the action to be executed. Vertically layered architectures are usually divided into two types: *one-pass* architectures and *two-pass* architectures. In the former type, the agent's decision-making process flows sequentially through each layer until the last layer generates an action. In two-pass architectures, information flows up the architecture (the first pass) and then back down. There exist some remarkable similarities between the principle of two-pass vertically layered architectures and the way organizations and enterprises work in the sense that information flows up to the highest levels and orders then flow down. In both one-pass and two-pass vertically layered architectures the complexity of interactions between layers is reduced. Since there are n - 1 edges between n layers, if each layer is capable of suggesting m actions, there are at most $m^2(n-1)$ interactions to be considered between layers. Clearly, this is a much simpler level of interaction than the one a horizontally layered architecture forces us to have. This simplicity comes at a cost, and that cost is flexibility. In order for a vertically layered architecture to make a decision, control must pass between each different layer. Vertically layered architectures are not flawless, and failures in any layer can have serious consequences for an agent's performance. In the next section we'll study a particular case of horizontally layered architecture: touring machines.

Touring Machines

Touring machines represent horizontally layered architectures composed of three layers (modeling layer, planning layer, and the reactive layer). Figure 3-12 illustrates a touring machine.

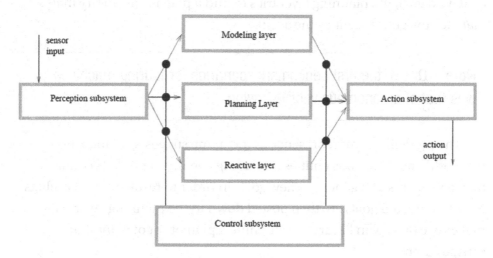

Figure 3-12. *Touring machine*

The reactive layer provides immediate responses to changes detected in the environment as a set of situation action rules resembling those of the Subsumption architecture. In the next pseudocode we illustrate a reactive rule of an autonomous vehicle agent. This example shows the obstacle-avoidance rule of the vehicle:

```
rule-1: obstacle-avoidance
if (in_front(vehicle, observer)
andspeed(observer) > 0
andseparation(vehicle, observer) <vehicleThreshHold)
then
change_orientation(vehicleAvoidanceAngle)
```

The planning layer is responsible for the agent's proactive behavior; in other words, it's responsible for what the agent will do in the long run. In order to do its planning, the layer maintains a library of plans; these plans are essentially hierarchically structured plans that the touring machines elaborate upon at runtime to decide what to do. Therefore, in order to achieve a goal, the planning layer tries to find a plan in the library that matches the goal sought by the agent.

Note   One of the first benchmark scenarios for touring machines was that of autonomous vehicle driving.

The modeling layer represents, as the name suggests, a model of the world and its various entities (including agents). It predicts conflicts between agents and generates new goals in order to resolve these conflicts. Newly generated goals are then posted down to the planning layer, which makes use of its plan library to determine a plan or set of plans that satisfies them.

All three layers are related to a control subsystem that decides which layer has control over the agent. This subsystem consists of a set of control rules that can either restrain information between layers or act over the output of layers as shown in the next pseudocode, which illustrates a control rule:

```
censorRule_1:
if (entity(bigObstacle) in perceptions)
then
removeSensoryRecord(layerReact, entity(bigObstacle))
```

This control rule prevents the reactive layer from ever knowing that a big obstacle has been detected. The reactive layer would be, in most scenarios, the most appropriate layer for dealing with obstacle avoidance, but under different scenarios it might be better to pass this perception to other layers. In this case, since the sensor detected a big obstacle that might be visible from a long distance away, the planning layer may need to find a plan that considers a big obstacle and changes the agent's route.

InteRRaP

InteRRaP (Integration of Rational Reactive behavior and Planning) is a vertically layered two-pass architecture composed of three layers (cooperation layer, planning layer, and behavior layer) similar to the ones found in touring machines. Figure 3-13 illustrates an InteRRaP.

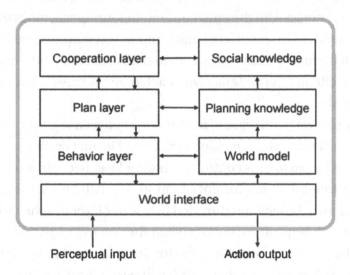

Figure 3-13. *InteRRaP architecture*

The behavior layer (lowest) deals with the reactive behavior; the planning layer (middle) deals with regular planning to achieve the agent's goals; and the cooperation layer (uppermost) deals with social interactions in multi-agent environments. A knowledge base is associated with every layer; each knowledge base represents the world in a manner that is convenient for its corresponding layer.

The highest knowledge base represents the set of plans and actions of other agents in the environment; the middle knowledge base represents the plans and actions of the agent itself; and the lowest-level knowledge base represents raw information about the environment.

Note   Knowledge bases distinguish InteRRaP from touring machines.

The main difference between InteRRap and touring machines is the way they interact with the environment. In touring machines every layer was connected to perceptual input and action output, creating the necessity of having a control subsystem to deal with conflicts between layers. In InteRRap layers interact with each other as they seek to fulfill a common goal.

There exist two main types of interactions between layers in InteRRap: *bottom-up activation* and *top-down execution.* The first occurs when a lower layer is forced to pass control to a higher layer because it is not capable of dealing with the current situation. The latter occurs when a higher layer uses the facilities provided by a lower layer to achieve its goals. Typical flow will begin at the bottom when the reactive layer receives perceptual input; if this layer is capable of dealing with that perceptual input received it will do so; otherwise, it will pass control to the planning layer. If the planning layer is capable of dealing with the situation it will probably make use of top-down execution; otherwise, it will keep moving control higher to the next layer. In this way control flows from the lowest layer to a higher (if necessary) layer and back down again.

Summary

Throughout this chapter we introduced the concept of agents, looking at some of their most relevant properties and examining a practical problem where we transformed the cleaning robot from Chapter 2 into a cleaning agent that followed the agent's model of an action function that receives a set of percepts and outputs an action. We also added state to this agent and compared it to a stateless agent that executes random actions. Finally, we presented various agent architectures: reactive, deliberative, and hybrid.

In the following chapter, we will look at a very interesting problem (Mars Rover) that will show us how agent architectures can be implemented in a real-life scenario.

CHAPTER 4

Mars Rover

Following the route (agents) started during the last chapter, we will devote Chapter 4 to the introduction of a Mars Rover AI that is based on a hybrid architecture that includes a reactive layer for its immediate decisions and uses the BDI (Beliefs, Desires, Intentions) paradigm for implementing its deliberative layer. This practical problem will help us reinforce all the knowledge acquired in Chapter 3 (agent properties, agent state, architectures, and so on) and will aid us in understanding how we can assemble it all in a real-world problem.

Space exploration is a fascinating topic that combines well with the area of AI and has millions of followers worldwide. Since the conditions of space are pretty difficult and risky for humans, the use of robots is frequent and necessary. Therefore, the idea of using AI for machines that are involved in space exploration is logical, and many studies of it have been made in recent years.

The practical problem addressed throughout this chapter will include a visual application (Windows Forms) that shows the execution of a Mars Rover at any moment in a discrete environment of n x m (rows x columns). This application simulates the Mars environment with various rocks that are considered obstacles by the agent and hidden spots of water or remnants of water. The program will also show us its planning (sequence of actions conforming a plan will be denoted in yellow) and how it manages beliefs, desires, and intentions. The goal of a Mars Rover

© Arnaldo Pérez Castaño 2018
A. Pérez Castaño, *Practical Artificial Intelligence*,
https://doi.org/10.1007/978-1-4842-3357-3_4

is basically scientific research, and in our case there is the very important task of finding vestiges of any type of water on Mars, plus trying to remain active and avoid obstacles.

Note   *Spirit* and *Opportunity* are two of the most popular Mars Rovers; they both made incredible discoveries and exceeded their life expectancies by a big margin. *Spirit* was launched in June 2003, *Opportunity* in July 2003. *Spirit* remained active until 2010 (seven years of life) when its wheels were trapped in sand, and *Opportunity*, as of the writing of this book, remains active and roving Mars.

What's a Mars Rover?

Mars is today a desolate, dry planet that when seen from a distance appears to resemble our home planet of Earth very little. However, when approaching Mars' orbit we can see on the surface what could have been ancient, now dried out lakes and canyons, suggesting that Mars may have harbored—three or four million years ago—not only water but also life.

Life in space is tough; it's highly complicated for humans to survive out there, it's risky, dangerous and reaching some of the closest planets could take many years, so in an effort to facilitate the research of other worlds, multiple space agencies (NASA, CSA, ESA, and so on) have been designing robots—or, as they are typically called, rovers—for the exploration and research of planets.

A *Mars Rover* is an automated motor vehicle that is loaded up with cameras to analyze its surroundings, research instruments to dig in and maybe analyze interesting rocks, communication equipment with which to send pictures and data and receive commands, solar panels to provide energy to itself, and so on (Figure 4-1). Rovers have the task of exploring

Mars and collecting significant data that will hopefully lead to the conclusion of the existence of water on the planet in the past—or maybe to the discovery of ancient life.

Figure 4-1. *Mars Rover*

Mars Rovers tend to move very slowly, at nearly two inches per second (approximately 0.09 miles per hour). After all the trouble and cost that is involved when taking a rover to Mars, engineers prefer to play it safe and drive carefully; no one would like to see a $2.5 billion rover upside down because it was driving too fast. Another important point: most rovers receive a daily set of commands or instructions from the team on Earth; these instructions tell the rover where to go or what to do. In this sense, one could say that classic rovers are not as autonomous as we might think; they do of course include some autonomous behavior because the team on Earth is not on Mars and cannot watch their every step live. Therefore, the AI of the rover takes care of deciding when a rock is too big to go over (obstacle) or when the color and texture of a rock make it interesting to be examined. One could say that rovers are sort of autonomous and follow orders very well, kind of like human soldiers do. The mission of the rover is a two-sided job; on one side we have the engineers on Earth, planning their daily moves, their large-scale strategies, and so forth, and on the other side we have the rovers, executing these actions, exploring, collecting data, and sending it back to Earth.

In this chapter, we will be demonstrating how to develop an AI for a completely autonomous Mars Rover that will consider obstacles in the terrain and will be searching for water under a hybrid architecture that includes a BDI (Beliefs, Desires, Intentions) deliberative mechanism and uses statistics and probabilities for injecting itself with new beliefs that will be drawn as conclusions from its state (past history).

Note Mars is usually known as the Red Planet because of its reddish tint in the night sky. In general, Mars is mostly rust colored because of the iron in its soil. When exposed to the small amount of oxygen in the Martian atmosphere, the iron oxidizes, or rusts. That "rusty dust" can also blow into the air, turning the sky into a peach color.

Mars Rover Architecture

Let's take a brief moment to examine the hybrid architecture that we will be proposing for our Mars Rover AI (Figure 4-2).

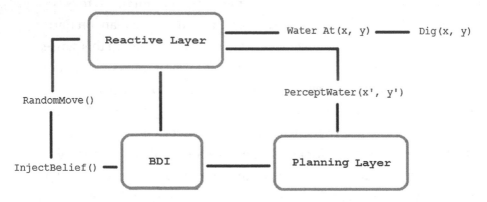

Figure 4-2. *Mars Rover architecture*

The architecture is composed of three layers (reactive, BDI, and planning); different percepts or events (denoted in the smaller font in Figure 4-2) can cause a layer to execute. For instance, if there's water at the rover's current position then the reactive layer will act and conduct the rover to dig in that spot immediately. If there's a percept related to water in nearby areas the reactive layer will also be triggered. The rover will incorporate a variable or field named SenseRadius that will determine the circle surrounding it and represent its field of view; the rover will be capable of perceiving everything in that circle. Since we are dealing with a discrete environment this circle will be an approximation of a real circle; in other words, it will be the discrete version of a circle.

Note   Mars Rovers like *Spirit* or *Opportunity*, both made by NASA, have fish-eye cameras or wide-angle cameras that allow them to catch a general view of the terrain in front of them. The photos these cameras take are analyzed to decide whether a certain rock on the path is too big to go over, and so on.

If the rover has some initial beliefs and there are no percepts of significant interest then control passes from the reactive layer to the BDI layer, where a process starts at the beliefs set; in this process the beliefs set is updated. A belief that we may have today could be proven wrong tomorrow. As for the rover, a location on the terrain where it believes there may be water could be incorrect, and as a result this database of beliefs must be constantly updated as new percepts arrive. In a second stage, desires are generated from beliefs. For the rover, its beliefs will consist of possible water locations and its desires will be these possible water locations ordered by proximity using the Manhattan distance (also known as Block distance) as measure. Thus, going to the closest water location will become the current intention of the rover.

In order to accomplish its current intention the rover uses its plan library (in the planning layer) and selects a plan fitting the selected intention. Since we are considering, in this example, only intentions associated with possible water locations our plan library will merely consist of one type of plan: path finding.

Path-finding algorithms solve the problem of finding the shortest path between two given points; these algorithms not only consider obstacles on the grid/terrain but also the cost of each possible path. Some of its representatives are Breadth First Search (BFS), Djistkra's algorithm, and A* search. For our rover, we developed BFS, the most inefficient of them all but also the simplest. The others perform better by using heuristics, dynamic programming, and so forth and avoid considering costly paths.

Once the rover has explored all of its beliefs it will wander around (making random moves) until it reaches a certain number of actions. At this point, we will inject beliefs into the rover by using a data structure (dictionary) that maintains its state, or past history, as a set of visited cells along with their visit frequency (number of times it has visited a cell), and a deliberation process that consists of applying simple concepts of probability and statistics.

In this deliberation process the terrain known by the rover is divided into four equal (or almost equal) sectors (could be divided into 2^n sectors for further precision), and for each sector and each (`location, frequency_visits`) pair in that sector we calculate the *relative frequency* and sum up the results obtained in each individual sector, having as the final result four Total Relative Frequency values (one for each sector). The Relative Frequency (RF) calculation is made with the following formula:

$$RF(c) = \frac{freq(c)}{N}$$

where *freq(c)* represents the number of times cell *c* has been visited and *N* is the total number of elements in the set (sector) to which *c* belongs. Then, for each sector *S* its Total Relative Frequency would be:

$$TRF(S) = \sum_{i=0}^{N} RF(c_i)$$

In the end, the rover will choose to "inject" the belief of water location in a corner of the sector with the lowest Total Relative Frequency, which should be the one least visited in the past. We could say that this approach is pretty much a heuristic; i.e., we have specific knowledge about this problem and we are embedding it, trying to achieve a better behavior from the rover in its task. This heuristic and others associated with this problem will be very simple and even naïve; the purpose right now is to illustrate how to create a hybrid agent architecture. Therefore, heuristics will not be at the core of this chapter. As a quick note, the strategy or heuristic where we always choose a corner of the selected sector for injecting a belief can be greatly improved in the same way the sector division and selection processes can be greatly improved.

Now that we have gotten a glimpse of our rover's architecture and how it will actually make decisions every step of the way, it's time to present its code.

Mars Rover Code

The Mars Rover is coded in a C# class containing the following fields, properties, and constructor (Listing 4-1).

Listing 4-1. Mars Rover Fields, Variables, and Constructor

```
public class MarsRover
    {
        public Mars Mars { get; set; }
        public List<Belief> Beliefs { get; set; }
        public Queue<Desire> Desires { get; set; }
```

```
        public Stack<Intention> Intentions { get; set; }
        public List<Plan> PlanLibrary { get; set; }
        public int X { get; set; }
        public int Y { get; set; }
        public int SenseRadius { get; set; }
        public double RunningOverThreshold { get; set; }
        // Identifies the last part of the terrain seen by the
        Rover
        public List<Tuple<int, int>> CurrentTerrain { get; set; }
        public Plan CurrentPlan { get; set; }
        public List<Tuple<int, int>> WaterFound { get; set; }
        private double[,] _terrain;
        private static Random _random;
        private Dictionary<Tuple<int, int>, int> _perceivedCells;
        private int _wanderTimes;
private const int WanderThreshold = 10;

        public MarsRover(Mars mars, double [,] terrain, int
        x, int y, IEnumerable<Belief> initialBeliefs, double
        runningOver, int senseRadious)
{
            Mars = mars;
            X = x;
            Y = y;
_terrain = new double[terrain.GetLength(0), terrain.GetLength(1)];
            Array.Copy(terrain, _terrain, terrain.GetLength(0)
            * terrain.GetLength(1));
            Beliefs = new List<Belief>(initialBeliefs);
            Desires = new Queue<Desire>();
            Intentions = new Stack<Intention>();
            PlanLibrary = new List<Plan>
```

```
                {
                    new  Plan(TypesPlan.
                    PathFinding, this),
                };
    WaterFound = new List<Tuple<int, int>>();
    RunningOverThreshold = runningOver;
    SenseRadius = senseRadious;
    CurrentTerrain = new List<Tuple<int, int>>();
    _random = new Random();
    _perceivedCells = new Dictionary<Tuple<int,
    int>, int>();
}
}
```

The MarsRover class contains the following fields and variables:

- Mars: an object-oriented representation of the world or environment of Mars. The agent will use this object to inquire about water locations and obstacles on the actual terrain of Mars.

- X, Y: are both integers that represent the current position of the rover in the grid/Mars terrain.

- _terrain: matrix representing the Mars world or terrain as the rover has it conceived initially, before landing there and before it can be updated by means of perceptions. It is like a preconception of Mars given by engineers; it's their map and could have mistakes, so it must be updated.

- `Beliefs`: list representing the set of beliefs the rover has; these could have come from a set of initial beliefs coded by engineers before the rover landed on Mars, like for instance, `WaterAt(2,3)`, etc., or the beliefs that the rover injects itself later through some deliberative logic process

- `Desires`: queue representing the set of desires the rover has; desires are born from beliefs and updated considering current intentions (if any). In the case of the rover, desires will consist of probable water locations, always ordered or prioritized by proximity.

- `Intentions`: stack of intentions the rover has; the one at the top represents the current intention and the one for which there's a plan in motion

- `PlanLibrary`: represents a list of plans the rover can execute depending on the intention taken

- `WaterFound`: list of water locations found on Mars (if any)

- `RunningOverThreshold`: double value that indicates the threshold by which rocks on the terrain are considered obstacles for the rover

- `SenseRadius`: integer value that represents the radius of vision of the rover; i.e., the radius of the circle whose center is the current position of the rover and determines its "sight" around

- `CurrentTerrain`: represents the current terrain of the rover; i.e., the one defined by the circle of radius `SenseRadius`. This data structure is updated as the rover moves.

- `CurrentPlan`: represents the current plan being executed by the rover

- `_random`: variable for obtaining random values (for when the rover wanders around)

- `_perceivedCells`: data structure storing the number of times a cell has been visited. It's used for the `Statistics-Probability` component of the rover in deciding where to inject a belief of water when it has wandered around long enough.

- `_wanderTimes`: integer value conveying the number of times the rover has wandered around

- `WanderThreshold`: integer value that determines the number of actions the rover can take as "wandering around." Once the rover executes `WanderThreshold` actions it will stop wandering and will auto inject a belief.

The `Mars` object (representation of Mars world) uses the class shown in Listing 4-2 as a blueprint.

Listing 4-2. Mars Class

```
public class Mars
{
    private readonly double[,] _terrain;

    public Mars(double[,] terrain)
    {
        _terrain = new double[terrain.GetLength(0),
        terrain.GetLength(1)];
```

```
        Array.Copy(terrain, _terrain, terrain.GetLength(0)
        * terrain.GetLength(1));
    }

    public double TerrainAt(int x, int y)
    {
        return _terrain[x, y];
    }

    public bool WaterAt(int x, int y)
    {
        return _terrain[x, y] < 0;
    }
}
```

The Mars class is pretty straightforward; it incorporates a matrix describing the terrain (elevations) and two methods that allow the rover to inquire about the situation of the environment at a given location. This terrain represents the real Martian terrain; the rover also incorporates a representation of Mars' environment, but this is a representation based on engineers' maps and so forth. It's not going to be as accurate as the actual terrain. Thus, the rover will have to deal with this object to make sure its data on the Martian environment is accurate and, if not, update it.

In order to work with beliefs, desires, and intentions we code them all as classes. The Intention class inherits from the Desire class (Listing 4-3).

Listing 4-3. Belief, Desire, and Intention Classes

```
public class Belief
    {
        public TypesBelief Name { get; set; }
        public dynamic Predicate;
```

```csharp
    public Belief(TypesBelief name, dynamic predicate)
    {
        Name = name;
        Predicate = predicate;
    }

    public override string ToString()
    {
        var result = "";
        var coord = Predicate as List<Tuple<int, int>>;

        foreach (var c in coord)
            result += Name + " (" + c.Item1 + "," + c.Item2
            + ")" + "\n";

        return result;
    }
}

public class Desire
{
    public TypesDesire Name { get; set; }
    public dynamic Predicate;
    public List<Desire> SubDesires { get; set; }

    public Desire() { SubDesires = new List<Desire>(); }

    public Desire(TypesDesire name)
    {
        Name = name;
        SubDesires = new List<Desire>();
    }
```

```csharp
public Desire(TypesDesire name, dynamic predicate)
{
    Name = name;
    Predicate = predicate;
    SubDesires = new List<Desire>();
}

public Desire(TypesDesire name, IEnumerable<Desire>
subDesires)
{
    Name = name;
    SubDesires = new List<Desire>(subDesires);
}

public Desire(TypesDesire name, params Desire[]
subDesires)
{
    Name = name;
    SubDesires = new List<Desire>(subDesires);
}

public List<Desire> GetSubDesires()
{
    if (SubDesires.Count == 0)
        return new List<Desire>() { this };

    var result = new List<Desire>();

    foreach (var desire in SubDesires)
        result.AddRange(desire.GetSubDesires());

    return result;
}
```

```csharp
    public override string ToString()
    {
        return Name.ToString() + "\n";
    }
}

public class Intention: Desire
{
    public static Intention FromDesire(Desire desire)
    {
        var result = new Intention
                        {
                            Name = desire.Name,
                            SubDesires = new List<Desire>
                            (desire.SubDesires),
                            Predicate = desire.Predicate
                        };

        return result;
    }
}
```

Beliefs are usually encoded as predicates, so we included a dynamic (could be anything) Predicate property to represent them. In this case, the rover will have as predicate a List<Tuple<int, int>> indicating beliefs of water locations. To adapt the class to hold different types of predicates, only the override ToString() method would need to change.

Desires not only include predicates but also subdesires, as explained in Chapter 3. The GetSubDesires() method will be in charge of getting leaves from the desires tree. Recall from Chapter 3 that a given desire may have subdesires that must be satisfied before the actual desire can be fulfilled, and these leaves or primary desires are the ones the agent must execute before any other (as the others depend on or are a consequence of the leaf desires).

Finally, intentions inherit from desires. Remember: Intentions are a subset of desires, and we may have multiple desires, but not all of them need to be realistic at a given time; `therefore,` intentions are those desires to which we decide to commit at some point. To be able to convert a desire into an intention we included the `FromDesire()` method.

To define and easily work with a finite set of beliefs, desires, percepts, actions, and so on we declared the following (Listing 4-4) enums.

Listing 4-4. Enum for Beliefs, Desires, Percepts, Plans, and Actions

```
public enum TypePercept
{
    WaterSpot, Obstacle, MoveUp, MoveDown, MoveLeft, MoveRight
}

public enum TypesBelief
{
    PotentialWaterSpots, ObstaclesOnTerrain
}

public enum TypesDesire
{
    FindWater, GotoLocation, Dig
}

public enum TypesPlan
{
    PathFinding
}

public enum TypesAction
{
    MoveUp, MoveDown, MoveLeft, MoveRight, Dig,
    None
}
```

To be able to handle percepts and plans a lot better we will incorporate into our program `Percept` and `Plan` classes as illustrated in Listing 4-5.

Listing 4-5. Percept and Plan Classes

```
public class Percept
    {
        public TypePercept Type { get; set; }
        public Tuple<int, int> Position { get; set; }

public Percept(Tuple<int, int> position, TypePercept percept)
        {
            Position = position;
Type = percept;
        }
    }

public class Plan
    {
        public TypesPlan Name { get; set; }
        public List<Tuple<int, int>> Path { get; set; }
        private MarsRover _rover;

        public Plan(TypesPlan name, MarsRover rover)
        {
            Name = name;
            Path = new List<Tuple<int, int>>();
            _rover = rover;
        }
```

```
public TypesAction NextAction()
{
    if (Path.Count == 0)
        return TypesAction.None;

    var next = Path.First();
    Path.RemoveAt(0);

    if (_rover.X > next.Item1)
        return TypesAction.MoveUp;
    if (_rover.X < next.Item1)
        return TypesAction.MoveDown;
    if (_rover.Y < next.Item2)
        return TypesAction.MoveRight;
    if(_rover.Y > next.Item2)
        return TypesAction.MoveLeft;

    return TypesAction.None;
}

public void BuildPlan(Tuple<int, int> source,
Tuple<int, int> dest)
{
    switch (Name)
    {
            case TypesPlan.PathFinding:
                Path = PathFinding(source.Item1,
                source.Item2, dest.Item1, dest.Item2).
                Item2;
                break;
    }
}
```

```
private Tuple<Tuple<int, int>, List<Tuple<int, int>>>
PathFinding(int x1, int y1, int x2, int y2)
{
    var queue = new Queue<Tuple<Tuple<int, int>,
    List<Tuple<int, int>>>>();
    queue.Enqueue(new Tuple<Tuple<int, int>,
    List<Tuple<int, int>>>(new Tuple<int, int>(x1, y1),
    new List<Tuple<int, int>>()));
    var hashSetVisitedCells = new HashSet<Tuple
    <int, int>>();

    while(queue.Count > 0)
    {
        var currentCell = queue.Dequeue();
        var currentPath = currentCell.Item2;
        hashSetVisitedCells.Add(currentCell.Item1);
        var x = currentCell.Item1.Item1;
        var y = currentCell.Item1.Item2;

        if (x == x2 && y == y2)
            return currentCell;

        // Up
        if (_rover.MoveAvailable(x - 1, y) &&
        !hashSetVisitedCells.Contains(new Tuple<int,
        int>(x - 1, y)))
        {
            var pathUp = new List<Tuple<int,
            int>>(currentPath);
            pathUp.Add(new Tuple<int, int>(x - 1, y));
            queue.Enqueue(new Tuple<Tuple<int, int>,
            List<Tuple<int, int>>>(new Tuple<int,
            int>(x - 1, y), pathUp));
        }
```

```
// Down
if (_rover.MoveAvailable(x + 1, y) &&
!hashSetVisitedCells.Contains(new Tuple<int,
int>(x + 1, y)))
{
    var pathDown = new List<Tuple<int,
    int>>(currentPath);
    pathDown.Add(new Tuple<int, int>(x + 1, y));
    queue.Enqueue(new Tuple<Tuple<int, int>,
    List<Tuple<int, int>>>(new Tuple<int,
    int>(x + 1, y), pathDown));
}
// Left
if (_rover.MoveAvailable(x, y - 1) &&
!hashSetVisitedCells.Contains(new Tuple<int,
int>(x, y - 1)))
{
    var pathLeft = new List<Tuple<int,
    int>>(currentPath);
    pathLeft.Add(new Tuple<int, int>(x, y - 1));
    queue.Enqueue(new Tuple<Tuple<int, int>,
    List<Tuple<int, int>>>(new Tuple<int,
    int>(x, y - 1), pathLeft));
}
// Right
if (_rover.MoveAvailable(x, y + 1) &&
!hashSetVisitedCells.Contains(new Tuple<int,
int>(x, y + 1)))
{
    var pathRight = new List<Tuple<int,
    int>>(currentPath);
    pathRight.Add(new Tuple<int, int>(x, y + 1));
```

```
            queue.Enqueue(new Tuple<Tuple<int, int>,
            List<Tuple<int, int>>>(new Tuple<int,
            int>(x, y + 1), pathRight));
        }
    }

    return null;
}

public bool FulFill()
{
    return Path.Count == 0;
}
}
```

The Percept class is very simple; we are merely using it to make it easier for us to know where a percept has occurred. By using this class we can save the percept location. The Plan class, on the other hand, is a bit more complicated.

The Plan class contains a property List<Tuple<int, int>> Path, which defines the Path the agent created as a result of executing a plan; in this case, a path-finding plan. The BuildPlan() method will allow us to build different types of plans. It's supposed to act as a plan-selection mechanism. The NextAction() method updates the Path property by returning and deleting the next action to execute in the present plan. Finally, the PathFinding() method implements the Breadth First Search (BFS) algorithm for finding the optimal route from a given source to a given destination or location in the terrain. We'll see more of this algorithm in a future chapter; for now let us consider it an essential algorithm for different graph-related tasks and remember that it starts at the source, discovering new steps of the path from source to destination and escalating by levels (Figure 4-3). For this purpose it uses a queue for enqueuing all non-visited neighbors of the cell being examined at the time.

The FulFill() method determines when a plan has been completely executed.

D	5	4	3	4
5	4	3	2	3
4	3	2	1	2
3	2	1	S	1
4	3	2	1	2

Figure 4-3. *BFS is capable of discovering paths by levels; S is the source and D the destination. Each numbered cell determines a level in the search; i.e., level 1, 2, etc.*

Now that we have gotten acquainted with all the classes that our Mars Rover will be using, let's dive into the Mars Rover AI code.

Resembling the method implemented for the agent from Chapter 3, our Mars Rover includes a GetPercepts() method (Listing 4-6) that provides a list of percepts perceived by the agent at the current time and in its radius of sight.

Listing 4-6. GetPercepts() Method

```
public List<Percept> GetPercepts()
        {
            var result = new List<Percept>();

            if (MoveAvailable(X - 1, Y))
                result.Add(new Percept(new Tuple<int,int>
                (X - 1, Y), TypePercept.MoveUp));
```

```
    if (MoveAvailable(X + 1, Y))
        result.Add(new Percept(new Tuple<int, int>
        (X + 1, Y), TypePercept.MoveDown));

    if (MoveAvailable(X, Y - 1))
        result.Add(new Percept(new Tuple<int, int>
        (X, Y - 1), TypePercept.MoveLeft));

    if (MoveAvailable(X, Y + 1))
        result.Add(new Percept(new Tuple<int,
        int>(X, Y + 1), TypePercept.MoveRight));

    result.AddRange(LookAround());

    return result;
}
```

The GetPercepts() method makes use of the MoveAvailable() and LookAround() methods, both illustrated in Listing 4-7.

Listing 4-7. MoveAvailable() and LookAround() Methods

```
    public bool MoveAvailable(int x, int y)
    {
        return x >= 0 && y >= 0 && x < _terrain.
        GetLength(0) && y < _terrain.GetLength(1)
        && _terrain[x, y] < RunningOverThreshold;
    }

private IEnumerable<Percept> LookAround()
    {
        return GetCurrentTerrain();
    }
```

159

Since we want to code our Mars Rover to be as generic as possible in the way it "looks around" (one may have a different definition of what it is to look around), the final implementation of this functionality is given by the GetCurrentTerrain() method shown in Listing 4-8.

Listing 4-8. GetCurrentTerrain() Method

```
public IEnumerable<Percept> GetCurrentTerrain()
      {
          var R = SenseRadius;
          CurrentTerrain.Clear();
          var result = new List<Percept>();

          for (var i = X - R > 0 ? X - R : 0; i <= X + R; i++)
          {
              for (var j = Y; Math.Pow((j - Y), 2) + Math.
              Pow((i - X), 2) <= Math.Pow(R, 2); j--)
              {
                  if (j < 0 || i >= _terrain.GetLength(0))
                  break;
                  // In the circle
                  result.AddRange(CheckTerrain(Mars.
                  TerrainAt(i, j), new Tuple<int, int>(i,
                  j)));
                  CurrentTerrain.Add(new Tuple<int, int>(i, j));
                  UpdatePerceivedCellsDicc(new Tuple<int,
                  int>(i, j));
              }
```

```
for (var j = Y + 1; (j - Y) * (j - Y) + (i - X)
* (i - X) <= R * R; j++)
{
    if (j >= _terrain.GetLength(1) || i >=
    _terrain.GetLength(0)) break;
    // In the circle
    result.AddRange(CheckTerrain(Mars.
    TerrainAt(i, j), new Tuple<int, int>(i, j)));
    CurrentTerrain.Add(new Tuple<int, int>(i, j));
    UpdatePerceivedCellsDicc(new Tuple<int,
    int>(i, j));
}
}

    return result;
}
```

The method from Listing 4-8 includes several loops that depend on the circle circumference formula:

$$(x-h)^2 + (y-k)^2 = r^2$$

where (h, k) represent the center of the circle, in this case the agent's location; r represents the radius of the circle, or in this case the SenseRadius. These loops allow the rover to track every cell at distance SenseRadius of its current location. Within these loops we make calls to the UpdatePerceivedCellsDicc() and CheckTerrain() methods (Listing 4-9). The first simply updates the visited cells dictionary that we use in the Statistics and Probability component to inject new beliefs to the rover.

The latter checks a given cell from the terrain to see if it's an obstacle or a water location. It also updates the internal _terrain data structure the rover has initially and maintains later by updating the value that corresponds to the perceived coordinate.

Listing 4-9. UpdatePerceivedCellsDicc() and CheckTerrain()
Methods

```
    private void UpdatePerceivedCellsDicc(Tuple<int,
    int> position)
    {
        if (!_perceivedCells.ContainsKey(position))
            _perceivedCells.Add(position, 0);
        _perceivedCells[position]++;
}

    private IEnumerable<Percept> CheckTerrain
    (double cell, Tuple<int, int> position)
{

        var result = new List<Percept>();

        if (cell > RunningOverThreshold)
            result.Add(new Percept(position,
            TypePercept.Obstacle));
        else if (cell < 0)
            result.Add(new Percept(position,
            TypePercept.WaterSpot));
        // Update the rover's internal terrain
        _terrain[position.Item1, position.Item2] = cell;

        return result;
    }
```

The method responsible for generating the next action to be executed
by the rover is the Action() method shown in Listing 4-10.

Listing 4-10. Action() Method

```
public TypesAction Action(List<Percept> percepts)
{
    // Reactive Layer
    if (Mars.WaterAt(X, Y) && !WaterFound.Contains
    (new Tuple<int, int>(X, Y)))
        return TypesAction.Dig;

    var waterPercepts = percepts.FindAll(p =>
    p.Type == TypePercept.WaterSpot);

    if (waterPercepts.Count > 0)
    {
        foreach (var waterPercept in waterPercepts)
        {
            var belief = Beliefs.FirstOrDefault(b =>
            b.Name == TypesBelief.PotentialWaterSpots);
            List<Tuple<int, int>> pred;
            if (belief != null)
                pred = belief.Predicate as List<Tuple
                <int, int>>;
            else
            {
                pred = new List<Tuple<int, int>>
                {waterPercept.Position};
                Beliefs.Add(new Belief(TypesBelief.
                PotentialWaterSpots, pred));
            }
            if (!WaterFound.Contains
            (waterPercept.Position))
                pred.Add(waterPercept.Position);
```

```
            else
            {
                pred.RemoveAll(
                    t => t.Item1 == waterPercept.
                    Position.Item1 && t.Item2 ==
                    waterPercept.Position.Item2);
                if (pred.Count == 0)
                    Beliefs.RemoveAll(b => (b.Predicate as
                    List<Tuple<int, int>>).Count == 0);
            }
        }

        if (waterPercepts.Any(p => !WaterFound.
        Contains(p.Position)))
            CurrentPlan = null;
    }

    if (Beliefs.Count == 0)
    {
        if (_wanderTimes == WanderThreshold)
        {
_wanderTimes = 0;
            InjectBelief();
        }
_wanderTimes++;
        return RandomMove(percepts);
    }
    if (CurrentPlan == null || CurrentPlan.FullFill())
    {
        // Deliberative Layer
        Brf(percepts);
```

```
        Options();
        Filter();
    }

    return CurrentPlan.NextAction();
}
```

In this method we incorporate the reactive and deliberative layers of the agent. The first lines correspond to the reactive layer, and different scenarios are considered that demand an Fimmediate response:

1. There's water at the current location of the rover, and that spot has not been discovered before.

2. There's a percept of a possible water location in the surrounding areas (defined by the circle with radius SenseRadius) of the rover. In this case, and always checking that the possible water location has not been already found, we add a water belief to the rover.

3. If the water location perceived at step 2 has not been previously found then the current plan is deleted. A new one considering the new belief will be built.

4. If the rover has no beliefs it will execute a random action (Listing 4-11); i.e., wanders around. Once this "wandering around" reaches a certain number of actions (ten, in this case) then a belief is injected.

The four previous steps make up the reactive layer of our agent; the last part of the method composed of the Brf(), Options(), and Filter() methods represent the deliberative layer (BDI architecture). The InjectBelief() method is also part of this deliberative layer as it involves a "deliberative" process where the agent decides its next course of action.

Listing 4-11. RandomMove() Method

```
private TypesAction RandomMove(List<Percept> percepts)
        {
            var moves = percepts.FindAll(p => p.Type.
            ToString().Contains("Move"));
            var selectedMove = moves[_random.Next(0, moves.Count)];

            switch (selectedMove.Type)
            {
                case TypePercept.MoveUp:
                    return TypesAction.MoveUp;
                case TypePercept.MoveDown:
                    return TypesAction.MoveDown;
                case TypePercept.MoveRight:
                    return TypesAction.MoveRight;
                case TypePercept.MoveLeft:
                    return TypesAction.MoveLeft;
            }

            return TypesAction.None;
        }
```

The Statistics and Probability component of the rover, and the one that allows it to inject beliefs based on its past history, is represented by the InjectBelief() method, which can be seen in Listing 4-12 along with its helper methods.

Listing 4-12. InjectBelief(), SetRelativeFreq(), and RelativeFreq()
Methods

```
private void InjectBelief()
        {
            var halfC = _terrain.GetLength(1) / 2;
            var halfR = _terrain.GetLength(0) / 2;

            var firstSector = _perceivedCells.Where(k => k.Key.
            Item1 < halfR && k.Key.Item2 < halfC).ToList();
            var secondSector = _perceivedCells.Where(k => k.Key.
            Item1 < halfR && k.Key.Item2 >= halfC).ToList();

            var thirdSector = _perceivedCells.Where(k => k.Key.
            Item1 >= halfR && k.Key.Item2 < halfC).ToList();
            var fourthSector = _perceivedCells.Where(k => k.Key.
            Item1 >= halfR && k.Key.Item2 >= halfC).ToList();

            var freq1stSector = SetRelativeFreq(firstSector);
            var freq2ndSector = SetRelativeFreq(secondSector);
            var freq3rdSector = SetRelativeFreq(thirdSector);
            var freq4thSector = SetRelativeFreq(fourthSector);

            var min = Math.Min(freq1stSector, Math.
            Min(freq2ndSector, Math.Min(freq3rdSector,
            freq4thSector)));

            if (min == freq1stSector)
                Beliefs.Add(new Belief(TypesBelief.
                PotentialWaterSpots, new List<Tuple<int, int>>
                { new Tuple<int, int>(0, 0) }));
```

```
        else if (min == freq2ndSector)
            Beliefs.Add(new Belief(TypesBelief.Potential
            WaterSpots, new List<Tuple<int, int>> { new
            Tuple<int, int>(0, _terrain.GetLength(1) - 1) }));
        else if (min == freq3rdSector)
            Beliefs.Add(new Belief(TypesBelief.Potential
            WaterSpots, new List<Tuple<int, int>> { new
            Tuple<int, int>(_terrain.GetLength(0) - 1, 0)
            }));
        else
            Beliefs.Add(new Belief(TypesBelief.Potential
            WaterSpots, new List<Tuple<int, int>> { new
            Tuple<int, int>(_terrain.GetLength(0) - 1,
            _terrain.GetLength(1) - 1) }));
    }

    private double SetRelativeFreq(List<KeyValuePair<Tuple
    <int, int>, int>> cells)
    {
        var result = 0.0;

        foreach (var cell in cells)
            result += RelativeFrequency(cell.Value,
            cells.Count);

        return result;
    }

    private double RelativeFrequency(int absFreq, int n)
    {
        return (double) absFreq/n;
    }
```

As it was detailed in the last section, the relative frequency is calculated for every cell of a given sector and then summed up in the `SetRelativeFreq()` method to obtain the total frequency of the group of cells. Note that in this case we decided to divide the terrain into four equal sectors, but you may decide to do it in as many sectors as you deem necessary or to the level of detail you believe necessary, like you would do in a QuadTree. One could even decide to divide the terrain into a certain number of sectors considering the `SenseRadius` of the rover and the time it wanders around. These values are all related, and most of them are considered in the heuristics attached to the rover. In this case—and seeking simplicity in the example proposed—we choose to attach truly naïve heuristics for the rover; for instance, always injecting a water belief at a corner of the selected sector could be a bad idea in different scenarios, as it's not going to work well every time. Thus, the sector selection and cell-within-sector selection mechanisms need to be more generic for the rover to perform well in multiple environments. Let's keep in mind that the heuristics presented here can be greatly improved, and as a result the rover will improve its performance.

Note   A QuadTree is a tree data structure where each internal node has exactly four children. They are often used to partition a two-dimensional space or region by recursively subdividing it into four quadrants or regions.

Lastly, let's examine the deliberative layer and all its methods, starting with the Beliefs Revision Function (Listing 4-13).

Listing 4-13. Brf() Method

```
public void Brf(List<Percept> percepts)
{
    var newBeliefs = new List<Belief>();

    foreach (var b in Beliefs)
    {
        switch (b.Name)
        {
            case TypesBelief.PotentialWaterSpots:
                var waterSpots = new List<Tuple<int,
                int>>(b.Predicate);
                waterSpots = UpdateBelief(TypesBelief.
                PotentialWaterSpots, waterSpots);
                if (waterSpots.Count > 0)
                    newBeliefs.Add(new Belief(TypesBelief.
                    PotentialWaterSpots, waterSpots));
                break;
            case TypesBelief.ObstaclesOnTerrain:
                var obstacleSpots = new List<Tuple<int,
                int>>(b.Predicate);
                obstacleSpots = UpdateBelief
                (TypesBelief.ObstaclesOnTerrain,
                obstacleSpots);
                if (obstacleSpots.Count > 0)
                    newBeliefs.Add(new Belief
                    (TypesBelief.ObstaclesOnTerrain,
                    obstacleSpots));
                break;
        }
    }

    Beliefs = new List<Belief>(newBeliefs);
}
```

In the Brf() method we examine every belief (possible water locations, possible obstacle locations) and update them, creating a new set of beliefs. The UpdateBelief() method is illustrated in Listing 4-14.

Listing 4-14. UpdateBelief() Method

```
private List<Tuple<int, int>> UpdateBelief(TypesBelief belief,
IEnumerable<Tuple<int, int>> beliefPos)
    {
        var result = new List<Tuple<int, int>>();

        foreach (var spot in beliefPos)
        {
            if (CurrentTerrain.Contains(new Tuple<int,
            int>(spot.Item1, spot.Item2)))
            {
                switch (belief)
                {
                    case TypesBelief.PotentialWaterSpots:
                        if (_terrain[spot.Item1, spot.
                        Item2] >= 0)
                            continue;
                        break;
                    case TypesBelief.ObstaclesOnTerrain:
                        if (_terrain[spot.Item1, spot.
                        Item2] < RunningOverThreshold)
                            continue;
                        break;
                }
            }
            result.Add(spot);
        }

        return result;
    }
```

In the UpdateBelief() method we check every belief against the currently perceived terrain. If there's a wrong belief—like, for instance, we thought or believed we would find water at location (x, y) and it happens that we were just there and there's nothing—then that belief must be deleted.

The Options() method, which is responsible for generating desires, is shown in Listing 4-15.

Listing 4-15. Options() Method

```
public void Options()
{
    Desires.Clear();

    foreach (var b in Beliefs)
    {
        if (b.Name == TypesBelief.PotentialWaterSpots)
        {
            var waterPos = b.Predicate as List<Tuple
            <int, int>>;
            waterPos.Sort(delegate(Tuple<int, int>
            tupleA, Tuple<int, int> tupleB)
                        {
                            var distA = Manhattan
                            Distance(tupleA,
                            new Tuple<int,
                            int>(X, Y));
                            var distB = Manhattan
                            Distance(tupleB,
                            new Tuple<int,
                            int>(X, Y));
                            if (distA < distB)
                                return 1;
```

```
                    if (distA > distB)
                         return -1;
                       return 0;
                 });
        foreach (var wPos in waterPos)
            Desires.Enqueue(new Desire
            (TypesDesire.FindWater, new Desire
            (TypesDesire.GotoLocation, new Desire
            (TypesDesire.Dig, wPos))));
}
        }
     }
```

We will consider only one type of desire—the desire to find water at specific locations. Thus, using the set of beliefs as a base, we generate desires and sort them by proximity using the distance (Listing 4-16) as the proximity measure.

Listing 4-16. Manhattan Distance

```
public int ManhattanDistance(Tuple<int, int> x, Tuple<int,
int> y)
{
return Math.Abs(x.Item1 - y.Item1) + Math.Abs(x.Item2 - y.Item2);
}
```

Using the set of desires, we push new intentions into our Intentions set in the Filter() method; if there's no plan in motion for the current intention then we choose one using the ChoosePlan() method (Listing 4-17).

Listing 4-17. Filter() and ChoosePlan() Methods

```csharp
    private void Filter()
{
        Intentions.Clear();

         foreach (var desire in Desires)
        {
            if (desire.SubDesires.Count > 0)
            {
                var primaryDesires = desire.
                GetSubDesires();
                primaryDesires.Reverse();
                foreach (var d in primaryDesires)
                    Intentions.Push(Intention.
                    FromDesire(d));
            }
            else
                Intentions.Push(Intention.
                FromDesire(desire));
        }

        if (Intentions.Any() && !ExistsPlan())
            ChoosePlan();
    }

    private void ChoosePlan()
    {
        var primaryIntention = Intentions.Pop();
        var location = primaryIntention.Predicate as
        Tuple<int, int>;
```

```
    switch (primaryIntention.Name)
    {
        case TypesDesire.Dig:
            CurrentPlan = PlanLibrary.First(p =>
            p.Name == TypesPlan.PathFinding);
            CurrentPlan.BuildPlan(new Tuple<int,
            int>(X, Y), location);
            break;
    }
}
```

To conclude, the ExistsPlan() method determines if there's a plan in motion, and the ExecuteAction() method executes the action selected by the agent (Listing 4-18). The latter method is also responsible for updating the WaterFound data structure with the locations where water has been found.

Listing 4-18. ExistsPlan() and ExecuteAction() Methods

```
    public bool ExistsPlan()
    {
        return CurrentPlan != null && CurrentPlan.Path.
        Count > 0;
    }

public void ExecuteAction(TypesAction action, List<Percept>
percepts)
    {
        switch (action)
        {
            case TypesAction.MoveUp:
                X -= 1;
                break;
```

```
            case TypesAction.MoveDown:
                X += 1;
                break;
            case TypesAction.MoveLeft:
                Y -= 1;
                break;
            case TypesAction.MoveRight:
                Y += 1;
                break;
            case TypesAction.Dig:
                WaterFound.Add(new Tuple<int, int>(X, Y));
                break;
        }
    }
```

In the next section, we'll take a look at our Mars Rover in action as it is executed in a Windows Forms Application that we created for experimenting and seeing how its AI works on a test world.

Mars Rover Visual Application

As mentioned at the beginning of this chapter, we created a Windows Forms application with which to test our Mars Rover and see how it would do on a test Mars world with hidden water locations and obstacles along the way. This example will not only help us to understand how to set up the MarsRover and Mars classes, but it will also demonstrate how the AI presented during this chapter will perform its decision-making process under different scenarios. The complete details of the Windows Form application (Listing 4-19) are beyond the scope of this book; we will simply present a fragment of it to illustrate to readers where the graphics are coming from. For further reference, the source code associated with this book can be consulted.

Listing 4-19. Fragment of Windows Forms Visual Application Code

```
public partial class MarsWorld : Form
    {
        private MarsRover _marsRover;
        private Mars _mars;
        private int _n;
        private int _m;

        public MarsWorld(MarsRover rover, Mars mars, int n, int m)
        {
            InitializeComponent();
            _marsRover = rover;
            _mars = mars;
            _n = n;
            _m = m;
        }

        private void TerrainPaint(object sender, PaintEventArgs e)
        {
            var pen = new Pen(Color.Wheat);
            var waterColor = new SolidBrush(Color.Aqua);
            var rockColor = new SolidBrush(Color.Chocolate);
            var cellWidth = terrain.Width/_n;
            var cellHeight = terrain.Height/_m;

            for (var i = 0; i < _n; i++)
                e.Graphics.DrawLine(pen, new Point(i *
                cellWidth, 0), new Point(i * cellWidth, i *
                cellWidth + terrain.Height));

            for (var i = 0; i < _m; i++)
                e.Graphics.DrawLine(pen, new Point(0, i *
                cellHeight), new Point(i * cellHeight +
                terrain.Width, i * cellHeight));
```

```
if (_marsRover.ExistsPlan())
{
    foreach (var cell in _marsRover.CurrentPlan.Path)
    {
        e.Graphics.FillRectangle(new SolidBrush
        (Color.Yellow), cell.Item2 * cellWidth,
        cell.Item1 * cellHeight,
        cellWidth, cellHeight);
    }
}

for (var i = 0; i < _n; i++)
{
    for (var j = 0; j < _m; j++)
    {
        if (_mars.TerrainAt(i, j) > _marsRover.
        RunningOverThreshold)
            e.Graphics.DrawImage(new
            Bitmap("obstacle-transparency.png"),
            j*cellWidth, i*cellHeight,
            cellWidth, cellHeight);
        if (_mars.WaterAt(i, j))
            e.Graphics.DrawImage(new Bitmap("water-
            transparency.png"), j * cellWidth,
            i * cellHeight, cellWidth, cellHeight);

        // Draw every belief in white
        foreach (var belief in _marsRover.Beliefs)
        {
            var pred = belief.Predicate as
            List<Tuple<int, int>>;
            if (pred != null && !pred.Contains(new
            Tuple<int, int>(i, j)))
                continue;
```

```
    if (belief.Name == TypesBelief.
    ObstaclesOnTerrain)
    {
        e.Graphics.DrawImage(new
        Bitmap("obstacle-transparency.
        png"), j * cellWidth, i *
        cellHeight, cellWidth, cellHeight);
        e.Graphics.DrawRectangle(new
        Pen(Color.Gold, 6), j * cellWidth, i
        * cellHeight, cellWidth, cellHeight);
    }
    if (belief.Name == TypesBelief.
    PotentialWaterSpots)
    {
        e.Graphics.DrawImage(new
        Bitmap("water-transparency.png"),
        j * cellWidth, i * cellHeight,
        cellWidth, cellHeight);
        e.Graphics.DrawRectangle(new
        Pen(Color.Gold, 6), j * cellWidth, i
        * cellHeight, cellWidth, cellHeight);
    }

}
}

e.Graphics.DrawImage(new Bitmap("rover-
transparency.png"), _marsRover.Y * cellWidth,
_marsRover.X * cellHeight, cellWidth, cellHeight);
```

```
var sightColor = Color.FromArgb(80, Color.Lavender);
_marsRover.GetCurrentTerrain();

        foreach (var cell in _marsRover.CurrentTerrain)
            e.Graphics.FillRectangle(new SolidBrush
            (sightColor), cell.Item2 * cellWidth, cell.
            Item1 * cellHeight, cellWidth, cellHeight);
    }

    private void TimerAgentTick(object sender, EventArgs e)
    {
        var percepts = _marsRover.GetPercepts();
        agentState.Text = "State: Thinking ...";
        agentState.Refresh();
        var action = _marsRover.Action(percepts);
        _marsRover.ExecuteAction(action, percepts);

        var beliefs = UpdateText(beliefsList, _marsRover.
        Beliefs);
        var desires = UpdateText(beliefsList, _marsRover.
        Desires);
        var intentions = UpdateText(beliefsList,
        _marsRover.Intentions);

        if (beliefs != beliefsList.Text)
            beliefsList.Text = beliefs;
        if (desires != desiresList.Text)
            desiresList.Text = desires;
        if (intentions != intentionsList.Text)
            intentionsList.Text = intentions;
        foreach (var wSpot in _marsRover.WaterFound)
```

```
        {
            if (!waterFoundList.Items.Contains(wSpot))
                waterFoundList.Items.Add(wSpot);
        }
        Refresh();
    }

    private string UpdateText(RichTextBox list, IEnumerable
    <object> elems)
    {
        var result = "";

        foreach (var elem in elems)
            result += elem;

        return result;
    }

    private void PauseBtnClick(object sender, EventArgs e)
    {
        if (timerAgent.Enabled)
        {
            timerAgent.Stop();
            pauseBtn.Text = "Play";
        }
        else
        {
            timerAgent.Start();
            pauseBtn.Text = "Pause";
        }
    }
}
```

From this code we may notice that the visual application consists of a grid where we have included Play/Pause buttons and used a timer to control rover actions and execute them every second.

In order to set up our Mars Rover and world we would need to define a set of initial beliefs, a terrain for the rover, and a real terrain of Mars (Listing 4-20).

Listing 4-20. Setting Up the Mars Rover and World

```
var water = new List<Tuple<int, int>>
          {
              new Tuple<int, int> (1, 2),
              new Tuple<int, int> (3, 5),
          };

    var obstacles = new List<Tuple<int, int>>
          {
              new Tuple<int, int> (2, 2),
              new Tuple<int, int> (4, 5),
          };

    var beliefs = new List<Belief> {
          new Belief(TypesBelief.PotentialWaterSpots, water),
          new Belief(TypesBelief.ObstaclesOnTerrain,
          obstacles),
          };

    var marsTerrain = new [,]
                    {
                              {0, 0, 0, 0, 0, 0, 0, 0, 0, 0},
                              {0, 0, 0, 0, 0, 0, 0, 0, 0, 0},
                              {0, 0, 0, 0, 0, 0, 0, 0, 0, 0},
                              {0, 0, 0.8, -1, 0, 0, 0, 0, 0, 0},
                              {0, 0, 0.8, 0, 0, 0, 0, 0, 0, 0},
```

```
                          {0, 0, 0, 0, 0, 0, 0, 0, 0, 0},
                          {0, 0, 0, 0, 0, 0, 0, 0, 0, 0},
                          {0, 0, 0, 0, 0, 0, 0, 0, 0, 0},
                          {0, 0, 0, 0, 0, 0.8, 0, 0, 0, 0},
                          {0, 0, 0, 0, 0, 0, 0, 0, 0, 0}
        };

var roverTerrain = new [,]
                {
                          {0, 0, 0, 0, 0, 0, 0, 0, 0, 0},
                          {0, 0, 0, 0, 0, 0, 0, 0, 0, 0},
                          {0, 0, 0, 0, 0, 0, 0, 0, 0, 0},
                          {0, 0, 0.8, 0, 0, 0, 0, 0, 0, 0},
                          {0, 0, 0.8, 0, 0, 0, 0, 0, 0, 0},
                          {0, 0, 0, 0, 0, 0, 0, 0, 0, 0},
                          {0, 0, 0, 0, 0, 0, 0, 0, 0, 0},
                          {0, 0, 0, 0, 0, 0, 0, 0, 0, 0},
                          {0, 0, 0, 0, 0, 0.8, 0, 0, 0, 0},
                          {0, 0, 0, 0, 0, 0, 0, 0, 0, 0}
        };

        var mars = new Mars(marsTerrain);
        var rover = new MarsRover(mars, roverTerrain, 7, 8,
        beliefs, 0.75, 2);

        Application.EnableVisualStyles();
        Application.SetCompatibleTextRenderingDefault(false);
        Application.Run(new MarsWorld(rover, mars, 10, 10));
```

Once we run the application, a GUI like the one illustrated in Figure 4-4 will show up. In this program, one can easily differentiate water locations (water drops images) from obstacle locations (rocks images).

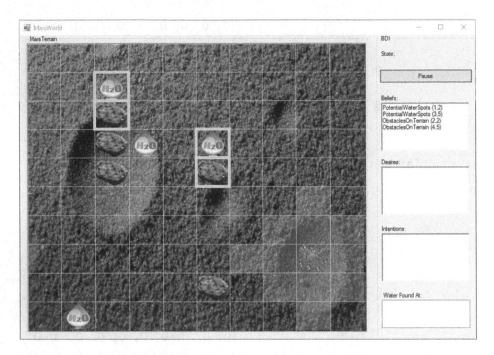

Figure 4-4. *Windows Forms application showing the rover, its SenseRadius, beliefs of water locations and obstacles marked as yellow squares, and actual water and obstacle locations without any yellow square surrounding them*

Notice the light-color cells surrounding the rover at all times; these are the cells that the rover can "see" or perceive at any given moment and are defined by the SenseRadius parameter (defined as a [Manhattan distance] value of 2 in the setup code) and the "discrete" circle whose radius is precisely the SenseRadius and whose center is the rover's current location.

On the right side of the application we have a panel with various information sections, such as Beliefs, Desires, Intentions, WaterFoundAt. All of these are Windows Forms controls and ultimately use the ToString() overrides presented in the last section.

The time to see our Mars Rover agent in action has come. Let's see what happens when we run the application (Figure 4-5).

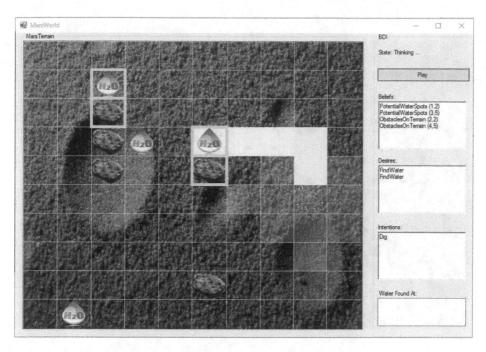

Figure 4-5. *The rover creates a plan to go to location (3, 5), its closest probable water location, and so it creates a plan or sequence of actions (denoted in yellow cells) to get there and dig in.*

Notice that the plan (sequence of actions) or path returned by our path-finding algorithm is denoted in yellow with the purpose of making it easier for us to comprehend where the rover is going and why. In this case, the rover is going after its closest water-location belief. Once it gets there (Figure 4-6), it discovers that its belief was wrong and there was no water in the pursued location as there was no obstacle in a cell adjacent to that water-location belief. The good news is that while exploring that area the rover perceived a water location nearby (in its sensing circle) and so it adventures to go there to find out more.

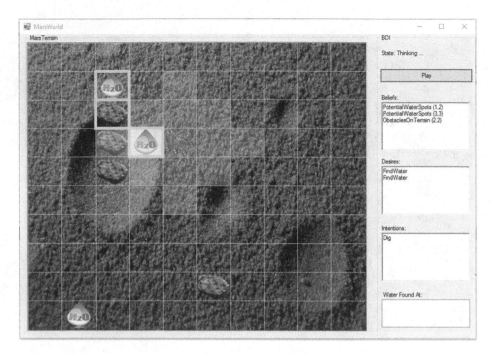

Figure 4-6. *The rover perceives a water location while exploring a belief and finds the first water location on Mars*

The previous location sought by the agent is a water location, so the WaterFound data structure is updated, and the rover has found water on Mars! Afterward, it continues pursuing its next belief (Figure 4-7): water at (1, 2).

Once again when approaching (entering its perception or sense radius), the next water-location belief is discarded by the agent as well as ` another obstacle-location belief, and so the beliefs set is updated.

Now that the rover has exhausted its beliefs set it will wander around (during ten actions; it was hardwired like that in the code, see Figure 4-8) until our Statistics and Probability deliberative component is activated and causes the rover to inject itself with a new belief that is drawn from logical conclusions. In this case—and imitating what our human mind would do, because we are merely trying to mimic what a human would do in this situation—we would think that it's more likely, or that our chances of finding water are far greater, in an unexplored area. In the "Heuristics and Metaheuristics" chapter 14 we will see that this concept is known as *diversification* and is very common in metaheuristics such as Genetic Algorithm, Tabu Search, and so on.

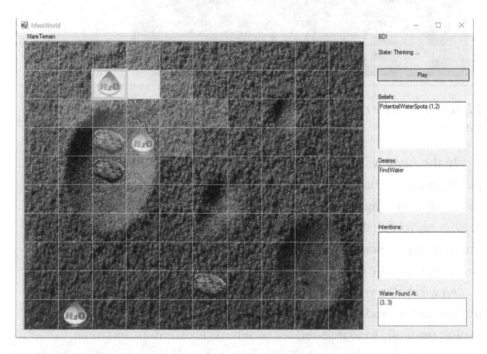

Figure 4-7. *The rover discards both a water-location belief and an obstacle-location belief*

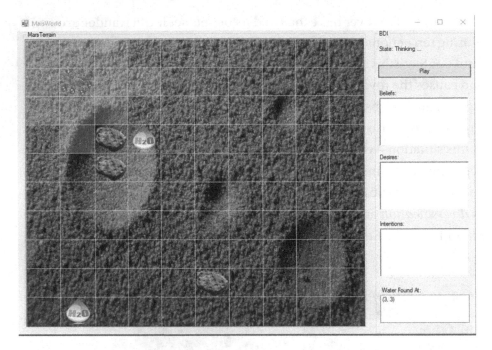

Figure 4-8. *The rover wanders around after having exhausted its beliefs set*

In the same way we can have a diversification stage to explore poorly visited or unexplored areas of the terrain we can also have an intensification stage to better explore areas where water has been previously found; that is, promising areas of the terrain. In our case the intensification phase could involve having the rover wander around in some sector of the terrain.

As we shall see in future chapters, finding a balance between the intensification and diversification stages (sometimes called the explore-exploit tradeoff) in search-related problems is essential, and most problems we face in our daily lives are search problems or optimization problems that in the end are search problems, as we search in the space of all possible solutions for one that is the best or optimal. Thus, many problems can be reduced to merely searching, and this is a complicated task that typically requires cleverness.

Continuing with our Mars Rover example, Figure 4-9 shows the rover after it finishes its wandering-around stage and injects itself with a belief of water at the lower-left corner cell of the third sector, and so it sets course to reach that cell.

The injection of this belief allows the rover to find an actual water location that was in the vicinity of the injected water-location belief. Thus, by diversifying the search to unexplored areas we found an actual water location (Figure 4-10). This process is repeated again; the rover wanders around (random moves), eventually injects a new belief, and moves to that location (Figure 4-11).

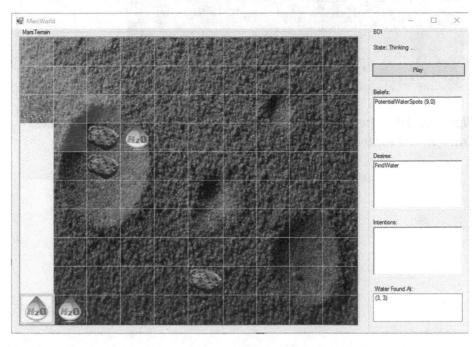

Figure 4-9. *The rover injects itself with a belief of a possible water location on the lower-left corner of the third sector*

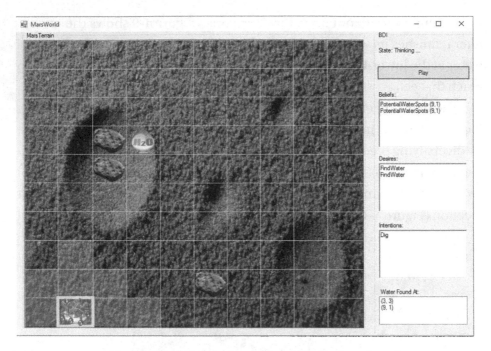

Figure 4-10. *The rover follows the injected belief and in the process finds an actual water location*

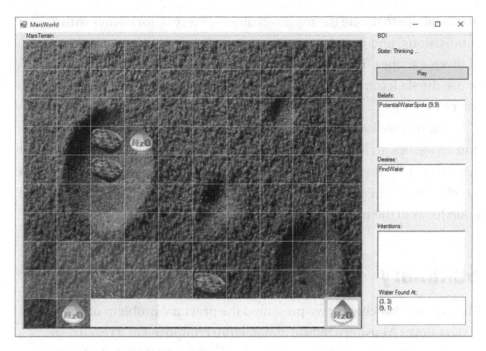

Figure 4-11. *The rover repeats the process, wanders around, and then injects a new water-location belief*

The Mars Rover presented in this chapter has multiple features that can be refined to improve its performance. For instance, the WanderThreshold may be adjusted since the rover spends more and more time on Mars, looking to prolong the time it stays wandering in a certain area; this decision may be dependent on the square area of the sector where it's wandering. The strategy of always choosing a corner of the less-frequently visited sector to inject the water-location belief can also change and be made dependent on various conditions related to the rover's history or state. The choice can also be made randomly; i.e., choose a random cell in the selected sector to inject the water-location belief or maybe choose the least-visited cell in that sector. The division of the terrain may also change; we could use a set of division patterns collected

191

in a database to divide the terrain in different ways (not always with 2^n subdivisions) and give the rover the opportunity to explore different areas of diverse shapes. The possibilities are endless, and it's up to the reader to use the skeleton provided in this chapter and create their perfect Mars Rover.

Now that we have examined a complete practical problem of an agent and an agent's architecture, we can move forward and explore multi-agent systems in which various agents coexist and maybe collaborate or compete to achieve certain goals that could be common to them all. This will be the main focus of the next chapter.

Summary

Throughout this chapter we presented the practical problem of designing a Mars Rover AI using a hybrid architecture composed of a reactive layer and a deliberative layer that implements the BDI (Beliefs, Desires, and Intentions) paradigm. The Mars Rover example included a visual application (Windows Forms) that demonstrated how the rover reacts to different scenarios, how it's able to plan via a path-finding algorithm, and how it's able to provide timely responses to immediately perceived situations. We also presented a Statistics and Probability component in the agent that acts as a deliberative component and allows it to explore unexplored or poorly visited areas of the terrain.

CHAPTER 5

Multi-Agent Systems

Thus far we have studied agents as single entities interacting with the environment; in real life many problems can be solved much more quickly and efficiently when multiple agents collaborate to achieve a common goal.

Recall the cleaning agent from Chapters 2 and 3; this agent was dealing with the problem of cleaning an entire terrain on its own. Undoubtedly, this task could be completed much quicker if various cleaning robots were on the terrain communicating and helping each other to complete, in a shorter time, the task that for a single agent would take much longer and at higher resource consumption.

Nowadays, multi-agent systems (MAS) are applied in real-world applications such as computer games, military defense systems, air traffic control, transportation, graphic information systems (GIS), logistics, medical diagnosis, and so on. Other uses involve mobile technologies, where they are applied to achieve automatic, dynamic load balancing and high scalability.

Throughout this chapter we will examine multi-agent systems in which multiple agents may collaborate, coordinate, communicate, or compete to achieve a certain goal. MAS fall into an area where *distributed systems* and AI join to form what is known as *distributed artificial intelligence.* At the end of this part, which will take the next three chapters, we will present a practical problem where various cleaning robots will collaborate to clean a room.

© Arnaldo Pérez Castaño 2018
A. Pérez Castaño, *Practical Artificial Intelligence*,
https://doi.org/10.1007/978-1-4842-3357-3_5

Note   Multi-agent systems represent distributed computing systems. As with any distributed system, they are composed of a number of interacting computational entities. However, unlike classical distributed systems, their constituent entities are intelligent and have the capacity to have intelligent interactions with one another.

What's a Multi-Agent System?

As occurred with the *logic* and *agent* terms previously presented, there's no global agreement on a definition for *multi-agent system*. In this book, we'll provide a personal definition that we regard as logical and that considers other MAS definitions taken from the scientific literature.

A *multi-agent system (MAS)* is a set S of agents that interact with each other in either a competitive manner—looking to achieve the goals defined by the subset S' of agents to which they belong (S' belongs to a partition of S)—or a collaborative manner—seeking to achieve a common goal defined in S. Additionally, it can happen that every agent in S is acting to achieve its own goals; in such cases we say that we are dealing with an *independent* MAS.

In Table 5-1 we can see a first and very frequent scenario of an MAS being applied to air traffic control; in this scenario, Agent Controller 1 (A1) deals directly with pilots and collaborates with Agent Controller 2 (A2) in finding them a runway available for landing. Refer to Table 5-1 for a complete dialogue between the two collaborative agents.

Table 5-1. *MAS Example in Air Traffic Control Scenario*

Pilot	Agent Controller 1 (A1)	Agent Controller 2 (A2)
To A1: Can I land?		
	To A2: Any runway available?	
		To A1: Runway P.
	To Pilot: Clear for P.	
To A1: OK		
	To A2: Runway P is busy now.	

Now that we have introduced a self-definition for the MAS term we'll continue presenting other relevant, related concepts.

A *coalition* is said to be a subset of the set of agents; for an MAS such as basketball, baseball, or soccer games there are always two coalitions—the two teams competing.

A *strategy* is a function that receives the current state of the environment and outputs the action to be executed by a coalition. The strategy for Team A usually depends on the actions executed by each agent in Team B at the current moment.

A *platform*, also known as a *multi-agent infrastructure*, is a framework, base, or support that describes the agent architecture, the multi-agent organization, and their relations or dependencies. It allows agents to interact without taking into consideration the properties of such a platform (centralized or not, embedded into the agents or not, and so on), and it usually provides agents with a set of services (agent location and so forth) depending on the system needs, with the aim of enhancing MAS activity and organization; it is considered a tool for agents.

Agent architecture describes the layers or modules constituting a single agent as well as the relations and interactions among them. For instance, agents (in the context of MAS) regularly have a communication module to augment communication with users and other agents. As we know (from Chapters 3 and 4), some types of agents also have a planning layer. Normally, incoming messages arriving at the communication module will affect the planning layer by some connection, and the planning layer may create outgoing messages to be handled by the communication module.

A *multi-agent organization* describes the manner in which multiple agents are organized to form an MAS. Relations, interactions between agents, and their specific roles within the organization constitute a multi-agent organization. Agent architecture is not part of the multi-agent organization even though interrelations among them are common.

An agent is said to be *autonomous* in an MAS if it's autonomous with respect to every other agent in the set of agents making up the MAS; in other words, if it's beyond the control or power of any other agent.

An MAS is *discrete* if it is independent and the goals of the agents bear no relation to one another. Thus, discrete MAS involve no cooperation as each agent will be going its own way trying to achieve its own goals.

Modularity is one of the benefits of MAS; sometimes solving a complex problem is subdivided into easier subproblems of the original problem, and each agent can be specialized in the solution of one of these particular types of problem, therefore leading to *reusability*. Imagine an MAS dealing with a city disaster like an earthquake. Such an MAS would be composed of different agents (policemen, firemen, and so forth) where each agent would be devoted to a single task and all of them would have the global assignment of establishing order and saving lives.

Problem solving through MAS leads to *efficiency*; the solution to a problem can often be achieved much quicker if various concurrent, parallel agents are working at the same time to solve the problem.

An MAS also provides improved *reliability* because we may have multiple agents taking care of a single task, and if one of them fails then the others can continue its work by distributing among the rest.

One last important benefit that MAS provides us is *flexibility;* we can add or delete agents from an MAS at will, and different agents that have complementary skills may form coalitions to work together and solve problems.

In the following sections we'll be exploring some key concepts in the area of distributed AI and especially on the topic of MAS: communication, cooperation, negotiation, and coordination. We'll also take a deeper look at some of the concepts previously presented.

Note   One of the services a platform can offer is agent location; in other words, the facility by which an agent or a third party is able to locate another agent in an MAS environment.

Multi-Agent Organization

Earlier in the chapter we provided a definition for the term *multi-agent organization*. In this section, we will detail some of the most common multi-agent organizations one can find:

- *Hierarchical*: organization in which agents can only communicate by following a hierarchical structure. Because of this restriction there's no need to have an agent-location mechanism. Instead a set of *facilitators* act as middle men and receive and send all messaging between agents. These facilitators are usually at the upper levels of the hierarchy. Consequently, lower levels usually depend on higher levels. Communication is really reduced in this type of organization.

- *Flat or Democracy*: organization in which agents can communicate directly with one another. There's no fixed structure in this type of organization, but agents can form their own structures if they judge it is necessary to solve some specific task. Furthermore, no control of one agent over another is assumed. Agent location must be provided as part of the infrastructure or platform or the system must be closed; in other words, every agent must know about the others at all times. This type of organization can lead to communication overhead.

- *Subsumption*: organization in which agents (subsumed) can be components of other agents (container). This type of organization resembles that of the hierarchical model except that in this case subsumed agents surrender all control to their container agents. As occurs with the hierarchical organization, it involves low communication overhead.

- *Modular*: organization in which the MAS is composed of various modules, and each of these can be conceived of as a stand-alone MAS. The partition of the system into modules is usually done by considering measures such as geographical vicinity or a necessity for extreme interaction among agents and services within the same module. Modularity increases the efficiency of task execution and reduces communication overhead.

Hybrids of these organization types and dynamic changes from one style to another are possible. From the multi-agent organizations detailed in the previous points we can easily see that communication plays a vital role in defining the architecture and way of functioning of agents. We'll devote the next section to explaining some key aspects of this very important topic.

Note   In recent years, a large variety of agent architectures have been proposed. In the case of MAS architectures, this number greatly decreases because for an agent to be incorporated in an MAS it must be equipped with vital components (communication, coordination, and so on) that would allow it to properly interact with other agents.

Communication

Agents in an MAS must coordinate their actions to solve problems. In this scenario, coordination is achieved by means of communication, which plays a vital role in providing agent interaction and facilitating not only coordination but also information sharing and cooperation.

In the last section we discussed MAS organizations and how they can affect agent communication depending on the type of organization they are in. Now, we'll look at some detailed aspects of this topic.

The communication link established between agents can be classified as:

- Point to Point: agents communicate directly with each other

- Broadcast/Multicast: agents are capable of sending information to a subset of the set of agents. If this subset equals the set of agents then the agent is broadcasting; otherwise, it is multicasting.

- Mediated: communication between agents is mediated by a third party (facilitators; see Figure 5-1).

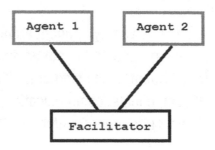

Figure 5-1. *Agent 1 and Agent 2 communicate via a facilitator acting as middle man*

Considering the nature of the medium by which messages travel from one agent to another, communication can be classified as:

- Direct routing: Messages are sent directly to other agents with no loss of signal.

- Signal-propagation routing: Agents send a signal whose intensity decreases as distance increases.

- Public-notice routing: using blackboard systems

Blackboard systems and *direct message passing* are two options for establishing agent communication.

A blackboard system (Figure 5-2) represents a common, shared space for every agent to place their data, information, and knowledge. Each agent can write and read from the blackboard at any given time, and in this centralized system there's no direct communication between agents. The blackboard also acts as a dispatcher, handling agent requests, data of the common problem, current state of the solution, current task of each agent, and so on. Since the blackboard system consists of a shared resource, one must be aware of all the concurrent issues that can arise in such a model (various agents trying to access the same info, agents using partial, not updated data written by other agents, and so on).

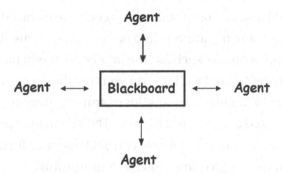

Figure 5-2. *The blackboard system is a centralized, common space for all agents to place and share their information*

In the other variant (message passing), information is passed from one agent (sender) to another (receiver). Communication among agents means more than communication in distributed systems; therefore, it is more appropriate to speak about interaction instead of communication. When we communicate we perform more than an exchange of messages with a specified syntax and a given protocol, as in distributed systems. Therefore, a more elaborate type of communication that tends to be specific to MAS is communication based on the *Speech Act Theory* (Searle, 1969; Vanderveken, 1994), which is the one that best describes the message-passing alternative for establishing agent communication.

Speech Act Theory

The origin of the Speech Act Theory (also called Communicative Act Theory) can be traced back to John Austin's book *How to Do Things with Words* (1962); most treatments of communication in MAS are inspired in this theory. The main point behind this theory is that we should consider communication as a form of action. Furthermore, Austin noticed that some utterances are like physical actions and appear to change the state of the world. Examples of this could be a declaration of war or simply "I declare you man and wife."

201

Austin argued that all communications could be phrased via declarative forms using the appropriate *performative* verbs. Therefore, a simple *informative* phrase such as "the jazz concert will take place on October 10th" can be treated as "I inform you that the jazz concert will take place on October 10th." *Directives*—as, for example, "give me that bottle of rum"—can be treated as "I request (demand) that you give me that bottle of rum." A *commissive* such as "I'll give you $100 for your furniture" can be treated as "I promise I'll give you $100 for your furniture."

Everything we utter is said with the intention of satisfying some goal; a theory of how utterances are used to achieve intentions is Speech Act Theory, and by using the different types of speech acts agents can interact effectively.

Note   Communicative act theories are theories of language use; they try to explain how language is used by people every day to achieve their goals and intentions.

Examples of some speech-act constructs are presented here:

- **Inform** other agents about some data.

- **Query** others about their state or current situation.

- **Answer** questions.

- **Request** others to act.

- **Promise** to do something.

- **Offer** deals.

- **Acknowledge** offers and requests.

Searle (1969) classified speech acts into the following categories:

- **Representatives:** when we are informing, asserting, claiming, describing; for example, it's cloudy

- **Directives:** an attempt to make the hearer do something; in other words, requesting, commanding, advising, forbidding; for example, bring me that bottle of rum

- **Commissives:** when we commit the speaker to do something, such as when promising, agreeing, offering, threatening, inviting; for example, I promise I'll bring you tea

- **Expressives:** when the speaker expresses a mental state; in other words, congratulating, thanking, apologizing; for example, I'm sorry you did not make it to Harvard

- **Declarations:** when the speaker brings about a state of affairs; in other words, declaring, marrying, arresting; or example, I declare (pronounce) you man and wife

A speech act has two components: a performative verb (for example, inform, declare, request, and so on) and a propositional content (for example, the bottle is open). Constructing speech acts involves combining a performative verb with a propositional content. See the following examples:

```
Performative = inform
Content = the bottle is open
Speech act = the bottle is open.

Performative = request
Content = the bottle is open
Speech Act = please open the bottle.
```

```
Performative = inquiry
Content = the bottle is open
Speech Act = is the bottle open?

Performative = refuse
Content = the bottle is open
Speech Act = I refuse to open the bottle

Performative = agree
Content = the bottle is open
Speech Act = I agree to open the bottle
```

In the same way we typically create a language for communication among co-workers at work, an MAS containing different agents that might be running in different machines, under different operating systems requires an agent communication language standardized to allow the exchange of messages in a standard format.

Agent Communication Languages (ACL)

Agent *communication languages* began to emerge in the 1980s; at first, they were dependent on the projects for which they were created and also on the internal representation of the agents that used them; there were no standard languages at that time.

Around the same time, but more generic than its predecessors, appeared the Knowledge Query and Manipulation Language, commonly known as KQML. It was created by the DARPA Knowledge Sharing Effort and was supposed to be a complement to the studies being made on knowledge-representation technologies, specifically on ontologies.

KQML is comprised of two parts: the language itself acts as an "outer" language, and the Knowledge Interchange Format (KIF) acts as an "inner" language; the first describes performatives, while the latter describes propositional content and is largely based on first-order predicate calculus. KQML represents knowledge that relies on the construct of a knowledge base; thus, instead of using a specific internal representation, it assumes that each agent maintains a knowledge base described in terms of knowledge assertions. KQML proposed a number of performatives such as *query* and *tell*. The idea was that each performative could be given semantics based on the effect it had on the knowledge bases of the communicating agents. Moreover, an agent would send a tell performative for some content only if it believed in the content sent; in other words, if it thought the content belonged in its knowledge base. An agent that receives a tell performative for some content would insert that content into its knowledge base; in other words, it would begin believing what it was told.

Note   An ontology is an explicit description of a domain (concepts, properties, restrictions, individuals, and so on). It defines a vocabulary and is used to share an understanding of the structure of information among computer agents or humans. In the Blocks World, `Block` represents a concept and `OnTop` represents a relationship.

The elegance of KQML is that all information for understanding the content of the message is included in the communication itself. Its generic syntax is described in Figure 5-3; notice it resembles the Lisp programming language:

```
(KQML-performative
:sender <word>
:receiver <word>
:language <word>
:ontology <word>
:content <expression>
...
)
```

Figure 5-3. *Basic structure of a KQML message*

In the following lines we show an example of a KQML dialogue between AgentX and AgentY:

```
 (stream-about
:sender AgentX
:receiver AgentY
:language KIF
:ontology CleaningTerrains
     :query
:reply-for query_from_AgentY
:content cell_i cell_j
)

(query
:sender AgentX
:receiver AgentY
:content(> (dirt cell_i) (0))
)

(tell
:sender AgentX
:receiver AgentY
:content(= (cell_j) (1))
)

(eos
:sender AgentX
:receiver AgentY
:query
:reply-for query_from_AgentY
)
```

In this little fragment of a KQML message, AgentX asks AgentY if there's dirt at cell i; it also replies to a previous query received from AgentY and tells it that cell j has 1 of dirt; eos stands for *End of Signal*. Note that the value of the content field is written in the language defined by the language tag, in this case KIF.

Note   KIF, a particular logic language, has been proposed as a standard to describe things within expert systems, databases, intelligent agents, and so on. One could say that KIF is a mediator used in the translation of other languages. Even though KQML is usually combined with KIF as content language, it can also be used in combination with other languages like Prolog, Lisp, Scheme, and so on.

In 1996, the Foundation for Intelligent Physical Agents (FIPA), a stand-alone non-profit organization now part of IEEE Computer Society, started working on several specifications for agent-based applications; one of these specifications was for an ACL of the same name as the organization; i.e., FIPA-ACL.

The basic structure of FIPA is quite similar to that of KQML, as illustrated in Figure 5-4.

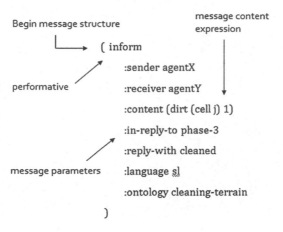

Figure 5-4. Components of a FIPA message

The parameters admitted by the FIPA language specification are the following:

- `:sender` — who sends the message
- `:receiver` — who is the recipient of the message
- `:content` — content of the message
- `:reply-with` — identifier of the message
- `:reply-by` — deadline for replying to the message
- `:in-reply-to` — identifier of the message being replied to
- `:language` — language in which the content is written
- `:ontology` — ontology used to represent the domain
- `:protocol` — communication protocol to be followed
- `:conversation-id` — identifier of the conversation

Table 5-2 details some FIPA performatives and the purpose for which they were created.

Table 5-2. *Some FIPA Performatives*

Performative	Passing Info	Requesting Info	Negotiation	Perform Actions	Error Handling
accept-proposal			x		
agree				x	
cancel		x		x	
cfp			x		
confirm	x				
disconfirm	x				x
failure					
inform	x				
inform-if	x				
inform-ref	x				
not-understood					x
propose			x		
query-if		x			
query-ref		x			
refuse				x	
reject-proposal			x		
request				x	
request-when				x	
request-whenever				x	
subscribe		x			

Inform and Request represent two basic performatives, while the others are defined in terms of these. Their meaning is composed of two parts: a precondition list that states what must be true for the speech act to succeed and a rational effect—i.e., what the sender of the message hopes to achieve.

In the FIPA inform performative, content is a statement, and sender informs the receiver that a given proposition is true; sender states the following:

- Some proposition is true.

- The receiving agent must also believe that the proposition is true.

- The receiver has no knowledge whatsoever of the truth of the proposition.

The next lines show an example of a FIPA inform performative:

```
(inform
:sender(agent-identifier :x)
:receiver(agent-identifier :y)
:content dirt( cell_i, 0 )
        :language Prolog
)
```

On the other hand, content in the request performative consists of an action; in this case, the sender requests the receiver to perform some action; sender states the following:

- The action content is to be performed.

- Recipient is capable of performing this action.

- Does not believe that receiver already intends to perform the action.

In this section, we analyzed a critical topic in MAS design: communication. Even though this is an essential aspect of every MAS, there are other components that are also relevant, one of which is coordination. We need our agents to coordinate and avoid problems like having two of them executing the same action at the same time (both trying to go through the same door at the same time) when it might be impossible. Coordination will be the focus point of the next section.

Coordination & Cooperation

An agent that is part of an MAS exists and performs its decision making in an environment where other agents exist as well. To avoid chaos and to ensure rational behavior in this environment we need our agents to coordinate and achieve their goals in a concise, logical manner. There are two main criteria points for assessing MAS: coherence and coordination.

Coherence refers to how well the MAS behaves considering some criteria of evaluation (solution quality, efficiency in applying resources, logical decision making, and so forth). A common problem for an MAS is how it can maintain overall coherence while lacking explicit global control. In such cases, agents must be able on their own to determine goals they share with other agents; they must also determine common tasks, avoid unnecessary conflicts, and collect knowledge. Having some form of organization among the agents is useful in this scenario.

Coordination refers to the ability of agents to avoid, by means of synchronization, irrational activities in which two or more agents could be involved. It implies the consideration of the actions of other agents when planning and executing one agent's actions. It is also a means to achieve the coherent behavior of the MAS, and it may imply *cooperation*. When agents in an MAS cooperate, they work toward achieving common goals. When they are *competing*, they have opposite goals. Coordination in both cases is essential because the agent must take into account the actions of others when competing or asking for a given resource or offering a service. Examples of coordination include ensuring the actions of agents are synchronized, providing opportune information to other agents, and avoiding redundant problem solving.

Cooperation is coordination among non-antagonistic agents. Typically, to cooperate successfully, each agent must maintain a model of the other agents and also develop a model of future interactions; this implies sociability.

For agents in an MAS to work together they must be able to share tasks and information. If we had an MAS where agents were designed by different individuals then we could end up having an MAS with various goals, all derived from different agents. Alternatively, if we are responsible for designing the entire system then we can have agents helping each other whenever we deem necessary; our best interest is going to be their best interest. In this cooperative model we say that agents are *benevolent* because they are working all together to achieve a common goal. A benevolent MAS, or those in which all agents are benevolent, simplifies the design task of the system significantly.

When agents represent the interests of individuals, organizations, companies, and so on, we say that they are *self-interested*. These agents will have their own set of goals, apart from the goals of other agents in the MAS, and will act to achieve them even at the expense of other agents' welfare; this could potentially lead to conflict between some of them.

Note   Self-interested agents complicate the design task of an MAS seriously. For an MAS with self-interested agents, we typically have to incorporate mechanisms for intelligent behavior, such as those based on game theory or rule-based algorithms.

Figure 5-5 illustrates a tree with some of the possible approaches for achieving coordination.

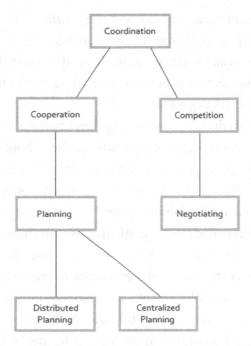

Figure 5-5. *Taxonomy for agent coordination possibilities*

A basic strategy for cooperation in an MAS is to decompose and then distribute tasks among agents. This divide-and-conquer approach can certainly reduce the complexity of the global task because by dividing it into smaller subtasks the global solution can be obtained in a shorter time and using fewer resources. In general, *task sharing* can be divided into three stages:

- Problem decomposition (Divide)

- Sub-problem solution

- Solution synthesis (Conquer)

In the problem decomposition stage the global problem is divided into subproblems, typically by a recursive or hierarchical procedure. Deciding how to do the division is a design choice and is problem dependent. Deciding who makes the problem decomposition and how it's made can

213

be left to an agent that we appoint as *task distributor*. This agent may not take care of anything other than distributing tasks among other agents in what would be a centralized design. Alternatively, it could be part of the subproblem solution team and act as any other agent but with the special attribute of being a work organizer.

Once the problem decomposition stage has provided us with a division of the global problem, each agent contributes to the subproblem assigned. During this process agents may need to share some information and update others on their current situation. Finally, in the solution synthesis stage all solutions to subproblems are joined (recursively or hierarchically).

In this cooperative model we can distinguish two main activities that will most likely be present during MAS execution: task sharing and results sharing. In the first, components of the task are distributed to agents, while in the latter partial or complete results are also distributed.

We can use a Subscribe/Notify (Publisher/Subscriber) pattern for results sharing; in such a pattern an object (subscriber) subscribes to another object (informant), requesting a notification for when event evt occurs. Once evt has occurred the informant notifies the subscriber of its occurrence, and they proactively exchange information in this manner.

At this point we have some unanswered questions. How is the process of allocating or matching tasks to agents done? How do we assemble a solution from the solved parts? In order to answer the first question we will look at a task-sharing protocol known as Contract Net.

Note   Some of the commonly used mechanisms for task sharing include the Market mechanism, where tasks are assigned to agents by generalized agreement or mutual selection; multi-agent planning, where planning agents have the responsibility of task assignment; and Contract Net protocol, one of several task-sharing mechanisms.

Negotiation Using Contract Net

The Contract Net mechanism is an interaction mechanism for task sharing among agents. It follows the model used by entities (governments, corporations, and so forth) to regulate the exchange of goods and services. Contract Net offers a solution to the problem of finding an appropriate agent to work on a task.

The agent who wants a task done is called *manager*. The candidate agents who can fulfill the task are known as *contractors*. The Contract Net process can be summarized in the next stages (Figure 5-6):

1. *Announcement*: The manager sends out an announcement of the task, which includes a specification of the task to be achieved. This specification must include a description of the task, any constraints (deadlines, etc.), and meta task info (bids must be submitted prior to deadline, due date, etc.). The announcement is broadcast.

2. *Bidding*: Agents receive the broadcast corresponding to the manager's announcement and decide for themselves whether they want to bid for the task. In this process they must take into account various factors like capacity to carry out the task and being able to meet all constraints. If they finally decide to bid then they submit a *tender*.

3. *Awarding*: The manager must choose between bids and decide on an agent to award the contract to. The result of this process is communicated to every agent that submitted a bid.

4. *Expediting*: The winner or successful contractor expedites the task.

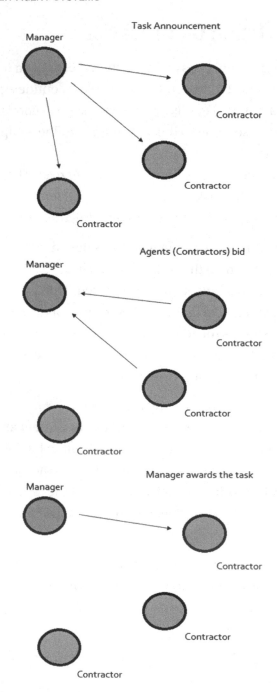

Figure 5-6. *Contract Net process*

Generally, any agent can act as manager and any agent can act as contractor by replying to task announcements. Because of this flexibility, task decomposition can be taken further to different depth levels. Furthermore, if a contractor is unable to complete or provide a suitable solution for a task then the manager can look for other contractor candidates, and as long as there are agents in the MAS the manager can seek a candidate contractor that at some point in time will be available to execute a task according to the manager's requirements.

From the contractor's perspective, he receives various offers (announcements) from various managers and decides upon what he thinks is the best offer. This decision is made based on some criteria (proximity, reward, etc.), and he sends a bid to the corresponding manager.

From the manager's perspective, he receives and evaluates bids for each task announcement. Any bid for a given task that is considered satisfactory will be accepted and always before the expiration time of the task announcement is met. Afterward, the manager notifies the winning contractor and possibly all other candidates who sent a bid with an "award notice" announcement that the task has been awarded.

Perhaps one could say that a negative point of the Contract Net mechanism is that the awarded agent does not have to be the best or most suitable agent for the task, as the most suitable agent for the task could be busy at award time.

Note   There exist several reasons why a manager may not receive bids on an announcement. All agents might be busy at the time of receiving the announcement, a candidate contractor (agent) ranks the task announced below other offered tasks, or no contractor is capable of working on the announced task.

The FIPA-ACL specification was projected to support the Contract Net negotiation mechanism. The `cfp` (call for proposals) performative is used to announce the task; the `propose` and `refuse` performatives are used to propose or refuse a proposal; `accept` and `reject` are used to accept or decline a proposal, and `inform` and `failure` are used to communicate completion of the task with its corresponding result.

Social Norms & Societies

Classical AI has been concerned with designing single agents that incorporate reasoning and control logics implemented using a von Neumann architecture. However, agents are not always in isolation; they exist in an environment where they might find other agents and be in need of some type of interaction to complete their task in an optimal manner. Thus, it's logical to see agents as a society where well-known rules govern their behavior and actions. Sociability is vital in cooperative MAS and aims to aid true peer-to-peer distributed and flexible paradigms that recent applications require and where agents can find their utmost contribution.

A *social commitment* in an MAS is an obligation created between an agent and another agent or group of agents, constraining the behavior of the first to follow a given prearranged commitment or rule. Imagine an MAS where agents must stay together at the same line of work in a 2D space, but AgentX moves faster than the remaining agents and always tends to go ahead and leave the team behind. A social commitment from this agent to the others could be to always stay in the same line and not move ahead and leave someone behind.

To establish rules for an MAS, we can design *social norms* or *laws* to rule agents' behavior (Figure 5-7). A social law is a set of constraints, and a *constraint* comes in the form of a pair (S, A) stating that an agent cannot execute an action A while being in state S.

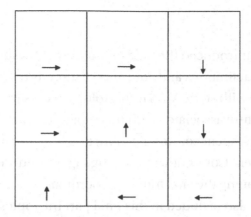

Figure 5-7. *Social law determining agent movement in a grid of 3 × 3.*
This law prevents collisions.

The set of *focal states* is the set of states we want our agent to have
access to; thus, from any focal state there must exist a path to the
remaining focal states. A *useful* law is one that does not stop agents from
getting to one state from another; the law from Figure 5-5 is a useful law.

Now that we have set the grounds for MAS terminology, concepts,
and ideas we will introduce in the following chapter a complete
practical application consisting of multi-agent communication
software that allows various agents to exchange messages using a WCF
Publisher/Subscriber pattern in a two-sided (service, client) program.
This communication program will be used later (in Chapter 7) to create
a complete example of a multi-agent system where a set of cleaning
robots will communicate, coordinate, and cooperate to clean an n x m
room of its dirt.

Summary

In this chapter, we introduced the field of multi-agent systems. We presented various definitions and concepts that set us on the right path to getting acquainted with some MAS terminology necessary for diving into the scientific literature associated with this topic. We examined multi-agent organizations, agent communication, and its subfields (Speech Act Theory and Agent Communication Languages), and we concluded the chapter by detailing the vital topics of coordination and cooperation among agents. We also included in this final part the topics of negotiation and social norms. In the next chapter, we'll present a very interesting practical problem where we'll have a set of N agents exchanging messages in a WCF application created under the Publisher/Subscriber pattern.

CHAPTER 6

Communication in a Multi-Agent System Using WCF

In the previous chapter, we examined the basics of multi-agent systems (MAS) and got acquainted with concepts like MAS platform, coordination, cooperation, and communication. In this chapter, we will describe an application that uses *Windows Communication Foundation* (WCF) to create a network of agents capable of interacting with and passing messages among each other. This application will use the Publisher/Subscriber design pattern to set up the communication component that every agent in the MAS will incorporate. We will use the application described throughout this chapter again in the next chapter, adapting it as the communication module of every agent in an MAS consisting of cleaning agents whose task is cleaning a room of its dirt.

WCF emerged in 2006 as a development kit and eventually became part of the .NET Framework; it's an *application programming interface* (API) for developing connected systems where both security and reliability in any communication between internal systems of an organization or systems over the internet is possible and provided. It is designed to offer a manageable approach to distributed computing, broad interoperability,

© Arnaldo Pérez Castaño 2018
A. Pérez Castaño, *Practical Artificial Intelligence*,
https://doi.org/10.1007/978-1-4842-3357-3_6

and direct support for service orientation. WCF represents Microsoft's alternative to a platform that collects a set of industry standards that define different protocols, service interactions, type conversion, marshalling, and so forth. It provides developers with the fundamental predesigned tools that every network application might require, and its first release included many useful facilities for creating services (hosting, service-instance management, asynchronous calls, reliability, transaction management, disconnected queued calls, security, and so on).

Applications built using WCF as the runtime environment will allow us to use Common Language Runtime (CLR) types as services and will allow us to consume other services as CLR types. Concepts such as service, contract, binding, endpoint, and others will be explained throughout this chapter as we develop our MAS communication example.

Note   Windows Communication Foundation (WCF) is a framework for developing and deploying services on Windows. Using WCF, we can build service-oriented applications (SOAs). WCF replaced the older ASMX web services technologies.

Services

A *service* is a functional component made accessible to its consumers via a network that could be the internet or a local internal network. A calculator could very well be a service offered to different clients in a network so they can connect to the service and request any operation between any given numbers. In a service-oriented application (SOA) we aggregate services the same way we aggregate objects when developing an object-oriented application; the service becomes the first-class citizen in this type of application.

Services communicate using any communication protocol previously agreed on, and they can use any language, platform, versioning, or framework without needing to have any agreement on those. Thus, one can say that services are dependent on the communication protocol applied but independent in any other area.

The *client* of a service is the part making use of the service's functionality. In the calculator service example the client would be the program requesting that the calculator solve mathematical expressions. The client can be any type of program, from a console application to a Windows Forms, an ASP.NET MVC site, a WPF program, or another service. In WCF, the client never interacts with the service directly, not even with a local service. Instead, the client always uses a proxy to forward calls to the service. The proxy acts as a middle man, presenting the same operations as the service in addition to some proxy-related methods.

Note   There has been an evolution from applications where functions were the first-class citizen to applications where objects were the first-class citizen (object-oriented programming), passing through component-oriented applications (component-object model, COM) and leading to the most recent step in this evolution, service-oriented applications (SOAs).

WCF most often uses *Simple Object Access Protocol* (SOAP) messages to communicate; SOAP is a protocol for data exchange. It can be seen as a set of components that can be invoked, published, and discovered. These messages are independent of transport protocols, and, contrasting with web services, WCF services can communicate over a variety of transports, not just HTTP. WCF clients are capable of interoperating with non-WCF services, and WCF services can interact with non-WCF clients.

Contracts

We deal with contracts often in our daily life, especially in business-related affairs, to make sure parts engaging in a relationship agree on various points. In WCF, a *contract* is a standard way of describing what a service does; it's a way for service consumers and providers to correlate correctly. In an SOA application, having a properly defined contract can give its consumers a pretty good idea of how to work with the service even though they might not know how it's implemented.

WCF defines various types of contracts:

- *Service Contract, Operation Contract*: used to represent a service and describe the operations that the client can perform on the service

- *Data Contract*: used to represent an agreement on the data that will be exchanged between the service and the client. WCF defines implicit contracts for built-in types such as `int` and `string` and gives you the option of defining explicit data contracts for custom types.

- *Fault Contract*: used to define which errors are raised by the service by associating custom exception types with certain service operations and describing how the service handles and propagates errors to its clients

- *Message Contract*: used by the service to interact directly with messages, altering its format or manipulating the service messages to modify other features like the SOAP header and so forth

There are different ways or patterns for defining contracts in WCF; we could define them using the *One-Way* pattern, the *Request–Response* pattern, or the *Duplex* pattern. These are all message-exchange patterns.

- *One-Way*: When an operation has no returned values and the client application is not interested in the success or failure of the invocation, we may have this "fire & forget" invocation called One-Way. After the client issues the call, WCF generates a request message, but no reply message will ever head back to the client. Consequently, One-Way operations can't return values, and any exception thrown on the service side will not make its way back to the client.

- *Request–Response*: In this pattern, a service operation call consists of a message sent and a reply expected from the service. Operations using this pattern have an input parameter and an associated return value. The client is always the one to initiate communication between the parties.

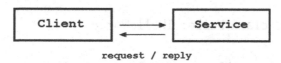

request / reply

- *Duplex*: This exchange pattern allows for a random number of messages to be sent by a client and received in any order. It resembles a conversation where each word spoken is seen as a message. Any part can initiate communication.

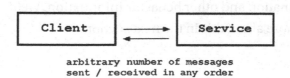

arbitrary number of messages
sent / received in any order

In order to implement a service in WCF you typically go through the following steps:

1. Define the service contract. A service contract specifies the signature of a service, the data it exchanges, and other contractually required data. The following code shows the service version of the very classic Hello World program:

    ```
    [ServiceContract]
                            interface IHelloWorld
    {
    [OperationContract(IsOneWay = true)]
                            void HelloMessage();
    }
    ```

2. Implement the contract by inheriting from the service contract definition (prearrangement interface) and create the class that implements the contract:

    ```
    public class Hello: IHelloWorld
    {
            public void HelloMessage()
            {
                Console.WriteLine("Hello World");
            }
    }
    ```

3. Configure the service by specifying endpoint information and other behavior information. We'll see more about this in the next section.

4. Host the service in IIS or in an application; it could be a console application, Windows Forms, WPF, ASP .NET, etc.

5. Create a client application; it could be a console application, Windows Forms, WPF, ASP .NET, etc.

Note that methods declared on the IHelloWorld service contract that do not have the OperationContract attribute will not be considered as WCF methods; in other words, they won't be invokable over WCF applications. You can mix non-WCF methods with WCF methods with the intention of having some subliminal processing, but only for that purpose.

Bindings

WCF allows us to send messages using different transport protocols, such as HTTP, HTTPS, TCP, MSMQ, and so on, and using different XML representations, such as text, binary, or MTOM (Message Transport Optimization Mechanism); this last one is known as the message encoding in WCF. Furthermore, we can improve specific messaging interactions using a suite of SOAP protocols, such as the multiple WS-X (WSHttpBinding, WSDualHttpBinding, etc.) specifications. Improvements could be related to security, reliable messaging, and transactions. These communication concepts (transport, message encoding, and protocol) are vital to understanding what happens on the wire at runtime.

In WCF, bindings are represented by the System.ServiceModel. Channels.Binding class, and all binding classes must derive from this base class; Table 6-1 illustrates some of the built-in bindings that WCF provides.

Table 6-1. *WCF Built-in Bindings*

Binding Class	Transport	Message Encoding	Message Version
BasicHttpBinding	HTTP	Text	SOAP 1.1
WSHttpBinding	HTTP	Text	SOAP 1.2 WS-Addressing 1.0
WSDualHttpBinding	HTTP	Text	SOAP 1.2 WS-Addressing 1.0
NetTcpBinding	TCP	Binary	SOAP 1.2
NetPeerTcpBinding	P2P	Binary	SOAP 1.2
NetMsmqBinding	MSMQ	Binary	SOAP 1.2
CustomBinding	Up to you	Up to you	Up to you

Bindings like BasicHttpBinding and WSHttpBinding were created for scenarios where interoperability is essential. Thus, they both use HTTP as the transport protocol and simple text for message encoding. On the other hand, bindings that have the Net prefix are optimized to function with the .NET Framework on both ends (service, client). As a result, these bindings are not designed for interoperability and perform better in Windows environments. A binding is part of another component of a WCF application known as an endpoint; endpoints will be the topic of the next section.

Note   As of .NET Framework 4.5 the NetPeerTcpBinding binding has been marked as obsolete and may disappear in the future.

Endpoints

WCF services are exposed through service endpoints that provide access points for clients to exploit the functionality provided by the WCF service. Service endpoints consist of what is known as the *ABC* of a service. *A* stands for *Address*, which defines where the service is (for example, http://localhost:9090/mas/). *B* stands for *Binding*, which defines how to communicate with the service, and *C* stands for *Contract*, which defines what the service can do. Hence, an endpoint can be seen as a tuple <A, B, C>: an address, a binding, and a contract.

We must define endpoints in both our service and client applications; this can be done programmatically or through the app.config file, as shown in the next example (Listing 6-1).

Listing 6-1. Defining Two Endpoints in the app.config File

```
<service name = "HelloWorld">
<endpoint
      address  = "net.tcp://localhost:8001/service/"
      binding  = "netTcpBinding"
      contract = "IHelloWorld"
   />
<endpoint
      address  = "http://localhost:8002/otherService/"
      binding  = "wsHttpBinding"
      contract = "IHelloWorld"
   />
</service>
```

There's no significant technical difference in the programmatic way and the configuration setting of the app.config file way for defining endpoints in WCF. Eventually .NET will parse the app.config file and execute its defined configuration in a programmatic manner. Now that we have been over the basics of WCF, we will look at the Publisher/Subscriber pattern that WCF supports and that we will be using in communicating with various agents.

Publisher/Subscriber Pattern

Real-time applications are those that provide a live feed or update (basketball game, baseball game, and so on) of a particular event occurring at a short, prior time from the time the feed is provided. Real-time apps implement one of two possible mechanisms for giving updated information to clients: *pushing* and *pulling*.

To understand how these mechanisms work, let's imagine a scenario where we would like to be updated on the results of a baseball game. We are part of a network that consists of a server, which has the updated information (live updates), and several other computers. Assuming we get the live feed in our browser (client) via HTTP, and considering the use of a pulling mechanism, our computer would be constantly sending update requests and pulling new information (if any) from the server. It would basically be like asking the server from time to time "Do you have anything new for me?" On the other hand, if we were to follow a pushing mechanism our client would tell the server, "Keep me updated on the score of this game," and the server would automatically "push" updates to the client whenever they were available. The Publisher/Subscriber model follows the latter approach, the pushing mechanism; the server plays the role of publisher and the client the role of subscriber, and it requires a duplex service to be established between both parts.

A *duplex* service consists of two contracts, one at the server and another at the client. The contract implemented at the server will be used by the subscriber (client) to subscribe for a particular data feed. The contract implemented at the client will be used by the server to make a call whenever new data needs to be "pushed." The contract implemented at the client side is known as a *callback contract*. We'll see more of the Publisher/Subscriber pattern, as well as callback contracts and duplex services, in the following sections when we look at a practical problem that puts all these pieces together in a complete, functional example.

Practical Problem: Communicating Among Multiple Agents Using WCF

In this section, we will create a WCF application where several agents contribute to a shared message list and each agent is aware of the current message list; in other words, everyone has an updated copy of the actual list. The service in this scenario acts as a message broker, sending new messages coming from a given agent to all other agents. This is an application that clearly follows the Publisher/Subscriber pattern; in Figure 6-1 we can see its architecture.

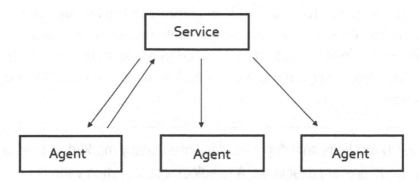

Figure 6-1. *An agent adds a message to the list and the service communicates the updated list to all other agents*

Beginning with the implementation process, we first need to define our service contract. Since we are going to create a duplex application, the service contract definition will need to be accompanied by a callback contract. The callback contract specifies the operations that the service can invoke on the client. To create a WCF service in Visual Studio, go to the Solution Explorer and right-click in the project or folder you wish to be the container of the project; select "Add a New Item," then look for the "WCF Service" option (Figure 6-2).

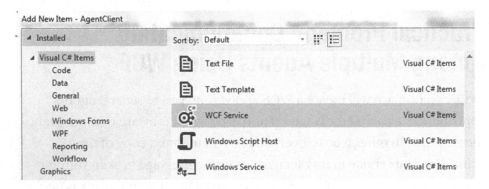

Figure 6-2. *Adding a WCF service to our project*

Once you add the service you will see two files have been added to your project—a class (contract implementation) and an interface (service contract). You'll also notice the addition of references to namespaces System.ServiceModel and System.ServiceModel.Description, which are the namespaces containing the binding classes, the ServiceHost class, and so forth.

Note   Operations on a duplex service are usually marked as OneWay = true to prevent deadlocks. A deadlock occurs when various units are waiting on the others to finish and as a consequence neither ever does.

The implementations of both the service and callback contracts are illustrated in Listing 6-2.

Listing 6-2. Service and Callback Contracts

```
[ServiceContract(CallbackContract = typeof(IAgentCommunication
Callback))]
    public interface IAgentCommunicationService
    {

        [OperationContract(IsOneWay = true)]
        void Subscribe();

        [OperationContract(IsOneWay = true)]
        void Send(string from, string to, string message);
}

public interface IAgentCommunicationCallback
{
        [OperationContract(IsOneWay = true)]
        void SendUpdatedList(List<string> messages);
}
```

Notice that in the previous code we are defining a relationship by specifically telling the service contract that its callback contract is IAgentCommunicationCallback. Thus, we are telling the service to use that callback contract to notify the client (notification will be achieved by calling the SendUpdateList() method on the callback) whenever new updates are available. The service contract contains two operations: Subscribe(), which subscribes the agent to the service, and Send(), which sends a new message to the message list. The callback contract has an operation named SendUpdatedList(), which is used to send the latest message list to all agents.

Note   All operations in `IAgentCommunicationService` and
`IAgentCommunicationCallback` return void because that's a
requirement of the attribute setting `IsOneWay` = `true`. One-Way
operations will block until the outbound data has been written to the
network connection.

Now that we know the agreement on operations established by the
service and callback, let's look at their concrete implementations.
Listing 6-3 shows the service implementation.

Listing 6-3. Service Implementation

```
[ServiceBehavior(InstanceContextMode = InstanceContextMode.
Single, ConcurrencyMode = ConcurrencyMode.Multiple)]
    public class AgentCommunicationService :
    IAgentCommunicationService
    {
        private static List<IAgentCommunicationCallback> _callback
        Channels = new List<IAgentCommunicationCallback>();
        private static List<string> _messages = new List<string>();
        private static readonly object _sycnRoot = new object();

        public void Subscribe()
        {
            try
            {
                var callbackChannel =
                    OperationContext.Current.GetCallbackChannel
                    <IAgentCommunicationCallback>();

                lock (_sycnRoot)
                {
```

```
        if (!_callbackChannels.Contains(callbackChannel))
        {
            _callbackChannels.Add(callbackChannel);
            Console.WriteLine("Added Callback
            Channel: {0}", callbackChannel.GetHash
            Code());
            callbackChannel.SendUpdatedList(_messages);
        }
    }
}
catch
{
}
}

public void Send(string from, string to, string message)
{
    lock (_sycnRoot)
    {
        _messages.Add(message);

        Console.WriteLine("-- Message List --");
        _messages.ForEach(listItem => Console.
        WriteLine(listItem));
        Console.WriteLine("------------------");

        for (int i = _callbackChannels.Count - 1;
        i >= 0; i--)
        {
            if (((ICommunicationObject)_callback
            Channels[i]).State != CommunicationState.
            Opened)
            {
```

```
                    Console.WriteLine("Detected Non-Open
                    Callback Channel: {0}", _callback
                    Channels[i].GetHashCode());
                    _callbackChannels.RemoveAt(i);
                    continue;
                }

                try
                {
                    _callbackChannels[i].SendUpdatedList
                    (_messages);
                    Console.WriteLine("Pushed Updated List
                    on Callback Channel: {0}", _callback
                    Channels[i].GetHashCode());
                }
                catch (Exception ex)
                {
                    Console.WriteLine("Service threw
                    exception while communicating on
                    Callback Channel: {0}", _callback
                    Channels[i].GetHashCode());
                    Console.WriteLine("Exception Type:
                    {0} Description: {1}", ex.GetType(),
                    ex.Message);
                    _callbackChannels.RemoveAt(i);
                }
            }
        }
    }
}
```

Notice the `AgentCommunicationService` class has the
attributes `InstanceContextMode` = `InstanceContextMode.Single`,
`ConcurrencyMode` = `ConcurrencyMode.Multiple` defined by the
`ServiceBehavior` class; as its name suggests, this class allows us to define
various behaviors for the service. The first sets it as a `Singleton` class;
thus, all service calls will be handled by the same service instance, and
all agents will refer to the same message and client callback channel list,
as those fields were declared static. The latter allows for concurrency to
occur and for you to have a multi-thread service, thus permitting each call
to be handled in parallel. The synchronization of the service object will be
handled using the *SyncRoot* pattern and the `lock` statement in C#.

Note   Locking public objects is not a good practice. A public object
can be locked by anyone, creating unexpected deadlocks. As a result,
you should use caution when locking an object that is exposed to the
outside world. The SyncRoot pattern guarantees that this scenario
does not occur by using a private, internal object to do the locking.

The `lock` statement acts as a key for objects. Imagine a man who wants
to enter a room and obtains a key from the owner, and while he is in the
room no one else can access it. When he leaves he gives the key back to the
owner so the next person in the line can obtain the key and enter the room.
The code that prevents multiple threads from accessing and modifying
data simultaneously is called *thread-safe* code.

The `Subscriber()` method (operation) gets the callback channel of the
client and checks whether it has been added in the callback channel list,
adding it in case it has not been. If the client has not accessed the service
before it sends it the `latestMessage` list.

In the `Send()` method we must ensure that only one thread at a time
obtains access to the list, as that's the reason for the `lock` statement. Once
we have added the message we loop through every callback channel and

inform the rest of the agents (clients) of the new addition by calling their
SendUpdatedList() method. This iteration process is done backward
because we will need to remove any channel that may have changed its
state to close or throw an exception.

As mentioned before, we need to create a Proxy class to interact with the
service. To create a duplex proxy we need to design a class that inherits from
DuplexClientBase<T> and then create the service contract (Listing 6-4).

Listing 6-4. Proxy Implementation

```
public class AgentCommunicationServiceClient : DuplexClientBase
<IAgentCommunicationService>, IAgentCommunicationService
    {
        public AgentCommunicationServiceClient(Instance
        Context callbackInstance, WSDualHttpBinding binding,
        EndpointAddress endpointAddress)
            : base(callbackInstance, binding, endpointAddress)
{ }

        public void Subscribe()
        {
            Channel.Subscribe();
        }

        public void Send(string from, string to, string message)
        {
            Channel.Send(from, to, message);
        }
    }
```

As we can see from Listing 6-4, the implementation of the proxy class is
pretty straightforward—simply forward every call to the Channel property
(of type IAgentCommunicationService) provided by the parent class

DuplexClientBase<IAgentCommunicationService>. In the Send method,
we included arguments string from, string to. We'll use these
arguments in the next chapter to filter messages from and to agents.

The concrete implementation of the callback contract class is shown in
Listing 6-5.

Listing 6-5. Callback Contract Implementation

```
[CallbackBehavior(UseSynchronizationContext = false)]
    public class AgentCommunicationCallback : IAgent
    CommunicationCallback
    {
public event EventHandler<UpdatedListEventArgs>
ServiceCallbackEvent;
 privateSynchronizationContext _syncContext = AsyncOperation
 Manager.SynchronizationContext;

        public void SendUpdatedList(List<string> items)
        {
            _syncContext.Post(new SendOrPostCallback(OnService
            CallbackEvent), new UpdatedListEventArgs(items));
        }

        private void OnServiceCallbackEvent(object state)
        {
            EventHandler<UpdatedListEventArgs> handler =
            ServiceCallbackEvent;
            var e = state as UpdatedListEventArgs;

            if (handler != null)
            {
                handler(this, e);
            }
        }
    }
```

Let's remember that the callback contract is the one handling the "push updates" received from the service contract. By default, the callback contract synchronizes all calls on the current synchronization context. If your client is a Windows Forms application this behavior would result in the code's being executed on the user-interface thread, which is not a good idea.

In order to communicate the results obtained on the operation thread to the UI thread we will use `AsyncOperationManager`, a class that .NET incorporates for concurrency management. This class contains a `SynchronizationContext` property, which returns the synchronization context for the application calling it. The purpose, in the end, for using these classes is sharing data between the UI thread and the operation thread.

Note   A synchronization context provides a way to queue a unit of work to a particular context. It could allow worker threads to dispatch messages to the UI synchronization context. Only the UI synchronization context is allowed to manipulate the UI controls; therefore, if we attempted to update the UI from another context it would result in an illegal operation, causing an exception to be thrown.

We'll use the `Post` method of the `SynchronizationContext` class to asynchronously queue messages to the UI synchronization context. The `Post` method takes two arguments: a delegate called `SendOrPostCallback` representing the callback method we need to execute after the message is dispatched to the UI synchronization context, and an object that is submitted to the delegate. We create the `SendOrPostCallback` delegate by passing in the `OnServiceCallbackEvent` method that has been implemented in the `Callback` class. We also create an instance of the `UpdatedListEventArgs` (Listing 6-6) class and submit the new list of messages in the constructor. The delegate and the event arguments class instance are used as arguments to the Post method. In this manner, our event-invocation method is capable of obtaining the event arguments when it is being marshalled from the worker thread to the UI thread. Subscribers (clients such as Windows Forms, console application, and so on) to our ServiceCallbackEvent can then handle the event when it is triggered.

Setting the UseSynchronizationContext attribute to *false* allows the callback operations to be distributed among different threads.

Listing 6-6. Class Used as Event Argument to Update the Message List on the Client Application (Windows Forms)

```
public class UpdatedListEventArgs : EventArgs
    {
        public List<string> MessageList { get; set; }

        public UpdatedListEventArgs(List<string> messages)
        {
            MessageList = messages;
        }
    }
```

Now that we have presented concrete implementations for all contracts, let's present the application acting as host for the service (Listing 6-7).

Listing 6-7. Service Being Hosted in a Console Application

```
static void Main(string[] args)
        {
            // Step 1 Create a URI to serve as the base address.
            var baseAddress = new Uri("http://localhost:9090/");
```

```
// Step 2 Create a ServiceHost instance
var selfHost = new ServiceHost(typeof(Agent
CommunicationService), baseAddress);

try
{
    // Step 3 Add a service endpoint.
    selfHost.AddServiceEndpoint(typeof(IAgent
    CommunicationService),
        new WSDualHttpBinding(WSDualHttpSecurity
        Mode.None), "AgentCommunicationService");

    // Step 4 Enable Metadata Exchange and Add MEX
    endpoint
    var smb = new ServiceMetadataBehavior {
    HttpGetEnabled = true };
    selfHost.Description.Behaviors.Add(smb);
    selfHost.AddServiceEndpoint(ServiceMetadata
    Behavior.MexContractName,
        MetadataExchangeBindings.
        CreateMexHttpBinding(), baseAddress + "mex");

    // Step 5 Start the service.
    selfHost.Open();
    Console.WriteLine("The service is ready.");
    Console.WriteLine("Listening at: {0}",
    baseAddress);
    Console.WriteLine("Press <ENTER> to terminate
    service.");
    Console.WriteLine();
    Console.ReadLine();

    // Close the ServiceHostBase to shut down the
    service.
```

```
            selfHost.Close();
        }
        catch (CommunicationException ce)
        {
            Console.WriteLine("An exception occurred: {0}",
            ce.Message);
            selfHost.Abort();
        }
    }
```

The steps for creating the service are clearly presented in Listing 6-7. In this case, we are hosting our service in a console application. Notice that we will not be using or editing the app.config file; on the contrary, all binding, address, and contract configuration is made programmatically.

Note   The WCF bindings supporting duplex services are WSDualHttp Binding, NetTcpBinding, and NetNamedPipeBinding.

The client application will be a Windows Forms application that has the code shown in Listing 6-8.

Listing 6-8. Client Application

```
public partial class AgentClient : Form
    {
        private const string ServiceEndpointUri = "http://
        localhost:9090/AgentCommunicationService";
        public AgentCommunicationServiceClient Proxy { get; set; }

        public AgentClient()
        {
```

```
        InitializeComponent();
        InitializeClient();
    }

    private void InitializeClient()
    {
        if (Proxy != null)
        {
            try
            {
                Proxy.Close();
            }
            catch
            {
                Proxy.Abort();
            }
        }

        var callback = new AgentCommunicationCallback();
        callback.ServiceCallbackEvent +=
        HandleServiceCallbackEvent;

        var instanceContext = new InstanceContext(callback);
        var dualHttpBinding = new WSDualHttpBinding(WSDual
        HttpSecurityMode.None);
        var endpointAddress = new EndpointAddress(Service
        EndpointUri);
        Proxy = new AgentCommunicationServiceClient(instance
        Context, dualHttpBinding, endpointAddress);
        Proxy.Open();
        Proxy.Subscribe();
    }
```

```
private void HandleServiceCallbackEvent(object sender,
UpdatedListEventArgs e)
{
    List<string> list = e.MessageList;

    if (list != null && list.Count > 0)
        messageList.DataSource = list;
}

private void SendBtnClick(object sender, EventArgs e)
{
    Proxy.Send("", "", wordBox.Text.Trim());
    wordBox.Clear();
}
}
```

As expected, the client application (Figure 6-3) contains a field of type AgentCommunicationServiceClient, which represents the proxy it will be using for subscribing and communicating with the service. The HandleServiceCallbackEvent is the event that will be triggered when a new message is added to the list; this is directly related to the callback contract and the OnServiceCallbackEvent event we recently described. The SendBtnClick event is fired when a user clicks the Send button of the client's UI and sends a new message.

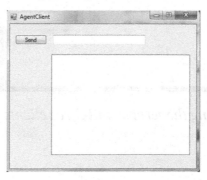

Figure 6-3. *Client UI in Windows Forms*

Now that we have all the pieces together, let's test the application and see how different agents communicate and receive messages.

First, let's run the console application that is hosting the service.

Note   You would typically need administrator rights to launch the service application. If you are experiencing any issues running the application, try running it as administrator.

Then, let's run as many clients as we want. In this case, we would be satisfied by just executing three clients. The scenario described would be the one illustrated in Figure 6-4.

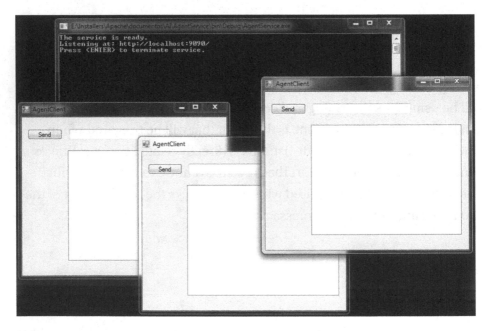

Figure 6-4. *Executing the service and three clients*

Now we can play with the application and send messages from any of the clients. The result will be a shared list of all messages as seen in Figure 6-5.

Figure 6-5. *Agents exchanging messages in a WCF Publisher/Subscriber application*

In the next chapter, we will slightly modify the WCF communication application introduced in the last few sections to adjust it to our multi-agent system of cleaning agents example. In the cleaning agents MAS program, clients will be agents that will be communicating through a WCF service that is acting as a message broker (publisher). Concepts examined in Chapter 5, such as cooperation, coordination, Contract Net, and social laws will be covered again in the cited example and in a practical manner will be implemented via classes and methods in C#.

Summary

In this chapter, we explained some of the basics of WCF (services, contracts, addresses, bindings, and endpoints) and also a common pattern in network applications, the Publisher/Subscriber model. We introduced and described duplex services and some of their features, like the callback contract. We implemented a WCF program that simulated the communication of several agents, using a service hosted on a console application as message broker and a Windows Forms application for clients. In the following chapter, we will insert this application into a much bigger program that simulates the process of a multi-agent system whose task is getting rid of all the dirt in an n x m room.

CHAPTER 7

Cleaning Agents: A Multi-Agent System Problem

Throughout Chapters 5 and 6 we studied multi-agent systems (MAS) and multi-agent communication. We introduced concepts such as agent platform, agent architecture, coordination, cooperation, social laws, and much more; we also detailed a practical problem where we created a multi-agent communication module using Windows Communication Foundation (WCF).

In this chapter, we'll analyze a complete practical problem where we will put all the pieces together and develop an MAS where n cleaning agents will be dealing with the task of cleaning an n x m room of its dirt. This problem will allow us to include many of the concepts and definitions studied before and also attach the WCF communication module created in Chapter 6 as the MAS communication module that every agent in the system will integrate.

The cleaning problem is a great benchmark or scenario by which to understand how we can use an MAS to solve a task, such as cleaning, in a much shorter time and using fewer resources than with just a single agent.

© Arnaldo Pérez Castaño 2018
A. Pérez Castaño, *Practical Artificial Intelligence*,
https://doi.org/10.1007/978-1-4842-3357-3_7

Note   Every robot in the cleaning problem will be using WCF at the core of their communication module and Windows Forms to display messages received.

Program Structure

The application will have a structure like the one depicted in Figure 7-1. The program comprises Communication, GUI (Graphical User Interface), Negotiation, Planning, and Platform modules. The Communication and Planning modules will not be analyzed in this chapter (except for the communication language, `FipaAcl` C# class) as they were previously studied. For further reference please download the source code associated with this book.

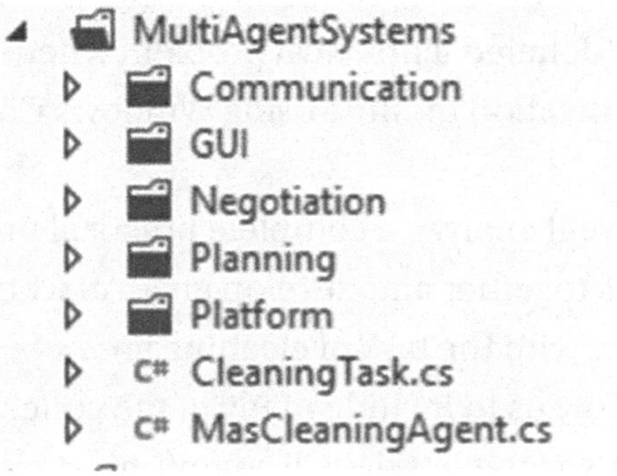

Figure 7-1. *Program structure*

The GUI module will contain two Windows Forms applications—one for graphically representing the room with every agent on it and their interactions, the other for representing the agent message board.

The Negotiation module will contain an implementation of the Contract Net task-sharing method, with every stage implemented as a static C# method within a `ContractNet` class.

The Platform module will contain an implementation of an agent platform and some of its functionalities (agent location via dictionary, Decide Roles service for task sharing, references to manager and contractors, and so forth). It will serve as support for other classes.

Within the Communication module we'll include the Agent Communication Language (ACL) module, which contains a tiny, simplified version of a `FIPA-ACL`, including a few performatives.

Note   In order to simplify the planning task in this MAS example, we will assume that the number of columns (M) is always divisible by the number of agents (S) in the MAS, i.e., $M \% S == 0$. This will allow us to simply assign M / S columns to each agent for cleaning.

Cleaning Task

To represent and encode the cleaning task we have created the class illustrated in Listing 7-1.

Listing 7-1. CleaningTask Class

```
public class CleaningTask
{
        public int Count { get; set; }
        public int M { get; set; }
        public List<Tuple<int, int>> SubDivide { get; set; }
        public IEnumerable<string> SubTasks { get; set; }
```

```csharp
public CleaningTask(int m, int agents)
{
    M = m;
    Count = agents;
    SubDivide = new List<Tuple<int, int>>();
    Divide();
    SubTasks = BuildTasks();
}

/// <summary>
/// For the division we assume that M % Count = 0, i.e.
/// the number of columns is always divisible by the
    number of agents.
/// </summary>
private void Divide()
{
    var div = M / Count;

    for (var i = 0; i < M; i += div)
        SubDivide.Add(new Tuple<int, int>(i, i + div - 1));
}

private IEnumerable<string> BuildTasks()
{
    var result = new string[SubDivide.Count];

    for (var i = 0; i < SubDivide.Count; i++)
        result[i] = "clean(" + SubDivide[i].Item1 + ","
        + SubDivide[i].Item2 + ")";

    return result;
}
}
```

The class contains the following fields or properties:

- `Count`: integer representing the number of agents participating in the cleaning task

- `M`: integer representing the number of columns in the room

- `SubDivide`: `List<Tuple<int, int>>` representing the equitable column division made considering the number of agents and columns

- `SubTasks`: `IEnumerable<string>` representing the set of tasks that need to be executed in order to complete the global task (cleaning the entire room). Each task is defined in a self-created inner language that our mini `FipaAcl` will be using.

On the other hand, the `CleaningTask` class exposes these methods:

- `Divide()`: divides the global task of cleaning a room into smaller subtasks. Each subtask will consist of a subset of contiguous columns to be cleaned. It stores in the `SubDivide` property a set of tuples, each defining a range of columns to be cleaned; e.g., (0, 2) will indicate the subtask of cleaning columns 0 up to 2.

- `BuildTasks()`: returns an `IEnumerable<string>` containing every subtask in a self-created language that will be used later for transmitting information via the communication module and using FIPA as ACL.

In trying to maintain a well-modularized application, the `CleaningTask` class merely deals with operations related to cleaning issues. In the next section, we'll take a look at the Cleaning Agent platform.

Cleaning Agent Platform

The Cleaning Agent platform is represented by the CleaningAgentPlatform class, whose code can be seen in Listing 7-2.

Listing 7-2. CleaningAgentPlatform Class

```
public class CleaningAgentPlatform
{
        public Dictionary<Guid, MasCleaningAgent> Directory {
        get; set; }
        public IEnumerable<MasCleaningAgent> Agents { get; set; }
        public IEnumerable<MasCleaningAgent> Contractors { get;
        set; }
        public MasCleaningAgent Manager { get; set; }
        public CleaningTask Task { get; set; }

        public CleaningAgentPlatform(IEnumerable<MasCleaning
        Agent> agents, CleaningTask task)
        {
            Agents = new List<MasCleaningAgent>(agents);
            Directory = new Dictionary<Guid, MasCleaningAgent>();
            Task = task;

            foreach (var cleaningAgent in Agents)
            {
                Directory.Add(cleaningAgent.Id, cleaningAgent);
                cleaningAgent.Platform = this;
            }

            DecideRoles();

        }
```

```
public void DecideRoles()
{
    // Manager Role
    Manager = Agents.First(a => a.CleanedCells.Count ==
    Agents.Max(p => p.CleanedCells.Count));
    Manager.Role = ContractRole.Manager;
    // Contract Roles
    Contractors = new List<MasCleaningAgent>(Agents.
    Where(a => a.Id != Manager.Id));
    foreach (var cleaningAgent in Contractors)
        cleaningAgent.Role = ContractRole.Contractor;
    (Contractors as List<MasCleaningAgent>).Add(Manager);
}
}
```

This class contains the following properties or fields:

- Directory: dictionary containing the ID of the agent and a reference to it as key–value pairs

- Agents: IEnumerable containing the set of agents

- Contractors: IEnumerable containing the set of contractors in a Contract Net

- Manager: reference to the manager in a Contract Net

- Task: cleaning task to be executed

This class contains two functions: a constructor and the DecideRoles() method. In the constructor, we initialize every property and then add every agent to the directory, referencing the Platform property of agents to point to *this* platform. The DecideRoles() method decides which agent is selected as manager, while the rest are regarded as contractors. In this case, the criteria for manager selection is to select the agent with the highest number of cells cleaned; this is equivalent to saying "Pick the most experienced agent, the one who has worked the most."

Note   In this case, we also add the manager to the list of contractors because we would like him not only to direct the operation but also to take part in it and clean a range of columns of the room as any other contractor would do.

Contract Net

The Contract Net task-sharing mechanism is represented by the ContractNet class; the role assumed by each agent is defined in the ContractRole enum. Both are described in Listing 7-3.

Listing 7-3. ContractNet Class

```
public class ContractNet
{

        public static IEnumerable<string>
        Announcement(CleaningTask cleaningTask,
        MasCleaningAgent manager, IEnumerable<MasCleaningAgent>
        contractors, FipaAcl language)
        {
            var tasks = cleaningTask.SubTasks;

            foreach (var contractor in contractors)
            {
                foreach (var task in tasks)
                    language.Message(Performative.Cfp,
                    manager.Id.ToString(),
                    contractor.Id.ToString(), task);
            }
```

```
        return tasks;
    }

    public static void Bidding(IEnumerable<string> tasks,
    IEnumerable<MasCleaningAgent> contractors)
    {
        foreach (var contractor in contractors)
            contractor.Bid(tasks);
    }

    public static void Awarding(List<string> messages,
    MasCleaningAgent manager, IEnumerable<MasCleaningAgent>
    contractors, CleaningTask task, FipaAcl language)
    {
        var agentsAssigned = new
        List<Tuple<MasCleaningAgent, Tuple<int, int>>>();
        var messagesToDict = messages.ConvertAll(FipaAcl.
        MessagesToDict);

        // Processing bids
        foreach (var colRange in task.SubDivide)
        {
            var firstCol = colRange.Item1;
            var secondCol = colRange.Item2;
            // Bids for first column
            var bidsFirstCol = new List<KeyValuePair
            <MasCleaningAgent, List<Tuple<double,
            Tuple<int, int>>>>();
// Bids for second column
var bidsSecondCol = new List<KeyValuePair<MasCleaningAgent,
                List<Tuple<double, Tuple<int, int>>>>();
```

```
                    foreach (var contractor in contractors)
                    {
// Skip agents that have been already assigned
                        if (agentsAssigned.Exists(tuple => tuple.
                        Item1.Id == contractor.Id))
                            continue;

                    var c = contractor;
// Get messages from current contractor
                        var messagesFromContractor = messagesToDict.
                        FindAll(m => m.ContainsKey("from") &&
                        m["from"] == c.Id.ToString());

                        var bids = FipaAcl.GetContent(messagesFrom
                        Contractor);
// Bids to first column in the range column
var bidsContractorFirstCol = bids.FindAll(b => b.Item2.Item2 ==
                        firstCol);
// Bids to second column in the range column
var bidsContractorSecondCol = bids.FindAll(b => b.Item2.Item2
                        == secondCol);

                        if (bidsContractorFirstCol.Count > 0)
                        {
                            bidsFirstCol.Add(
                                new KeyValuePair<MasCleaningAgent,
                                List<Tuple<double, Tuple<int,
                                int>>>>(contractor,
                                        bidsContractorFirstCol));
                        }
                        if (bidsContractorSecondCol.Count > 0)
                        {
```

```
            bidsSecondCol.Add(
                new KeyValuePair<MasCleaningAgent,
                List<Tuple<double, Tuple<int,
                int>>>>(contractor,
                        bidsContractorSecondCol));
    }
}

// Sorts to have at the beginning of the list
the best bidders (closest agents)
bidsFirstCol.Sort(Comparison);
bidsSecondCol.Sort(Comparison);

var closestAgentFirst = bidsFirstCol.
FirstOrDefault();
var closestAgentSecond = bidsSecondCol.
FirstOrDefault();

// Sorts again to find closest end
if (closestAgentFirst.Value != null)
    closestAgentFirst.Value.Sort(Comparison);

if (closestAgentSecond.Value != null)
    closestAgentSecond.Value.Sort(Comparison);

// Assigns agent to column range
if (closestAgentFirst.Value != null &&
closestAgentSecond.Value != null)
{
    if (closestAgentFirst.Value.First().Item1 >=
    closestAgentSecond.Value.First().Item1)
        agentsAssigned.Add(new
        Tuple<MasCleaningAgent, Tuple<int,
        int>>(closestAgentSecond.Key,
        closestAgentSecond.Value.First().Item2));
```

```
                else
                    agentsAssigned.Add(new
                    Tuple<MasCleaningAgent, Tuple<int,
                    int>>(closestAgentFirst.Key,
                    closestAgentFirst.Value.First().Item2));
            }
            else if (closestAgentFirst.Value == null)
                agentsAssigned.Add(new
                Tuple<MasCleaningAgent, Tuple<int,
                int>>(closestAgentSecond.Key,
                closestAgentSecond.Value.First().Item2));
            else
                agentsAssigned.Add(new
                Tuple<MasCleaningAgent, Tuple<int,
                int>>(closestAgentFirst.Key,
                closestAgentFirst.Value.First().Item2));
        }

                // Transmits the accepted proposal for
                each agent.
        foreach (var assignment in agentsAssigned)
            language.Message(Performative.Accept, manager.
            Id.ToString(),
                assignment.Item1.Id.ToString(), "clean(" +
                assignment.Item2.Item1 + "," + assignment.
                Item2.Item2 + ")");
    }

    private static int Comparison(Tuple<double, Tuple<int,
    int>> tupleA, Tuple<double, Tuple<int, int>> tupleB)
    {
        if (tupleA.Item1 > tupleB.Item1)
            return 1;
```

```
    if (tupleA.Item1 < tupleB.Item1)
        return -1;
    return 0;
}

private static int Comparison(KeyValuePair<MasCleaning
Agent, List<Tuple<double, Tuple<int, int>>>>
bidsAgentA, KeyValuePair<MasCleaningAgent,
List<Tuple<double, Tuple<int, int>>>> bidsAgentB)
{
    if (bidsAgentA.Value.Min(p => p.Item1) >
    bidsAgentB.Value.Min(p => p.Item1))
        return 1;
    if (bidsAgentA.Value.Min(p => p.Item1) <
    bidsAgentB.Value.Min(p => p.Item1))
        return -1;
    return 0;
}
}

public enum ContractRole
{
    Contractor, Manager, None
}
```

This class contains the following static methods:

- Announcement(): a message is sent from the manager
  to every contractor, announcing every task to be
  completed

- Bidding(): each agent is asked for a bid that considers
  the set of tasks to be completed. Bidding on the
  agent side is executed in the Bid() method of the
  MasCleaningAgent class.

- `Awarding()`: method executing the final stage of the task-sharing mechanism. To award a range of columns x - x' to a contractor (agent), it calculates the distance of every agent to the four ends of that column range—i.e., cells(0, x), (n - 1, x) at the first column and cells(0, x'), (n - 1, x') at the second column—and then awards that column range to the agent that is the closest (minimum Block or Manhattan distance) to any of the four ends. The bid of the agent contains a `tuple<int, int>` defining the closest end and a double representing the distance to that end. Refer to the code comments for more details.

- *Comparison()*: Both methods relate to sorting a list of elements by considering a double value that indicates its distance to a column.

Every method was created as a service of the class; in other words, as a static method that requires no instance of the class to be called.

FIPA-ACL

In order to communicate cleaning-related issues among agents, we created a tiny language for processing these types of commands. This mini-language resembles the `FIPA language` and contains an inner language that merely includes the `clean(x, y)` statement telling agents to clean all columns from x to y. The `FipaAcl` class and the `Performative` enum are both illustrated in Listing 7-4.

Listing 7-4. FipaACL Class

```
public class FipaAcl
{
        public AgentCommunicationServiceClient Communication {
        get; set; }

        public FipaAcl(AgentCommunicationServiceClient
        communication)
        {
            Communication = communication;
        }

        public void Message(Performative p, string senderId,
        string receiverId, string content)
        {
            switch (p)
            {
                case Performative.Accept:
                    ThreadPool.QueueUserWorkItem(delegate {
                    Communication.Send(senderId, receiverId,
                    "accept[content:" + content + ";]"); });
                    break;
                case Performative.Cfp:
                    ThreadPool.QueueUserWorkItem(delegate {
                    Communication.Send(senderId, receiverId,
                    "cfp[content:" + content + ";]"); });
                    break;
```

```
        case Performative.Proposal:
            ThreadPool.QueueUserWorkItem(delegate {
            Communication.Send(senderId, receiverId,
            "proposal[from:" + senderId + ";content:" +
            content + "]"); });
            break;
    }
}

public static string GetPerformative(string task)
{
    return task.Substring(0, task.IndexOf('['));
}

public static string GetInnerMessage(string task)
{
    return task.Substring(task.IndexOf('[') + 1,
    task.LastIndexOf(']') - task.IndexOf('[') - 1);
}

public static Dictionary<string, string>
MessageToDict(string innerMessage)
{
    var result = new Dictionary<string, string>();
    var items = innerMessage.Split(';');
    var contentItems = new List<string>();

    foreach (var item in items)
        if (!string.IsNullOrEmpty(item))
            contentItems.AddRange(item.Split(':'));

    for (int i = 0; i < contentItems.Count; i += 2)
        result.Add(contentItems[i], contentItems[i + 1]);

    return result;
}
```

```
    public static Dictionary<string, string>
    MessagesToDict(string message)
    {
        return MessageToDict(GetInnerMessage(message));
    }

    public static List<Tuple<double, Tuple<int, int>>>
    GetContent(List<Dictionary<string, string>
    messagesFromContractor)
    {
        var result = new List<Tuple<double, Tuple<int,
        int>>>();

        foreach (var msg in messagesFromContractor)
{
            var content = msg["content"];
            var values = content.Split(',');
            result.Add(new Tuple<double, Tuple<int,
            int>>(double.Parse(values[0]),
                new Tuple<int, int>(int.Parse(values[1]),
                int.Parse(values[2])))));
}

        return result;
    }
}

public enum Performative
{
    Accept, Cfp, Inform, Proposal
}
```

Notice that every agent communication is executed using the `QueueUserWorkItem` method of the `ThreadPool` class. Starting a new thread can be a very expensive operation; therefore, we use the thread-pool facilities to reuse threads and reduce cost. In this manner, we queue methods for execution under different threads that are drawn from the thread pool.

The `FipaACL` class includes an `AgentCommunicationServiceClient` communication property (recall from Chapter 6 that `AgentCommunicationServiceClient` is the proxy that establishes communication between client and service) that is used to transmit messages to other agents. `FipaACL` incorporates the following methods:

- `Message()`: depending on the type of performative, creates and sends a new message using the `senderId`, `receiverId`, and `content` strings provided as arguments.

- `GetPerformative()`: gets the performative of the message provided as argument; e.g., for a message such as `cfp[content: clean(0,2)]` the performative would be `cfp`

- `GetInnerMessage()`: gets the inner message; e.g., if the entire message is something like `cfp[from: 2312; content: clean(0,2)]` then `from: 2312; content: clean(0,2)` represents the inner message

- `MessageToDict()`: assuming an inner message is supplied as argument, it translates that inner message into a dictionary; e.g., from an inner message such as `from: 2312; content: clean(0,2)` the resulting dictionary would be `{ 'from': 2312, 'content': 'clean(0,2)' }`

- `MessagesToDict()`: gets the inner message of a message submitted as an argument and returns the dictionary resulting from the `MessageToDict()` method

- `GetContent()`: gets the set of values contained within the content label of the inner message. It assumes each message corresponds to a contractor's bid; therefore, it contains three elements: a distance double and a pair of integers matching a column range; e.g., `2.0, 1, 1` will add the tuple `<2.0, <0, 2>>`

The only components of the MAS cleaning example presented in this chapter that use the `FipaAcl` class are the `ContractNet` and `MasCleaningAgent` classes; the latter will be the topic of the next section.

MAS Cleaning Agent

Agents in the cleaning MAS example are objects of the `MasCleaningAgent` class, which contains the set of properties, fields, and constructor shown in Listing 7-5.

Listing 7-5. MasCleaningAgent Class, Including Fields, Properties, and Constructor

```
public class MasCleaningAgent
    {
        public Guid Id { get; set; }
        public int X { get; set; }
        public int Y { get; set; }
        public bool TaskFinished { get; set; }
        public Timer ReactionTime { get; set; }
        public FipaAcl Language { get; set; }
```

```
        public CleaningAgentPlatform Platform { get; set; }
        public List<Tuple<int, int>> CleanedCells;
        public ContractRole Role { get; set; }
        public Color Color;
        public bool AwaitingBids { get; set; }
        public bool AwaitingTaskAssignment { get; set; }
        public bool AnnouncementMade { get; set; }
        public bool TaskDistributed { get; set; }
        public Plan Plan { get; set; }
        public bool InCleaningArea { get; set; }
        public List<Tuple<int, int>> AreaTobeCleaned;
        private readonly int[,] _room;
        private readonly Form _gui;
        private Messaging _messageBoardWin;
        private readonly List<Tuple<double, Tuple<int,
        int>>> _wishList;

        public MasCleaningAgent(Guid id, int[,] room, Form gui,
        int x, int y, Color color)
        {
Id = id;
 X = x;
Y = y;
 _room = room;
CleanedCells = new List<Tuple<int, int>>();
Role = ContractRole.None;
_wishList = new List<Tuple<double, Tuple<int, int>>>();
Color = color;
 _gui = gui;
Run();
        }
}
```

This class exposes the following properties and fields:

- `Id`: represents a unique identifier for the agent

- `X`: integer representing the x-coordinate of the agent in the room

- `Y`: integer representing the y-coordinate of the agent in the room

- `TaskFinished`: Boolean value indicating whether the task has been completed

- `ReactionTime`: timer defining the reaction time of the agent; i.e., the frequency by which it executes an action

- `Language`: mini-Fipa language represented by the `FipaAcl` class that will be used for parsing and transmitting messages

- `Platform`: agent platform used for different services (agent location) and for deciding the role (manager or contractor) of each agent. It's represented by the `CleaningAgentPlatform` class.

- `CleanedCells`: list of `Tuple<int, int>` indicating the cells on the terrain that have already been cleaned by the agent

- `Role`: role assumed by the agent (contractor, manager, none)

- `Color`: color used by the agent on the room; i.e., on the Windows Forms picture box representing the room

- `AwaitingBids`: Boolean value indicating whether the agent is awaiting a bid (for the manager role)

- `AwaitingTaskAssignment`: Boolean value indicating whether the agent is awaiting a task assignment (for the contractor role)

- `AnnouncementMade`: Boolean value indicating whether an announcement has been made (for the manager role)

- `TaskDistributed`: Boolean value indicating whether tasks have been distributed (for the manager role)

- `Plan`: instance of the `Plan` class used for executing path-finding algorithms. This is the `Plan` class presented in Chapter 4, "Mars Rover."

- `InCleaningArea`: Boolean value indicating whether the agent is in the cleaning area assigned by the manager after a Contract Net task-sharing mechanism has been executed

- `AreaTobeCleaned`: list of cells the agent must clean

- `_room`: reference to the integer matrix representing the room to be cleaned. A value greater than 0 in any cell represents dirt; a value of 0 indicates the cell is clean.

- `_gui`: reference to the Windows Forms object that represents the room

- `_messageBoardWin`: reference to the Windows Forms representing the message board where all messages received by the agent will be displayed

- `_wishList`: list of `Tuple<double, Tuple<int, int>>` representing the wish list or bid list (for the contractor role) of the agent. The second item indicates a cell of the room, and the first item indicates the distance to that cell. This field is used in the bidding process to find the closest column end.

In the constructor, we initialize various fields and properties and eventually call the Run() method (Listing 7-6), which will set up everything to start running the agent.

Listing 7-6. Run() Method Starts the Agent by Enabling the Timer and Connecting the Tick Event to the ReactionTimeOnTick() Method

```
private void Run()
        {
_messageBoardWin = new Messaging (Id.ToString())
                                {
                                        StartPosition =
                                        FormStartPosition.
                                        WindowsDefaultLocation,
                                        BackColor = Color,
                                        Size = new Size
                                        (300, 300),
                                        Text = Id.ToString(),
                                        Enabled = true
                                };

            Language = new FipaAcl(_messageBoardWin.Proxy);
            _messageBoardWin.Show();

            ReactionTime = new Timer { Enabled = true,
            Interval = 1000 };
            ReactionTime.Tick += ReactionTimeOnTick;
        }
```

In the Run() method we initialize the _messageBoardWin variable as an instance of the Messaging class (Form class that will contain all messages received by the agent). We also initialize the Language property, passing as an argument the proxy created in the Messaging class. Finally, the Timer

271

of the agent is enabled and subscribed to the ReactionTimeOnTick (Listing 7-7). This method, which will be executed every second, causes the agent to take action.

Listing 7-7. ReactionTimeOnTick() Method Executed

```
private void ReactionTimeOnTick(object sender, EventArgs
eventArgs)
{
        // There's no area assigned for cleaning
        if (AreaTobeCleaned == null)
        {
            if (Role == ContractRole.Manager &&
            AnnouncementMade && !TaskDistributed)
            {
                ContractNet.Awarding(_messageBoardWin.
                Messages, Platform.Manager, Platform.
                Contractors, Platform.Task, Language);
                TaskDistributed = true;
            }
            if (Role == ContractRole.Manager &&
            !AnnouncementMade)
            {
                ContractNet.Announcement(Platform.Task,
                Platform.Manager, Platform.Contractors,
                                        Language);
                AnnouncementMade = true;
                Thread.Sleep(2000);
            }
            if (Role == ContractRole.Contractor &&
            AwaitingTaskAssignment || Role == ContractRole.
            Manager && TaskDistributed)
```

```
        {
            AreaTobeCleaned = SetSocialLaw
            (_messageBoardWin.Messages);
        }
        if (Role == ContractRole.Contractor &&
        !AwaitingTaskAssignment)
        {
            Thread.Sleep(2000);
            ContractNet.Bidding(_messageBoardWin.
            Messages, Platform.Contractors);
            AwaitingTaskAssignment = true;
        }
    }
    else
    {
        if (!InCleaningArea)
        {
            if (Plan == null)
            {
                Plan = new Plan(TypesPlan.PathFinding,
                this);
                Plan.BuildPlan(new Tuple<int, int>(X, Y),
                AreaTobeCleaned.First());
            }
            else if (Plan.Path.Count == 0)
                InCleaningArea = true;
        }

        Action(Perceived());
    }
    _gui.Refresh();
}
```

Notice that we put the thread to sleep for 2000 milliseconds to wait for certain operations of other agents to complete. This time may need to be increased as the cardinality of the set of agents increases.

The ReactionTimeOnTick() method uses a logic that depends on two scenarios: the agent has a cleaning area assigned or no area has been assigned. If no area has been assigned, that indicates no task sharing has been accomplished among agents, and so a Contract Net mechanism must be started. The different scenarios for when no cleaning area has been defined for the agent are the following:

- If the agent is a manager and an announcement has been made and tasks have not been distributed yet then the agent must enter an awarding phase.

- If the agent is a manager and no announcement has been made then the agent must enter an announcement phase.

- If the agent is a contractor and is awaiting a task assignment or the agent is a manager and tasks have been distributed then it should assign an area to be cleaned by setting a social law; we will detail this social law soon.

- If the agent is a contractor and is awaiting a task assignment then it must enter a bidding phase.

The bidding process of the agent follows the logic described by the code shown in Listing 7-8.

Listing 7-8. Bid Method of the Agent

```
public void Bid(IEnumerable<string> tasks)
        {
            var n = _room.GetLength(0);
            _wishList.Clear();
```

```
foreach (var task in tasks)
{
    var innerMessage = FipaAcl.GetInnerMessage(task);
    var messageDict = FipaAcl.
    MessageToDict(innerMessage);
    var content = messageDict["content"];
    var subtask = content.Substring(0, content.
    IndexOf('('));
    var cols = new string[2];

    switch (subtask)
    {
        case "clean":
            var temp = content.Substring(content.
            IndexOf('(') + 1, content.Length -
            content.IndexOf('(') - 2);
            cols = temp.Split(',');
            break;
    }

    var colRange = new Tuple<int, int>(int.
    Parse(cols[0]), int.Parse(cols[1]));

    for (var i = colRange.Item1; i < colRange.
    Item2; i++)
    {
        // Distance to extreme points for each column
        var end1 = new Tuple<int, int>(0, i);
        var end2 = new Tuple<int, int>(n - 1, i);

        var dist1 = ManhattanDistance(end1, new
        Tuple<int, int>(X, Y));
```

```
                    var dist2 = ManhattanDistance(end2, new
                    Tuple<int, int>(X, Y));

                    _wishList.Add(new Tuple<double, Tuple<int,
                    int>>(dist1, end1));
                    _wishList.Add(new Tuple<double, Tuple<int,
                    int>>(dist2, end2));
                }
            }

            _wishList.Sort(Comparison);

            foreach (var bid in _wishList)
                Language.Message(Performative.Proposal,
                Id.ToString(), Platform.Manager.Id.ToString(),
                bid.Item1 + "," + bid.Item2.Item1 + "," + bid.
                Item2.Item2);
        }
```

The Bid() method receives the list of tasks as input, parses every task message contained in the list, and then, having the column range detailed in each incoming message task, finds the distance to the four possible column ends. Finally, it sorts the _wishList of all possible distances to column ends and transmits them (as proposals) to the manager ordered from lowest to highest.

When a cleaning area has been assigned, the agent must design a plan (path-finding technique from Chapter 4) to reach its cleaning area. Once in its cleaning area, the agent will follow a social law defined by the method illustrated in Listing 7-9.

Listing 7-9. SetSocialLaw() Method

```
private List<Tuple<int, int>> SetSocialLaw(List<string> messages)
{
        if (!messages.Exists(m => FipaAcl.
        GetPerformative(m) == "accept"))
            return null;

        var informMsg = messages.First(m => FipaAcl.
        GetPerformative(m) == "accept");
var content = FipaAcl.MessageToDict(FipaAcl.
GetInnerMessage(informMsg));
        var directive = content["content"];
var temp = directive.Substring(directive.IndexOf('(') + 1,
directive.Length - directive.IndexOf('(') - 2);
var pos = temp.Split(',');
var posTuple = new Tuple<int, int>(int.Parse(pos[0]), int.
Parse(pos[1]));
var colsTuple = new Tuple<int, int>(posTuple.Item2, posTuple.
Item2 + _room.GetLength(1) / Platform.Directory.Count - 1);

        var result = new List<Tuple<int, int>>();
        var startRow = _room.GetLength(0) - 1;
        var dx = -1;

        // Generate path to clean
        for (var col = colsTuple.Item1; col <= colsTuple.
        Item2; col++)
        {
            startRow = startRow == _room.GetLength(0) - 1 ?
            0 : _room.GetLength(0) - 1;
            dx = dx == -1 ? 1 : -1;
```

```
        for (var row = startRow; row < _room.GetLength(0)
        && row >= 0; row+=dx)
            result.Add(new Tuple<int, int>(row, col));
    }

    return result;
}
```

While in their cleaning area, and for the purpose of having an ordered, uniform way of executing their cleaning task, the SetSocialLaw() method will define the path followed by agents during their cleaning process; this social law is illustrated in Figure 7-2.

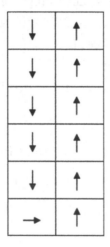

Figure 7-2. *Social law followed by agents*

If there's an active plan (for going to the designated cleaning area) then a move from this plan is executed and deleted from the plan's path. According to the percepts received (clean, dirty), the agent will choose to update its state or clean the dirty cell. If the area to be cleaned still contains some unvisited cells, then we move to that cell. If the area to be cleaned has no more cells, then the task can be considered finished. This is the process executed by the Action() method seen in Listing 7-10.

Listing 7-10. Action() Method

```
public void Action(List<Tuple<TypesPercept, Tuple<int, int>>>
percepts)
        {
            if (Plan.Path.Count > 0)
            {
                var nextAction = Plan.NextAction();
                var percept = percepts.Find(p => p.Item1 ==
                nextAction);
                Move(percept.Item1);
                return;
            }

            if (percepts.Exists(p => p.Item1 == TypesPercept.
               Clean))
                UpdateState();
            if (percepts.Exists(p => p.Item1 == TypesPercept.
            Dirty))
            {
                Clean();
                return;
            }

            if (AreaTobeCleaned.Count > 0)
            {
                var nextCell = AreaTobeCleaned.First();
                AreaTobeCleaned.RemoveAt(0);
                Move(GetMove(nextCell));
            }
```

```
        else
        {
            if (!TaskFinished)
            {
                TaskFinished = true;
                MessageBox.Show("Task Finished");
            }
        }
    }
```

Other methods of the MasCleaningAgent class, such as Clean(), IsDirty(), Move(), GetMove(), UpdateState(), ManhattanDistance(), MoveAvailable(), and Perceived() share a high degree of similitude with methods of the same name defined in the example from Chapter 2; thus, we will not be including their codes in this chapter. For further reference please consult the source code associated with this book.

GUI

As mentioned before, we will include in the project two Windows Forms applications—one for showing a list of messages received by the agent and another for graphically representing the room. The Messaging class of the message board acts as a client; it incorporates the code presented in the last chapter in the client's Windows Forms application. The service in this case is called from a console application in similar fashion to the one we detailed in Chapter 6. Even though the code of the Room class is merely a Windows Forms code, we present it in Listing 7-11 to serve as reference.

Listing 7-11. Room Class

```
public partial class Room : Form
{
        public List<MasCleaningAgent> CleaningAgents;
        private int _n;
        private int _m;
        private int[,] _room;

        public Room(int n, int m, int[,] room)
        {
            _n = n;
            _m = m;
            _room = room;
            CleaningAgents = new List<MasCleaningAgent>();
            InitializeComponent();
        }

        private void RoomPicturePaint(object sender,
        PaintEventArgs e)
        {
            var pen = new Pen(Color.Wheat);
            var cellWidth = roomPicture.Width / _m;
            var cellHeight = roomPicture.Height / _n;

            // Draw room grid
            for (var i = 0; i < _m; i++)
                e.Graphics.DrawLine(pen, new Point
                (i * cellWidth, 0), new Point(i * cellWidth,
                i * cellWidth + roomPicture.Height));
```

```
        for (var i = 0; i < _n; i++)
            e.Graphics.DrawLine(pen, new Point(0, i *
            cellHeight), new Point(i * cellHeight +
            roomPicture.Width, i * cellHeight));

        // Draw agents
        for (var i = 0; i < CleaningAgents.Count; i++)
            e.Graphics.FillEllipse(new SolidBrush
            (CleaningAgents[i].Color), CleaningAgents[i].Y
            * cellWidth, CleaningAgents[i].X * cellHeight,
            cellWidth, cellHeight);

        // Draw Dirt
        for (var i = 0; i < _n; i++)
        {
            for (var j = 0; j < _m; j++)
                if (_room[i, j] > 0)
                    e.Graphics.DrawImage(new Bitmap("rock-
                    transparency.png"), j * cellWidth, i *
                    cellHeight, cellWidth, cellHeight);
        }
    }

    private void RoomPictureResize(object sender, EventArgs e)
    {
        Refresh();
    }
}
```

In the Room class, we implemented the Paint event and the
PictureResize event of the PictureBox, where all elements (dirt, agents)
are graphically represented. Agents are drawn as ellipses of a color defined

by the Color agent property, and dirt is drawn as images. When agents clean dirty cells, the dirt will vanish (image no longer painted), and the global task will end when no cell contains a picture of dirt.

Running the Application

Now that we've finished building an MAS program that incorporates all topics described in the preceding three chapters, let us run and look at the complete application and how the agents cooperate, coordinate, and are actually capable of cleaning an n x m room. Remember we are assuming the number of columns is divisible by the number of agents, which simplifies our planning process. The reader can easily change this strategy, transforming it into a more general strategy—one that will allow him to plan the cleaning task for any number of agents.

We embed the WCF service in the console application where we also declare all agents, platform, and the room GUI (Listing 7-12).

Listing 7-12. Setting Up and Starting the Application in a Console Application Project

```
var room = new [,]
            {
                {0, 0, 0, 0, 0, 0, 0, 0, 0, 0},
                {0, 0, 0, 0, 0, 0, 0, 0, 0, 0},
                {0, 0, 0, 0, 0, 0, 1, 0, 0, 0},
                {0, 0, 0, 0, 0, 0, 0, 0, 0, 0},
                {2, 0, 0, 1, 0, 0, 0, 0, 0, 0},
                {0, 0, 0, 0, 0, 0, 0, 0, 0, 1},
                {0, 0, 0, 0, 0, 0, 0, 0, 0, 0},
                {0, 0, 0, 0, 0, 0, 0, 1, 0, 0},
                {0, 0, 0, 0, 0, 0, 0, 0, 0, 0},
                {0, 0, 0, 0, 0, 0, 0, 0, 0, 0}
            };
```

```
            Application.EnableVisualStyles();
            Application.SetCompatibleTextRenderingDefault(false);

            const int N = 10;
            const int M = 10;
            var roomGui = new Room(N, M, room);

            // Starts the WCF service.
            InitCommunicationService();

var clAgent1 = new MasCleaningAgent(Guid.NewGuid(), room,
            roomGui, 0, 0, Color.Teal);
            var clAgent2 = new MasCleaningAgent(Guid.NewGuid(),
            room, roomGui, 1, 1, Color.Yellow);
            var clAgent3 = new MasCleaningAgent(Guid.NewGuid(),
            room, roomGui, 0, 0, Color.Tomato);
            var clAgent4 = new MasCleaningAgent(Guid.NewGuid(),
            room, roomGui, 1, 1, Color.LightSkyBlue);
            var clAgent5 = new MasCleaningAgent(Guid.NewGuid(),
            room, roomGui, 1, 1, Color.Black);
roomGui.CleaningAgents = new List<MasCleaningAgent> { clAgent1,
clAgent2, clAgent3, clAgent4, clAgent5 };
            var platform = new CleaningAgentPlatform(roomGui.
            CleaningAgents, new CleaningTask(M, roomGui.
            CleaningAgents.Count));

            Application.Run(roomGui);
```

The InitCommunicationService() method contains the exact lines of code as in the agent service detailed in Chapter 6. The result is the one shown in Figure 7-3, where the MAS application starts by having all agents exchange messages in a Contract Net mechanism.

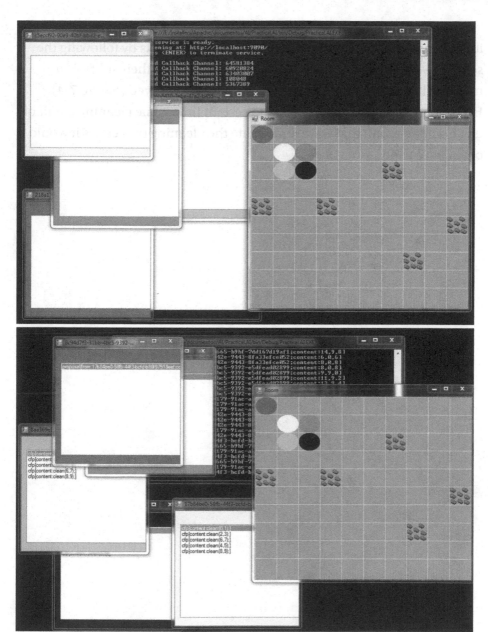

Figure 7-3. *Agents exchanging messages in a Contract Net mechanism; messages received are shown in their Message Board windows*

Once an agreement has been reached and every agent is aware of its designated cleaning area, the cleaning process starts by following the social law previously described. When they complete their subtask, a message box with a "Task Finished" message is displayed (Figure 7-4). Each agent thread is put to sleep for a certain time while cleaning a unit of dirt from the room; that way we simulate the cleaning process as it would occur in real life.

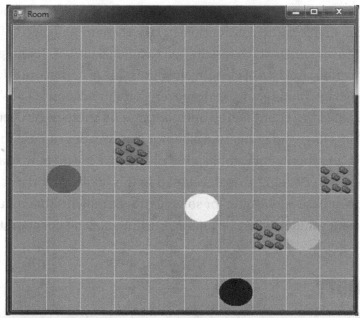

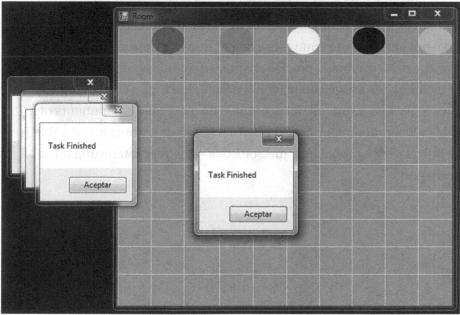

Figure 7-4. *Agents cleaning their designated area and displaying the "Task Finished" message once they have completed cleaning their area*

We have finally reached the closing stages of our cleaning agent MAS application. In this particular example, a 10 x 10 room was successfully cleaned by five agents, which distributed the global task of cleaning the entire room into subtasks of cleaning just portions of it; these portions were defined by column ranges. Moreover, communication via a WCF service resulted in a coordination and cooperation strategy. As occurred with the Mars Rover program from Chapter 4, the reader can use this example in an experimental application or improve it with new strategies or methods. The cleaning MAS developed in this book can serve as the foundation or base application for solving other problems that require a more efficient solution when various agents interact and collaborate.

Summary

Chapter 7 ends for now the "Agents" topic of this book, the closing practical problem not only encompassing many of the points studied in Chapters 5 and 6 but also going beyond the scope of detail included in those chapters to be the most thorough, precise chapter up to this point. Going back to the cleaning MAS application, you'll notice that topics such as logic, first-order logic, and agents are incorporated as inevitable components of a multi-agent program. In Chapter 8, we'll begin describing an area that is deeply related to probability and statistics—the very interesting topic of simulation.

CHAPTER 8

Simulation

Modeling is a basic tool of the human mind that provides us with the ability to create abstract versions of the world, or part of it. These abstract versions can embody a convenient, simplified representation of a situation, object, and so forth and can be used to find a solution to a given problem. Modeling involves imagination and creativity; it underlies our capacity to communicate, generalize, and express meaning or patterns in an intelligent manner.

It is usually accepted that modeling is a way of making decisions and predictions about the world and that the purpose of a model must be well defined and understood before the model is created. Models are typically classified as *descriptive* (they explain or describe the world) or *prescriptive* (they formulate optimal solutions to problems and are related to the area of optimization). Examples of models of the first type are maps, 3D objects created using computer graphics, or video games. Models of the latter type are heavily related to math and specifically to optimization; in these models, we define a set of constraints for a problem and a goal function to be optimized.

Every model possesses three basic features:

- *Reference*: It represents something, either from the real world or an imaginary world; e.g., building, city.

- *Purpose*: It has a logical intention with respect to that which it references; e.g. study, analysis.

- *Cost-effectiveness*: It is more effective to use the model than the reference, e.g. blueprint vs. real building, map vs. real city.

© Arnaldo Pérez Castaño 2018
A. Pérez Castaño, *Practical Artificial Intelligence*,
https://doi.org/10.1007/978-1-4842-3357-3_8

Simulation is considered a variety of modeling whose purpose is comprehension, planning, prediction, and manipulation. It can be defined broadly as a behavioral or phenomenological approach to modeling; that is, a simulation is an active behavioral analog of its referent.

Note   Modeling is one of the most important processes that occurs in the human mind. When modeling we try to create abstract versions of our reality, simplifying it many times to help us solve a problem. Examples of models are maps (such as Google Maps), which represent abstract versions of the world.

What Is Simulation?

As occurs with the *logic* and *agent* words (it seems like the AI community should get together and try to agree on several definitions), there's no consensus on what the word *simulation* means. There is, however, a consensus on the fact that *simulation* is an imitative and dynamic type of modeling used to model phenomena that must be researched or understood for some reason.

When we implement a simulation as a computer program we obtain high flexibility; being in a programming-language environment means that in principle it is possible to refine, maintain, evolve, and extend a computer simulation in ways that are difficult to match in any other environment. Modern programming languages such as C# facilitate the development of modular data and program code, allowing new simulations to be built using pieces or modules of existing ones.

Computer simulation is usually divided into *analytic* and *discrete-event* approaches. The analytic approach involves mathematical analysis and problems that can be understood or approximated from an analytic perspective. For instance, if the reality being modeled can be accurately described by a set of differential equations (as in the flow of heat over a surface), analytic solutions for those equations can be used to generate the time-dependent behavior required for the simulation. The mathematical elegance of analytic simulation makes it in many scenarios cryptic and incomprehensible; by reducing reality to an abstract mathematical relationship the understanding required could get obscured. There are also cases in which analytic solutions are known but feasible means of computing these solutions are not available. Nonetheless, analytic simulations are indispensable in many situations, particularly when dealing with complex physical phenomena involving enormous numbers of relatively small and relatively similar entities whose individual interactions are relatively simple and whose aggregate interactions follow the "law of large numbers"; in other words, they permit statistical treatment. In such cases, analytic models often represent at least one form of complete understanding.

Note   There is a large class of problems that are not well enough understood to be handled analytically—i.e., for which no formal mathematical solutions exist. These problems are modeled and simulated by means of discrete-event simulations (DES).

When we have a system that is composed of several entities, and we understand each entity in isolation and also their pairwise interactions, but fail to comprehend the behavior and relations of the system as a whole, then we can make use of a simulation to encode the pairwise interactions and then run the simulation to try to approximate the relations or behavior of the system as a whole; one of these simulations is known as a discrete-event simulation (DES).

Discrete-Event Simulation

Time is essential in a DES, and the simulation can be seen as a succession of discrete events in which entities interact. Time advances in a discrete manner by means of fixed ticks or a simulated clock.

A DES is often the last alternative for modeling certain kinds of intractable problems. Its power lies in its capacity to expose patterns of interaction for the whole system that cannot be acknowledged in other ways. It's frequently possible to enumerate and describe a collection of entities and their properties, relations, and immediate interactions without knowing where these interactions lead. If this knowledge is encoded in a DES simulation and the behavior of the resulting model is observed, then we could acquire a better understanding of the system and the interaction among its entities; this is typically the main purpose behind the development of a DES.

When developing a DES there are six key elements to consider:

- *Objects*, which represent elements of the system, have properties, relate to events, consume resources, and enter and leave queues over time. In an airport simulation (soon to be examined), objects would be airplanes. In a health-care system, objects might be patients or organs. In a warehouse system, objects would be products in stock. Objects are supposed to interact with each other or the system and can be created at any time during the simulation.

- *Properties*, which are features particular to every object (size, takeoff time, landing time, sex, price, and so on), are stored in some manner and help determine a response to a variety of scenarios that might arise during the simulation; such values can be modified.

- *Events*, which are incidents that can occur in the system and are usually related to objects, can be things like the landing of an airplane, the arrival of a product to a warehouse, the appearance of a particular disease, and so forth. Events can occur and reoccur in any order.

- *Resources*, which are elements that provide services to objects (for example, a runway at the airport, storage cells in a warehouse, and doctors at a clinic), are finite. When a resource is occupied and an object needs it, the object must queue and wait until the resource is available. We'll see such a scenario in the practical problem of this chapter.

- *Queues*, which are the means by which objects are organized to await the release of some resource that's currently occupied, can have a maximum capacity and can have different calling approaches: First-In-First-Out (FIFO), Last-In-First-Out (LIFO), or based on some criteria or priority (disease progression, fuel consumption, and the like).

- *Time* (as mentioned before and occurs in real life) is essential in simulation. To measure time, a clock is started at the beginning of the simulation and can be used to track particular periods of time (departure or arrival time, transportation time, time spent with certain symptoms, and so on). Such tracking is fundamental because it allows you to know when the next event should occur.

Discreet Events Simulation (DES) are closely related to probability and statistics because they model real-life scenarios where randomized and probabilistic events occur; DES must rely on probabilistic distributions, random variables, and other statistics and probability tools for events generation.

Probabilistic Distributions

A discrete random variable is one whose set of values is finite or countably infinite; in other words, its values can be listed as a finite or infinite sequence, such as 1, 2, 3 . . . and so on. The probability distribution for a discrete random variable is any graph, table, or formula that assigns a probability to each possible value. The sum of all probabilities must be 1, and each individual probability must be between 0 and 1. For example, when we throw a fair die (all sides equally probable), the discrete random variable X representing the possible outcomes will have the probability distribution $X(1) = 1/6$, $X(2) = 1/6$, ..., $X(6) = 1/6$. All sides are equally probable, so the assigned probability for every value of the random variable is 1/6.

Parameter μ will indicate the mean (expected value) in their corresponding distributions. The mean represents the value that the random variable takes on average. In other words, it's the sum E=[(each possible outcome) × (probability of that outcome)], where E denotes the mean. In the case of the die, the mean would be E = 1/6 + 2/6 + 3/6 + 4/6 + 5/6 + 6/6 = 3.5. Notice that the result 3.5 is actually halfway between all possible values the die can take; it's the expected value when the die is rolled a large number of times.

Parameter $\sigma 2$ will indicate the variance of the distribution. Variance represents the dispersion of possible values of the random variable; it's always non-negative. Small variances (close to 0) indicate values are close to each other and the mean; high variances (close to 1) indicate great distance among values and from the mean.

Poisson is a discrete distribution expressing probabilities concerning the number of events per time unit (Figure 8-1). It's usually applied when the probability of an event is small and the number of opportunities for its occurrence is large. The number of misprints in a book, airplanes arriving at an airport, cars arriving at traffic lights, and deaths per year in a given age group are all examples of applications of the Poisson distribution.

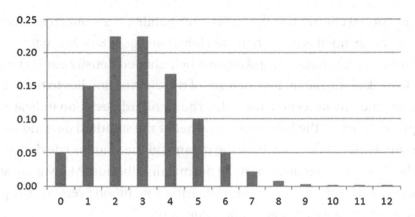

Figure 8-1. *Poisson distribution*

An exponential distribution expresses time between events in a Poisson process (Figure 8-2). For instance, if you're dealing with a Poisson process describing the number of airplanes arriving at an airport during a certain time then you may be interested in a random variable that would indicate how much time passed before the first plane arrived. An exponential distribution can serve this purpose, and it could also be applied to physics processes; for example, to represent the lifetime of particles where the λ parameter would indicate the rate at which the particle ages.

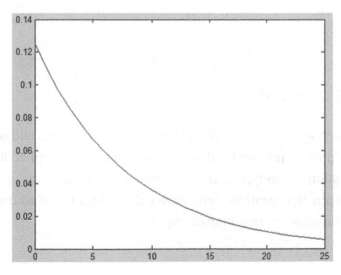

Figure 8-2. *Exponential distribution*

295

The normal distribution describes a probability that converges around a central value, no bias left or right, as shown in Figure 8-3. Normal distributions are symmetric and possess bell-shaped density curves with a single peak at the mean. Fifty percent of the distribution lies to the left of the mean and fifty percent to the right. The standard deviation indicates the spread or belt of the bell curve; the smaller the standard deviation the more concentrated the data. Both the mean and the standard deviation must be defined as parameters of the normal distribution. Many natural phenomena strongly follow a normal distribution: blood pressure, people's height, errors in measurements, and many more.

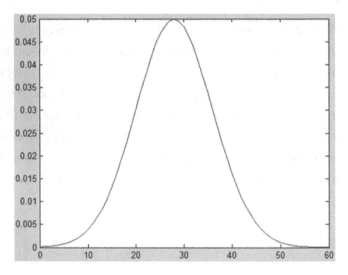

Figure 8-3. *Normal distribution*

So far we have described what a DES is, its components, and some of the most important probability distributions that can be applied for event time-generation in this type of simulation. In the next section, we will start looking at a practical problem, where we will see how to put all the pieces together in an airport simulation example.

Practical Problem: Airport Simulation

Let's imagine a scenario in which we would like to simulate the operation of a five-runway airport where airplanes transporting a certain number of passengers arrive, spend some time at the airport to refuel, and eventually depart in a timeframe that depends, among others, on the probability that the airplane might have gotten broken up. This is the airport simulation that we will be implementing in this chapter. The IDistribution, Poisson, and Continuous classes (interfaces) seen in future code are part of the MathNet.Numerics package.

The time between arrival to the airport of one plane and another distributes as a Poisson function with a lambda parameter specified by Table 8-1.

Table 8-1. *Arrivals of Airplanes at the Airport According to Timeframes*

Time	Lambda
06:00–14:00	7 mins
14:00–22:00	10 mins
22:00–06:00	20 mins

When an airplane arrives at the airport it lands on an available runway, selecting it uniformly from any of the available runways. If there's no runway available, the airplane is enqueued into a line of airplanes asking permission to land. Once the airplane finally lands, it processes its cargo in an amount of time that distributes by an exponential function whose parameter gets its value by considering the number of passengers traveling on the plane, as shown in Table 8-2.

Table 8-2. *Time to Process Cargo for Any Airplane and Dependant on Number of Passengers*

Passengers	Lambda
0–150	50 mins
150–300	60 mins
300–450	75 mins

While an airplane is processing its cargo, it's considered to be occupying the runway. An airplane can get broken down with a probability of 0.15, in which case the reparation will distribute by an exponential function with parameter lambda = 80 mins.

In order to start analyzing the code of our airport simulation, let's consider the Airplane class as described in Listing 8-1.

Listing 8-1. Airplane Class

```
public class Airplane
    {
        public Guid Id { get; set; }
        public intPassengersCount{ get; set; }
        public double TimeToTakeOff{ get; set; }
        public intRunwayOccupied{ get; set; }
        public bool BrokenDown{ get; set; }

        public Airplane(int passengers)
        {
            Id = Guid.NewGuid();
PassengersCount = passengers;
RunwayOccupied = -1;
        }
    }
```

The `Airplane` class contains the following properties:

- `Id`: It's initialized in the constructor and will uniquely identify every airplane.

- `PassengersCount`: defines the number of passengers in the airplane

- `TimeToTakeOff`: defines the time (in minutes) at which the airplane is supposed to take off from the landing strip

- `RunwayOccupied`: identifies whether an airplane is occupying a runway at the airport, and, if so, this property matches the index of the runway being occupied. When its value is less than 0 it means the airplane is not occupying any runway.

- `BrokenDown`: has value True if the airplane has broken down, False otherwise

In Listing 8-2 we can see the `AirportEvent<T>` abstract class, which will serve as the parent of the other three classes representing different events taking place in the `AirportSimulation`. The intention is to shorten the code, compacting all lines that can be logically compacted or included in one single parent class, thus taking advantage of inheritance in C#.

Listing 8-2. AirportEvent<T> Abstract Class

```
public abstract class AirportEvent<T> where T: IComparable
 {
        protected double[] Parameters;
        protected List<Tuple<T, T>> Frames;
        public double[] DistributionValues;
        public List<IDistribution> Distributions;
```

```
        protected AirportEvent(params double[] lambdas)
        {
            Distributions = new List<IDistribution>();
DistributionValues = new double[lambdas.Length];
            Frames = new List<Tuple<T, T>>();
            Parameters = lambdas;
        }

        public virtual void SetDistributionValues(Distribution
        Type type)
        {
foreach (var lambda in Parameters)
            {
                switch (type)
                {
                    case DistributionType.Poisson:
Distributions.Add(new Poisson(lambda));
                        break;
                    case DistributionType.Exponential:
Distributions.Add(new Exponential(lambda));
                        break;
                }
            }
            // Sampling distributions
            for (vari = 0; i<Frames.Count; i++)
DistributionValues[i] = type == DistributionType.Poisson
                                    ? ((Poisson)
                                    Distributions[i]).Sample()
                                    : (1 - ((Exponential)
                                    Distributions[i]).
                                    Sample()) *
                                    Parameters[i];
        }
```

```
public virtual double GetEvtFrequency(T elem)
{
    for (vari = 0; i<Frames.Count; i++)
    {
        if (elem.CompareTo(Frames[i].Item1) >= 0
        &&elem.CompareTo(Frames[i].Item2) < 0)
            return DistributionValues[i];
    }

    return -1;
}
}

public enumDistributionType
{
    Exponential, Poisson
}
```

Note   In the AirportEvent<T> class we are requiring, by use of
the where keyword, that the T parameter be of type IComparable.
We need this prerequisite to be able to compare them later in the
most generic way possible.

The AirportEvent<T> class includes the following properties:

- Parameters: an array of doubles storing the lambda
  parameters to be used in the different distributions

- Frames: a list of tuples of type T defining the timeframes
  or numeric frames of an event, corresponding with a
  probability distribution and a parameter as indicated
  in Tables 8-1 and 8-2. The cardinality of this list must
  match that of the Parameters array and also of the next
  two properties that we will list.

- `DistributionValues`: array of doubles used to store at index i the value resulting from calculating the probability distribution i using parameter i from array `Parameters`

- `Distributions`: list of distributions to be used; when calculating a probability distribution we consider some parameter lambda, and the value resulting from this calculation is stored in the `DistributionValues` array

Apart from the previous properties, the class also includes the following methods:

- `SetDistributionValues()`: depending on the type of distribution indicated as argument, it adds new distributions to the `Distributions` list and samples these distributions with the `Parameters` specified, leaving every sampled value in the `DistributionValues` array

- `GetEvtFrequency()`: This method receives as argument a type T, which is `Icomparable`, and compares it against the time or numeric frames to decide the portion to which it belongs and therefore the distribution value for it. For instance, if frames are (0, 100), (100, 200), (200, 250) and T = 110, then T would fall into the second frame and match the second (`index=1`) distribution value.

Additionally, we have the `DistributionType` enum indicating the two types of distributions that we will be considering in this example (Poisson, Exponential).

The `AirplaneEvtArrival` (Listing 8-3) class inherits from `AirportEvent<T>`; in this case, T becomes a `TimeSpan`. This class represents the event that an airplane arrived at the airport.

Listing 8-3. AirplaneEvtArrival<TimeSpan> Class

```
public class AirplaneEvtArrival :AirportEvent<TimeSpan>
   {
       public AirplaneEvtArrival(params double[] lambdas) :
       base(lambdas)
       {
Frames = new List<Tuple<TimeSpan, TimeSpan>>
                       {
                            new Tuple<TimeSpan,
                            TimeSpan>(new TimeSpan(0, 6, 0,
                            0), new TimeSpan(0, 14, 0, 0)),
                            new Tuple<TimeSpan,
                            TimeSpan>(new TimeSpan(0, 14, 0,
                            0), new TimeSpan(0, 22, 0, 0)),
                            new Tuple<TimeSpan,
                            TimeSpan>(new TimeSpan(0, 22, 0,
                            0), new TimeSpan(0, 6, 0, 0))
                       };
       }
   }
```

The class merely contains a constructor, where the Frames list is defined as a set of tuples where each tuple details a time range.

Similarly, the AirplaneEvtProcessCargo class (Listing 8-4), which also inherits from AirportEvent<int>, defines in its constructor a list of Frames containing tuples of integers that indicate ranges of passengers. These ranges ultimately match some value (in minutes) that is the time it takes to process that amount of passengers (recall Table 8-2).

Listing 8-4. AirplaneEvtProcessCargo<int> Class

```
public class AirplaneEvtProcessCargo :AirportEvent<int>
    {
        public AirplaneEvtProcessCargo(params double[] lambdas)
        : base(lambdas)
        {
            Frames = new List<Tuple<int, int>>
                        {
                                new Tuple<int, int>(0, 150),
                                new Tuple<int, int>(150, 300),
                                new Tuple<int, int>(300, 450)
                        };
        }

        public double SampleAt(intelem)
        {
            for (vari = 0; i<Frames.Count; i++)
            {
                if (elem.CompareTo(Frames[i].Item1) >=0&&elem.
                CompareTo(Frames[i].Item2) < 0)
return  (1 - ((Exponential) Distributions[i]).Sample()) *
Parameters[i];
            }

            return -1;
        }
    }
```

The class also contains a SampleAt() method, which returns the probability distribution value of the element supplied as argument and considers the range imposed on the class by the Frames list.

In Listing 8-5 we can see the `AirplaneEvtBreakdown` class, which inherits from `AirportEvent<TimeSpan>`; its code is very simple, as it simply calls the constructor of its parent class.

Listing 8-5. AirplaneEvtBreakdown<TimeSpan> Class

```
public class AirplaneEvtBreakdown :AirportEvent<TimeSpan>
    {
public AirplaneEvtBreakdown(params double[] lambdas): base(lambdas)
{
}
    }
```

Lastly, the `Simulation` class includes various properties, fields, and constructor, as shown in Listing 8-6.

Listing 8-6. Constructor, Fields, and Properties of the Simulation Class

```
public class Simulation
    {
        public TimeSpanMaxTime{ get; set; }
        private TimeSpan _currentTime;
        private readonlyAirplaneEvtArrival _arrivalDistribution;
        private readonlyAirplaneEvtProcessCargo
        _processCargoDistribution;
        private readonlyAirplaneEvtBreakdown _airplaneBreakdown;
        private readonly bool [] _runways;
        private readonlyint _planeArrivalInterval;
        private readonly Queue<Airplane> _waitingToLand;
        private readonly List<Airplane> _airplanes;
        private List<Airplane> _airplanesOnLand;
        private static readonly Random Random = new Random();
```

```
        public Simulation(TimeSpanstartTime, TimeSpanmaxTime,
        IEnumerable<Airplane> airplanes)
        {
MaxTime = maxTime;
            _runways = new bool[5];
            _arrivalDistribution = new AirplaneEvtArrival(7, 10, 20);
            _processCargoDistribution = new
            AirplaneEvtProcessCargo(50, 60, 75);
            _airplaneBreakdown = new AirplaneEvtBreakdown(80);
            _waitingToLand = new Queue<Airplane>();
            _airplanes = new List<Airplane>(airplanes);
            _airplanesOnLand = new List<Airplane>();
            _currentTime = startTime;
            // For 1st day set distribution values.
            _arrivalDistribution.SetDistributionValues
            (DistributionType.Poisson);
            _processCargoDistribution.SetDistributionValues
            (DistributionType.Exponential);
            _airplaneBreakdown.SetDistributionValues(Distribution
            Type.Exponential);
            _planeArrivalInterval = (int) _arrivalDistribution.
            GetEvtFrequency(startTime);
        }
}
```

The properties and fields of the Simulation class are as follows:

- MaxTime: the maximum time the simulation will last

- _currentTime: current time in the simulation

- _arrivalDistribution: object describing the event of an airplane arrival

- _processCargoDistribution: object describing the event of an airplane processing its cargo

- `_airplaneBreakdown`: object describing the event of an airplane being broken down

- `_runways`: set of runways at the airport

- `_planeArrivalInterval`: interval by which an airplane arrives at the airport. This value is calculated using the `_arrivalDistribution`.

- `_waitingToLand`: queue of airplanes waiting for an available runway to land

- `_airplanes`: list of airplanes arriving at the airport

- `_airplanesOnLand`: list of airplanes that have already landed at the airport

- `Random`: random variable

The constructor of the `Simulation` class receives as arguments the start time and end time of the simulation and the list of airplanes scheduled to land at the airport. Inside the constructor, we initialize the fields and properties according to the values described in Tables 8-1 and 8-2.

In the `Execute()` method (Listing 8-7) we execute the simulation; everything occurs within an outer `while` loop that runs until the current time of the simulation exceeds the maximum time allowed.

Inside the outer `while` loop, we first try to give landing permission to airplanes that have been queued for landing. We'll soon examine the `TryToLand()` method, which attempts to perform a landing for some airplane. Then, we take care of the airplane arrival event, checking first if there are still airplanes waiting to land and if the current time in minutes leaves a remainder of zero when divided by the interval by which airplanes are supposed to arrive at the airport; this is equivalent to saying that the current minute belongs to the residual class defined by the value of the arrival-time interval previously calculated.

Ultimately, we loop through every airplane on land, checking for those that must depart at the current minute or looking into the possibility of an airplane's having a breakdown. We also update the list of airplanes and airplanes on land and the list of runways occupied at any given moment. To conclude and start another cycle of the simulation, we add a minute to the current time.

Listing 8-7. Execute() Method

```
public void Execute()
        {
            while (_currentTime<MaxTime)
            {
Console.WriteLine(_currentTime);

                // Process airplanes on queue for landing
foreach (var airplane in _waitingToLand)
                {
                    if (!TryToLand(airplane))
                        break;
                }

                // Plane arrival event
                if (_currentTime.Minutes % _planeArrivalInterval
                == 0 && _airplanes.Count> 0)
                {
varnewPlane = _airplanes.First();
                    _airplanes.RemoveAt(0);
Console.WriteLine("Plane {0} arriving ...", newPlane.Id);

                    if (TryToLand(newPlane))
                        _airplanesOnLand.Add(newPlane);
                }
```

```
                // For updating list of airplanes on the ground
varnewAirplanesOnLand = new List<Airplane>();
                // Update airplane status for this minute
foreach (var airplane in _airplanesOnLand)
                {
airplane.TimeToTakeOff--;
                    if (airplane.TimeToTakeOff<= 0)
                    {
                        _runways[airplane.RunwayOccupied] = false;
airplane.RunwayOccupied = -1;
Console.WriteLine("Plane {0} took off", airplane.Id);
                    }
                    else
newAirplanesOnLand.Add(airplane);

                    // Odds of having a breakdown
                    if (Random.NextDouble() < 0.15 &&
                    !airplane.BrokenDown)
                    {
airplane.BrokenDown = true;
airplane.TimeToTakeOff += _airplaneBreakdown.
DistributionValues.First();
Console.WriteLine("Plane {0} broke down, take off time is now
{1} mins", airplane.Id, Math.Round(airplane.TimeToTakeOff, 2));
                    }
                }

            _airplanesOnLand = new List<Airplane>(newAirplanes
            OnLand);
```

```
            // Add a minute
            _currentTime = _currentTime.Add(new TimeSpan
            (0, 0, 1, 0));
        }
    }
```

In Listing 8-8, we can see the RunwayAvailable() and TryToLand() methods. The first is very simple and allows us to know whether there's a runway available, returning its index in that case. The latter tries to provide landing permission to an airplane by checking first if there are runways available. Assuming there is, then it updates the corresponding list and properties and sets the time the airplane will consume at the airport; i.e., its takeoff time. In case there's no runway available, the airplane is enqueued for an eventual landing.

Listing 8-8. RunwayAvailable() and TryToLand() Methods

```
    public intRunwayAvailable()
    {
        return _runways.ToList().IndexOf(false);
    }

    public bool TryToLand(Airplane newPlane)
    {
varrunwayIndex = RunwayAvailable();
        if (runwayIndex>= 0)
        {
            _runways[runwayIndex] = true;
newPlane.RunwayOccupied = runwayIndex;
newPlane.TimeToTakeOff = _processCargoDistribution.
SampleAt(newPlane.PassengersCount);
```

```
Console.WriteLine("Plane {0} landed successfully", newPlane.Id);
Console.WriteLine("Plane {0} time for take off {1} mins",
newPlane.Id, Math.Round(newPlane.TimeToTakeOff, 2));
                return true;
            }

            _waitingToLand.Enqueue(newPlane);
            return false;
        }
    }
```

To initialize and test the simulation we can rely upon the code shown in Listing 8-9, which corresponds to a console application in C#.

Listing 8-9. Initiating the Simulation

```
var airplanes = new List<Airplane>
                            {
                                new Airplane(100),
                                new Airplane(300),
                                new Airplane(50),
                                new Airplane(250),
                                new Airplane(150),
                                new Airplane(200),
                                new Airplane(120)
                            };

var sim = new Simulation.Airport.Simulation(new TimeSpan(0, 13,
0, 0), new TimeSpan(0, 15, 0, 0), airplanes);
sim.Execute();
```

Once we execute the simulation we will get a peek at the various events taking place in the simulation, such as time, airplane arriving, airplane taking off, airplane broke down, and so on. These will all be printed in the console application, as Figure 8-4 illustrates.

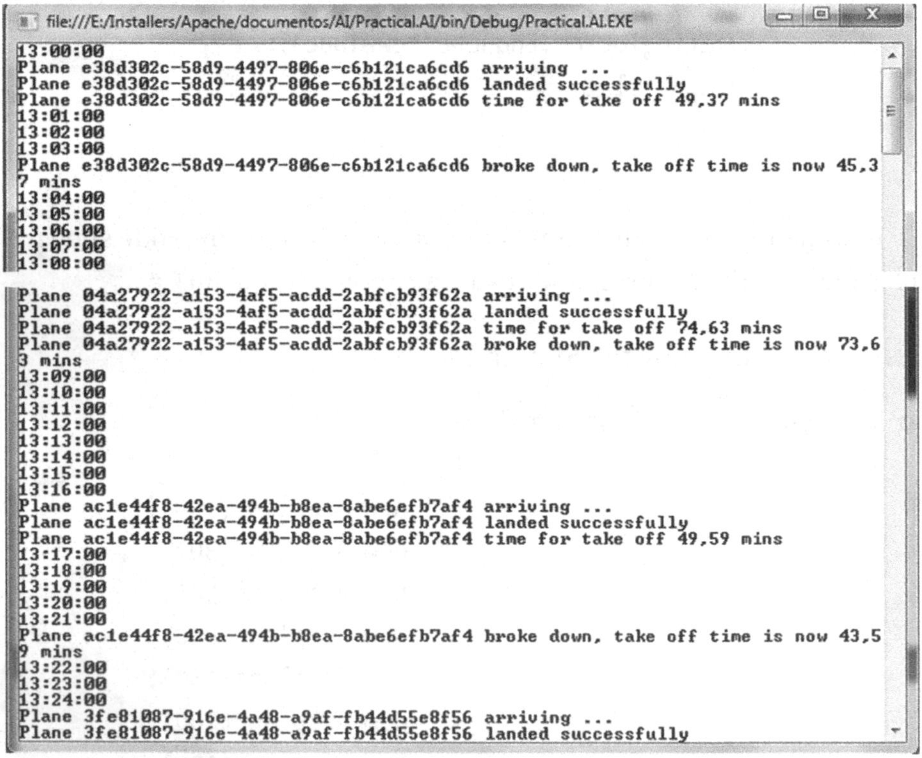

Figure 8-4. Console application displaying diverse events occurring at the simulation

In our airport simulation we considered events such as arrival, departures, and breakdowns. As usual, the suggestion to the reader is to try to expand the simulation and consider new events or maybe adjust the parameters to make them fit a more realistic scenario.

Summary

Throughout this chapter, we introduced the concepts of modeling and simulation. We described what a discrete-events simulation (DES) is and also described its components (events, queue, and so forth). We studied various probabilistic distributions and their relation to simulation applications. Ultimately, we presented a full example where we simulated the functioning of an airport during a given time and were able to see how every piece came together to create a program that simulated the working hours of an airport while considering several events (arrivals, departures, breakdowns). In the following chapter, we will start diving into the interesting and vast world of supervised learning.

CHAPTER 9

Support Vector Machines

In this chapter, we'll begin the study of *supervised learning*, a branch of machine learning whose algorithms resemble the type of learning we would have at school where we learn from experience and from many examples introduced by a professor during class or training.

Many supervised learning algorithms are composed of two phases: a training phase where the learner is presented with a set of training data, having each data as a vector along with its correct classification, and a prediction phase where the learner, having learned the function that corresponds to the training data, is now supposed to predict the correct classification or value of new incoming data. For instance, a training data set could be defined as follows:

```
{ { (2, 3), 1}, { (1, 1), -1}, { (3, 3), 1}  }
```

Notice that each pair (x, y) is accompanied by a classification or class, in this case 1 or -1.

The training data is usually expressed as a pair (v, c) where v is an n-dimensional vector (typically known as a *feature vector*) representing different properties of an object and c is the classification or label of that object considering the problem at hand. The object could be anything, from people, flowers, and chemical compounds to cities, states, and

© Arnaldo Pérez Castaño 2018
A. Pérez Castaño, *Practical Artificial Intelligence*,
https://doi.org/10.1007/978-1-4842-3357-3_9

basically anything we can imagine or can be classified. The vector could indicate various properties of the object, such as location, height, weight, strength, sex, population, oxygen, and so on.

In general, the learning process of a classification (we'll examine soon what *classification* means in this context) supervised learning algorithm follows the following points:

- *Training*: From the training data received as input, a function $f(x)$ is inferred. This function describes the structure of the data and attempts to classify new input data considering the structure learned from the training data.

- *Prediction*: Assuming a new data x has been received, it classifies it as $f(x)$; i.e., uses the learned function f to classify the new input data.

Two of the most significant problems that supervised learning tries to solve are *classification* and *regression*.

In the first type of problem, we map incoming data into a predefined, discrete number of categories. Therefore, we categorize incoming data by labeling it with some class. In such cases, we claim that the supervised learning algorithm is a *classifier*. In the latter problem, we do not categorize or classify an object; rather, we provide an estimate of the odds of some variable belonging to a class. In this type of problem we are interested in finding a good relation that represents the set of data. This relation could be embodied by the line that best approximates this set as it occurs in a type of regression known as *linear regression*; a method that solves this type of problem is known as a *regressor*.

Note   In classification algorithms, output variables take on discrete, categorical values. In regression algorithms, output variables take continuous, real values. A regression algorithm would predict the temperature on a given day; a classification algorithm would simply tell us whether it's going to be hot or not.

In Figure 9-1 we can graphically see the difference between a classifier and a regressor. The classifier (b) is able to partition the space into various subspaces or classes (two classes in Figure 9-1), and the regressor (a) simply tries to find a structure (line in Figure 9-1) that best approximates the shape of the set of data at hand; because this set has a linear structure a linear regressor is a good approximator.

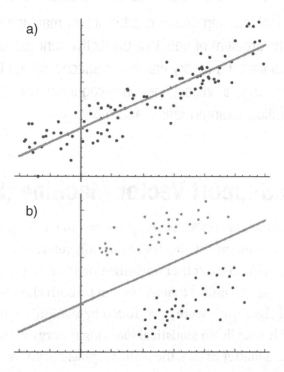

Figure 9-1.   *a) represents a regressor and b) represents a classifier*

Throughout this chapter, we'll be studying support vector machine algorithms, which are applied in data classification and consequently are regarded as classifiers. The purpose of this chapter is to describe the support vector machine algorithm and present the full code in C# of such an algorithm, accompanied by a visual application in Windows Forms to validate the results obtained(graphically shown) and serve as a tool for testing and clarification. We'll use two approaches when developing our support vector machine. One will use an optimization library to find a solution to the optimization problem that support vector machines attempt to solve, and the second will use Platt's Sequential Minimal Optimization (SMO) algorithm to find a solution for the same problem. We'll soon examine what element support vector machine provides us that allows us to predict the class of new incoming data.

Note   Statistical learning theory is a branch of machine learning dealing with the problem of finding a predictive function based on data. Statistical learning theory has led to successful applications in fields such as computer vision, speech recognition, text classification, pattern recognition, bioinformatics, and more.

What Is a Support Vector Machine (SVM)?

A *support vector machine* (SVM) is an optimization technique usually applied to classification problems. It's commonly referred to as a classifier but has also been adapted to other optimization problems such as regression; thus, we can affirm that SVMs can be both classifiers and regressors. SVM algorithms were introduced by Vladimir Vapnik during the 1960s and rely heavily on statistical learning theory and mathematical optimization. As a matter of fact, the training phase of an SVM reduces to solving an optimization problem that provides us with a set of weights and a value (bias) that allows us to classify new incoming data.

As occurs with many areas of machine learning, SVMs are about learning structure from data. In the binary classification case (only two classes), an SVM algorithm finds the hyperplane that gives the widest margin with respect to vectors on the frontier of each class.

A *hyperplane* of an n-dimensional space is the subspace of n - 1 dimension. For example, when $n = 1$ our space is a line, therefore its hyperplanes are points; when $n = 2$ our space is the usual two-dimensional coordinate space, thus its hyperplanes are lines; when $n = 3$ our space is the three-dimensional space, therefore its hyperplanes are two-dimensional planes, and so on. Figure 9-1 b) shows a two-dimensional space with an orange line that represents a hyperplane in that space.

Note   SVMs are used for text-classification tasks such as category assignment, detecting spam, and sentiment analysis. It is also commonly used for image-recognition challenges, performing particularly well in aspect-based recognition and color-based classification. SVMs also play a vital role in many areas of handwritten-digit recognition, such as postal-automation services.

We may also notice that this hyperplane separates the blue points from the red points; we can say that this is a *classifying hyperplane* because it's separating the space into two classes. As illustrated in Figure 9-2, there can be multiple classifying hyperplanes for a given classification problem.

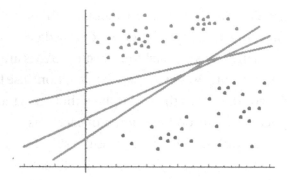

Figure 9-2. *Various possible classifying hyperplanes for a classification problem*

For future incoming data, not every hyperplane will have the same efficacy. Intuitively, we would like to have a classifying hyperplane that would produce the greatest margin between the two classes so that new data to be predicted will have a better chance of being correctly classified.

The distance between the hyperplane and the nearest data point from either set (blue or red points) is known as the *margin* (Figure 9-3). The goal of SVMs is to choose a classifying hyperplane with the greatest possible margin between the hyperplane and any point within the training set in either class. As mentioned before, this gives us a better chance of having new incoming data correctly classified; in this sense, we can affirm that SVMs search for the optimal hyperplane to classify data.

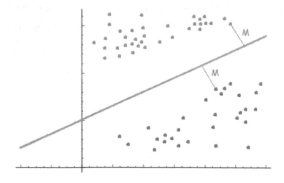

Figure 9-3. *Margin M defined by the classifying hyperplane*

To find the optimal hyperplane for a training data set we need to find the classifying hyperplane that provides the greatest possible margin between the two classes. As a result, the training phase of SVMs consists of an optimization problem (more precisely, a quadratic programming problem) where we maximize the value 2 x M; in other words, two times the margin will determine the full width of the "street" defined by the hyperplanes passing through the set of support vectors (Figure 9-4). Vectors defining this margin are known as *support vectors.*

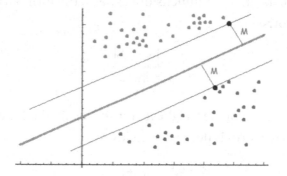

Figure 9-4. *Support vectors denoted as black points*

To obtain a formula for M, let's first remember that in a two-dimensional space the formula for a line (hyperplane in 2D) is $Ax + By + C = 0$. This expression can be generalized to the point of deducing the general expression of any hyperplane according to the formula $wx + b = 0$, where w is a vector known as *weight vector* and b (matches C in the line equation) is a real value known as *bias* or *intercept*; this value determines the shift of the hyperplane from the origin of its space. Therefore, when $b = 0$ it means the hyperplane passes through the origin $(0, 0, ... 0)$; w is a normal vector to the hyperplane and defines its orientation.

Now that we have a formula for the hyperplane, we can obtain the value of M by finding the distance from the support vectors (marked as black points in Figure 9-4) to the hyperplane. Recall that in a two-dimensional space the distance from a point (x', y') to a line is given by the following formula:

$$M = \frac{|Ax' + By' + C|}{\sqrt{A^2 + B^2}}$$

In general form, in the n-dimensional space, the formula for M can be deduced as follows:

$$M = \frac{|wx + b|}{\|w\|}$$

where $\|w\|$ is the norm of the weight vector w. Recall that for a vector $v = (v1, v2 \ldots vn)$ its norm is defined as follows:

$$\|v\| = v_1^{\ 2} + v_2^{\ 2} + \ldots + v_n^{\ 2}$$

Any hyperplane can be represented in an infinite number of ways by scaling w and b. This type of normalization or scaling is analogous to the type of scaling we use with percentages sometimes; instead of referring to a percentage as 85 percent we simply work with numbers in the range [0, 1] and find a direct mapping from 85 percent to the equivalent 0.85. In our case, we have the classifying hyperplane and also two other hyperplanes that are parallel to the classifying hyperplane and pass through the support vectors of each class. By means of normalization, we can express these hyperplanes as follows:

$$wx + b = 1$$
$$wx + b = -1$$

This representation is known as the *canonical hyperplane*; under this representation, assuming a normalization of values and the fact that we are trying to find the distance from a point in the classifying hyperplane to any of the hyperplanes formed by support vectors, we can adjust M's equation as follows:

$$M = \frac{|wx + b|}{\|w\|} = \frac{1}{\|w\|}$$

Thus, the total margin to be maximized would be $2 \times M = 2 / \|w\|$. Notice that maximizing this value is equivalent to minimizing the following:

$$\frac{\|w\|^2}{2}$$

At this point we know we need to minimize the previous function in order to find a (weight vector, bias) pair that maximizes the margin between the classifying hyperplane and both classes. Now we need to define under what set of constraints such optimization will occur.

We already have an equation for the hyperplanes passing through support vectors. Since support vectors define the border of each class in space, these hyperplanes determine our constraints, as we need every data point to be on one side or the other of these hyperplanes (Figure 9-5). Thus, we end up having the following constraints:

$$wx + b \geq 1$$

$$wx + b \leq -1$$

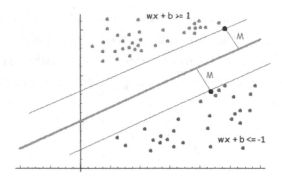

Figure 9-5. *Blue points satisfy equation wx + b >= 1 and red points satisfy equation wx + b <= -1*

The first equation applies to the case when the classification of data point *x* equals *yi* = 1; otherwise when *yi* = -1. Remember for each data point *x* we have its corresponding classification in the data-set training.

The previous constraints can be combined into one:

$$y_i \left(wx_i + b \right) \geq 1$$

Finally, the optimization problem that SVMs solve is formulated as follows:

$$\min_{w,\, b} \frac{\|w\|^2}{2}$$

$$\text{subject to:} \ \ y_i \left(wx_i + b \right) \geq 1$$

Let's remember at this moment that the optimization problem just presented corresponds to a linear SVM classifier; in other words, we are assuming the set of training data to be linearly separable. The SVM classifier function would then be as follows:

$$\text{sign} \left(wx + b \right)$$

$$\text{sign}(x) = \begin{cases} -1 & \text{if } x < 0 \\ 0 & \text{if } x = 0 \\ 1 & \text{if } x > 0 \end{cases}$$

Note that if *wx + b >= 1* then data point *x* belongs to class 1; otherwise, *x* belongs to class -1. As we can see, merely having *w, b* as the weight vector and bias of the optimal classifying hyperplane will allow us to classify new incoming data.

Even though at the moment we have reached a formulation for an optimization problem whose solution would indeed lead us to finding the maximum margin of a classifying hyperplane, this formulation is typically disregarded for one that facilities the computational effort and the optimization itself. This new formulation is based on Lagrange multipliers and the Wolfe dual-problem equivalence.

Duality represents a key role in optimization theory, and many optimization problems have an associated optimization problem called the *dual*. This alternative formulation of the problem possesses a set of solutions that are related to the solutions of the original (known as *primal*) problem. In particular, for a broad class of problems the primal solutions can be easily calculated from the dual ones. Moreover, in the specific case of the problem we are dealing with in this chapter, the dual formulation provides us with easier-to-handle constraints that are also well suited for kernel functions (we'll examine them soon).

A constrained optimization problem such as ours can be solved by means of the *Lagrangian method*. This method allows us to find the maximum or minimum of a multi-variable function subject to a set of constraints. It reduces the constrained problem to an unconstrained problem by adding *n + k* variables, *k* being the number of constraints of the original problem. These new variables are known as *Lagrange multipliers*. Using this transformation, the resulting problem will include equations that are easier to solve than the ones in the original problem.

The Lagrangian of a function $f(x)$ having constraints $g_i(x)=0 (i=1...m)$ is the following:

$$L(x, \alpha) = f(x) + \sum_{i=1}^{m} \alpha_i g_i(x)$$

Notice the new formulation has no constraints; they have been encapsulated in the only function now present, L(x, α). In this case, the α_i represents the Lagrangian multipliers. Let's substitute the objective function and constraints of our primal problem into L(w, b, α):

$$L(w, b, \alpha) = \frac{\|w\|^2}{2} - \sum_{i=1}^{m} \alpha_i \left(y_i (wx_i + b) - 1 \right)$$

The previous expression uses the *generalized Lagrangian* form that not only encompasses equality constraints but also inequalities $g_i(x) \le 0$ or equivalently $-g_i(x) \ge 0$. Once we have introduced the Lagrangian multipliers, we just need to find the dual form of the problem. In particular, we'll find the Wolfe dual form of the problem. For this purpose, we minimize L with respect to w, b, which is achieved by solving the following equations where $\nabla_x L(w, b, \alpha)$ denotes the gradient of L with respect to x:

$$\nabla_w L(w, b, \alpha) = 0$$

$$\nabla_b L(w, b, \alpha) = 0$$

The derivative of L with respect to w yields the following result:

$$\nabla_w L(w, b, \alpha) = w - \sum_{i=1}^{m} \alpha_i y_i x_i = 0$$

This implies the following:

$$w = \sum_{i=1}^{m} \alpha_i y_i x_i$$

As for the gradient with respect to b, the result is as follows:

$$\nabla_b L(w, b, \alpha) = \sum_{i=1}^{m} \alpha_i y_i = 0$$

Substituting the new formula obtained for w and considering that $\sum_{i=1}^{m} \alpha_i y_i = 0$, we can adjust L(w, b, α) as follows:

$$L(w, b, \alpha) = \sum_{i=1}^{m} \alpha_i - \frac{1}{2} \sum_{i, j=1}^{m} y_i y_j \alpha_i \alpha_j x_i x_j$$

Notice that since x_i, x_j are vectors, $x_i x_j$ denotes their inner product. So, finally, we have reached the expression of the dual problem, and in fact the optimization problem that most SVM libraries and packages solve because of the advantages previously mentioned. The complete optimization problem would be as follows:

$$\max_{\alpha} L(w, b, \alpha) = \sum_{i=1}^{m} \alpha_i - \frac{1}{2} \sum_{i, j=1}^{m} y_i y_j \alpha_i \alpha_j x_i x_j$$

$$\text{s.t} \quad \sum_{i=1}^{m} \alpha_i y_i = 0$$

$$\alpha_i \geq 0 \quad i = 1, \ldots m$$

In the next section, we'll see a practical problem where the previous problem (dual) will be solved using an optimization library in C#. Such a problem will help us understand some of the concepts and ideas that have been introduced in this chapter.

Note   The gradient of a function *f* is usually denoted by the symbol
∇ preceding the function name (∇f). It's a vector formed by the
derivatives of *f* with respect to every variable and indicates the
direction of the maximum increment of *f* at a given point. For
instance, assuming *f* is the function that maps every point in space
with a given pressure, then the gradient will indicate the direction in
which pressure will change more quickly from any point (*x*, *y*, *z*).

Practical Problem: Linear SVM in C#

To develop our Linear SVM, we will create a class named
LinearSvmClassifier that has the following fields or properties
(Listing 9-1).

Listing 9-1. Properties and Fields of Our Linear SVM

```
public class LinearSvmClassifier
{
        public List<TrainingSample>TrainingSamples{ get; set; }
        public double[] Weights;
        public double Bias;
        public List<Tuple<double, double>>SetA{ get; set; }
        public List<Tuple<double, double>>SetB{ get; set; }
        public List<Tuple<double, double>> Hyperplane
        { get; set; }
        private readonlydouble[] _alphas;
public intModelToUse = 1;
```

```
public LinearSvmClassifier(IEnumerable<TrainingSample>training
Samples)
        {
TrainingSamples = new List<TrainingSample>(trainingSamples);
        Weights = new double[TrainingSamples.First().
        Features.Length];
SetA = new List<Tuple<double, double>>();
SetB = new List<Tuple<double, double>>();
        Hyperplane = new List<Tuple<double, double>>();
        _alphas = new double[TrainingSamples.Count];
    }
}

public class TrainingSample
{
        public int Classification { get; set; }
        public double[] Features { get; set; }

        public TrainingSample(double [] features, int
        classification)
        {
        Features = new double[features.Length];
Array.Copy(features, Features, features.Length);
        Classification = classification;
    }
  }
```

Each property or field is described as follows:

- TrainingSamples: list of TrainingSample objects;
  each object represents a data point accompanied by
  its classification. The TrainingSample class illustrated
  in Listing 9-1 merely consists of a Features array of
  doubles and an integer Classification.

- `Weights`: double array representing the weights in an SVM model

- `Bias`: double value representing the bias or intercept in an SVM model

- `SetA`: list of `Tuple<double, double>` representing points in the training data that satisfy $wx + b >= 1$. It's only used in the prediction stage.

- `SetB`: list of `Tuple<double, double>` representing points in the training data that satisfy $wx + b <= -1$. It's only used in the prediction stage.

- `Hyperplane`: list of `Tuple<double, double>` representing points in the training data that satisfy $wx + b = 0$; i.e., points that lie in the hyperplane. It's only used in the prediction stage.

- `_alphas`: array of doubles representing the alphas in the dual problem in SVMs

- `ModelToUse`: determines the training method used during the training phase of our SVM

The `Training()` method where we encoded the dual-optimization problem is illustrated in Listing 9-2. We are using the Accord.NET library as an optimization tool for solving the SVM model. You can download Accord.NET from Nuget via the web or by using the Nuget Package Manager provided by Visual Studio.

Listing 9-2. Training() Method Where We Model the Dual-Optimization Problem Using Accord.NET

```
public void Training()
{
var coefficients = new Dictionary<Tuple<int, int>, double>();
ModelToUse = 1;

        for (vari = 0; i<TrainingSamples.Count; i++)
        {
            for (var j = 0; j <TrainingSamples.Count; j++)
coefficients.Add(new Tuple<int, int>(i, j),
                            -1 * TrainingSamples[i].
Classification * TrainingSamples[j].Classification *
TrainingSamples[i].Features.Dot(TrainingSamples[j].Features));
        }

var q = new double[TrainingSamples.Count, TrainingSamples.Count];
q.SetInitValue(coefficients);

        // This variable contains (1, 1, ..., 1)
var d = Enumerable.Repeat(1.0, TrainingSamples.Count).ToArray();
var objective = new QuadraticObjectiveFunction(q, d);

        // sum(ai * yi) = 0
var constraints = new List<LinearConstraint>
                                {
                                        new LinearConstraint(d)
                                        {
VariablesAtIndices=Enumerable.Range(0, TrainingSamples.Count).
ToArray(),
ShouldBe = ConstraintType.EqualTo,
                                                Value = 0,
```

```
CombinedAs = TrainingSamples.Select(t =>t.Classification).
ToArray().ToDouble()
                                                    }
                                    };

// 0 <= ai
            for (vari = 0; i<TrainingSamples.Count; i++)
            {
constraints.Add(new LinearConstraint(1)
                                    {
VariablesAtIndices = new[] { i },
ShouldBe = ConstraintType.GreaterThanOrEqualTo,
                                        Value = 0
                                    });
            }

var solver = new GoldfarbIdnani(objective, constraints);
            if (solver.Maximize())
            {
var solution = solver.Solution;
UpdateWeightVector(solution);
UpdateBias();
            }
            else
Console.WriteLine("Error ...");
 }
```

To solve the optimization problem, we'll be making use of the constraint-optimization problem solver GoldfarbIdnani; this and many others can be found in the Accord.NET library. There exist different ways to specify the objective function and constraints in the constructor of the GoldfarbIdnani class; in this case we have opted

to indicate the objective as a `QuadracticObjectiveFunction` class
and the set of constraints as instances of the `LinearConstraint` class.
The `QuadracticObjectiveFunction`, which represents the objective
function, was declared by specifying the Hessian matrix of the
objective function and the vector of linear terms. As we can see from
Listing 9-2, the `Training()` method starts by storing a set of values
into a `Dictionary<Tuple<int, int>, double>`, where the first item
(`Tuple<inti, int j>`) indicates the variables i, j to which the coefficient
belongs in the Hessian matrix.

Note   The Hessian matrix H of a function f of n variables is an $n \times n$
matrix containing the second derivatives of f with respect to each of
the n variables. We can say that f is convex if and only if H is positive
semidefinite; i.e., all its eigenvalues are positive.

The Hessian of the objective function with respect to variables α_i has
the following form:

$$-1 * \left[y_i y_j x_i x_j \right]_{mxm}$$

This matrix is negative semidefinite, which indicates that our problem
is concave, not convex. If H is positive semidefinite our problem is convex,
meaning any optimizer that converges to a local minimum will converge
to a global minimum because the two sets of minima coincide for convex
problems. Moreover, this can be accomplished in polynomial time and
can exploit the quadratic structure of the problem; therefore, it will be fast
in practice. On the contrary, if H has at least one negative eigenvalue then
your problem is nonconvex. When H has at least one negative eigenvalue,
the problem is known to be NP-hard.

The set of linear constraints is easily defined in the `Training()` method
using Accord.NET objects and properties, which are self-explanatory;

the only property that could raise some doubts is the CombineAs property
of the LinearConstraint object. CombineAs allows us to indicate
the scalar coefficients accompanying the variables specified in the
VariablesAtIndices property, in this case $\alpha_i y_i$.

The UpdateWeightVector() and UpdateBias() methods shown in
Listing 9-3 are in charge of updating the weight vector and bias according
to the formulas previously described.

Listing 9-3. Methods for Updating Weights and Bias of the
Classifying Hyperplane

```
private void UpdateWeightVector(double [] alphas)
    {
varlen = TrainingSamples.First().Features.Length;

        for (vari = 0; i<len; i++)
        {
            for (var j = 0; j <TrainingSamples.Count; j++)
                Weights[i] += TrainingSamples[j].
                Classification*alphas[j]*
TrainingSamples[j].Features[i];
        }
    }

    private void UpdateBias()
        {
var x = TrainingSamples.First().Features;
        Bias = 1;

        for (vari = 0; i<x.Length; i++)
            Bias -= Weights[i] * x[i];
}
```

There's one final method used within the `Training()` method that must be explained: the `SetInitValue()` method, which belongs to an extension class that we created to simplify the code and avoid unnecessary loops and ideas that do not correspond to the core functionality of the methods that actually use them. This extension class, along with its methods, is illustrated in Listing 9-4.

Listing 9-4. Class with Extension Methods

```
public static class ArrayDoubleExtended
{
    public static void SetInitValue(this double[,] q,
    Dictionary<Tuple<int, int>, double> coefficients,
    double epsilon = 0.000001)
    {
        for (vari = 0; i<q.GetLength(0); i++)
        {
            for (var j = 0; j <q.GetLength(1); j++)
            {
q[i, j] = coefficients[new Tuple<int, int>(i, j)];
                if (i == j)
q[i, j] -= epsilon;
            }
        }
    }

    public static IEnumerable<int>GetIndicesFromValues(this
    double [] toCompare, params double [] values)
    {
var result = new List<int>();

        for (vari = 0; i<toCompare.Length; i++)
            if (values.Contains(toCompare[i]))
result.Add(i);
```

```
            return result;
        }

        public static IEnumerable<double>RoundValues(this
        double [] list, int decimals)
        {
var result = new double[list.Length];

            for (vari = 0; i<list.Length; i++)
                result[i] = Math.Round(list[i], decimals);

            return result;
        }
    }
```

The SetInitValue() method fills the values of the Hessian matrix with those of the coefficient dictionary formerly explained. Note the epsilon value decrementing every value in the main diagonal by a tiny quantity. This is necessary since our function is not convex; therefore, we alter these values just a little bit, looking to change it into a positive semidefinite matrix. We must later consider the numerical error that will derive from this twist. The GoldfarbIdnani solver will not give us a solution if the matrix does not satisfy this condition.

The GetIndicesFromValues() method saves indices of the values contained in both arrays, and RoundValues() rounds an array of values by the number of decimals indicated. Finally, the Predict() method is shown in Listing 9-5.

Listing 9-5. Predict() Method

```
public void Predict(IEnumerable<double[]>elems)
{
varroundWeights = Weights.RoundValues(2).ToArray();
varroundBias = new [] {Bias}.RoundValues(2).ToArray();
```

```
foreach (var e in elems)
            {
var @class = Math.Sign(e.Dot(roundWeights) +  ModelToUse *
roundBias.First());
                if (@class >= 1)
SetA.Add(new Tuple<double, double>(e[0], e[1]));
                else if (@class <= -1)
SetB.Add(new Tuple<double, double>(e[0], e[1]));
                else
Hyperplane.Add(new Tuple<double, double>(e[0], e[1]));
            }
}
```

In the Predict() method, we start by rounding the weights and bias values, then for each element or new data point we get its class by using the hyperplane equation that is well known to us already ($wx + b$). If its class is greater than or equal to 1 we add it to SetA; if it's less than or equal to -1 we add it to SetB; otherwise it must be that $wx + b = 0$ and so it belongs to the classifying hyperplane.

In order to test our hyperplane equation and see how well it separates or classifies our data points, we have created a Windows Forms application that uses the OxyPlot library to plot the graphic. You can obtain OxyPlot via the web on Nuget or by using the Nuget Package Manager included with Visual Studio. Listing 9-6 shows the SvmGui class of our Windows Forms application.

Listing 9-6. SvmGui Windows Forms Class Where We Plot the Results Obtained

```
public partial class SvmGui : Form
    {
        private readonlyMainViewModel _plot;
```

```
        public SvmGui(double [] weights, double bias, int
        model, IEnumerable<Tuple<double, double>>setA,
        IEnumerable<Tuple<double, double>>setB,
        IEnumerable<Tuple<double, double>> hyperplane = null)
        {
InitializeComponent();

            _plot = new MainViewModel(weights, bias, model,
            setA, setB, hyperplane);
var view = new OxyPlot.WindowsForms.PlotView
                        {
                            Width = Width,
                            Height = Height,
                            Parent = this,
BackColor = Color.WhiteSmoke,
                            Model = _plot.Model
                        };
        }
    }
```

As we can see, the class is very simple; we just need to create a
PlotModel, which is done by the MainViewModel class, and a PlotView
that displays this model. The MainViewModel class is illustrated in
Listing 9-7.

Listing 9-7. MainViewModel Class Where the Model to Be Plotted Is
Created

```
public class MainViewModel
    {
        public PlotModel Model { get; set; }
```

```
public MainViewModel(double[] weights, double
bias, int model, IEnumerable<Tuple<double,
double>>setA, IEnumerable<Tuple<double, double>>setB,
IEnumerable<Tuple<double, double>> hyperplane = null)
{
    Model = new PlotModel{ Title = "SVM by SMO" };
varscatterPointsA = setA.Select(e => new ScatterPoint(e.Item1,
e.Item2)).ToList();
varscatterPointsB = setB.Select(e => new ScatterPoint(e.Item1,
e.Item2)).ToList();
var h = new List<ScatterPoint>();

    if (hyperplane != null)
        h = hyperplane.Select(e => new ScatterPoint
        (e.Item1, e.Item2)).ToList(); ;

varscatterSeriesA = new ScatterSeries
                                {
MarkerFill = OxyColor.FromRgb(255, 0, 0),
ItemsSource = scatterPointsA,
                                };
varscatterSeriesB = new ScatterSeries
                                {
MarkerFill = OxyColor.FromRgb(0, 0, 255),
ItemsSource = scatterPointsB
                                };

varscatterSeriesH = new ScatterSeries
                                {
MarkerFill = OxyColor.FromRgb(0, 255, 255),
ItemsSource = h
                                };
```

339

```
Model.Series.Add(scatterSeriesA);
Model.Series.Add(scatterSeriesB);
Model.Series.Add(scatterSeriesH);
Model.Series.Add(GetFunction(weights, bias, model));
        }

        public FunctionSeriesGetFunction(double [] w, double b,
        int model)
        {
const int n = 10;
var series = new FunctionSeries();

            for (var x = 0.0; x < n; x += 0.01)
{
for (var y = 0.0; y < n; y += 0.01)
{
                    //adding the points based x,y
varfunVal = GetValue(x, y, w, b, model);

                    if (Math.Abs(funVal) <= 0.001)
series.Points.Add(new DataPoint(x, y));
                }
            }

        return series;
        }

        public double GetValue(double x, double y, double [] w,
        double b, int model)
        {
            w = w.RoundValues(5).ToArray();
            b = new [] {b}.RoundValues(5).ToArray().First();
            return w[0] * x  + w[1] * y + model * b;
        }
    }
```

The constructor of the class receives all necessary values (weights, bias, etc.) and creates different scatter-point series: one for points satisfying $wx + b >= 1$, another for points satisfying $wx + b <= -1$, and lastly one for points in the hyperplane—those that satisfy $wx + b = 0$. Additionally, the GetFunction() method plots the line corresponding to the hyperplane. Note that in this case we are considering the numeric error introduced by adding epsilon to values in the main diagonal of the Hessian matrix; therefore, we accept as hyperplane points those that yield a class value less than or equal to 0.001. The GetValue() method finds the class of the incoming data using our RoundValues() extension method.

We can run the code from a console application as shown in Listing 9-8.

Listing 9-8. Console Application Where Our SVM Will Be Created and Executed

```
vartrainingSamples = new List<TrainingSample>
                            {
                                    new TrainingSample(new
                                    double[] {1, 1}, 1),
                                    new TrainingSample(new
                                    double[] {1, 0}, 1),
                                    new TrainingSample(new
                                    double[] {2, 2}, -1),
                                    new TrainingSample(new
                                    double[] {2, 3}, -1),
                            };

varsvmClassifier = new LinearSvmClassifier(trainingSamples);
svmClassifier.Training();
```

```
svmClassifier.Predict(new List<double[]>
                                    {
                                                new double[] {1, 1},
                                                new double[] {1, 0},
                                                new double[] {2, 2},
                                                new double[] {2, 3},
                                                new double[] {2, 0},
                                                new []    {2.5, 1.5},
                                                new []    {0.5, 1.5},
                                    });

Application.EnableVisualStyles();
Application.SetCompatibleTextRenderingDefault(false);
Application.Run(new SvmGui(svmClassifier.Weights,
svmClassifier.Bias, svmClassifier.ModelToUse, svmClassifier.
SetA, svmClassifier.SetB, svmClassifier.Hyperplane));
```

Once we execute the preceding code, the result obtained can be seen in Figure 9-6.

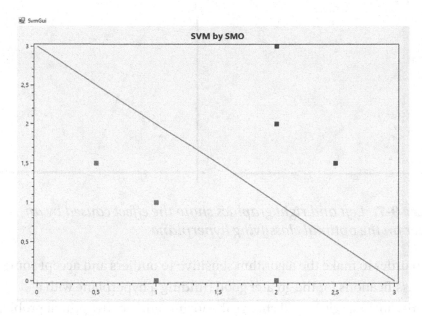

Figure 9-6. *Plot showing the classifying hyperplane and points on one side and the other*

So far we have assumed that the set is linearly separable, but what if it's not, or what if there's no perfect separation between the two classes? These concerns will be the main topic of the following sections, where we'll examine the non-linearly separable case of SVMs and the imperfect separation case.

Imperfect Separation

In some cases finding the optimal classifying hyperplane as we have considered it thus far is not the most suitable option. For instance, Figure 9-7 illustrates the effect an outlier point has on deciding the optimal classifying hyperplane. The single red point on the upper-left corner of the right graphic is causing the hyperplane to significantly swing, changing its direction and resulting in a much smaller margin than the one on the left graphic.

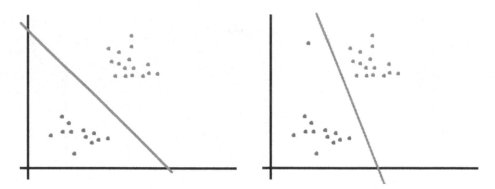

Figure 9-7. *Left and right graphics show the effect caused by an outlier on the optimal classifying hyperplane*

In order to make the algorithm sensitive to outliers and accept some misclassifications for the greater good (finding a hyperplane with a considerable margin), we'll change the formulation of the primal problem and introduce a set of *slack* variables and a constant C that will control how the misclassification will be handled.

The new formulation of the primal problem is the following:

$$\min_{w,\, b} \frac{\|w\|^2}{2} + C\sum_{i=1}^{m} \xi_i$$
$$\text{subject to}: y_i\left(wx_i + b\right) \geq 1 - \xi_i$$
$$\xi_i \geq 0 \ i = 1\ldots m$$

A direct result of this reformulation is that training data is now permitted to have a margin of less than 1, and whenever a training data has a functional margin of $1 - \xi_i$ ($\xi > 0$), that cost or penalization is paid at the objective function, which is increased by $C * \xi_i$. The parameter C controls the relative weighting between the goals of making $\|w\|^2$ small (as we examined earlier, this makes the margin large) and ensuring that most training data will have a margin of at least 1.

Seeking to reach the dual form again, we introduce the Lagrangian form and set the derivatives with respect to w and b to zero again. We will skip the full calculation, which is left to the reader; the final result would be the following:

$$\max_{\alpha} L(w, b, \alpha) = \sum_{i=1}^{m} \alpha_i - \frac{1}{2} \sum_{i,\,j=1}^{m} y_i y_j \alpha_i \alpha_j x_i x_j$$

$$\text{s.t} \quad \sum_{i=1}^{m} \alpha_i y_i = 0$$

$$0 \le \alpha_i \le C \ i = 1, \ldots m$$

As we can see, the dual form of the reformulated problem is basically the same as before; the only difference lies in the fact that the previous $\alpha_i \ge 0$ constraint is now the box constraint $0 \le \alpha_i \le C$. The calculation of b also changes; we'll see it shortly when we examine the SMO algorithm.

Note   The reformulated problem is known as the soft-margin SVM as opposed to the hard-margin SVM described before. For a soft-margin SVM, we allow training data to lie inside the margin, or to be misclassified, and we want the overall error measured by the sum of slack variables to be minimized.

Non-linearly Separable Case: Kernel Trick

Up to this point, we have assumed the training data set to be linearly separable, but what happens when neither the training data set nor the function being learned have a linear structure? This scenario is illustrated in Figure 9-8.

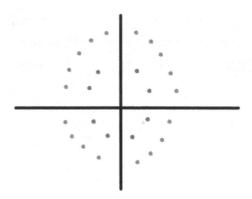

Figure 9-8. *Non-linear case*

As the reader can verify, there's no possible way to divide the two classes (red and blue points) in the graphic using a hyperplane. What's the solution in this scenario? The SVM solution is to map or transform the training data into a higher, richer space; find a classifying hyperplane in that higher space and then transform the result back to the original space. The mapping is accomplished through a *feature mapping* function that goes from the original space (R^2 in the previous example) to a higher space (R^3), thus increasing the dimensionality of the data (Figure 9-9).

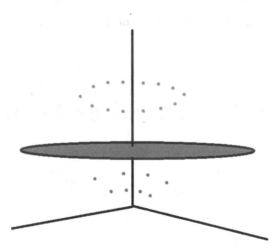

Figure 9-9. *Data mapped from 2D space into 3D space*

For instance, a polynomial feature mapping $\varphi : R^2 \to R^3$ would transform the data as follows:

$$(x, y) \to \left(x^2, \sqrt{2} * xy, y^2 \right)$$

The decision function would now change its formulation to adjust to the new dimension of data as follows:

$$f(x) = w \cdot \varphi(x) + b$$

One problem with this approach is that the dimensionality of $\varphi(x)$ can get very large on some occasions; this would complicate the quadratic problem to be solved and also the explicit representation of w. Fortunately for us, sections ago we obtained the dual form of the problem in terms only of α_i and as an alternative for expressing w; hence, the new decision equation or classifying hyperplane equation can be stated as follows:

$$f(x) = \sum_{i=1}^{m} \alpha_i \varphi(x_i) \cdot x + b$$

In this context, we say that $K(x_i, x) = \varphi(x_i) \cdot \varphi(x)$ is a *kernel* function; this function will replace any inner product we may have in our formulation. The key point when using kernel functions is that the cost of computing their value can be significantly lower when compared to the cost of computing or even representing $\varphi(x)$; computing a kernel function does not imply computing $\varphi(x)$.

The *polynomial* kernel for instance, follows the formula shown here:

$$K(x, x') = (x \cdot x' + 1)^d$$

The reader can verify that computing this kernel will be far more efficient than computing explicitly $\varphi(x_i) \cdot \varphi(x)$, especially for large dimensions. Another relevant kernel is the *Gaussian* kernel, which is defined as

$$K(x', x) = e^{-\|x-x'\|^2 / 2\sigma^2}$$

where $\sigma > 0$, and it's chosen by the user. Intuitively, if $\varphi(x)$ and $\varphi(z)$ are close together, we might expect $K(x', x) = \varphi(x') \cdot \varphi(x)$ to be large. On the other hand, if $\varphi(x')$ and $\varphi(x)$ are far apart (nearly orthogonal to each other) then $K(x', x) = \varphi(x') \cdot \varphi(x)$ will be small. Thus, we can think of $K(x', x)$ as some measurement of how similar $\varphi(x')$ and $\varphi(x)$ are, or of how similar x' and x are.

The application of kernels is not reduced to SVMs. On the contrary, it has a much broader application in the area of artificial intelligence. Any learning algorithm that computes inner products can have them replaced by kernel functions, thus allowing a much more efficient way of working with higher-dimensional feature spaces.

Note   Not every function can be regarded as a kernel. It has been proven (Mercer's theorem) that a sufficient and necessary condition for a function to be considered a kernel is that its kernel matrix *K* be symmetric positive semidefinite. The kernel matrix associated with a training data set of *m* vectors is a square *m* x *m* matrix containing every possible combination of values *Kij = K(xi, xj)*.

Sequential Minimal Optimization Algorithm (SMO)

The *sequential minimal optimization (SMO)* algorithm was proposed by John Platt at Microsoft Research in 1998; at that time its purpose was to introduce an efficient method for training an SVM. Consequently, SMO avoids working with Quadratic Programming (QP) libraries and solves the optimization problem by analytically solving a large number of small optimization subproblems that involve any two Lagrange multipliers previously selected using a heuristic.

Two mathematical results or theorems are basic for understanding SMO's functioning. First, the *Karush-Kuhn-Tucker (KKT)* conditions as a generalization of Lagrange multipliers provide necessary, sufficient conditions for determining whether a solution of an optimization problem is optimal. Secondly, *Osuna's* theorem proves that a large QP problem can be broken down into a series of smaller QP subproblems. As long as at least one example that violates the KKT conditions is added to the examples for the previous subproblem, each step will reduce the overall objective function and maintain a feasible point that satisfies every constraint. Hence, a sequence of QP subproblems that always adds at least one violator will guarantee convergence. Osuna's theorem validates SMO's strategy of choosing only two multipliers when optimizing a QP subproblem of the major QP problem. In general, SMO heavily relies on the two previous results to justify its functioning.

Checking KKT conditions implies solving a system of equations where the gradient of the objective function plus all constraints and Lagrange multipliers are equal to zero. Having solved this system, which is left to the reader as an exercise, you would have the following conditions for the α_i to be considered as an optimal solution:

$$\alpha_i = 0 \leftrightarrow y_i u_i \geq 1$$
$$0 < \alpha_i < C \leftrightarrow y_i u_i = 1$$
$$\alpha_i = C \leftrightarrow y_i u_i \leq 1$$

In this case, u_i is the output or classification provided by the SVM for the *i*th training data. The geometric interpretations of these conditions are presented in Table 9-1.

Table 9-1. *Geometric Interpretation of Lagrange Multiplier Values and KKT Conditions*

Value	Interpretation
$\alpha_i = 0$	ith training data is correctly classified; might lie on the margin.
$0 < \alpha_i < C$	ith training data is correctly classified and lies on the margin (support vector).
$\alpha_i = C$	Three cases may arise in this scenario; either the ith training data is correctly classified and lies on the margin, or the ith training data is correctly classified and lies between the classifying hyperplane and the margin, or the ith data training is incorrectly classified because it is probably an outlier.

The SMO algorithm will terminate once all α_i satisfy the previous conditions to a certain, predefined tolerance, which is usually 10^{-3}.

Note   In Platt's original paper he assumed the formula for the classifying hyperplane to be *wx - b* instead of *wx + b*. Also, instead of maximizing the objective function *f(x)* of the dual problem described in this chapter, he minimized *-f(x)*; we know that's equivalent to our maximization problem because *min f(x) = max -f(x)*.

As described earlier, the algorithm optimizes two α_i at a time. First of all, and following Osuna's theorem, we must search for an α_i that violates KKT conditions; let this α_i be α_2. Then, using a heuristic, another α_i—let it be α_1—is also found. The first multiplier (α_2) is typically taken from the set of unbound multipliers (those that satisfy $0 < \alpha_i < C$).

Once we have selected α_2, the second multiplier α_1 is chosen to maximize $|E_1 - E_2|$, where $E_i = f(x_i) - y_i$ is the error committed by the SVM when correctly classifying the ith training data. This is the heuristic we mentioned before and is supposed to speed up the procedure. If we can't find such α_1 then we randomly choose an unbound training data point. If that also fails then we randomly choose any training data, and if *that* fails we reselect α_2.

After choosing α_1, α_2 the rest of the algorithm is reduced to updating these values. To carry out such an update we must guarantee that every α_i respects the constraints of the problem; i.e., $0 < \alpha_i < C$ and $\sum_{i=1}^{m} \alpha_i y_i = 0$. Since Osuna's theorem allows us to focus only on the QP subproblem composed of α_1, α_2 we must guarantee at each time that both Lagrange multipliers satisfy the following constraints:

$$0 < \alpha_1, \alpha_2 < C$$
$$\alpha_1 y_1 + \alpha_2 y_2 = k$$

The constraints that α_1, α_2 must satisfy can be graphically represented in a two-dimensional space as illustrated in Figure 9-10.

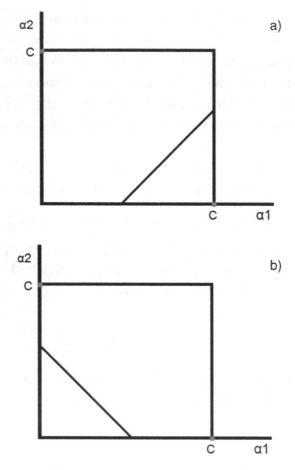

Figure 9-10. *Case a) occurs when y1 ≠ y2; case b) occurs when y1 = y2*

In order to maintain both α_1, α_2 in the constraint box and respect the linear constraint we must establish low (L) and high (H) bound values. If y1 ≠ y2 it can be proven that the following bounds apply to α_2:

$$L = \max\left(0, \alpha_2 - \alpha_1\right)$$
$$H = \min\left(C, C + \alpha_2 - \alpha_1\right)$$

If y1 = y2 then the line changes direction; therefore,

$$L = \max(0, \alpha_2 + \alpha_1 - C)$$
$$H = \min(C, \alpha_2 + \alpha_1)$$

Thus, the updated α_2—let's call it α_2^{new}, and we'll soon see how to compute it—after being calculated must be clipped against these bounds, and its clipped value would be as follows:

$$\alpha_2^{new, \, clipped} = \begin{cases} H & if \; \alpha_2^{new} \geq H \\ \alpha_2^{new} & if \; L < \alpha_2^{new} < C \\ L & if \; \alpha_2^{new} \leq L \end{cases}$$

Once we have obtained a final, clipped (if necessary) value for α_2^{new} we can easily obtain α_1^{new} using the equation of the linear constraint as shown in the next lines. In the α_1^{new} formula $s = y_1 y_2$ is a value introduced with the single purpose of clearing α_1^{new} from the following linear constraint equation:

$$\alpha_1^{new} = \alpha_1 + s\left(\alpha_2 - \alpha_2^{new, \, clipped}\right)$$

Up to this point we have gathered almost every piece of the SMO algorithm. Still, we are missing one very important component—the *learning rule* or *update rule* for α_2. Recall the objective function we want to optimize is as follows:

$$\min_{\alpha} L(w, b, \alpha) = \frac{1}{2} \sum_{i, \, j=1}^{m} y_i y_j \alpha_i \alpha_j K(x_i) K(x_j) - \sum_{i=1}^{m} \alpha_i$$

$$s.t \quad \sum_{i=1}^{m} \alpha_i y_i = 0$$

$$0 \leq \alpha_i \leq C \; i = 1, \ldots m$$

Note that this is the same problem we defined before but includes the kernel function *K* in the formulation and changes the objective from *max f(x)* to *min -f(x)*. This is the exact formulation solved in Platt's paper.

The expression for the update rule of α_2 is derived from the objective function by rewriting it in terms of α_1, α_2, then in terms of α_2 only (using the linear constraint equation), fixing all other α_i and finding the minimum of this rewritten objective by calculating its second derivative with respect to α_2. Rewriting it in terms of α_1, α_2 and fixing any other α_i term as a constant would yield the following:

$$\frac{1}{2}K_{11}\alpha_1^2 + \frac{1}{2}K_{22}\alpha_2^2 + sK_{12}\alpha_1\alpha_2 + v_1y_1\alpha_1 + v_2y_2\alpha_2 - \alpha_1 - \alpha_2 + P$$

where $K_{ij} = K(x_i, x_j)$, $v_i = \sum_{j=3}^{m} y_j\alpha_j K_{ij}$, $v_1y_1\alpha_1$ is the term that relates α_1 with all other variables, and equivalently $v_2y_2\alpha_2$ is the term that relates α_2 with all other variables. *P* is a constant representing the terms related to all other α_i. Using the linear constraint equation in the form

$$\alpha_1 + s\alpha_2 = w$$
$$s = y_1y_2$$

allows us to clear out α_1 from our rewritten equation and merely view it in terms of α_2.

$$\frac{1}{2}K_{11}(w - s\alpha_2)^2 + \frac{1}{2}K_{22}\alpha_2^2 + sK_{12}(w - s\alpha_2)\alpha_2$$
$$+ v_1y_1(w - s\alpha_2) + v_2y_2\alpha_2$$
$$- (w - s\alpha_2) - \alpha_2 + P$$

To find an expression of the minimum of the previous formulation, we find its second derivative with respect to α_2, which is the following:

$$(K_{11} + K_{22} - 2K_{12})\alpha_2 = s(K_{11} - K_{12})w + y_2(v_1 - v_2) + 1 - s$$

This takes into consideration that

$$v_i = \sum_{j=3}^{m} y_j \alpha_j K_{ij} = u_i + b^* - y_1 \alpha_1^* K_{1i} - y_2 \alpha_2^* K_{2i}$$

In the previous equation, every variable that has a subscript identifies its corresponding optimal value.

By substituting v_i and w in the second derivative formula and readjusting the terms we will finally obtain the update rule for α_2:

$$\alpha_2^{new} = \alpha_2 + \frac{y_2 (E_1 - E_2)}{K_{11} + K_{22} - 2K_{12}}$$

where $E_i = u_i - y_i$ and $K_{11} + K_{22} - 2K_{12}$ is known as the *learning rate* of the SVM.

One last step before diving into the implementation of the SMO algorithm is the calculation of the bias. We already know how to compute w, but what about the bias b? The bias will be computed as follows:

$$b_1 = E_1 + y_1 \left(\alpha_1^{new} - \alpha_1 \right) K_{11} + y_2 \left(\alpha_2^{new, \, clipped} - \alpha_2 \right) K_{12} + b$$
$$b_2 = E_2 + y_1 \left(\alpha_1^{new} - \alpha_1 \right) K_{12} + y_2 \left(\alpha_2^{new, \, clipped} - \alpha_2 \right) K_{22} + b$$

A mean of these values is calculated, so the final bias can be computed as follows:

$$b = \left(b_1 + b_2 \right) / 2$$

In case none of the α_i were clipped, it's guaranteed that $b = b_1 = b_2$. The new value for b is computed at the end of each step of the SMO algorithm. Having described every theoretical piece in detail, let's now look at the implementation of the algorithm in C#.

Practical Problem: SMO Implementation

The C# algorithm we'll describe in this section narrowly follows Platt's pseudocode seen in the original paper published in 1998. First, the access point to the algorithm is the TrainingBySmo() method shown in Listing 9-9; this is where the first α_i is selected. Also shown in Listing 9-9 is a tiny update that we need to do on our LinearSvmClassifier class, the one presented in previous sections and where the SMO algorithm will be embedded. This update consists of adding constant values *C*, *Epsilon*, and *Tolerance* as class properties or fields; additionally, every SMO-related method will be eventually added as well.

Listing 9-9. Start Point of the SMO Algorithm Where We Search for the First Lagrange Multiplier

```
public class LinearSvmClassifier
{
        private const double C = 0.5;
        private const double Epsilon = 0.001;
        private const double Tolerance = 0.001;
        ...
}

        public void TrainingBySmo()
        {
varnumChanged = 0;
varexamAll = true;
ModelToUse = -1;

            while (numChanged> 0 || examAll)
            {
```

```
numChanged = 0;
            if (examAll)
            {
                for (vari = 0; i<TrainingSamples.Count; i++)
numChanged += ExamineExample(i) ?1 : 0;
            }
            else
            {
var subset = _alphas.GetIndicesFromValues(0, C);
foreach (vari in subset)
numChanged += ExamineExample(i) ?1 : 0;
            }

            if (examAll)
examAll = false;
            else if (numChanged == 0)
examAll = true;
        }
    }
```

The `TrainingBySmo()` method declares two variables that will aid it in finding the two Lagrange multipliers: `numChanged` and `examAll`. The first, an integer variable, contains the number of unbound Lagrange multipliers suitable to accompany the first selected Lagrange multiplier α_2 to be optimized. If no unbound multiplier can be found, then `examAll` turns True, meaning all training data must be examined in the next loop execution.

The `ExamineExample()` method illustrated in Listing 9-10 starts by checking whether the given multiplier (α_2) violates the KKT conditions by more than the predefined tolerance value. Assuming it does, it then looks for the second Lagrange multiplier and jointly optimizes them by calling the `TakeStep()` method.

Listing 9-10. The ExamineExample() Method Looks for a Second
Lagrange Multiplier and Jointly Optimizes Them by Calling the
TakeStep() Method

```
        private bool ExamineExample(int i1)
        {
varyi = TrainingSamples[i1].Classification;
varai = _alphas[i1];
varerrorI = LFunctionValue(i1) - yi;

varri = yi * errorI;

            if ((ri< -Tolerance &&ai< C) ||
            (ri> Tolerance &&ai> 0))
            {
                for (var i2 = 0; i2 <TrainingSamples.Count; i2++)
                    if (TakeStep(i1, i2))
                        return true;
            }

            return false;
        }
```

The TakeStep() method (Listing 9-11) receives as arguments the
indices of the two selected Lagrange multipliers.

Listing 9-11. The TakeStep() Method Jointly Optimizes the Two
Lagrange Multipliers

```
        private bool TakeStep(inti, int j)
        {
            if (i == j)
                return false;
```

```
varyi = TrainingSamples[i].Classification;
varyj = TrainingSamples[j].Classification;

            // Checking bounds on aj
var s = yi*yj;
varerrorI = LFunctionValue(i) - yi;

            // Computing L, H
var l = Math.Max(0, _alphas[j] + _alphas[i] * s - (s + 1) / 2 * C);
var h = Math.Min(C, _alphas[j] + _alphas[i] * s - (s - 1) / 2 * C);

        if (l == h)
            return false;

        double newAj;

        // Obtaining new value for aj
var k12 = Kernel.Polynomial(2, TrainingSamples[i].Features,
TrainingSamples[j].Features);
var k11 = Kernel.Polynomial(2, TrainingSamples[i].Features,
TrainingSamples[i].Features);
var k22 = Kernel.Polynomial(2, TrainingSamples[j].Features,
TrainingSamples[j].Features);
var eta = 2*k12 - k11 - k22;
varerrorJ = LFunctionValue(j) - yj;

            if (eta < 0)
            {
newAj = _alphas[j] - TrainingSamples[j].
Classification*(errorI - errorJ)/eta;
                if (newAj< l)
newAj = l;
                else if (newAj> h)
newAj = h;
}
```

```
else
            {
var c1 = eta/2;
var c2 = yj * (errorI - errorJ) - eta * _alphas[j];
varlObj = c1*Math.Pow(l, 2) + c2*l;
varhObj = c1*Math.Pow(h, 2) + c2*h;

if (lObj>hObj + Epsilon)
newAj = l;
                else if (lObj<hObj - Epsilon)
newAj = h;
                else
newAj = _alphas[j];
            }

            if (Math.Abs(newAj - _alphas[j]) < Epsilon *
            (newAj + _alphas[j] + Epsilon))
                return false;

varnewAi = _alphas[i] - s * (newAj - _alphas[j]);
            if (newAi< 0)
            {
newAj += s*newAi;
newAi = 0;
            }
            else if (newAi> C)
            {
newAj += s * (newAi - C);
newAi = C;
            }
```

```
                // Updating bias & weight vector
UpdateBias(newAi, _alphas[i], newAj, _alphas[j], yi, yj,
errorI, errorJ, k11, k12, k22);
UpdateWeightVector(i, j, newAi, _alphas[i], newAj, _alphas[j],
yi, yj);

                _alphas[i] = newAi;
                _alphas[j] = newAj;

                return true;
        }
```

If the TakeStep() method achieves an optimization on both
Lagrange multipliers, then it returns True; otherwise, it returns False. The
LFunctionValue() and Kernel.Polynomial() methods are presented in
Listing 9-12. The first calculates the value of the objective function and the
latter is a static method of the Kernel class representing the polynomial
kernel. This class is intended to contain all kernel functions; since the
inner product is supposed to be a kernel function it has also been added to
this class.

Listing 9-12. LFunctionValue() Method, Which Calculates the Value
of the Objective Function and the Kernel Class

```
private double LFunctionValue(inti)
{
var result = 0.0;

for (int k = 0; k <TrainingSamples[i].Features.Length; k++)
result += Weights[k] * TrainingSamples[i].Features[k];

                result -= Bias;
                return result;
}
```

```
public class Kernel
{
        public static double Polynomial(double degree,
        double [] v1, double [] v2)
        {
            return Math.Pow(InnerProduct(v1, v2) + 1, degree);
        }

        private static double InnerProduct(double [] v1,
        double [] v2)
        {
var result = 0.0;

            for (vari = 0; i< v1.Length; i++)
                result += v1[i]*v2[i];

            return result;
        }
}
```

To conclude, let's present the methods in charge of updating the bias and weight vector of the SVM (Listing 9-13).

Listing 9-13. LFunctionValue() Method, Which Calculates the Value of the Objective Function and the Kernel Class

```
private void UpdateBias(double newAi, double oldAi, double newAj,
        double oldAj, double yi, double yj, double errorI,
        double errorJ,
        double k11, double k12, double k22)
        {
            double b1, b2, bNew;

            if (newAi> 0 &&newAi< C)
```

```
bNew = Bias + errorI + yi*(newAi - oldAi)*k11 + yj*(newAj -
oldAj)*k12;
            else
            {
                if (newAj> 0 &&newAj< C)
bNew = Bias + errorJ + yi * (newAi - oldAi) * k12 + yj *
(newAj - oldAj) * k22;
                else
                {
                    b1 = Bias + errorI + yi * (newAi - oldAi) *
                    k11 + yj * (newAj - oldAj) * k12;
                    b2 = Bias + errorJ + yi * (newAi - oldAi) *
                    k12 + yj * (newAj - oldAj) * k22;
bNew = (b1 + b2)/2;
                }
            }

            Bias = bNew;
        }

private void UpdateWeightVector(inti, int j, double newAi,
double oldAi,
        double newAj, double oldAj, double yi, double yj)
        {
var t1 = yi * (newAi - oldAi);
var t2 = yj * (newAj - oldAj);
varobjI = TrainingSamples[i].Features;
varobjJ = TrainingSamples[j].Features;

            for (var k = 0; k <objI.Length; k++)
                Weights[k] += t1 * objI[k] + t2 * objJ[k];
        }
```

Now that we have the entire SMO algorithm implemented, let's see the result, or classifying hyperplane, obtained by this algorithm, using the same graphical tool we used before (Windows Forms application, Figure 9-11).

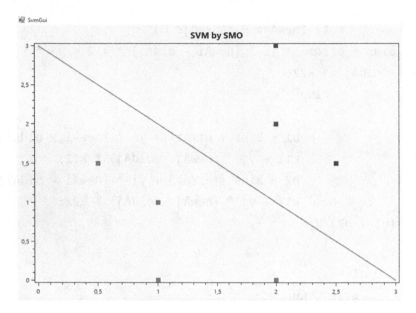

Figure 9-11. *Classifying hyperplane obtained by our implementation of the SMO algorithm*

A final question that has surely been on the reader's mind throughout this chapter is: How can I use SVMs for more than binary classification? How can I classify or label a new incoming data from a set of *n* classes? This problem, known as *multi-class SVM*, will not be addressed in detail in this book as it gets into methods that ultimately use the binary SVM classifier; we'll just give a general overview of them.

There are a lot of methods for multi-class SVM classification. Two classic options, which are not SVM specific, are:

- *One-vs-All classification (OVA)*: Suppose you have classes A, B, C, and D. Instead of doing a four-way classification, we train four different binary classifiers:

A vs. not(A), B vs. not(B), C vs. not(C), and D vs. not(D), resulting in four hyperplanes. Then, for any new incoming data, pick as class the hyperplane that gives the maximum value when calculating $wx + b$.

- *All vs All*: Train all possible pairs of classifications. Rank the classes by some factor (e.g., number of times selected) and pick the best.

Multi-class SVMs remain an ongoing research issue, and most methods proposed are typically constructed by combining several binary classifiers. Some methods also consider all classes at once. As it is computationally more expensive to solve multi-class problems, comparisons of these methods using large-scale problems have not been seriously conducted. Especially for methods solving multi-class SVMs in one step, a much larger optimization problem is required, so up to now experiments have been limited to small data sets.

This concludes our chapter on SVMs; it is now up to the reader to evolve the C# SVM herein proposed and use it as an experimentation tool or customize it to their needs.

Summary

In this chapter, we described the very interesting topic of support vector machines (SVMs) as optimization instruments oriented toward solving a particular machine learning problem—the problem of classification. We mainly focused on binary classification, even though in the last paragraphs we briefly mentioned some multi-class methods. We showed how to directly solve the dual-optimization problem of an SVM using the Accord .NET library, and we also explained and implemented the sequential minimal optimization (SMO) algorithm. We included a graphical application developed in Windows Forms that used OxyPlot and allowed us to display the hyperplane and data points of the problem.

CHAPTER 10

Decision Trees

Data mining is the process of discovering and extracting meaningful, useful information (patterns) from large data sets. Numerous data-mining techniques are inherited from AI, and particularly from machine learning and its subfield of supervised learning; among these techniques lies the classification technique.

Classification is a frequent task in data mining that solves a wide range of real-world problems, such as fraud, spam mail checking, credit scoring, bankruptcy prediction, medical diagnosis, pattern recognition, multimedia classification, and so on. It is recognized as a powerful way for companies to develop effective knowledge based on decision models to gain competitive advantages. In the previous chapter, we studied our first classifier, support vector machines. In this chapter, we'll present a popular classifier that presents us with a very intuitive way to classify a set of items: the decision tree.

In this chapter, we'll introduce decision trees (DTs) and describe their purpose and how they achieve said purpose. We'll present two of the most popular algorithms for generating DTs, which are ID3 (Interactive Dichotomizer 3) and C4.5, the latter being an extension of the first that includes multiple significant improvements. Both ID3 and C4.5 were developed by J. Ross Quinlan.

Additionally, and as we have done thus far, we'll develop a graphical application in Windows Forms using Microsoft Automatic Graph Layout to graphically represent the DT obtained after executing our algorithm.

© Arnaldo Pérez Castaño 2018
A. Pérez Castaño, *Practical Artificial Intelligence*,
https://doi.org/10.1007/978-1-4842-3357-3_10

> **Note**   Microsoft Automatic Graph Layout (MSAGL) is a .NET tool
> for graph layout and viewing. It was developed in Microsoft by
> Lev Nachmanson, Sergey Pupyrev, Tim Dwyer, and Ted Hart. Using
> MSAGL, we can build trees and graphs, we can label edges and
> nodes, and we can even define edge direction. On top of that, it offers
> many other facilities that we invite readers to check out.

What Is a Decision Tree?

A *decision tree (DT)* is a graphic representation of a decision-making
process that possesses high expressivity and can be easily interpreted
by humans. As occurs with support vector machines, DTs partition the
decision space into different classes using hyperplanes (Figure 10-1).

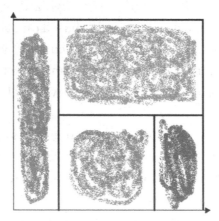

Figure 10-1. *Partition created using a DT*

As a tree, a DT consists of a root node, multiple internal nodes, and leaf nodes, which ultimately determine the classification of new incoming data. Since DTs are data structures obtained from supervised learning algorithms, these algorithms receive as input a set of training data and output a function (DTs can be seen as multivariate functions) that classifies new incoming data.

Unlike other algorithms like SVM or neural networks, DTs consider and use the set of attribute names in the training data set because they use them later to construct the tree. Every node in a DT is labeled with some attribute name, and edges leaving that node are labeled with the corresponding attribute values (assuming they are discrete and categorical); leaf nodes are labeled with goal attribute values. Hence, the set of attributes can be divided into non-goal and goal, where |goal| = 1. Table 10-1 illustrates several attributes and their corresponding values.

Table 10-1. *Attributes and Their Values*

Attribute	Type	Values
Outlook	non-goal	sunny, rainy, cloudy
Temperature	non-goal	warm, cold, temperate
Humidity	non-goal	high, normal
Wind	non-goal	strong, weak
Play Baseball	Goal	yes, no

An example of a training data set is shown in Table 10-2.

Table 10-2. *Training Data Set*

Outlook	Temperature	Humidity	Wind	Play Baseball
sunny	warm	high	weak	no
sunny	warm	high	strong	no
cloudy	warm	high	weak	yes
rainy	temperate	high	weak	yes
rainy	cold	normal	weak	yes
rainy	cold	normal	strong	no
cloudy	cold	normal	strong	yes
sunny	temperate	high	weak	no
sunny	cold	normal	weak	yes
rainy	temperate	normal	weak	yes
sunny	temperate	normal	strong	yes
cloudy	temperate	high	strong	yes
cloudy	warm	normal	weak	yes
rainy	temperate	high	strong	no

A DT derived from applying a learning method such as ID3 that uses the training data set presented in Table 10-2 could be the following (Figure 10-2).

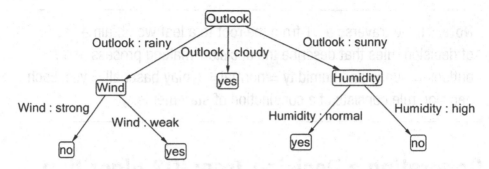

Figure 10-2. *Graphic of a DT matching the training data from Table 10-2 and created using MSAGL*

Once we have our DT, the question is, how do we classify new incoming data? To classify new data we just need to traverse the tree and match each attribute in the data vector with its corresponding value in the incoming data vector. For instance, let's assume x is a new incoming data and

$$X = (\text{cloudy, warm, normal, strong})$$

Then, seeking a classification for X, we start traversing the tree from the root (*Outlook*). Because *Outlook* in X equals "cloudy", we follow that edge and end up in the leaf node "Yes," which means *Play Baseball = Yes* under X's conditions or values.

Thus far, we know the purpose (classification) of DTs, we know what they look like, and we know how to classify new data once we have it (traversing the tree from the root, matching incoming data with attribute names). In the next section, we'll examine how to generate a DT, and we'll also identify some issues (such as overfitting) that could arise when generating a DT.

Note   If we traverse a DT from the root to a leaf we obtain a set of decision rules that describe the decision-making process; e.g., outlook = sunny and humidity = normal => play baseball = yes. Each decision rule consists of a conjunction of statements.

Generating a Decision Tree: ID3 Algorithm

Building an optimal decision tree is a key problem in supervised learning. In general, multiple decision trees can be constructed from a given set of attributes. While some of the trees are more accurate than others, the problem of finding the optimal tree is computationally infeasible because of the exponential size of the search space.

Most algorithms that have been developed for learning DTs are variations of a core algorithm (Hunt's) that employs a top-down, greedy search through the space of possible decision trees. Hunt's algorithm grows a decision tree in a recursive fashion by partitioning the training data set into sequentially more granular subsets. Assuming `TrainingData` represents the current training data set (which considers only columns matching non-goal attributes) at node N, then Hunt's pseudocode would follow the following steps:

1. In case `TrainingData` contains records that belong all to the same class, $C \rightarrow N$ will be a leaf node labeled C.

2. In case `TrainingData` is an empty set, $\rightarrow N$ will be a leaf node labeled with the most frequent class C. Remember, `TrainingData` only contains non-goal attribute columns; thus, C is taken from the goal-attribute column.

3. In case `TrainingData` contains records that belong
   to more than one class, use a test to select an
   attribute for splitting the data into smaller subsets
   and continue recursively applying the same
   procedure on each subset.

The ID3 algorithm uses the same idea as Hunt's algorithm; as a matter
of fact, if we were to look at ID3's pseudocode, it would be almost the same
as Hunt's pseudocode. The main difference lies in the attribute-splitting
test. ID3 uses the concepts of information gain and entropy to select the
attribute with the highest information gain, and then, as occurs in Hunt's
algorithm, creates a new node labeled with that attribute name. It then
creates edges going out of that new node, one for each value of the selected
attribute, and continues recursively in each new edge.

Note   Entropy and information gain are concepts drawn from
Information Theory, a scientific field that has its origins in a paper
published in 1948 by Claude Shannon, known as the Father
of the Information Age. It's the science of operations on data
such as compression, storage, statistical signal processing, and
communication.

A significant point to consider when generating a DT is the size of
the training data set. Recall that learning can be seen as approximating
a function that best describes the training data set. This is not merely
something that occurs in the machine learning area but also in real
life with humans. When we learn to drive, we learn a function that is
being described to us through a set of data that someone (instructor) is
providing; data such as you cannot go over people, you cannot continue
on a red light, you must go by the indicated speed limit, you handle the
steering wheel this way, you brake using this device, and so forth. Making

use of this data, we eventually learn a procedure or function that allows us to take an action or output (such as "stop," "continue") after receiving inputs into our "drive" function (such as "red light" or "people on the street"). Reasonably, the more quality data we receive the better we'll be able to learn an approximation of the function to which the training data set belongs. In Figure 10-3 we can see a graphic that describes the relation between the training data set size and the prediction quality offered by the resulting DT. As mentioned before, the larger the size of the training data set, the higher the chances are of correctly approximating the function to which it belongs.

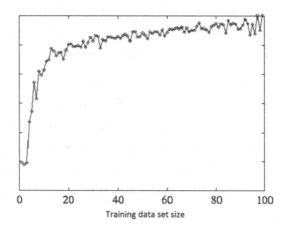

Training data set size

Figure 10-3. *Graphic describing how the prediction quality increases as the training data set size also increases*

In the following subsection we'll examine the ideas behind the use of entropy and information gain, two notions taken from Information Theory that constitute the splitting criteria used in algorithms like ID3 and its descendants.

Entropy and Information Gain

Entropy is a measure of chaos and uncertainty; high entropy means high disorder or chaos, while low entropy means low uncertainty or chaos (Figure 10-4). The entropy function is usually denoted as $H(x)$ where x is a vector containing probabilities; i.e., $x = p_1, p_2, \ldots, p_n$.

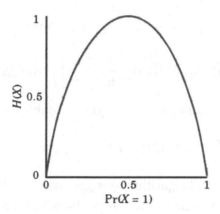

Figure 10-4. *Entropy function*

Looking at Figure 10-4, we can see what happens when probabilities p_i are midway; i.e., approximately 0.5. In such a case, we have high entropy (close to 1). Since there's a high uncertainty on every p_i, because their probabilities are nearly 0.5 (or 50 percent chance), meaning they can either occur or not uniformly (with the same probability), then the global uncertainty or chaos will be also high. When each p_i approximates 0 or 1 their entropy will be low because element probabilities indicate a low or high chance of occurrence, hence reducing uncertainty. The entropy function is the following:

$$H(X) = H([p_1, \ldots, p_n]) = -\sum_{i=1}^{n} p_i * \log_2 p_i$$

It satisfies the next set of properties:

1. $H(X) = H([p_1, \ldots, p_n]) \geq 0$.

2. $H(X) = H([p_1, \ldots, p_n]) = 0$, if it exists some $p_i = 1$.

3. $H(X) = H([p_1, \ldots, p_n]) \leq H\left(\left[\dfrac{1}{n}, \ldots, \dfrac{1}{n}\right]\right)$, the greatest

   entropy corresponds to the equis probable case.

4. $H(X) = H([p_1, \ldots, p_n, 0]) = H([p_1, \ldots, p_n])$.

Going back to the ID3 algorithm, our goal when splitting the tree will be to select the attribute that achieves the greatest reduction in entropy (disorder, chaos, uncertainty). How do we measure this expected reduction? We use a concept drawn from Information Theory known as *information gain* that has the following formula:

$$G(S, A) = H(S) - \sum_{v \in \text{Values}(A)} \frac{|S_{A=v}|}{|S|} * H(S_{A=v})$$

where S is the training data set for the current node in the DT, Values(A) represents the set of values corresponding to attribute A, and $S_{A=v}$ is the subset of S whose value for attribute A equals v.

Information gain can be defined as the expected reduction of entropy in S due to sorting on attribute A. It answers the question, How well is the resulting set going to be formed or ordered if we pick attribute A? Gain is calculated as the entropy of the entire set S minus the summation of the probability of $A = v$ in S; i.e. ($\frac{|S_{A=v}|}{|S|}$), times the entropy of subset $S_{A=v}$.

This is the test that ID3 uses in order to select an attribute for splitting the tree, and it will select that attribute which provides the highest gain. Now that we have gathered all the necessary pieces for building our ID3 algorithm, we'll start diving, from the next section on, into implementation issues and develop our ID3 method in C#.

Note   An ideal attribute would divide the training data set into subsets that are all positive or all negative (with regards to the goal attribute); i.e., that provide the maximum information gain.

Practical Problem: Implementing the ID3 Algorithm

To begin the implementation of our ID3 algorithm, we'll start by creating two classes (Listing 10-1) to handle attributes and the training data set.

Listing 10-1. Attribute and TrainingDataSet Classes

```
public class Attribute
{
        public string Name { get; set; }
        public string[] Values { get; set; }
        public TypeAttrib Type { get; set; }
        public TypeVal TypeVal{ get; set; }

        public Attribute(string name, string [] values,
        TypeAttrib type, TypeVal typeVal)
```

```
            {
                Name = name;
                Values = values;
                Type = type;
TypeVal = typeVal;
            }
}

    public enumTypeAttrib
    {
        Goal, NonGoal
    }

    public enumTypeVal
    {
        Discrete, Continuous
    }

public class TrainingDataSet
    {
        public string [,] Values { get; set; }
        public Attribute GoalAttribute{ get; set; }
        public List<Attribute>NonGoalAttributes{ get; set; }

        public TrainingDataSet(string [,] values,
        IEnumerable<Attribute>nonGoal, Attribute goal)
        {
            Values = new string[values.GetLength(0), values.
            GetLength(1)];
            Array.Copy(values, Values, values.GetLength(0) *
            values.GetLength(1));
            NonGoalAttributes = new List<Attribute>(nonGoal);
GoalAttribute = goal;
```

```
    if (NonGoalAttributes.Count + 1 != Values.GetLength(1))
        throw new Exception("Number of attributes must
        coincide");
  }
}
```

The `Attribute` class contains the following fields and properties:

- `Name`: property defining the name of the attribute

- `Values`: property defining the set of values for the attribute

- `Type`: property defining the type of attribute, either goal or non-goal

- `TypeVal`: property defining the type of value for the attribute, either discrete or continuous. We'll examine continuous attributes when we look at the C4.5 algorithm.

The `TrainingDataSet` class includes the following properties and fields:

- `Values`: matrix detailing values of the training data set

- `GoalAttribute`: defines the goal attribute of the training data set

- `NonGoalAttribute`: defines the set of non-goal attributes

As we can see, the `TrainingDataSet` class feeds from the `Attribute` class; a first piece of the `DecisionTree` class is shown in Listing 10-2.

Listing 10-2. DecisionTree Class

```
public class DecisionTree
    {
        public TrainingDataSetDataSet{ get; set; }
        public string Value { get; set; }
        public List<DecisionTree> Children { get; set; }
        public string Edge { get; set; }

        public DecisionTree(TrainingDataSetdataSet)
        {
DataSet = dataSet;
        }

        public static DecisionTreeLearn(TrainingDataSetdataSet,
        DtTrainingAlgorithm algorithm)
        {
            if (dataSet == null)
                throw new Exception("Data Set cannot be null");

            switch (algorithm)
            {
                default:
                    return Id3(dataSet.Values, dataSet.
                    NonGoalAttributes, "root");
            }
        }

        public DecisionTree(string value, string edge)
        {
            Value = value;
            Children = new List<DecisionTree>();
            Edge = edge;
        }
```

```
        public void Visualize()
        {
var form = new Form();
            //create a viewer object
var viewer = new GViewer();
            //create a graph object
var graph = new Graph("Decision Tree");
            //create the graph content

CreateNodes(graph);

            //bind the graph to the viewer
viewer.Graph = graph;
            //associate the viewer with the form
form.SuspendLayout();
viewer.Dock = DockStyle.Fill;
form.Controls.Add(viewer);
form.ResumeLayout();

            //show the form
form.ShowDialog();
        }

        private void CreateNodes(Graph graph)
{
varqueue = new Queue<DecisionTree>();
queue.Enqueue(this);
graph.CreateLayoutSettings().EdgeRoutingSettings.
EdgeRoutingMode = EdgeRoutingMode.StraightLine;
var id = 0;
```

```
            while (queue.Count> 0)
            {
varcurrentNode = queue.Dequeue();
                Node firstEnd;
                if (graph.Nodes.Any(n =>n.LabelText ==
                currentNode.Value))
firstEnd = graph.Nodes.First(n =>n.LabelText == currentNode.Value);
                else
firstEnd = new Node((id++).ToString()) { LabelText =
currentNode.Value };
graph.AddNode(firstEnd);

foreach (vardecisionTree in currentNode.Children)
                {
varsecondEnd = new Node((id++).ToString()) { LabelText =
decisionTree.Value };
graph.AddNode(secondEnd);
graph.AddEdge(firstEnd.Id, decisionTree.Edge, secondEnd.Id);
queue.Enqueue(decisionTree);
                }
            }
        }
}


    public enumDtTrainingAlgorithm
    {
        Id3,
    }
```

This class contains the following properties:

- Dataset: This is the method receiving the training data
  set as input and also the type of learning algorithm
  used during the learning phase.

- `Value`: defines the value of the node representing the root of this decision tree

- `Children`: defines the set of children for the current decision tree

- `Edge`: defines, as a string, the label of the edge connecting this node to its parent

Additionally, the `DecisionTree` class includes the following methods:

- `Learn()`: This is the method receiving the training data set as input and also the type of learning algorithm used during the learning phase.

- `Visualize()`: This method uses the MSAGL graphic tool to visualize the resulting tree after the learning phase is complete.

- `CreateNodes()`: This method executes a BFS algorithm to traverse the decision tree created by the ID3 algorithm, and as it traverses it creates an equivalent tree labeled using MSAGL facilities.

The ID3 algorithm and its supporting methods, all part of the `DecisionTree` class, are illustrated in Figure 10-3.

Listing 10-3. ID3 Algorithm

```
public static DecisionTree Id3(string [,] values,
List<Attribute> attributes, string edge)
{
    // All training data has the same goal attribute
vargoalValues = values.GetColumn(values.GetLength(1) - 1);
    if (goalValues.DistinctCount() == 1)
        return new DecisionTree(goalValues.First(), edge);
```

```
                // There are no NonGoal attributes
                if (attributes.Count == 0)
                    return new DecisionTree(goalValues.
                    GetMostFrequent(), edge);

                // Set as root the attribute providing the highest
                information gain
var attrIndexPair = HighestGainAttribute(values, attributes);
var attr = attrIndexPair.Item1;
var attrIndex = attrIndexPair.Item2;
var root = new DecisionTree(attr.Name, edge);

foreach (var value in attr.Values)
            {
var subSetVi = values.GetRowIndex(attrIndex, value,
ComparisonType.Equality);

                if (subSetVi.Count == 0)
root.Children.Add(new DecisionTree(goalValues.
GetMostFrequent(), value));
                else
                {
var newAttrbs = new List<Attribute>(attributes);
newAttrbs.RemoveAt(attrIndex);
var newValues = values.GetMatrix(subSetVi).
RemoveColumn(attrIndex);
root.Children.Add(Id3(newValues, newAttrbs, attr.Name + " : " +
value));
                }
            }

        return root;
    }
```

```
        private static Tuple<Attribute, int>HighestGainAttribute
        (string [,] values, IEnumerable<Attribute> attributes)
        {
            Attribute result = null;
varmaxGain = double.MinValue;
var index = -1;
vari = 0;

foreach (varattr in attributes)
            {
                double gain = Gain(values, i);

                if (gain >maxGain)
                {
maxGain = gain;
                    result = attr;
                    index = i;
                }
i++;
            }

            return new Tuple<Attribute, int>(result, index);
        }

        private static double Gain(string [,] values,
        intattributeIndex)
        {
varimpurityBeforeSplit = Entropy(values.
GetFreqPerDistinctElem(values.GetLength(1) - 1).GetProbabilities());
varimpurityAfterSplit= SubsetEntropy(values, attributeIndex);
            return impurityBeforeSplit - impurityAfterSplit;
        }
```

```
        private static double Entropy(IEnumerable<double>probs)
        {
            return -1 * probs.Sum(d =>LogEntropy(d));
        }

        private static double LogEntropy(double p)
        {
            return p >0 ? p * Math.Log(p, 2) : 0;
        }

        private static double SubsetEntropy(string[,] values,
        intcolumnIndex)
        {
varfreqDicc = values.GetFreqPerDistinctElem(columnIndex);
var result = 0.0;

var sum = freqDicc.Values.Sum();

foreach (var key in freqDicc.Keys)
        {
varrowIndex = values.GetRowIndex(columnIndex, key,
ComparisonType.Equality);
varfrequencyPerClass = values.GetFreqPerDistinctElem(values.
GetLength(1) - 1, rowIndex.ToArray());
                result += (freqDicc[key] / (double) sum) *
                Entropy(frequencyPerClass.GetProbabilities());
        }

        return result;
    }
}
```

In Listing 10-3, we are using several extension methods, some
belonging to the Accord .NET package and some others belonging to
an extension class that we created to support some of the operations
that necessarily need to be handled in the ID3 algorithm and that if
were included directly in the code of the method would obscure its
understanding, legibility, and clarity. Furthermore, since every method
in the class is self-descriptive and matches the pseudocode previously
presented, we'll focus on explaining the extension methods shown in
Listing 10-4; these methods belong to an extension class.

Listing 10-4. Extension Methods

```
public static string GetMostFrequent(this string[] values)
        {
vardicc = new Dictionary<string, int>();

foreach (var v in values)
            {
                if (!dicc.ContainsKey(v))
dicc.Add(v, 1);
else
dicc[v] += 1;
            }

varmaxVal = dicc.Max(e =>e.Value);
return dicc.First(p =>p.Value == maxVal).Key;
        }
        public static Dictionary<string,
        int>GetFreqPerDistinctElem(this string [,] values,
        intcolumnIndex, int [] rowIndex = null )
{
varfreqDicc = new Dictionary<string, int>();
```

```
            for (vari = 0; i< (rowIndex == null ?values.
            GetLength(0) : rowIndex.Length); i++)
            {
var row = rowIndex == null ?i : rowIndex[i];
                if (!freqDicc.ContainsKey(values[row, columnIndex]))
freqDicc.Add(values[row, columnIndex], 1);
                else
freqDicc[values[row, columnIndex]] += 1;
            }

        return freqDicc;
}

        public static List<int>GetRowIndex(this string[,]
        values, intcolumnIndex, string toCompare,
        ComparisonTypecomparisonType)
        {
var result = new List<int>();

            for (vari = 0; i<values.GetLength(0); i++)
            {
                switch (comparisonType)
                {
                        case ComparisonType.Equality:
                            if (values[i, columnIndex] ==
                            toCompare)
result.Add(i);

                        break;
                        case ComparisonType.NumericLessThan:
                            if (double.Parse(values[i, columnIndex])
                            <double.Parse(toCompare))
```

```
result.Add(i);
                            break;
                    case ComparisonType.NumericGreaterThan:
                        if (double.Parse(values[i, columnIndex])
                        >double.Parse(toCompare))
result.Add(i);

                        break;
              }
            }

        return result;
      }

      public static string[,] GetMatrix(this string[,]
      values, List<int>rowIndex)
      {
var result = new string[rowIndex.Count, values.GetLength(1)];
var j = 0;

foreach (vari in rowIndex)
          {
result.SetRow(j, values.GetRow(i));
j++;
          }

        return result;
      }

      public static IEnumerable<double>GetProbabilities(this
      Dictionary<string, int>dicc)
      {
var probabilities = new List<double>();
var sum = dicc.Values.Sum();
```

```
foreach (var e in dicc)
probabilities.Add((e.Value / (double) sum));

            return probabilities;
        }

public enumComparisonType
    {
Equality, NumericGreaterThan, NumericLessThan
    }
```

The descriptions of the previous extension methods are detailed here:

- GetMostFrequent(): returns the most frequent element from an array of strings received as argument; extension method of string []

- GetFreqPerDistinctElem(): returns the frequency (number of times it appears) of elements in the indicated column and in the indicated set of rows (if any, it's an optional argument); extension method of string [,]

- GetRowIndex(): returns the set of indices matching rows whose value at the column index received as argument satisfy the comparison criteria defined by ComparisonType and consider the comparison string detailed as argument; extension method of string [,]

- GetMatrix(): returns a new matrix containing only those rows whose index in the original matrix matches an integer in the list received as argument. It uses the SetRow() method belonging to Accord .NET; extension method of string [,]

- GetProbabilities(): returns the probability of
  each element *x* in the input dictionary as *value(x)*
  / total(S) where *total(S)* is the sum of all element
  values in the input dictionary; extension method of
  Dictionary<string, int>

Now that we have fully detailed every component of our ID3
implementation, let's see how to test our algorithm in a console
application by including the code shown in Listing 10-5.

Listing 10-5. Testing Our DecisionTree Class and the ID3 Algorithm
in a Console Application

```
var values = new [,]
                        {
{ "sunny", "warm", "high", "weak", "no" },
{ "sunny", "warm", "high", "strong", "no" },
{ "cloudy", "warm", "high", "weak", "yes" },
{ "rainy", "temperate", "high", "weak", "yes" },
{ "rainy", "cold", "normal", "weak", "yes" },
{ "rainy", "cold", "normal", "strong", "no" },
{ "cloudy", "cold", "normal", "strong", "yes" },
{ "sunny", "temperate", "high", "weak", "no" },
{ "sunny", "cold", "normal", "weak", "yes" },
{ "rainy", "temperate", "normal", "weak", "yes" },
{ "sunny", "temperate", "normal", "strong", "yes" },
{ "cloudy", "temperate", "high", "strong", "yes" },
{ "cloudy", "warm", "normal", "weak", "yes" },
{ "rainy", "temperate", "high", "strong", "no" },
                        };

varattribs = new List<Attribute>
                        {
```

391

```
                                    new Attribute("Outlook",
                                    new[] { "sunny", "cloudy",
                                    "rainy" }, TypeAttrib.
                                    NonGoal, TypeVal.Discrete),
                                    new Attribute("Temperature",
                                    new[] { "warm", "temperate",
                                    "cold" }, TypeAttrib.NonGoal,
                                    TypeVal.Discrete),
                                    new Attribute("Humidity",
                                    new[] { "high", "normal" },
                                    TypeAttrib.NonGoal, TypeVal.
                                    Discrete),
                                    new Attribute("Wind", new[]
                                    { "weak", "strong" },
                                    TypeAttrib.NonGoal, TypeVal.
                                    Discrete),
                                };

vargoalAttrib = new Attribute("Play Baseball", new[] { "yes",
"no" }, TypeAttrib.Goal, TypeVal.Discrete);
vartrainingDataSet = new TrainingDataSet(values, attribs,
goalAttrib);
vardtree = DecisionTree.Learn(trainingDataSet,
DtTrainingAlgorithm.Id3);
dtree.Visualize();
```

The result obtained after executing the code presented in Listing 10-5 can be seen in Figure 10-5; the reader can verify it exactly coincides with the DT shown in Figure 10-2. The same occurs with the training data set of Listing 10-5 and the one illustrated in Table 10-2.

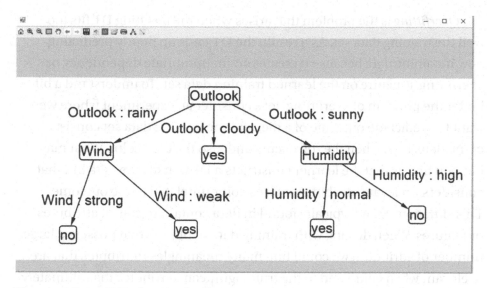

Figure 10-5. *DT obtained after executing our console application program*

At the moment, we have covered the basics of DTs, explained the functioning of the ID3 algorithm, and introduced a practical problem where we implemented the ID3 algorithm. In the upcoming sections we'll explain some of the difficulties or disadvantages of the ID3 algorithm and how its improved version, the C4.5 algorithm, overcomes these difficulties and provides a more efficient DT by applying pruning techniques to handle missing values and attributes whose values can be continuous instead of discrete.

C4.5 Algorithm

The C4.5 algorithm (Quinlan, 1993) represents an extension or enhancement over ID3's shortcomings. Its improvement lies in three main points: handling continuous attributes (remember ID3 deals only with categorical attributes), handling missing values, and taking care of overfitting issues by pruning the tree in the end.

Overfitting is the problem that arises when the resulting DT fits too well the training data set. As a result, the DT ends up poorly predicting new incoming data because it creates an inappropriate dependency or overfitting structure on the learned training data set. To understand a bit better the problem of overfitting, let's consider an experiment where we want to predict the outcome of a die, and the training data set consists of the date, time when the roll occurs and also the die's color. What may happen here is that the learner constructs a DT that fits the data but that considers irrelevant attributes such as color unrelated to the outcome. This situation can be typically found in data containing lots of attributes or features. When dealing with training data or objects that possess a large number of attributes, we could find many meaningless attributes that are irrelevant when compared to the truly significant attributes that ultimately decide the outcome of the upcoming data.

How can we approach this problem? There exist two major approaches to counteracting overfitting problems. First, to stop the growth of the tree in the early stages of the generation process and before reaching the point at which it perfectly classifies the training data set. Second, to prune the tree after it has been generated. The second approach has been more successful than the first, mainly because knowing when to stop the growth of the tree can be a tricky task. Once we begin the pruning process, a fundamental question is how to decide if a subtree is worth pruning; in other words, what criteria should we use for pruning, and how should we carry out this process?

Even though there are diverse strategies for carrying out the pruning process of a DT, the most popular approach relies on *cross-validation*, a statistical technique that divides the training data set S into subsets S_1, S_2 and then uses the first subset for training and generating a DT and the second subset for testing how well the resulting DT is performing on classifying data coming from validation set S_2. Cross-validation is combined with a post-pruning measure that gives us an assessment of how well the resulting DT will do after pruning. The most common measures are *error reduction* and *rule pruning*.

The pseudocode of the error-reduction criteria would be the following:

- Classify training data in the validation set S_2 using the DT (Figure 10-6).

- For each node X:

  - Find the sum of errors of the entire subtree rooted at X.

  - Calculate the error of the same training data but once X has been transformed into a leaf node and assigned the most common class of all of its descendants.

- Compare both values and prune the one with the highest reduction in error.

- Repeat until error is no longer reduced.

Figure 10-6 illustrates a subtree where a plus sign indicates a training data correctly classified and a minus sign represents a training data incorrectly classified.

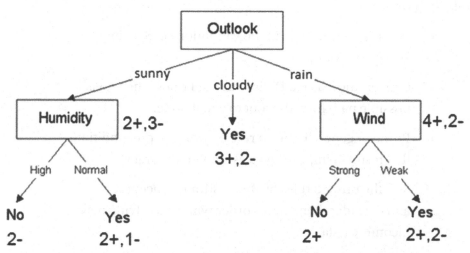

Figure 10-6. *Validation set consisting of 16 training data classified by the DT. A positive number indicates a training data correctly classified by the DT, and a minus indicates an error in classification*

The error-reduction measure is, at the same time, typically used in conjunction with a subtree simplification operator or pruning technique known as *subtree replacement* where each internal node of the DT happens to be a candidate node for pruning in a bottom-up approach that prunes a tree only after examining its subtrees. In this sense, pruning can be translated as deleting a subtree of the DT and replacing it with a leaf whose value corresponds to the most frequent class found in all leaves of the subtree, as the previous pseudocode describes.

A subtree is finally pruned if the resulting DT behaves worse than the previous one when tested against validation set S_2. Nodes in the DT are pruned iteratively, selecting always those that increase the efficiency of the resulting DT over the validation set. This will cause any leaf node created based on coincidental regularities while learning on the training data set to be pruned when double checking the validation set since the same coincidental regularities are not likely to also happen on the validation set.

The other criteria, rule pruning, converts the learned DT into a set of rules, one for each possible path from the root to a leaf node. It involves the following steps:

- Classify training data in the validation set S_2 using the DT (Figure 10-6).

- Convert the learned DT into a set of rules, one for each possible path from the root to a leaf node.

- Prune or generalize each rule by pruning preconditions that result in improving its estimated accuracy.

- Sort the pruned rules by their estimated accuracy and consider them in this order when classifying new incoming data.

In this sense, rule preconditions represent attribute tests from the root to a leaf node, and the value or classification at that leaf becomes the rule consequence or postcondition. For instance, if (outlook = sunny ∧ humidity = normal) is a precondition and playBaseball = yes is the consequent. Afterward, each rule is pruned by removing its precondition if its removal does not affect the estimated accuracy of the DT before pruning.

Another distinguishing feature of the C4.5 algorithm is that it uses a different measure for selecting the attribute to split on; instead of using information gain it uses *gain ratio*, whose formula is as follows:

$$\text{GainRatio}(S, A) = \frac{\text{Gain}(S, A)}{\text{SplitInformation}(S, A)}$$

where

$$\text{SplitInformation}(S, A) = -\sum_{i=1}^{n} \frac{|S_i|}{|S|} * \log_2 \frac{|S_i|}{|S|}$$

where S_i are the subsets after partitioning S with respect to attribute A containing n possible values. The gain ratio measure overcomes the downfalls of information gain, whose main disadvantage is favoring attributes with the largest number of values. For instance, consider a Date attribute with the many values it could include; because the size of this set might be huge it will probably divide the entire set of training data into smaller subsets whose entropy will be very low; hence, the information gain will be very high. Gain ratio penalizes those attributes with multiple values uniformly distributed.

Handling continuous attributes is one of the major advantages that C4.5 provides over its predecessor ID3. To handle continuous attributes, C4.5 partitions the set of values into a discrete set of intervals. It creates a binary decision node that divides the range of possible values into two subsets, those satisfying < X and those satisfying >= X where X is a threshold to be decided. This procedure assumes the existence of a total order in the set of continuous values. The key point is finding the value X (threshold) on which the partition will be made. The most common approach is to sort the values of the training data set in increasing order; loop through the list of sorted values while comparing goal attributes of consecutives elements $(i, i + 1)$; calculate (if and only if their goal attributes differ) the threshold as the average of those two consecutive elements (i.e., $X'=(L[i] + L[i+1])/2$); compute the information gain achieved on partitioning the attribute on the threshold X' (considering subsets of elements less than X', greater than X'; and select the one providing the highest information gain. Note that we consider consecutive elements only when their classes are different. We would never consider elements $L[i]$, $L[i + 1]$ (where L is the list of sorted values on the continuous attribute) if they both have the same class C (Figure 10-7).

Temperature	40	48	60	72	80	90
Play Baseball	no	no	yes	yes	yes	no

Figure 10-7. *After incrementally sorting values we examine those consecutive values whose goal attribute is different*

For handling missed values, there exist different strategies, and the process is usually executed prior to executing any DT learning algorithm. The simplest strategy is to simply ignore missed values, not considering them when calculating entropy. A smarter strategy would be to assign the most common value of that attribute in the training data set to the missing value. Lastly, a more complex approach would be to assign probabilities for each possible value of the missing attribute A and then create branches on that node for each probability calculated. For instance, assuming we have a binary attribute A whose values are P, Q, ten known values for this attribute, six for attribute P, four for value Q, then this approach would create two branches corresponding to the 0.6 probability of the attribute's having value P and another one related to the odds of the attribute's having value Q.

Practical Problem: Implementing the C4.5 Algorithm

In this section, we'll present an implementation of the C4.5 algorithm that will include different features such as handling continuous attributes and the gain ratio measure. The pruning techniques and strategies for handling missed values will be left to the reader as an exercise and as a way to complement the code herein presented. The main coding task to move from ID3 to C4.5 lies in the adaptation to handle continuous values; hence, we present it in this section.

As expected, ID3 and C4.5 share almost the same code. Base conditions are the same, and the main differences lie within the main body. Listing 10-6 shows the access point of the C4.5 algorithm; remember that this method is to be added to the DecisionTree class we have been developing throughout the chapter.

Listing 10-6. Main Body of C4.5 Algorithm

```
public static DecisionTreeC45(string [,] values,
List<Attribute> attributes, string edge)
        {
            // All training data has the same goal attribute
vargoalValues = values.GetColumn(values.GetLength(1) - 1);
            if (goalValues.DistinctCount() == 1)
                return new DecisionTree(goalValues.First(), edge);

            // There are no NonGoal attributes
            if (attributes.Count == 0)
                return new DecisionTree(goalValues.
                GetMostFrequent(), edge);

            // Set as root the attribute providing the highest
            information gain
```

```
varattrIndexPair = HighestGainAttribute(values, attributes);
varattr = attrIndexPair["attrib"] as Attribute;
varattrIndex = (int) attrIndexPair["index"];
var threshold = (int) attrIndexPair["threshold"];
var less = (List<int>) attrIndexPair["less"];
var greater = (List<int>) attrIndexPair["greater"];
var root = new DecisionTree(attr.Name, edge);
varsplittingVals = attr.TypeVal == TypeVal.Discrete ? attr.Values
                                                : new [] { "less"
                                                + threshold,
                                                "greater" +
                                                threshold } ;

foreach (var value in splittingVals)
            {
                List<int>subSetVi;

                if (attr.TypeVal == TypeVal.Discrete)
subSetVi = values.GetRowIndex(attrIndex, value, ComparisonType.
Equality);
                else
subSetVi = value.Contains("less") ? less : greater;

                if (subSetVi.Count == 0)
root.Children.Add(new DecisionTree(goalValues.
GetMostFrequent(), value));
                else
                {
varnewAttrbs = new List<Attribute>(attributes);
newAttrbs.RemoveAt(attrIndex);
varnewValues = values.GetMatrix(subSetVi).
RemoveColumn(attrIndex);
```

```
root.Children.Add(Id3(newValues, newAttrbs, attr.Name + " : " +
value));
                }
        }

        return root;
    }
```

In this case, TypeVal is an enum attached to the Attribute class that allows us to know whether an attribute is discrete or continuous. Notice the code is very similar to that of ID3, but a significant difference can be found in the HighestGainAttribute() method, which now provides us with more information, mainly information related to the continuous attribute handling. Such a method is illustrated in Listing 10-7.

Listing 10-7. HighestGainAttribute() Method for Continuous Attributes

```
        private static Dictionary<string, dynamic>HighestGain
        Attribute(string [,] values, IEnumerable<Attribute>attributes)
        {
            Attribute result = null;
varmaxGain = double.MinValue;
var index = -1;
            double threshold = -1.0;
vari = 0;
            List<int>bestLess = null;
            List<int>bestGreater = null;

foreach (varattr in attributes)
            {
                double gain = 0;
                Dictionary<string, dynamic>gainThreshold = null;
```

```
                    if (attr.TypeVal == TypeVal.Discrete)
                        gain = Gain(values, i);
                    if (attr.TypeVal == TypeVal.Continuous)
                    {
gainThreshold = GainContinuous(values, i);
                        gain = gainThreshold["gain"];
                    }

                    if (gain >maxGain)
                    {
maxGain = gain;
                        result = attr;
                        index = i;

                        if (gainThreshold != null)
                        {
                            threshold = gainThreshold["threshold"];
bestLess = gainThreshold["less"];
bestGreater = gainThreshold["greater"];
                        }
                    }
i++;
                }

            return new Dictionary<string, dynamic> {
{ "attrib" , result },
{ "index" , index },
{ "less" , bestLess },
{ "greater" , bestGreater },
{ "threshold" , threshold },
                                                     };
        }
```

In this new or continuous version of the `HighestGainAttribute()` method, we make a differentiation in regards to the attribute's being discrete or continuous. Also note that in this case the method returns a dictionary containing the selected attribute, its index, and, if the selected attribute is continuous, two lists of index positions (less, greater), along with the double-value threshold. For calculating the gain of a continuous attribute it uses the `GainContinuous()` method shown in Listing 10-8.

Listing 10-8. GainContinuous() Method for Calculating the Gain of Continuous Attributes

```
        private static Dictionary<string, dynamic>GainContinuous
        (string[,] values, inti)
        {
var column = values.GetColumn(i);
varcolumnVals = column.Select(double.Parse).ToList();
varbestGain = double.MinValue;
varbestThreshold = 0.0;
        List<int>bestLess = null;
        List<int>bestGreater = null;

columnVals.Sort();

        for (var j = 0; j <columnVals.Count - 1; j++)
        {
            if (columnVals[j] != columnVals[j + 1] &&
            values[j, values.GetLength(1) - 1] != values[j
            + 1, values.GetLength(1) - 1])
            {
var threshold = (columnVals[j] + columnVals[j + 1])/2;
var less = values.GetRowIndex(i, threshold.ToString(),
ComparisonType.NumericLessThan);
```

```
var greater = values.GetRowIndex(i, threshold.ToString(),
ComparisonType.NumericGreaterThan);

var gain = Gain(values, i, threshold, less, greater);
                    if (gain >bestGain)
                    {
bestGain = gain;
bestThreshold = threshold;
bestLess = less;
bestGreater = greater;
                    }
                }
            }

            return new Dictionary<string, dynamic>
                    {
{ "gain" , bestGain },
{ "threshold" , bestThreshold },
{ "less", bestLess },
{ "greater", bestGreater },
                    };
        }
```

In the GainContinuous() method we partition the set of possible values of a continuous attribute and create a binary distinction on the threshold value, which is, as we recall, the average of consecutive pairs (in the list of sorted values) yielding the highest information gain. Output in this case is a dictionary holding the gain, threshold double values, and the less, greater lists.

Remember that in C4.5 we use the GainRatio criteria for selecting the attribute to split on; the C# method calculating this measure is shown in Listing 10-9. In the same listing we can see the SplitInformation procedure on which GainRatio relies, as described in prior sections.

Listing 10-9. GainRatio() and SplitInformation()

```
private static double GainRatio(string[,] values,
intattributeIndex, double threshold = -1, List<int> less =
null, List<int> greater = null)
        {
            return Gain(values, attributeIndex, threshold,
            less, greater) / SplitInformation(values,
            attributeIndex);
        }

        private static double SplitInformation(string[,]
        values, intattributeIndex)
        {
varfreq = values.GetFreqPerDistinctElem(attributeIndex);
var total = freq.Sum(t =>t.Value);
var result = 0.0;

foreach (var f in freq)
                result += (double)f.Value / total * Math.
                Log((double)f.Value / total, 2);

            return -result;
        }
```

Since `GainRatio()` requires the computation of `Gain()`, we need to adapt it a little bit to the continuous case—the case where we have two sets of values, one less and the other greater than a calculated threshold. Listing 10-10 shows the adaptation of the `Gain()` method, which is enclosed in the `if(threshold >= 0)` statement.

Listing 10-10. Gain() Adaptation to Handle the Continuous Case

```
        private static double Gain(string [,] values,
        intattributeIndex, double threshold = -1, List<int>
        less = null, List<int> greater = null)
        {
varimpurityBeforeSplit = Entropy(values.
GetFreqPerDistinctElem(values.GetLength(1) - 1).GetProbabilities());
            double impurityAfterSplit = 0;

            if (threshold >= 0)
            {
varfreq = new Dictionary<string, int>{  {"less", less.Count},
{"greater", greater.Count}  };

                for (vari = 0; i<freq.Count; i++)
impurityAfterSplit += SubsetEntropy(values, attributeIndex,
freq, less, greater);
            }
            else
impurityAfterSplit = SubsetEntropy(values, attributeIndex);

            return impurityBeforeSplit - impurityAfterSplit;
        }
```

SubsetEntropy() is another method that we need to slightly modify to make it fit the continuous case and consider the less, greater set of values. This modification is illustrated in Listing 10-11.

Listing 10-11. Modification to the SubsetEntropy() Method

```
private static double SubsetEntropy(string[,] values,
intcolumnIndex, Dictionary<string, int>freqContinous = null,
        List<int> less = null, List<int> greater = null)
        {
```

```
var result = 0.0;
varfreqDicc = freqContinous ?? values.GetFreqPerDistinctElem
(columnIndex);

var total = freqDicc.Values.Sum();

foreach (var key in freqDicc.Keys)
            {
                List<int>rowIndex;

                switch (key)
                {
                    case "less":
rowIndex = less;
                        break;
                    case "greater":
rowIndex = greater;
                        break;
                    default:
rowIndex = values.GetRowIndex(columnIndex, key, ComparisonType.
Equality);
                        break;
                }

varfrequencyPerClass = values.GetFreqPerDistinctElem(values.
GetLength(1) - 1, rowIndex.ToArray());
                result += (freqDicc[key] / (double) total) *
                Entropy(frequencyPerClass.GetProbabilities());
            }

        return result;
        }
```

Note   The ?? operator is called the null-coalescing operator. It returns the left-hand operand if the operand is not null; otherwise, it returns the right-hand operand.

In order to test our C4.5 algorithm we can add the code from Listing 10-12 to a console application.

Listing 10-12. Testing Our C4.5 Algorithm in a Console Application

```
var values = new [,]
{ { "sunny", "12", "high", "weak", "no" },
{ "sunny", "12", "high", "strong", "no" },
{ "cloudy", "14", "high", "weak", "yes" },
{ "rainy", "12", "high", "weak", "yes" },
{ "rainy", "20", "normal", "weak", "yes" },
{ "rainy", "20", "normal", "strong", "no" },
{ "cloudy", "20", "normal", "strong", "yes" },
{ "sunny", "12", "high", "weak", "no" },
{ "sunny", "14", "normal", "weak", "yes" },
{ "rainy", "20", "normal", "weak", "yes" },
{ "sunny", "14", "normal", "strong", "yes" },
{ "cloudy", "20", "high", "strong", "yes" },
{ "cloudy", "20", "normal", "weak", "yes" },
{ "rainy", "14", "high", "strong", "no" }, };
varattribs = new List<Attribute>
                        {
                            new Attribute("Outlook", new[]
                            { "sunny", "cloudy", "rainy"
                            }, TypeAttrib.NonGoal,
                            TypeVal.Discrete),
```

```
                    new Attribute("Temperature",
                    new[] { "12", "14", "20" },
                    TypeAttrib.NonGoal, TypeVal.
                    Continuous),
                    new Attribute("Humidity",
                    new[] { "high", "normal" },
                    TypeAttrib.NonGoal, TypeVal.
                    Discrete),
                    new Attribute("Wind", new[]
                    { "weak", "strong" },
                    TypeAttrib.NonGoal, TypeVal.
                    Discrete),
                };
vargoalAttrib = new Attribute("Play Baseball", new[] { "yes",
"no" }, TypeAttrib.Goal, TypeVal.Discrete);
vartrainingDataSet = new TrainingDataSet(values, attribs, goalAttrib);
vardtree = DecisionTree.Learn(trainingDataSet,
DtTrainingAlgorithm.C45);
dtree.Visualize();
```

The result obtained after executing the code from Listing 10-12 can be
seen in Figure 10-8.

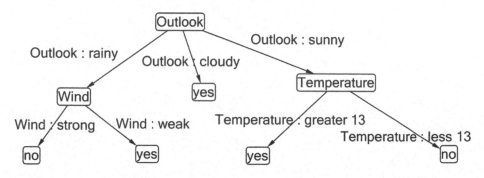

Figure 10-8. *Resulting DT after executing the code from Listing 10-12*

We didn't include any code related to the handling of missing values feature, but using the very simple strategy of ignoring them, we can create a C# method that receives the training data set as input, and examines each cell of the matrix replacing any unknown value with a 0, making it not count for entropy calculations. As mentioned before, pruning techniques are left to the reader for implementation and complementary exercise.

Summary

In this chapter, we examined DTs, an implementation of a classification model with a treelike data structure where decision rules can be found traversing the tree from the root to any leaf. We described the basic, most popular algorithm for generating DTs (ID3), and an implementation in C# was detailed; such an implementation included a Windows Forms application that graphically showed the resulting DT using MSAGL.

We also explained the C4.5 algorithm, an improved version of ID3 where continuous attributes, missing values in the training data set, and overfitting issues are handled. An implementation in C# of this algorithm included the most significant coding details, which lay mainly on the handling continuous attributes feature. Implementation of pruning techniques were left to the reader as an exercise.

CHAPTER 11

Neural Networks

In this chapter, we will be discussing artificial neural networks, a family of algorithms very popular in the area of supervised learning (and also applicable to unsupervised learning and reinforcement learning) that try to mimic or model the human brain's functioning to solve problems that, as with SVMs and DTs, rely on learning or approximating a function F defined by a table of training data in the form of pairs (data, classification). This function F is the result of the learning process and is known as the approximated or learned function. It is later used to classify or predict the class of new incoming data.

As we have seen so far, many of the algorithms, methods, and tools used in artificial intelligence— and especially in supervised learning—are closely related to other areas of knowledge, such as algebra, mathematical analysis, and mathematical optimization. Because learning in life relates to a process in which we "improve" or learn how to do certain things on a timeline (considering time), and that's precisely the goal of optimization algorithms—to optimize (either minimize or maximize) a function through iterative processes—then neural networks will not be the exception, and we will keep the same pattern of using optimization techniques to learn and construct a function that predicts the class of input data.

In this chapter, we'll introduce neural networks (NNs) and describe their functioning and how they simulate the way our neurons work all together. We'll implement the Perceptron algorithm, one of the oldest and simplest NN models. We will also implement the Adaline NN model

© Arnaldo Pérez Castaño 2018
A. Pérez Castaño, *Practical Artificial Intelligence*,
https://doi.org/10.1007/978-1-4842-3357-3_11

since it will be a useful introduction to the topic of multi-layer NNs; the optimization technique it uses resembles that of the last algorithm to be examined in this chapter, the popular backpropagation algorithm for learning in multi-layer NNs.

Note   NNs can be applied to multiple problems, among which it would be worth mentioning pattern, shape, face, and handwritten recognition, autonomous vehicle driving, and many others. The study of brain-style computation has its roots in the work of McCulloch and Pitts (1943) and later in Hebb's famous *Organization of Behavior* (1949).

What Is a Neural Network?

A *neuron* is a type of cell of the nervous system (Figure 11-1) that possesses a plasmatic membrane that allows it to receive stimulus from external elements and transmit signals to other neurons or to different types of cells of the human brain. The signals they either receive or send are electrochemical; thus, neurons are responsible for collecting, processing, and transmitting electrochemical signals. When several neurons are connected through their synapses they are said to be defining a neural network. In this network, a neuron fires or sends a signal when the excitation of all electrochemical signals received from all other neurons connected to it is high enough.

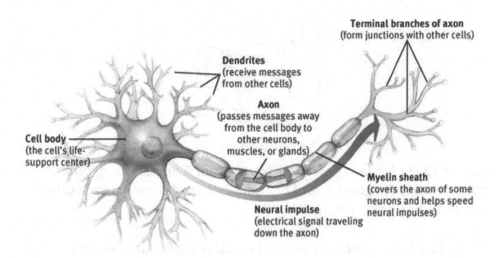

Figure 11-1. *Biological neuron; dendrites represent inputs of signals coming from other neurons and axons represent outputs for our neuron. One can think of the structure of a neuron as having input nodes called dendrites, output nodes called axons, and edges called synapses.*

Finding an analogous model in the mathematical AI world, a neuron can be seen as a mathematical object or function that receives numeric inputs $x1, x2, ..., xn$ from all neurons that connect to it and combines these values, calculating a *weighted sum* as a way to give a certain "relevance" to each connection by associating weight values $w1, w2, ..., wn$ with them. Thus, $X = w1 * x1 + w2 * x2 + ... + wn * xn$ is the value reaching the body of the neuron. The final outputted value can be either a signal or nothing (0). To determine the strength of the signal (output) we typically use something known as an *activation function*; this function determines the outputted value and will vary depending on the type of neuron used.

Hence, a *neural network (NN)* is a collection of the previously described neurons; relations between these neurons can be described as forming a graph where an edge from neuron i to neuron j indicates an input to neuron j and an output from neuron i going to neuron j (Figure 11-2).

413

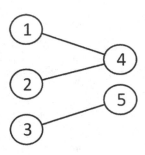

Figure 11-2. *NN as a graph; neurons 4 and 5 are receiving inputs from neurons 1, 2, and 3, and neurons 1, 2, and 3 are having output connections to neurons 4 and 5.*

In the following sections, we will be examining single-unit NNs, networks composed of a single neuron. In single-neuron networks, one can think of the inputs as coming from some unknown neurons and having values that match those of the vector representing the training data. The output would then serve as classification for the input training data.

Note   An artificial neuron can be seen as a mathematical function $F = A(x1 * w1 + \ldots + xn * wn)$ where xi are the inputs; wi the weights that are meant to strengthen or weaken the connection to other neurons, and A the activation function that ultimately determines the strength of the outputted signal.

Perceptron: Singular NN

The *Perceptron* is a single-NN unit that follows the same process stated before: it receives n inputs $x1, ..., xn$, then calculates the weighted sum $x1 * w1 + ... + xn * wn$ and finally applies an activation function to get an output or classification for the input data. With the Perceptron this function is usually as follows:

$$f(x) = \begin{cases} 1 & x \geq T \\ 0 & otherwise \end{cases}$$

T is a value known as the *threshold;* it's used to compare the weighted sum with a threshold and determine whether the signal should be sent or not. Thus, the Perceptron can be represented as shown in Figure 11-3.

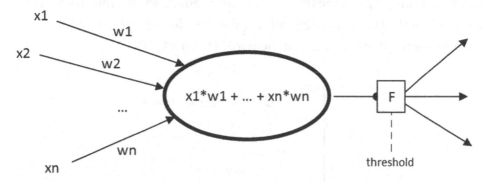

Figure 11-3. *The Perceptron computes a weighted sum of the inputs and weights, submits this value to the activation function F, and transmits the signal to other neurons if and only if F turns out to be greater than or equal to a given threshold.*

We already know how the flow of information works in the Perceptron; remember the purpose of the analyzed flow is to provide a classification for the input data. Now, how can we train it to correctly predict new incoming data?

First of all, the Perceptron is a linear classifier (recall from Chapter 9 that support vector machines were also linear classifiers); it tries to find a weight vector and a threshold value in such a way that the space of the problem is divided into classes A and B. The weight vector and the threshold value will define one of the possible classifying hyperplanes. If we were in 2D then the hyperplane would be a line, if we were in 3D then the hyperplane would be a plane, and so on. It will always occur that all points in the training data will lie on one side or the other of the classifying hyperplane if the training data set is linearly separable.

As we did in Chapter 9, let us consider the equation of a line, $y = mx + b$, where m is the slope of the line—or, in more general terms, the gradient of the line—and b is the bias determining the shift, left or right, of the line— i.e., the intercept of the line with the y-axis (Figure 11-4).

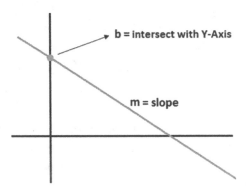

Figure 11-4. *Considering the equation of a line* $mx + b = y$, *then m defines the slope of the line and b its intercept with the y-axis, or equivalently its shift left or right*

Therefore, the training or learning process in a Perceptron will consist of an adjustment (made over time through several iterations) to the weights (slope of the line) and also to the bias in an attempt to find a line or hyperplane in the general case that correctly classifies all training data; in other words, to have a line that divides the training data set into two classes.

The Perceptron algorithm starts by setting random values for the weight vector, typically in the range [0, 1], and also for the bias. This will result in the construction of a random classifying hyperplane, or, in 2D (weight vector with two components), this scenario will result in the construction of a line that may or may not correctly classify the training data set. Then, in order to refine the classifying hyperplane and force it to correctly classify all examples, a loop through the entire training data set is made and each error detected in the classification of a single training data is corrected by increasing or decreasing the weight associated with the component of that training data; remember that for each component xi in any training data $(x1, ..., xn)$ we have associated some wi, and these are all combined in a weighted sum $x1 * w1 + ... + xn * wn$.

Note   The Convergence Theorem of the Perceptron states that for any data set that is linearly separable, the Perceptron learning rule is guaranteed to find a solution in a finite number of iterations.

As a result, the learning process of a Perceptron is basically an optimization technique where we improve the classifying hyperplane by slowly changing its slope or gradient and the bias to move it to a position where every training data would be correctly classified (Figure 11-5).

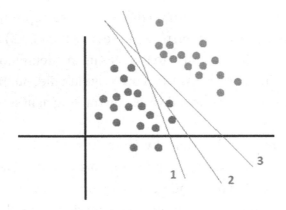

Figure 11-5. *In the graphic, line number 1 incorrectly classifies two of the red points; therefore, we modify weights and bias to move it to the right a little bit; then classifying hyperplane 2 also makes a mistake classifying one of the red points. Finally, classifying hyperplane 3 makes no mistakes and properly divides red from blue points.*

The pseudocode of the Perceptron algorithm is the following:

1. Initialize weights and bias to a random value in the range $[0, 1]$.

2. If the stopping condition is satisfied, end.

3. Loop through the entire training data set, picking each training data (x, y) one step at a time, x being the vector of features and y its classification.

4. Calculate the output y_x of the Perceptron for training data x.

5. In case $y != y_x$ then:

Correct each weight following the rule:

$$w_i = w_i + \alpha * (y - y_x) * x_i$$

Correct also the bias using the formula:

$$b = b + \alpha *(y - y_x)$$

6.   Go to step 2.

Step 5 of the pseudocode contains what is known as the *learning rule* of the Perceptron; all learning accomplished in the algorithm is encapsulated in the formula where weights are modified. In order to understand the learning formula let us reconstruct it from zero.

First, notice that when $w \cdot x < 0$ (where $\cdot$ represents the dot product, in this case the weighted sum mentioned so far) and the correct classification of x is positive, it can be geometrically interpreted as having the angle between ve ctors w and x with a value greater than 90 degrees, and consequently we would need to rotate w in x's direction to bring it to the positive space. Equivalently, if $w \cdot x > 0$ and the correct classification of x is negative (or less than zero), then the angle between vectors w and x is less than 90 degrees and w must be rotated away from x.

Note   The $a \bullet b$ operation represents the dot product between vectors a and b. Whenever a and b are perpendicular then $a \bullet b = 0$.

Thus, we already know that having a weight update of either $w + x$ or $w - x$ can be geometrically interpreted as moving w in the direction of x or in the opposite direction; this operation seeks to obtain a correct classification for training data x. Now, to merge the two previous cases into one, we will add the term $(y - y_x)$ as a multiplier of x. Let's analyze the possible values of this term to understand that it will always give us the correct sign for x.

- If $y = y_x$ then $y - y_x = 0$, which implies there's no change to the weight since the classification of x is correct.

- If $y > y_x$ then $y - y_x > 0$, which implies the weight needs to be increased because $y > y_x$; i.e., we need to increase the weight so that $w \cdot x$ provides us with a higher value and the training data classifies it as 1 instead of 0.

- If $y < y_x$ then $y - y_x < 0$, which implies the weight needs to be decreased because $y < y_x$. Analogous explanation to the previous point.

Accordingly, we now have the update rule justified as $w + (y - y_x) * x$, and we conclude we will multiply the last term by α, a value in the range $(0, 1)$ known as the *learning rate.*

The learning rate controls how quickly the Perceptron will learn, or, equivalently, how much we change the weights and bias at each step. From a geometrical perspective, it can be seen as how much we rotate the w vector toward or away from training data vector x. To guarantee convergence and to not step over the solution of the problem, we must choose small values for the learning rate; 0.05 is typically chosen.

Using a similar approach, we can deduct the formula for updating the bias, but this is left to the reader as an exercise.

Practical Problem: Implementing the Perceptron NN

To implement the Perceptron in C#, we'll create an abstract class named `SingleNeuralNetwork` that will allow us to easily develop the Perceptron and also any single-unit NN that we would need to implement, as they all share similar features in their structure and significant changes occur merely in their learning rules. This class is shown in Listing 11-1.

Listing 11-1. SingleNeuralNetwork Abstract Class

```
public abstract class SingleNeuralNetwork
    {
        public List<TrainingSample>TrainingSamples{ get; set; }
        public int Inputs { get; set; }
        public List<double> Weights { get; set; }
        public readonly Random Random = new Random();
        protected readonly double LearningRate;
        protected double Bias= 0.5;

        protected SingleNeuralNetwork(IEnumerable<TrainingSample>
        trainingSamples, int inputs, double learningRate)
        {
TrainingSamples = new List<TrainingSample>(trainingSamples);
            Inputs = inputs;
            Weights = new List<double>();
            for (vari = 0; i< Inputs; i++)
Weights.Add(Random.NextDouble());
LearningRate = learningRate;
        }

        public virtual void Training()
        {
        }

        public virtual double Predict(double[] features)
        {
var result = 0.0;

            for (vari = 0; i<features.Length; i++)
                result += features[i] * Weights[i];

            return result > -Bias ?1 : 0;
        }
```

```
        public List<double>PredictSet(IEnumerable<double[]> objects)
        {
var result = new List<double>();

foreach (varobj in objects)
result.Add(Predict(obj));

            return result;
        }
    }
```

The class contains the following fields or properties:

- **TrainingSamples**: It's the same class used in the SVM chapter; it contains a vector of features (double values) representing the training data and an integer defining the correct classification of that training data.

- **Inputs**: integer representing the number of inputs for the Perceptron

- **Weights**: list of double values representing the weight vector of the single-unit NN

- **Random**: field used to obtain random values

- **LearningRate**: the learning rate of the Perceptron

- **Threshold**: the threshold of the Perceptron; initial value set to 0.5

In the class constructor we initialize the weights to random values in the range [0, 1]; the constructor is followed by a set of methods, which are detailed here:

- **Training()**: virtual method that every class inheriting from **SingleNeuralNetwork** will implement in order to provide a training algorithm implementation.

We mark it as virtual instead of abstract because we are considering the case in which you would not like to include a training method for the single-unit NN but rather just use the fields and properties it includes.

- Predict(): calculates the weighted sum $S = w_i * x_i$ and checks whether $w_i * x_i + b > 0$ or, equivalently, that $w_i * x_i > -b$

- PredictSet(): using the previous method, predicts the classification of each data in the list submitted as argument

Remember the goal of the Perceptron is to find a classifying hyperplane that divides the set of data points into classes A and B. This division must guarantee that every element from class A lies on one side of the hyperplane and every element from class B lies on the other side. This hyperplane will satisfy (as it did in Chapter 9) the equation $wx + b = 0$. Thus, in the Predict() method, we classify any data point x for which $wx + b > 0$ as belonging to class 1; otherwise, we set it to be a member of class 0.

Finally, the Perceptron class, which inherits from the SingleNeuralNetwork abstract class, is illustrated in Listing 11-2.

Listing 11-2. Perceptron Class

```
public class Perceptron :SingleNeuralNetwork
    {
        public Perceptron(IEnumerable<TrainingSample>training
        Samples, int inputs, double learningRate)
            : base(trainingSamples, inputs, learningRate)
        { }
```

```csharp
        public override void Training()
        {
            while (true)
            {
varmissclasification = false;

foreach (vartrainingSample in TrainingSamples)
                {
var output = Predict(trainingSample.Features);
var features = trainingSample.Features;
                    if (output != trainingSample.Classification)
                    {
missclasification = true;
                        for (var j = 0; j < Inputs; j++)
                            Weights[j] += LearningRate*
                            (trainingSample.Classification -
                            output)*features[j];
Bias+= LearningRate * (trainingSample.Classification - output);
                    }
                }

                if (!missclasification)
                    break;
            }
        }
    }
```

As we can see, the implementation of the `Training()` method in the `Perceptron` class is almost a direct translation of the pseudocode previously detailed.

To test our algorithm we will create a console application with the code seen in Listing 11-3.

Listing 11-3. Testing the Perceptron Class in a Console Application

```
vartrainingSamples = new List<TrainingSample>
                                 {
new TrainingSample(new double[] {1, 1}, 0, new List<double> { 0 } ),
new TrainingSample(new double[] {1, 0}, 0, new List<double> { 0 } ),
new TrainingSample(new double[] {0, 1}, 0, new List<double> { 0 } ),
                                 new TrainingSample
                                 (new double[] {0, 0}, 0,
                                 new List<double> { 0 } ),
                                 new TrainingSample
                                 (new double[] {1, 2}, 1,
                                 new List<double> { 0 } ),
                                 new TrainingSample
                                 (new double[] {2, 2}, 1,
                                 new List<double> { 1 } ),
                                 new TrainingSample
                                 (new double[] {2, 3}, 1,
                                 new List<double> { 1 } ),
                                 new TrainingSample
                                 (new double[] {0, 3}, 1,
                                 new List<double> { 1 } ),
                                 new TrainingSample
                                 (new double[] {0, 2}, 1,
                                 new List<double> { 1 } ),};

var perceptron = new Perceptron(trainingSamples, 2, 0.01);
perceptron.Training();

vartoPredict = new List<double[]>
                                 {
                                 new double[] {1, 1},
                                 new double[] {1, 0},
```

```
                                    new double[] {0, 0},
                                    new double[] {0, 1},
                                    new double[] {2, 0},
new[] {2.5, 2},
new[] {0.5, 1.5},
                                    };

var predictions = perceptron.PredictSet(toPredict);

            for (vari = 0; i<predictions.Count; i++)
Console.WriteLine("Data: ( {0} , {1} ) Classified as: {2}",
toPredict[i][0], toPredict[i][1], predictions[i]);
```

The result obtained after executing the code in Listing 11-3 can be seen in Figure 11-6.

```
Data: ( 1 , 1 ) Classified as: 0
Data: ( 1 , 0 ) Classified as: 0
Data: ( 0 , 0 ) Classified as: 0
Data: ( 0 , 1 ) Classified as: 0
Data: ( 2 , 0 ) Classified as: 0
Data: ( 2.5 , 2 ) Classified as: 1
Data: ( 0.5 , 1.5 ) Classified as: 1
```

Figure 11-6. *Classification outputted by our Perceptron, considering the data set defined in Listing 11-3*

When implementing an NN or any supervised learning method, always remember that the larger the training data set the better the approximation or mapping the algorithm will be able to make from the tabular function defined in the training set to the one being built using the weight vector and bias. In Listing 11-3, our training data set is very small, so the Perceptron will most likely make classification mistakes on new incoming data. It did not happen in this example, but it could happen when adding data that significantly differs from the type of data in that small training set.

Adaline & Gradient Descent Search

Adaline (Adaptive Linear Neuron) is a NN model proposed by Bernard Widrow in 1960 whose network structure is the same as that of the Perceptron. The difference between Perceptron and Adaline lies in the learning rule used. The Adaline algorithm uses a learning rule known by several names: *Delta Rule, Gradient Descent,* or *Least Mean Square (LMS).* This learning rule is typically incorporated in multi-layer networks and especially in the backpropagation algorithm. Thus, Adaline serves as a good introduction to multi-layer networks and to the popular backpropagation algorithm.

The main idea with the Delta Rule is to minimize the squared error carried out when classifying a training data *x*:

$$E_x = \frac{\left(y_x - y_x'\right)^2}{2}$$

In this case, y_x is the correct classification for training data *x* and y'_x is the classification outputted by the NN.

Adaline is an *unthresholded* NN, meaning it does not consider a bias or threshold in its learning stage. Therefore, during training, its output (for a data point *x*) is simply computed as the sum of $w_i x_i$. To achieve a minimization of the squared error carried out when classifying a training data *x*, the algorithm relies on the fact that the gradient (vector formed by all partial derivatives) of a function indicates the direction of the steepest increase of *E* (Figure 11-7). Thus, by multiplying the gradient by -1 we will obtain the direction of the steepest decrement of *E* from any point, which will lead us to the minimum error carried out.

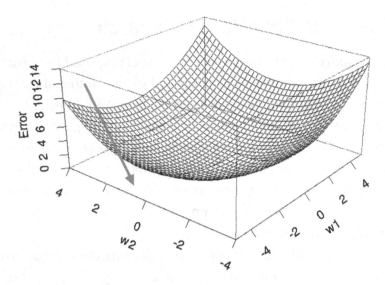

Figure 11-7. *The gradient denotes the direction of maximum increment of a function; its negation (blue arrow) indicates the direction of maximum decrement*

Thus, Adaline's training method is a type of *gradient descent search (GDS)* algorithm that determines the best weight vector by minimizing the global error E (remember E_x relates to the error carried out just on classifying training data x). In Adaline, the weight vector will initially contain random variables, and then these weights will be modified by taking small steps and moving downhill until we reach a point in the error surface that we consider "acceptable"; usually a small value for the maximum error on any training data point is considered acceptable. A gradient descent search is capable of finding the global minimum of a differentiable function.

To comprehend a little bit better the gradient descent method, let's see how it works by revising the following graphic (Figure 11-8). Also, let us consider that in a function $f : R \rightarrow R$, or a function of one variable x, the equation for updating the minimum value sought by the gradient descent method would be

$$x = x - \alpha * \frac{\partial f(x)}{\partial x}.$$

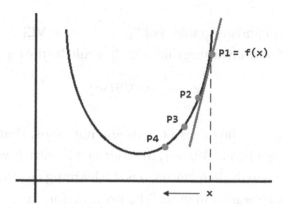

Figure 11-8. *Functioning of the gradient descent method*

In Figure 11-8, the GDS starts at point $p1 = f(x)$. According to the update formula, it calculates the derivative of f evaluated at point x and multiplied by the learning rate α. .ecause the derivative indicates the slope of f—and in this particular case the red line, which is the tangent line to point $p1$—has a positive slope, then $\alpha * \dfrac{\partial f(x)}{\partial x}$ will be a positive value

(recall $\alpha > 0$). Hence, the new value for x, let it be x', will be shifted to the left, and the new $p2 = f(x')$ will satisfy that $p2 < p1$. This procedure will continue until we reach the minimum, assuming α is small enough and will take smaller steps as it approaches the minimum; in other words, x will be slowly shifted to the left on new iterations.

Going back to the general case, and in order to find the steepest decrease of the error, we express E (the sum of all errors upon classifying each training data) in terms of w (weight vector). Notice that setting E in terms of w is always possible because $y'_x = w_i x_i$ for any given training data x; therefore, the function to minimize will be the following:

$$E(w) = \frac{\sum\limits_{i=1}^{n}(y_i - y'_i)^2}{2}$$

Hence, we will find the gradient of E(w)—let it be $\nabla E(w)$—and we will consider it in Adaline's learning rule, which would be the following:

$$w = w - \alpha * \nabla E(w)$$

Notice the sign on the rule is a minus and not a plus. That's because we must negate the gradient, $-\nabla E(w)$, in order to minimize E(w). As it was previously defined in the Perceptron, α is the learning rate that controls how fast we move toward a solution. The previous formula relates to the way we update the weight vector w, but how should we update a single weight? The rule for a single weight would be this:

$$w_i = w_i - \alpha * \frac{\partial E}{\partial w_i}$$

We substituted the gradient with its equivalent, the partial derivatives with respect to every weight w_i. After developing the term $\frac{\partial E}{\partial w_i}$ by calculating some derivatives and applying the chain rule, we will finally have the complete learning rule for GDS:

$$\frac{\partial E}{\partial w_i} = \sum_{j=1}^{n}\left(y_j - y_j'\right)*\left(-x_{ij}\right)$$

As before, y_j represents the correct classification of training data j, y_j' represents the classification outputted by the NN, and x_{ij} represents the ith input value of training data j—the input of training data j associated with weight w_i.

Even though GDS is, from a theoretical or mathematical perspective, an elegant method for finding a local minimum of a function, in practice it tends to be quite slow. Notice that to update a single weight you would need to go over the entire training data set, which could contain tens of thousands of training examples, so that would imply a lot of computations. Thus, for this practical reason, we typically use an approximated variant of GDS as the learning rule of Adaline; this variant is presented in the next section.

Stochastic Approximation

Stochastic gradient descent (SGD) or *incremental gradient descent* is an approximation procedure supplemental to GDS where weights are updated incrementally after the calculation of the error of each training data. Thus, it saves us from the computational trouble of having to loop over the entire training data set to compute the value of every weight. This is, in practice, the method used in Adaline and in other NN algorithms (backpropagation) that minimize the squared error by considering the correct classification of a training data and its output in the NN. The learning rule that uses stochastic approximation is known as the Delta Rule, the Adaline Rule, or the Widrow-Hoff Rule (after its creators). In Figure 11-9 we can see a very intuitive idea of the differences between GDS and SGD. In the first we move directly to the minimum of the error surface so we follow a straight path, while in the latter we move like a drunk person would; sometimes we lose balance and move to incorrect positions, but eventually we end up at the same point as GDS.

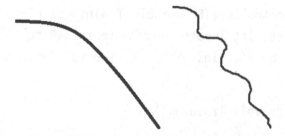

Figure 11-9.   *To the left the direct path that GDS would follow over the error surface to get to a minimum; to the right the "unbalanced" path followed by SGD*

The update rule using SGD would be as follows:

$$w_i = w_i + \alpha * (y_i - y_i') * x_i$$

Notice the similarity between this learning rule and the one described before for the Perceptron—it looks very similar. What's the main difference? The main difference is in the output of the NN while training. In Adaline we do not consider any threshold or activation function; therefore, $y_i' = w_i x_i$.

Note   When you combine several Adalines in a multi-layer network you obtain what is known as a Madaline.

Practical Problem: Implementing Adaline NN

After examining the theory behind Adaline's algorithm, it's time to finally implement the procedure in C#. For this purpose, we will create the class Adaline, shown in Listing 11-4.

Listing 11-4. Adaline Class

```
public class Adaline :SingleNeuralNetwork
    {
        public Adaline(IEnumerable<TrainingSample>training
        Samples, int inputs, double learningRate)
            : base(trainingSamples, inputs, learningRate)
        { }

public override void Training()
        {
            double error;
```

```
            do
            {
                error = 0.0;

foreach (vartrainingSample in TrainingSamples)
                {
var output = LinearFunction(trainingSample.Features);
varerrorT = Math.Pow(trainingSample.Classification - output, 2);

                    if (Math.Abs(errorT) < 0.001)
                        continue;

                    for (var j = 0; j < Inputs; j++)
                        Weights[j] +=  LearningRate *
                        (trainingSample.Classification - output) *
                        trainingSample.Features[j];

error = Math.Max(error, Math.Abs(errorT));
}
                }
            while (error > 0.25);
        }

        public double LinearFunction(double [] values)
        {
var summation = (from i in Enumerable.Range(0, Weights.Count)
                    select Weights[i]*values[i]).Sum();
            return summation;
        }

        public override double Predict(double[] features)
        {
            return LinearFunction(features) >0.5 ?1 : 0;
        }
    }
```

This class inherits from `SingleNeuralNetwork` and contains three methods. The second method is `LinearFunction()`, which simply computes the weighted sum $w_i x_i$. Remember, there's a difference between the prediction stage and the training stage in an Adaline. In the training or learning phase we compute the output of the NN as a weighted sum, but in the prediction phase we must use a categorical function to classify new incoming data; therefore, the prediction function is different from the learning function. In this case, our prediction function computes the weighted sum of the new data and outputs either 1 or 0 depending on whether the result of the weighted sum outputted a value greater than 0.5 or less than it.

The `Training()` method consists of a do ... while() statement where we verify if the maximum error carried out when classifying any training data exceeds 0.25. If it does, the loop will continue; otherwise, we will consider ourselves as being satisfied, and the method will end. Furthermore, we will not alter the weights if the error when classifying a training data is below 0.001. In Figure 11-10 we can see the result obtained after executing our Adaline on a small set of data.

```
Data: < 1 , 1 > Classified as: 0
Data: < 1 , 0 > Classified as: 0
Data: < 0 , 0 > Classified as: 0
Data: < 0 , 1 > Classified as: 0
Data: < 2 , 0 > Classified as: 0
Data: < 2,5 , 2 > Classified as: 1
Data: < 0,5 , 1,5 > Classified as: 1
```

Figure 11-10. *Result obtained after executing our Adaline on a small data set*

If we are curious about the functioning of the algorithm, we could set a breakpoint on the line `while (error > 0.25);` and then see how the maximum error diminishes after each iteration. The following values were the ones obtained on a series of iterations when we executed Adaline on the same training data set used in the Perceptron implementation: 3.2386, 1.7957, 1.0569, 0.6973, 0.5822, 0.5050, 0.4523, 0.4144, 0.3861, 0.3640, 0.3463, 0.3315, 0.3189, 0.3078, 0.2980, 0.2891, 0.2810, 0.2735, 0.2676, 0.2614, 0.2552, and 0.2491.

Multi-layer Networks

A *multi-layer network* is a type of NN in which we have multiple NNs grouped in layers and connected from one layer to the other. The NNs we have described so far (Perceptron, Adaline) were constituted by two layers: an input layer of multiple nodes and an output layer of a single node. The multi-layer NN shown in Figure 11-11 is composed of three layers: input, hidden, and output. It's also a *feed-forward* NN; in other words, all signals go from nodes in one layer to nodes in the next layer. Thus, a multi-layer NN is constructed by putting together many of our simple "neurons" arranged into layers and having the output of a neuron as the input of another neuron in the next layer.

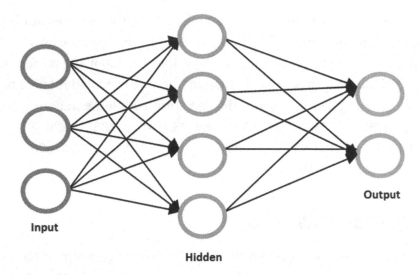

Figure 11-11. *Multi-layer, feed-forward, fully connected NN consisting of three layers: one for input units, one for hidden units (gray) and one for output units (green). Sometimes the input layer is not considered as a layer.*

Except for the input layer, which receives its inputs from the components (xi) of the training data, all other layers receive their inputs from the activation function of the previous layer. Every edge in a multi-layer NN represents a weight, and any edge leaving a node has its weight value multiplied by the activation function value of the node from which it originates. Thus, any node from layer L, where $L > 0$ (not the input layer), will have its input or activation value computed as follows:

$$A_{l,i} = g\left(\sum_{j=1}^{n} w_{l-1,j,i} A_{l-1,j} \right)$$

where n is the total number of units in layer $L - 1$, $A_{l,i}$ indicates the activation value of unit i at layer L, $w_{l-1,j,i}$ is the weight or edge going from unit j of layer $L - 1$ to unit i of layer L, and g is the activation function applied in the NN. Typically, g is chosen as the technically logical sigmoid function whose values range in the interval $[0, 1]$, and it is computed as follows:

$$sigmoid(x) = \frac{1}{1 + e^{-x}}$$

A very important property of the sigmoid function is that it's differentiable and continuous; remember that this property is significant to us because we will be calculating gradients and consequently derivatives.

One key element with multi-layer NNs is that they are capable of classifying non-linearly separable data sets. As a result, functions like *XOR* (Figure 11-12) that cannot be classified by linear NNs such as the Perceptron can be correctly classified by a simple multi-layer NN containing just one hidden layer.

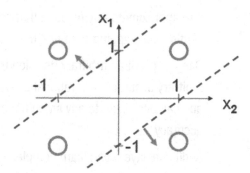

Figure 11-12. *XOR function; there's no line that would divide the red points from the green points*

We could think of multi-layer NNs as powerful mathematical functions able to approximate any tabular function we may have on the training data set. Each hidden layer represents a function, and the combination of layers can be seen as the composition of functions in mathematics. Thus, having n hidden layers could be seen as having the mathematical function $o(h1, h2 (\ldots hn(i(x)) \ldots))$ where o is the output layer, i the input layer, and hi the hidden layers.

Traditional NNs have a single hidden layer, and when they have more than one layer we are dealing with *deep neural networks* and *deep learning*. Table 11-1 illustrates the relationship between the number of hidden layers and the capacity of the resulting NN.

Table 11-1. *Relationship Between Number of Layers and Power of NNs*

Number Hidden Layers	Result
None	Only capable of representing linear separable functions or decisions
1	Can approximate any function that contains a continuous mapping from one finite space to another
2	Can represent an arbitrary decision boundary to arbitrary accuracy with rational activation functions and can approximate any smooth mapping to any accuracy
>2	Additional layers can learn complex representations (sort of automatic feature engineering).

It has been proven that a multi-layer NN with a single hidden layer is capable of learning any function. Hence, one may ask the question, if with a single hidden layer we can learn any function, then why do we need deep learning? The idea is that while the *universal approximation theorem* proves that, indeed, having a single hidden layer is enough for learning any continuous function, it does not state how easy it would be to complete this learning. Thus, for efficiency and accuracy reasons, we may need to add complexity to our NN architecture and include additional hidden layers in order to get a decent solution in a decent time.

The number of neurons in hidden layers is another important issue to consider when deciding on our NN architecture. Even though these layers do not directly interact with the external environment, they do have a remarkable influence on the final output. Both the number of hidden layers and the number of neurons in hidden layers must be carefully thought out.

Using too few neurons in the hidden layers will result in something called underfitting. Underfitting occurs when there are too few neurons in the hidden layers to effectively perceive signals in a complicated data set. Using too many neurons in hidden layers can result in several problems, the best known of which is overfitting, or when the weights adjust too well to the training data set and as a result the NN is unable to correctly predict new incoming data.

Note   The universal approximation theorem states that a feed-forward network with a single hidden layer containing a finite number of neurons can approximate any continuous function; this allows NNs to be considered as universal approximators.

Backpropagation Algorithm

As occurs in Adaline NNs, multi-layer NNs using backpropagation typically rely on the gradient descent method, and more specifically on the stochastic gradient approximation method, for adjusting the weights of the NN. They also seek to achieve the same goal as Adaline's algorithm— minimizing the error in the quadratic difference between the true classification of the data and the network output.

The idea with the backpropagation algorithm is that it serves as a mechanism for transporting the error taking place at the output layer to the final hidden layer (adjusting weights on the way), and from there to the previous hidden layer, and so on, backward; in other words, if o is the output layer and h_1, h_2, ..., h_n denote the hidden layers, then the backpropagation algorithm carries on the error from the output layer (equivalent to having the weights adjusted or the error minimized), from o to h_n, then from h_n to h_{n-1}, and so on until the error adjustment process reaches h_1. This functioning justifies the name *backpropagation*, because the output is computed from the input layer passing through layers h_1, h_2, ..., h_n and ending in the output layer, and then, once an output has been obtained, the weights are adjusted backward from output to the first hidden layer.

As mentioned before, the backpropagation algorithm relies on the gradient descent method, as does the Adaline method. The first difference we can call out between these two procedures is that with Adaline we only had one output node, but in multi-layer NNs and therefore in backpropagation we could be dealing with multiple output nodes arranged in an output layer; thus, the total error must be calculated as follows:

$$E(w) = \frac{\sum_{i=1}^{n}\sum_{j=1}^{k}\left(y_{ij} - y_{ij}'\right)^2}{2}$$

where n is the cardinality of the training data set, k the number of units in the output layer, y_{ij} the correct classification of training data i at node and position j from the output layer, and y'_{ij} the classification outputted for training data i at node j in the output layer of our NN.

The learning rule for every node in a backpropagation procedure resembles that of the Perceptron and Adaline. The rule, according to a stochastic approximation, is as follows:

$$w_{ij} = w_{ij} + \alpha * \delta_j * x_{ij}$$

In this case, w_{ij} indicates a weight going from node i into node j, α is the learning rate, x_{ij} is the activation value going from node i into node j (in the input layer these values coincide with the input values), and δ_j is the error at node j. Learning rules previously described did not have two subindices (w_{ij}) as they do now in the weight update rule of the backpropagation algorithm. Let's recall that backpropagation is intended to work on multi-layer NNs; therefore, we will have many nodes connected to other nodes so each edge ij has an associated w_{ij}.

So, we initially have every variable in the weight update formula except for δ_j; this term represents the error on classification and is the one we need to derivate with respect to the weights to find the gradient, and as a result the steepest descent with respect to w in the error surface. As stochastic approximation does, we iterate through every training data one at a time, which justifies that

$$\delta_j = -\frac{\partial E_d}{\partial \sum\limits_{i} w_{ij} * x_{ij}}$$

where E_d is the error associated with classifying training data d and w_{ij} is the weights associated with unit j. We know the formula for the global error $E(w)$, but that's not the formula we derivate to minimize w. Remember that stochastic approximation works on one training data at a time; therefore, we derivate the following equation:

$$E_d = \frac{\sum_{j=1}^{k}\left(y_j - y_j'\right)^2}{2}$$

In this case, k is the total number of nodes in the output layer, y_j is the correct classification for node j, and y_j' is the value outputted by our NN. Applying the chain rule and considering the case where the node on which we calculate the error term is either an output or a hidden unit, we can reach the next formulas:

- For nodes in the output layer,

$$\delta_j = -\frac{\partial E_d}{\partial \sum_i w_{ij} * x_{ij}} = \left(y_j - y_j'\right) * y_j' * \left(1 - y_j'\right)$$

- This implies,

$$w_{ij} = w_{ij} + \alpha * \left(y_j - y_j'\right) * y_j' * \left(1 - y_j'\right) * x_{ij}$$

- For nodes in the hidden layers,

$$\delta_j = -\frac{\partial E_d}{\partial \sum_i w_{ij} * x_{ij}} = y_j' * \left(1 - y_j'\right) * \sum_{k \in Stream} \delta_k * w_{kj}$$

- Stream, in this case, is the set of nodes whose inputs correspond to the output of node j. The previous formula implies that

$$w_{ij} = w_{ij} + \alpha * y'_j * \left(1 - y'_j\right) * \sum_{k \in \text{Stream}} \delta_k * w_{kj} * x_{ij}$$

Note that the weight-update formulas obtained assume we have sigmoid units; in other words, that we are using the sigmoid function as an activation function in every node of the NN. The general form of the weight-update rule for output and hidden layers respectively would be as follows:

$$w_{ij} = w_{ij} + \alpha * \left(y_j - y'_j\right) * G\left(y'_j\right) * x_{ij}$$

$$w_{ij} = w_{ij} + \alpha * G\left(y'_j\right) * \sum_{k \in \text{Stream}} \delta_k * w_{kj} * x_{ij}$$

where $G(y'_j)$ represents the derivative of the activation function evaluated at the value outputted by the activation, as we know this value can be expressed in terms of w. Recall that the sigmoid function's derivative is $F(x) * (1 - F(x))$; this is very easy to compute and work with and is one of the main reasons the sigmoid function is the classical activation function for multi-layer neural networks.

Figure 11-13 illustrates another popular activation function, the hyperbolic tangent, a symmetrical function whose output is in the range [-1;1] and that is denoted and calculated as follows:

$$\tanh(x) = \frac{\sinh(x)}{\cosh(x)} = \frac{e^x - e^{-x}}{e^x + e^{-x}}$$

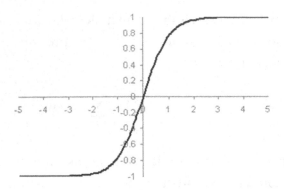

Figure 11-13. *Hyperbolic tangent function, which outputs values in the range (-1;1)*

Nowadays, a popular activation function that is replacing the sigmoid function and other similar smooth functions is the rectified linear unit, or ReLU (Figure 11-14). Unlike sigmoid and the smooth functions, ReLU doesn't have the shortcoming of the vanishing gradient issues seen in deep learning, such as when training a NN of more than three layers. Its equation is extremely simple:

$$ReLU(x) = max(0, x)$$

In other words, ReLUs let all positive values pass through unchanged, but just set any negative values to 0. Although newer activation functions are gaining traction, most deep neural networks these days use ReLU or one of its closely related variants.

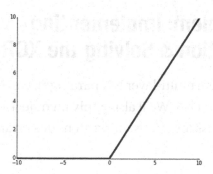

Figure 11-14. *ReLU function*

To comprehend a little bit better the flow backward in the backpropagation algorithm and the nodes or edges in which our variables will reside, let's examine Figure 11-15.

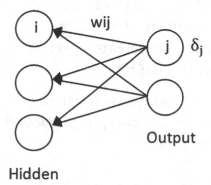

Figure 11-15. *Flow backward in the backpropagation algorithm. Weight wij is updated by considering the error term residing in node j.*

Now that we have a theoretical background on the functioning of the backpropagation algorithm, in the next section we will implement a `MultiLayerNetwork` class representing multi-layer NNs, and we will develop our backpropagation algorithm as a method of that class.

Practical Problem: Implementing Backpropagation & Solving the XOR Problem

To properly encode the multi-layer NN paradigm, we will create the class shown in Listing 11-5. We'll also apply an object-oriented approach to include a Layer class for representing all nodes arranged as a list of sigmoid units.

Listing 11-5. MultiLayerNetwork and Layer Classes

```
public class MultiLayerNetwork
    {
        public List<Layer> Layers { get; set; }
        public List<TrainingSample>TrainingSamples{ get; set; }
        public intHiddenUnits{ get; set; }
        public intOutputUnits{ get; set; }
        public double LearningRate{ get; set; }
        private double _maxError;

        public MultiLayerNetwork(IEnumerable<TrainingSample>tra
        iningSamples, int inputs, inthiddenUnits, int outputs,
        double learningRate)
        {
            Layers = new List<Layer>();
TrainingSamples = new List<TrainingSample>(trainingSamples);
LearningRate = learningRate;
HiddenUnits = hiddenUnits;
OutputUnits = outputs;

CreateLayers(inputs);
        }
```

```
private void CreateLayers(int inputs)
        {
Layers.Add(new Layer(HiddenUnits, TrainingSamples,
LearningRate, inputs, TypeofLayer.Hidden));
Layers.Add(new Layer(OutputUnits, TrainingSamples,
LearningRate, HiddenUnits, TypeofLayer.OutPut));
        }

        public List<double>PredictSet(IEnumerable<double[]> objects)
        {
var result = new List<double>();

foreach (varobj in objects)
result.Add(Predict(obj));

            return result;
        }

        public Layer OutPutLayer
        {
            get { returnLayers.Last(); }
        }

        public Layer HiddenLayer
        {
            get { returnLayers.First(); }
        }
    }

public class Layer
    {
        public List<SigmoidUnit> Units { get; set; }
        public TypeofLayer Type { get; set; }
```

```
    public Layer(int number, List<TrainingSample>tr
    ainingSamples, double learningRate, int inputs,
    TypeofLayertypeofLayer)
    {
        Units = new List<SigmoidUnit>();
        Type = typeofLayer;
        for (vari = 0; i< number; i++)
Units.Add(new SigmoidUnit(trainingSamples, inputs, learningRate));
    }
}

public enumTypeofLayer
{
    Hidden, OutPut
}
```

The Layer class contains two properties, a List of SigmoidUnit (we will soon examine this class) and a TypeofLayer Type that is an enum with two possible values: Hidden and OutPut. In the class constructor we simply add as many nodes to the layer as the number argument specifies. In the MultiLayerNetwork class we include properties to obtain the HiddenLayer or, if there's more than one, the first hidden layer and the OutputLayer.

The constructor of the MultiLayerNetwork class receives as arguments the training data set, the number of inputs, hidden nodes, and outputs; and the learning rate. It creates the set of layers by calling the CreateLayers() method. Finally, the PredictSet() method predicts or classifies a set of data received as an argument. The class also includes some properties or fields, most of which are self-descriptive. The _maxError field will be used to indicate the maximum error when classifying any training data in an iteration or epoch of the backpropagation algorithm.

Note   An iteration in a NN's learning algorithm is typically known as an *epoch*.

The SigmoidUnit class inherits from SingleNeuralNetwork, and its code is very simple (Listing 11-6). It merely overrides the Predict() method to compute the value of the sigmoid function with the features of the input data and the weight vector.

Listing 11-6. SigmoidUnit Class, Which Inherits from the SingleNeuralNetwork Abstract Class

```
public class SigmoidUnit :SingleNeuralNetwork
    {
        public double ActivationValue{ get; set; }
        public double ErrorTerm{ get; set; }

        public SigmoidUnit(IEnumerable<TrainingSample>training
        Samples, int inputs, double learningRate)
            : base(trainingSamples, inputs, learningRate)
        { }

        public override double Predict(double [] features)
        {
var result = 0.0;

            for (vari = 0; i<features.Length; i++)
                result += features[i] * Weights[i];

            return ActivationValue = 1/(1 + Math.Pow(Math.E,
            -result));
        }
    }
```

The Training() method representing the backpropagation algorithm is illustrated in Listing 11-7. In this method, we iterate over the training data set until the maximum error when predicting any training data becomes less than 0.001. We predict the output of the NN, and, because we are using SigmoidUnit nodes, the resulting value will be stored, as Listing 11-8 indicates, in the public property ActivationValue. Once this value has been calculated, we loop over the output units, computing their error terms, and later over nodes in the hidden layers, also computing their error terms. Recall from the last section that their computation is different. In the UpdateWeight() method we update the weights, and at the end of the loop we update the maximum error when classifying any training data.

Listing 11-7. Training() Method Representing Backpropagation Algorithm

```
public void Training()
{
    _maxError = double.MaxValue;

    while (Math.Abs(_maxError) > .001)
    {
foreach (vartrainingSample in TrainingSamples)
        {
Predict(trainingSample.Features);

            // Error term for output layer ...
            for (vari = 0; i<OutPutLayer.Units.Count; i++)
            {
OutPutLayer.Units[i].ErrorTerm = FunctionDerivative
(OutPutLayer.Units[i].ActivationValue, TypeFunction.Sigmoid) *
```

```
                                        (trainingSample.
                                        Classifications[i] -
                                        OutPutLayer.Units[i].
                                        ActivationValue);
    }

                    // Error term for hidden layer ...
                    for (vari = 0; i<HiddenLayer.Units.Count; i++)
                    {
varoutputUnitWeights = OutPutLayer.Units.Select(u =>u.
Weights[i]).ToList();
var product = (from j in Enumerable.Range(0, outputUnitWeights.Count)
                                        select outputUnitWei
                                        ghts[j]*OutPutLayer.
                                        Units[j].ErrorTerm).
                                        Sum();
HiddenLayer.Units[i].ErrorTerm = FunctionDerivative
(HiddenLayer.Units[i].ActivationValue, TypeFunction.Sigmoid) *
product;
                    }

UpdateWeight(trainingSample.Features, OutPutLayer);
UpdateWeight(trainingSample.Features, HiddenLayer);
_maxError = OutPutLayer.Units.Max(u =>Math.Abs(u.ErrorTerm));
            }
        }
```

In order to make our method as flexible as possible and interact easily with different activation functions, we coded the FunctionDerivative() method (Listing 11-8), which receives an activation value and a type of function (encoded as an enum) and outputs the derivative of the activation function evaluated at the activation value.

Listing 11-8. FunctionDerivative() Method and Enum Declaration
with Activation Functions Previously Mentioned

```
private double FunctionDerivative(double v, TypeFunctionfunction)
        {
            switch (function)
            {
                case TypeFunction.Sigmoid:
                    return v*(1 - v);
                case TypeFunction.Tanh:
                    return 1 - Math.Pow(v, 2);
                case TypeFunction.ReLu:
                    return Math.Max(0, v);
                default:
                    return 0;
            }
        }
public enumTypeFunction
    {
 Sigmoid, Tanh, ReLu
    }
```

By combining the previous method with the following (Listing 11-9)
sibling classes of the `SigmoidUnit` class (shown in Listing 11-6), we can
effortlessly change our model from one type of unit (Sigmoid, Tanh,
ReLU) to the other and experiment with different types of activation
functions.

Listing 11-9. Hyperbolic Tangent and ReLU Units

```
public class TanhUnit :SingleNeuralNetwork
    {
        public double ActivationValue{ get; set; }
        public double ErrorTerm{ get; set; }

        public TanhUnit(IEnumerable<TrainingSample>training
        Samples, int inputs, double learningRate)
            : base(trainingSamples, inputs, learningRate)
        { }

        public override double Predict(double [] features)
        {
var result = 0.0;

            for (vari = 0; i<features.Length; i++)
                result += features[i] * Weights[i];

ActivationValue = Math.Tanh(result);
            return ActivationValue;
        }
    }

public class ReLu :SingleNeuralNetwork
    {
        public double ActivationValue{ get; set; }
        public double ErrorTerm{ get; set; }

        public ReLu(IEnumerable<TrainingSample>trainingSamples,
        int inputs, double learningRate)
            : base(trainingSamples, inputs, learningRate)
        { }
```

```
        public override double Predict(double [] features)
        {
var result = 0.0;

            for (vari = 0; i<features.Length; i++)
                result += features[i] * Weights[i];

            return Math.Max(0, result);
        }
    }
```

Note that all "unit" classes can be grouped better depending on the hierarchy model used. For example, all classes include an ActivationValue and ErrorTerm properties that could be encapsulated in an upper class, and as a result we would obtain a better class design. This object-oriented design task will be left to the reader.

The UpdateWeight() method (Listing 11-10) is a direct translation of the weight-update rules presented in the last section. This method uses the ErrorTerm public property that we incorporated in the SigmoidUnit class to store the error of every node of the NN.

Listing 11-10. UpdateWeight() Method

```
        private void UpdateWeight(double[] features, Layer layer)
        {
varactivationValues =
layer.Type == TypeofLayer.Hidden ? features : HiddenLayer.
Units.Select(u =>u.ActivationValue).ToArray();

foreach (var unit in layer.Units)
        {
            for (vari = 0; i<unit.Weights.Count; i++)
```

```
unit.Weights[i] += LearningRate * unit.ErrorTerm *
activationValues[i];
                }
        }
```

Finally, in order to predict and classify new incoming data in the multi-layer NN, we code the `Predict()` method (Listing 11-11), which calculates the activation values from the nodes of each layer, starting from the input nodes in a feed-forward manner until it reaches the output layer. Then, to output a classification, it considers the set of values at the output layer and either outputs a classification that is mapped to a set of values (0, 1 in this case, depending on whether or not the outputted value is greater than 0.5) or simply outputs the index of the node in the output layer with the highest value; that's the purpose of the `ReturnIndexByHalf()` and `ReturnIndexByMax()` methods, respectively, also illustrated in Listing 11-11. Notice that the first method is developed such that it thinks about a NN with an output layer of a single node.

Listing 11-11. Classification-related Methods

```
        public double Predict(double[] features)
        {
            for (vari = 0; i<Layers.Count; i++)
            {
foreach (var unit in Layers[i].Units)
                {
varactivationValues =
i ==  0 ? features : HiddenLayer.Units.Select(u =>u.
ActivationValue).ToArray();
```

```
unit.Predict(activationValues);
                    }
                }

                return ReturnIndexByHalf();
        }

        private intReturnIndexByHalf()
        {
var unit = OutPutLayer.Units.First();
                return unit.ActivationValue< 0.5 ? 0 : 1;
        }

        private intReturnIndexByMax()
        {
var max = OutPutLayer.Units.Max(u =>u.ActivationValue);
                return OutPutLayer.Units.FindIndex(0, unit =>unit.
                ActivationValue == max);
        }
```

In order to test our multi-layer NN, we will see how it correctly classifies data from the XOR problem by having a NN structure composed of a hidden layer of three nodes and an output layer of a single node. We will also add a little modification to our TrainingSample class to contemplate the case where a training data may have a classification vector instead of a single value. A classification vector could be binary; for instance, (1, 0, 0) could indicate that the training data with which it associates is to be classified as red and not green or blue.

Both the new TrainingSample class and the setting for testing a multi-layer NN on the XOR problem are illustrated in Listing 11-12.

Listing 11-12. Slight Modification to TrainingSample Class and Setting Up for Testing Our MultiLayerNetwork Class for the XOR Problem

```
public class TrainingSample
    {
        public int Classification { get; set; }
        public List<double> Classifications { get; set; }
        public double[] Features { get; set; }

        public TrainingSample(double [] features, int
        classification, IEnumerable<double>clasifications = null )
        {
            Features = new double[features.Length];
Array.Copy(features, Features, features.Length);
            Classification = classification;
            if (clasifications != null)
                Classifications = new List<double>(clasifications);
        }
    }

vartrainingSamplesXor = new List<TrainingSample>
                                {
                                    new TrainingSample
                                    (new double[] {0, 0},
                                    -1, new List<double>
                                    { 0 } ),
                                    new TrainingSample
                                    (new double[] {1, 1},
                                    -1, new List<double>
                                    { 0 } ),
```

```
                                        new TrainingSample
                                        (new double[] {0, 1},
                                        -1, new List<double>
                                        { 1 } ),
                                        new TrainingSample
                                        (new double[] {1, 0},
                                        -1, new List<double>
                                        { 1 } ),
                            };

var multilayer = new MultiLayerNetwork(trainingSamplesXor, 2,
3, 1, 0.01);
vartoPredict = new List<double[]>
                            {
                                    new double[] {1, 1},
                                    new double[] {1, 0},
                                    new double[] {0, 0},
                                    new double[] {0, 1},
                                    new double[] {2, 0},
new[] {2.5, 2},
new[] {0.5, 1.5},
                            };

var predictions = multilayer.PredictSet(toPredict);

            for (vari = 0; i<predictions.Count; i++)
Console.WriteLine("Data: ( {0} , {1} ) Classified as: {2}",
toPredict[i][0], toPredict[i][1], predictions[i]);
```

The result obtained after executing the code from Listing 11-12 in a C# console application is shown in Figure 11-16.

```
Data: ( 1 , 1 ) Classified as: 0
Data: ( 1 , 0 ) Classified as: 1
Data: ( 0 , 0 ) Classified as: 0
Data: ( 0 , 1 ) Classified as: 1
Data: ( 2 , 0 ) Classified as: 1
Data: ( 2,5 , 2 ) Classified as: 0
Data: ( 0,5 , 1,5 ) Classified as: 1
```

Figure 11-16. *Result obtained after executing the code from Listing 11-12*

Up to this point we have examined different models of NNs; we examined the Perceptron model, which is unable to distinguish the scenario where we have more than two classes that cannot be separated by a hyperplane. We know Adalines are based on the gradient descent search method, which allows them to differentiate non-linearly separable data sets, and their learning rule serves as the learning paradigm for the backpropagation algorithm. Finally, we learned about multi-layer NNs, which use a multi-layer structure—which simulates the composition of mathematical functions——and are considered as universal approximators. In the next chapter, we will examine a very interesting application of NNs, one in which an AI will be able to understand our handwritten digits; such an application is called handwritten digit recognition.

Summary

In this chapter, we studied artificial neural networks, a powerful AI device capable of solving multiple problems by learning patterns acquired from labeled training data sets and by means of approximating a tabular function represented by the training data set. We described how learning is, at its core, highly related to optimization problems since it can be seen as a continuous improvement of doing some task. Equivalently, it can be viewed as a way of minimizing the error carried out while being in a learning stage that ends after several epochs or iterations or after having achieved a suitable learning error that would allow us to eventually predict, with a small error factor, the classification of new incoming data. We began by describing the Perceptron, then moved to Adalines, whose learning rule resembles that of multi-layer NNs, and proposed an object-oriented approach for implementing all of these NNs

CHAPTER 12

Handwritten Digit Recognition

In Chapter 11 we studied artificial neural networks (NNs), a supervised learning paradigm that mimics the way neurons in our brain work. The learning process in NNs consists of approximating a function described in a tabular manner via a training data set containing features of objects (inputs to the function to be approximated) and their corresponding classification (outputs of the function).

As described before, NNs are capable of learning a function described in a training data set by adjusting the set of weights linking their neurons. At the same time, neurons can be arranged in different layers, and the purpose of each layer is to improve the mathematical power of the NN. Recall that an NN is basically a mathematical function and that the addition of layers is similar to the operation of the composition of functions in mathematics; in other words, every layer can be seen as a function, and the NN as $F(L1(L2(\dots (LN(x))))$ where F is the NN and Li the layers within the NN.

NNs can be applied to multiple problems of science. Among these problems, it is worth mentioning face recognition, which is very popular nowadays and is being incorporated in mobile phones and other electronic devices, pattern recognition, shape recognition, autonomous vehicle driving, and the problem that will be the focus point of this chapter, *optical character recognition* (OCR), and, more specifically, a subproblem of OCR known as *handwritten digit recognition* (HDR).

© Arnaldo Pérez Castaño 2018
A. Pérez Castaño, *Practical Artificial Intelligence*,
https://doi.org/10.1007/978-1-4842-3357-3_12

Why choose HDR over all other possible problems to present as an illustrative example of NNs? First, HDR is not as far as you might imagine from the practical problems we examined in Chapter 11. Furthermore, a training data set for HDR typically consists of low-resolution images that can be easily reproduced by anyone, and the feature extraction process is very easy to accomplish. As we shall see soon, the entire image will be considered as input to the NN, and the image-processing stage will not be complicated for this problem, so it will not deviate us from our core topic, NNs.

In this chapter, we will implement an application in Windows Forms that will allow us to "hand paint" a digit and will give us the correct classification for that drawn digit. For example, if the drawn digit is 1, then the output should be 1; if it's 2 then output should be 2, and so on. In the back end, this application will use a slightly modified version of the multi-layer NN introduced in Chapter 11.

Note   NNs can be applied not only as supervised learning methods but also as unsupervised learning and reinforcement learning methods, which are other paradigms of machine learning.

What Is Handwritten Digit Recognition?

The recent digital revolution brought a dramatic change to our perspective of concepts such as communication and connectivity. Today, biometrics, the science of identifying or verifying the identity of a person based on physiological or behavioral characteristics, is playing a key role in authentication problems. Physiological characteristics could include fingerprints, iris, hand geometry, or facial image. Behavioral characteristics can be actions carried out by a person in a particular manner and may include recognition of signature, machine-printed characters, handwriting, and voice.

Some of the applications of OCR include postal address system, signature verification system, recognition of characters from form-filled applications, and so forth. OCR is basically of two types: *offline* character recognition and *online* character recognition. In the first case, an image coming from a scanner is typically accepted as input, and the recognition procedure tends to be more difficult than in the latter case because of the unavailability of contextual information and lack of prior knowledge such as text position, size of text, order of strokes, start point, stop point, and so on. In online character recognition, the system starts accepting input from the moment a pen from a hardware device, such as a graphic tablet, light pen, and so on, begins working; lots of information becomes available during the input process, such as current position, moment's direction, start points, stop points, and stroke orders. Handwritten character recognition usually comes under this category even though applications for the other one also exist.

Handwriting is the human way of communicating with each other using written media. With advancements in technology and developments in science, there have been a lot of changes in technology in terms of communication with computers through handwriting. Nowadays, a computer program is typically needed that is capable of receiving and recognizing an input in the form of handwriting data; this is what is known as *handwritten recognition.*

Handwritten digit recognition is a subset of handwritten recognition whose main purpose is to recognize handwritten digits; thus, the universe of characters in HDR is exclusively {0, 1, 2, 3, 4, 5, 6, 7, 8, 9}, and no other character will be correctly recognized.

Note   One of the most popular data sets for HDR is MNIST; divided in two subsets, one of them serves for training your NN and the other for testing its accuracy. It can be downloaded from `http://yann.lecun.com`.

Training Data Set

In order to train our multi-layer NN to recognize handwritten digits, we created the training data set shown in Figure 12-1.

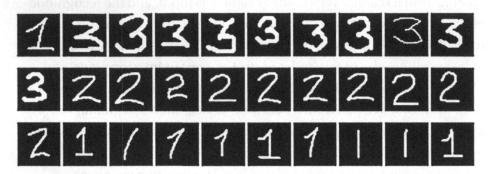

Figure 12-1. *Small training data set consisting of 30 images of 30 x 30 resolution*

This self-created training data set consists of merely 30 images containing handwritten digits in the range [1, 3], ten images for each digit. In this practical problem, we will not be incorporating the recognition of all digits; rather, we will focus on recognizing digits 1, 2, and 3. As we shall see very soon, extending the NN herein detailed to recognize all digits will not result in any complication to the reader in their future efforts.

We choose to have all images in 30 x 30 resolution because it simplifies the input layer of our NN, and the color selection (black background, white font) simplifies our feature-extraction phase.

Multi-layer NN for HDR

The NN we will be modeling to solve the HDR problem will not differ too much from the model of the multi-layer NN proposed in Chapter 11. Recall that because of the universal approximation theorem we know that having a single hidden layer in a multi-layer NN is always enough for learning or approximating any continuous function. Also, recall that deep learning (NNs involving various hidden layers) does not exist in vain and that its purpose is to provide more accurate and efficient results in those problems where having a single hidden layer would not provide accurate or feasible enough results. Having multiple hidden layers can help us obtain a more accurate, efficient solution in a shorter time. For the problem at hand, we will settle for having a multi-layer NN with a single hidden layer.

The input layer will be a direct mapping from the image pixels into the nodes of this layer; therefore, if we have a 30 x 30 image, our input layer will contain 900 nodes, one for each pixel, and their values will be 0 if the pixel color is black and 1 in any other case (Figure 12-2). This is not the most accurate strategy we can use for extracting features to be fed to our NN, but it will work for this simple example. Other feature-extraction strategies consider getting the pixel intensity values and having those values scaled to the range [0, 1].

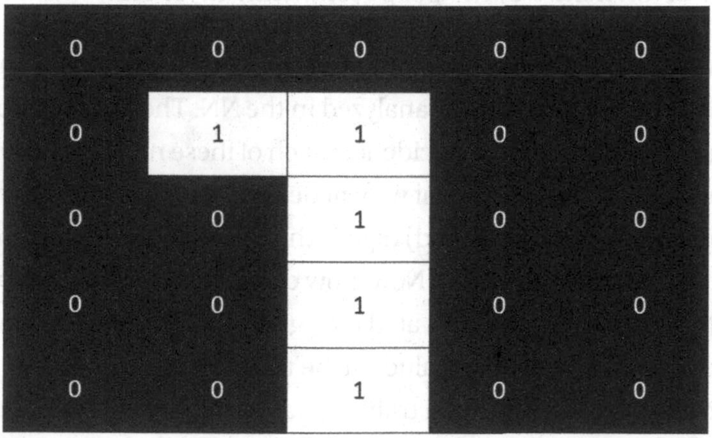

Figure 12-2. *Feature extraction by mapping every black pixel to 0 and any other pixel to 1*

The output layer will contain three nodes, one for each of the digits (1, 2, 3) being considered for recognition. The definitive structure of the proposed multi-layer NN is illustrated in Figure 12-3.

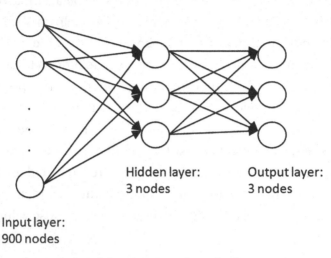

Figure 12-3. *Structure of the proposed multi-layer NN*

At this point, the reader may wonder how we decide from the output layer the classification of the data being analyzed in the NN. The fact that we have three nodes in this layer is no coincidence; each of these nodes is supposed to match a digit out of the three that we will be recognizing. The first node matches or outputs (if it is activated) digit 1, the second node matches digit 2, and the third node outputs digit 3. Now, how do we choose a node to be the output of the network or to be activated for a given training data? Simple—the node with the highest activation value will be the node chosen as output.

The correct classification of a training data will be represented as a vector of three components; two of these will have value 0 and one will have value 1. The component having 1 as its value indicates the correct classification of the training data. For example, the vector (1, 0, 0) denotes 1 as the correct classification of a training data, the vector (0, 1, 0) indicates 2 as the correct classification, and (0, 0, 1) marks 3 as the proper classification for the training data being analyzed.

To conclude, it's essential to mention that in the proposed NN we will not consider an initialization of weights as random values in the range [0, 1]; rather, we will set them up as random values in the range [-0.5, 0.5]. The reasons behind this change are numerical and are also related to performance. Because we will have an input layer with many nodes, the weighted sum of these input values will result in sigmoid activation values very close to 1, which will undermine the performance of our NN and prevent us from converging toward a minimization of the error and consequently prevent us from achieving a decent solution. As a note of advice, remember that even the initialization of weights is an issue to consider when designing your NN as it can affect the NNs overall performance.

Implementation

As mentioned before, we will be developing a Windows Forms application that will allow us to draw a digit on a picture box, and then by clicking on a Classification button we will obtain the classification of the drawn digit. Simply to gain elegance and expressiveness in the code, we will work with the following class (Listing 12-1), which is a direct descendant of the MultiLayerNetwork class introduced in Chapter 11.

Listing 12-1. HandwrittenDigitRecognitionNn Class Representing a NN for HDR

```
public class HandwrittenDigitRecognitionNn : MultiLayerNetwork
    {
        public HandwrittenDigitRecognitionNn(IEnumerable<Training
        Sample> trainingDataSet, int inputs, int hiddenUnits,
        int outputs, double learningRate)
```

```
        :base(trainingDataSet, inputs, hiddenUnits,
        outputs, learningRate)
    {

    }
}
```

An instance of this class will be added to the HandwrittenRecognitionGui class, inheriting from Windows.Forms.Form and containing most of the code detailed in this chapter. The part of this class where fields and properties are declared can be seen in Listing 12-2.

Listing 12-2. HandwrittenRecognitionGui Class Representing the Visual Application

```
public partial class HandwrittenRecognitionGui : Form
    {
        private bool _mouseIsDown;
        private Bitmap _bitmap;
        private const int NnInputs = 900;
        private const int NnHidden = 3;
        private const int NnOutputs = 3;
        private HandwrittenDigitRecognitionNn _
        handwrittenDigitRecogNn;
        private bool _weightsLoaded;

public HandwrittenRecognitionGui()
        {
            InitializeComponent();
            _bitmap = new Bitmap(paintBox.Width, paintBox.Height);
        }
}
```

These fields or properties can be described as follows:

- _mouseIsDown: used in mouse-related events to determine whether a mouse button (left click) has been pressed

- _bitmap: bitmap image used to store what the user draws on the picture box and then submit it to the NN for classification

- NnInputs: number of nodes in the input layer of the NN

- NnHidden: number of nodes in the hidden layer of the NN

- NnOutputs: number of nodes in the output layer of the NN

- _handwrittenDigitRecogNn: instance of the NN class

- _weightsLoaded: determines whether the set of weights has been loaded to the application. Once we train the NN the set of weights found will be saved in a file for future use; therefore, this variable will control the reading of the file containing those weights.

The HandRecognitionGui class will be complemented by adding different methods for handling mouse-related events in the picture-box control, which we added to the application in Design mode. We will see how the application looks very soon. These methods linked to mouse events are shown in Listing 12-3.

Listing 12-3. Mouse-Event Methods in the Picture Box Where We Will Be Drawing Digits to Be Classified

```
private void PaintBoxMouseDown(object sender, MouseEventArgs e)
    {
        if (e.Button == MouseButtons.Left)
            _mouseIsDown = true;
    }

    private void PaintBoxMouseMove(object sender,
    MouseEventArgs e)
    {
        if (_mouseIsDown)
        {
            var point = paintBox.PointToClient(Cursor.
            Position);
            DrawPoint((point.X), (point.Y), Color.
            FromArgb(255, 255, 255, 255));
        }
    }

    private void PaintBoxMouseUp(object sender,
    MouseEventArgs e)
    {
        _mouseIsDown = false;
    }

    public void DrawPoint(int x, int y, Color color)
    {
        var pen = new Pen(color);
        var gPaintBox = paintBox.CreateGraphics();
        var gImg = Graphics.FromImage(_bitmap);
        gPaintBox.DrawRectangle(pen, x, y, 1, 1);
        gImg.DrawRectangle(pen, x, y, 1, 1);
    }
```

From Listing 12-3 we can see that we have captured three mouse events: MouseDown (when user presses a mouse button on the control), MouseMove (when user moves the mouse over the control), and MouseUp (when user stops pressing a button on the control). These three events combined with the _mouseIsDown variable give us the necessary tools to construct a simple, straightforward mechanism for determining when the user is drawing on the control and saving that drawing both on the picture box and on the auxiliary bitmap image that we eventually submit to the NN for classification. Once the user has drawn a digit on the picture box control and clicked on the Classification button (we will soon take a look at the final GUI) an image-processing stage begins where we extract features from the image using the next method (Listing 12-4).

Listing 12-4. Extracting features

```csharp
private double [,] GetImage(Bitmap bitmap)
        {
        var result = new double[bitmap.Width, bitmap.Height];

        for (var i = 0; i < bitmap.Width; i++)
        {
            for (var j = 0; j < bitmap.Height; j++)
            {
                var pixel = bitmap.GetPixel(i, j);
                result[i, j] = pixel.R + pixel.G + pixel.B
                == 0 ? 0 : 1;
            }
        }

        return result;
        }
```

In the GetImage() method, we build a matrix of binary values; a value of 0 on a given (*i*, *j*) coordinate of the resulting matrix will indicate a pixel of black color in the image associated with the picture box, while a value of 1 indicates any other color.

In our visual application we will include a Train button whose method for the click event can be seen in Listing 12-5. In this method, we load the set of 30 x 30 images forming the training data set; we process each image and create an equivalent TrainingSample object. Then, we start the training process and save the resulting set of weights in a weights.txt file.

Listing 12-5. Load the Training Data Set, Train the NN, and Save the Resulting Weights

```
private void TrainBtnClick(object sender, EventArgs e)
        {
            var trainingDataSet = new List<TrainingSample>();
            var trainingDataSetFiles = Directory.
            GetFiles(Directory.GetCurrentDirectory() +
            "\\Digits");

            foreach(var file in trainingDataSetFiles)
            {
                var name = file.Remove(file.LastIndexOf(".")).
                Substring(file.LastIndexOf("\\") + 1);
                var @class = int.Parse(name.Substring(0, 1));
                var classVec = new[] {0.0, 0.0, 0.0};
                classVec[@class - 1] = 1;
                var imgMatrix = GetImage(new Bitmap(file));
                var imgVector = imgMatrix.Cast<double>().
                Select(c => c).ToArray();
                trainingDataSet.Add(new
                TrainingSample(imgVector, @class, classVec));
            }
```

```
_handwrittenDigitRecogNn = new HandwrittenDigit
RecognitionNn(trainingDataSet, NnInputs, NnHidden,
NnOutputs, 0.002);
_handwrittenDigitRecogNn.Training();

var fileWeights = new StreamWriter("weights.txt",
false);

foreach (var layer in _handwrittenDigitRecogNn.Layers)
{
    foreach (var unit in layer.Units)
    {
        foreach (var w in unit.Weights)
            fileWeights.WriteLine(w);
        fileWeights.WriteLine("*");
    }
    fileWeights.WriteLine("-");
}

fileWeights.Close();

MessageBox.Show("Training Complete!", "Message");
}
```

To classify the digit drawn on the picture box, we add the Classify button. The method triggered when the click event occurs is illustrated in Listing 12-6. In this method, we check for the existence of the weights.txt file, load the set of weights if the file exists, or output a warning message in any other case. If the weights have not been loaded then we run the ReadWeights() method and eventually execute the Predict() method of the NN and save the resulting classification in the classBox textbox.

Listing 12-6. Method Executed After the Classify Button Has Been Clicked

```
private void ClassifyBtnClick(object sender, EventArgs e)
        {
            if (Directory.GetFiles(Directory.
            GetCurrentDirectory()).Any(file => file ==
            Directory.GetCurrentDirectory() + "weights.txt")) {
                MessageBox.Show("Warning", "No weights file,
                you need to train your NN first");
               return;
            }

            if (!_weightsLoaded)
            {
                ReadWeights();
                _weightsLoaded = true;
            }

            var digitMatrix = GetImage(_bitmap);
            var prediction = _handwrittenDigitRecogNn.
            Predict(digitMatrix.Cast<double>().
            Select(c => c).ToArray());
            classBox.Text = (prediction + 1).ToString();
        }
```

The ReadWeights() method, acting as an auxiliary mini-parser, is in charge of reading the file of weights and assigning them to every node in the NN (Listing 12-7). Weights are stored one per line in the file, and weights belonging to different units will be separated by a line containing a "*" symbol, which marks the end of the weights assignment to a given unit and the start of another one. The same thing occurs with the "-" symbol but at the layer level.

Listing 12-7. ReadWeights() Method

```
private void ReadWeights()
        {
            _handwrittenDigitRecogNn = new HandwrittenDigitRe
            cognitionNn(new List<TrainingSample>(), NnInputs,
            NnHidden, NnOutputs, 0.002);
            var weightsFile = new StreamReader("weights.txt");
            var currentLayer = _handwrittenDigitRecogNn.
            HiddenLayer;
            var weights = new List<double>();
            var j = 0;

            while (!weightsFile.EndOfStream)
            {
                var currentLine = weightsFile.ReadLine();

                // End of weights for current unit.
                if (currentLine == "*")
                {
                    currentLayer.Units[j].Weights = new
                    List<double>(weights);
                    j++;
                    weights.Clear();
                    continue;
                }

                // End of layer.
                if (currentLine == "-")
                {
                    currentLayer = _handwrittenDigitRecogNn.
                    OutPutLayer;
                    j = 0;
```

```
            weights.Clear();
            continue;
        }

        weights.Add(double.Parse(currentLine));
    }

    weightsFile.Close();
}
```

Finally, let's execute and take a look at our Handwritten Digit Recognition visual application (Figure 12-4).

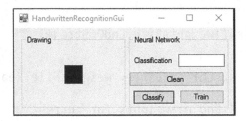

Figure 12-4. *·HDR visual application*

Now that we have completely developed the application, let's see how it would perform after different drawings of digits 1, 2, and 3 are presented to the NN.

Testing

Going back to Figure 12-4, we can see the drawing space in our application is the picture box control with a black background; it is in this picture box that we will draw different digits to eventually obtain a classification by clicking the Classify button. Let's examine some tests (Figure 12-5).

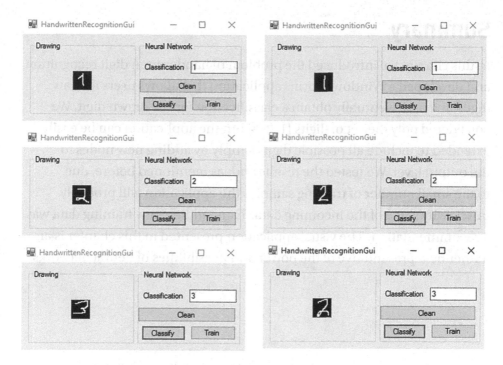

Figure 12-5. *Classification of handwritten digits*

In the same way as we can obtain a correct classification for many handwritten digits in this application, it could happen that for others we get an incorrect classification. The reason behind this inaccuracy, as the reader may expect at this point, is the very small training data set used while training the NN. To obtain higher accuracy we would need many more samples with different styles of handwriting.

Summary

In this chapter we introduced the problem of handwritten digit recognition and developed a Windows Forms application that allows users to draw digits in it and eventually obtain a classification for the drawn digit. We considered only the set of digits {1, 2, 3} but the application can be easily extended to include all possible digits simply by adding new nodes to the output layer. We tested the results and, as mentioned before, due to the small number of training samples the application will probably misclassify some of the incoming data. Thus, adding new training data was a recommendation. The visual application presented in this chapter is an authentic representative of the power and possibilities of neural networks.

CHAPTER 13

Clustering & Multi-objective Clustering

Thus far, we have discussed several methods related to supervised learning. In these methods, we approximated a function from a training data set containing labeled data. In this chapter, we will begin addressing unsupervised learning, a paradigm of machine learning where we deduce a function and the structure of data from an unlabeled data set.

Unsupervised learning (UL) methods no longer have a "training" data set. Consequently, the training phase in UL disappears because data does not have an associated classification; the correct classification is considered unknown. Therefore, UL is far more subjective than supervised learning is, since there is no simple goal for the analysis such as prediction of a response. The general goal of UL methods, as imprecise as it may sound, is to find patterns that describe the structure of the data being analyzed. Because obtaining unlabeled data from a lab instrument or any measurement device is usually easier than obtaining labeled data, UL methods are being applied more and more to multiple problems that require learning the structure of data.

© Arnaldo Pérez Castaño 2018
A. Pérez Castaño, *Practical Artificial Intelligence*,
https://doi.org/10.1007/978-1-4842-3357-3_13

In this chapter, we will explore one of the most important learning tasks associated with UL, which is clustering, as well as a variant of it where we consider several objective functions to be minimized or maximized at the same time, which is called multi-objective clustering. A method of the broad family of clustering algorithms will be described and implemented throughout the chapter; namely, we will implement the k-means method. Moreover, some measures for determining object and cluster similarity will be also implemented.

Note   Both supervised and unsupervised learning algorithms represent techniques of knowledge extraction frequently used in data-mining applications.

What Is Clustering?

Clustering is a broad family of algorithms whose purpose is to partition a set of objects into groups or clusters, trying to ensure that objects in the same group have the highest similarity possible and objects in different groups have the highest dissimilarity possible. Similarity in this case is related to a property of the objects; it could be height, weight, color, bravery, or any other quality that our data set includes, typically in a numeric form. Figure 13-1 illustrates clustering based on object color.

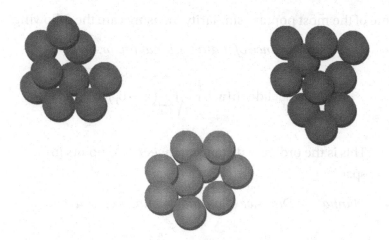

Figure 13-1. *Clustering a set of objects based on their color*

Clustering finds applications in various areas of science and business, such as astronomy, psychology, medicine, economics, fraud avoidance, architecture, demographic analysis, image segmentation, and more.

A clustering algorithm is usually composed of three elements:

- *Similarity Measure*: function used to determine the similarity between two objects. In the example from Figure 13-1, a similarity function could be *Color(x, y)* outputting an integer that determines the equivalence between objects *x* and *y* in regard to their colors. Typically, the larger the value outputted the greater the dissimilarity is between *x* and *y*; the smaller the value outputted the more similar *x* and *y* will be.

- *Criterion or Objective Function*: function used to evaluate the quality of a clustering

- *Optimization or Clustering Algorithm*: an algorithm that minimizes or maximizes the criterion function

Some of the most popular similarity measures are the following:

- *Euclidean Distance of n-dimensional vectors a, b:*

$$\text{Euclidean}(a, b) = \sqrt{\sum_{i=1}^{n}(a_i - b_i)^2}$$

  This is the ordinary distance between two points in space.

- *Manhattan Distance of n-dimensional vectors a, b:*

$$\text{Manhattan}(a, b) = \sum_{i=1}^{n}|a_i - b_i|$$

  This is an approximation of the Euclidean Distance, and it's cheaper to compute.

- *Minkowski Distance of cells that belong to an n x m matrix T; p is a positive integer and is a generalization of the previously detailed distances:*

$$\text{Minkowski}_p(T_k, T_h) = \sqrt[p]{\sum_{i=1}^{m}(T_{ki} - T_{hi})^2}$$

Among the criterion or objective functions used for determining or evaluating the quality of a clustering we can find the following:

- *Intra-class Distance*, also known as *Compactness*: as its name suggests with its "intra" (on the inside, within) prefix, it measures how close data points in a cluster (group) are to the cluster centroid. The cluster *centroid* is the average vector of all data points in a cluster. The Sum of Squared Errors is typically used as the mathematical function to measure this distance.

- *Inter-class Distance*, also known as *Isolation* or
  Separation: as its name suggests from the "inter"
  (between) prefix, it measures how far clusters are from
  each other.

The family of clustering algorithms can be divided into hierarchical, partitional, and Bayesian algorithms. Figure 13-2 illustrates the relation between the different families of clustering algorithms.

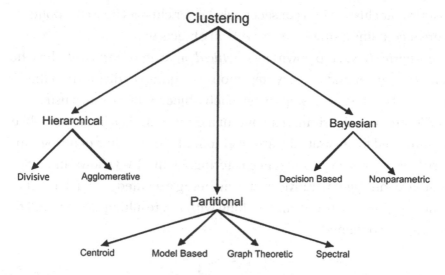

Figure 13-2. *Clustering algorithms family*

In this book, we will discuss hierarchical and partitional algorithms; Bayesian clustering algorithms try to generate a posteriori distribution over the set of all possible partitions of the data points. This family of algorithms is highly related to areas such as probability and statistics, so it will be left to the reader as supplementary research.

Note   Clustering is a well-known NP-hard problem, meaning no polynomial time solution for the problem can be developed or designed on a deterministic machine.

Hierarchical Clustering

Hierarchical algorithms discover new clusters from previously discovered clusters; hence, new clusters become descendants of parent clusters after being nested within them, and the hierarchical relation is established that way. Hierarchical algorithms can be classified as agglomerative or divisive.

An *agglomerative* (a.k.a bottom-up) *hierarchical* algorithm starts with each object as a separate cluster of size 1 and then begins merging the most similar clusters into consecutively larger clusters up to the point where it contains a single cluster with all objects in it.

A *divisive* (a.k.a top down) *hierarchical* algorithm starts with the whole set in one cluster and in every step chooses a group to divide from the current set of clusters. It stops when each object is a separate cluster.

Hierarchical algorithms can output a dendrogram, a binary tree–like diagram used to illustrate the arrangement of clusters. In a dendrogram, every level represents a different clustering. Figure 13-3 shows an example of an agglomerative clustering being executed over a data set formed by points a, b, c, d, and e, along with the resulting clusters and the dendrogram obtained.

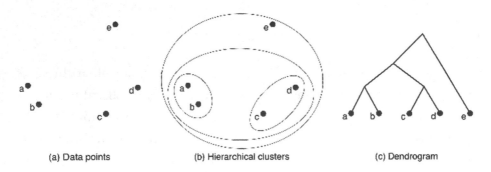

(a) Data points   (b) Hierarchical clusters   (c) Dendrogram

Figure 13-3. *Agglomerative clustering example*

484

Because points a, b and c, d respectively are the nearest ones, they are clustered together. Afterward, clusters {a, b}, {c, d}, being the nearest ones, are grouped together and {e} is left as another cluster. Finally, all data points are merged into a cluster that contains all data points; in this case, we executed a bottom-up procedure. How do we determine clusters' similarity or distance? The previously detailed measures or distances give us the similarity between two data points, but what about cluster similarity? The measures described in the next lines output the similarity between clusters:

- *Average Linkage Clustering*: determines the similarity between clusters C1 and C2 by finding the similarity or distance between all pairs (x, y) where x belongs to C1 and y to C2. These values are added and eventually divided by the total number of objects in both C1 and C2. Thus, ultimately, what we calculate is an average or mean of the distance between C1 and C2.

- *Centroid Linkage Clustering*: determines the similarity between clusters C1 and C2 by finding the similarity or distance between any pair (x, y) where x is the centroid of C1 and y the centroid of C2.

- *Complete Linkage Clustering*: determines the similarity between clusters C1 and C2 by outputting the maximum similarity or distance between any pair (x, y) where x is an object from C1 and y is an object from C2.

- *Single-Linkage Clustering*: determines the similarity between clusters C1 and C2 by outputting the minimum similarity or distance between any pair (x, y) where x is an object from C1 and y is an object from C2.

The pseudocode of an agglomerative hierarchical clustering demonstrates how easy it is in principle to implement this type of algorithm:

```
AgglomerativeClustering (dataPoints)
{
Initialize each data point in dataPoints as a single cluster
while (numberClusters> 1)
 find nearest clusters C1, C2 according to a cluster similarity
 measure
merge(C1, C2)
end
}
```

The agglomerative algorithm represents a more efficient approach than that of the divisive algorithm, but the latter often provides a more accurate solution. Notice that the divisive algorithm begins operating with the whole data set; thus, it's able to find the best division or partition into two clusters at the original data set, and from that point on it's able to find the best possible division within each cluster. The agglomerative method, on the other hand, at the moment of merging does not consider the global structure of data, so it's restricted to analyzing merely pairwise structure.

Note   In the 1850s during a cholera epidemic, London physician John Snow applied clustering techniques to plot the locations of cholera deaths on the map. The clustering indicated that death cases were located in the vicinity of polluted wells.

Partitional Clustering

Partitional algorithms partition a set of n objects into k clusters or classes. In this case, k (number of clusters or classes) can be fixed a priori or be determined by the algorithm when optimizing the objective function.

The most popular representative of the family of partitional clustering algorithms is k-means (MacQueen, 1967).

K-means is one of the simplest unsupervised learning methods for finding a clustering of a set of objects. It follows a simple procedure to partition a given data set into k clusters, where k is a number fixed a priori. In its initialization phase it defines k centroids, one for each cluster. There are different approaches for defining centroids. We could choose k random objects from the data set as centroids (naïve approach) or choose them in a more sophisticated way by selecting them to be as far as possible from each other. The choice made can affect performance later, as the initial centroids will influence the final outcome.

The main body of the k-means algorithm is formed by an outer loop that verifies whether a stopping condition has been reached; this outer loop contains an inner loop that passes through all data points. Within this inner loop—and while examining a data point P—we decide the cluster to which P should be added by comparing the distance of P to the centroid of every cluster, and ultimately we add it to the cluster with the nearest associated centroid.

Once all data points have been examined for the first time—in other words, the inner loop ends for the first time—a primary phase of the algorithm has been completed and an early clustering has been obtained. At this point, we need to refine our clustering; therefore, we recalculate the k centroids obtained in the previous step (recall that centroids are the average vector of their respective clusters), which will give us new centroids. The inner loop is executed again if the stopping condition has not been met, adding every data point to the cluster with the nearest new associated centroid. This is the main process of k-means; notice that the k centroids change their location step-by-step until no more changes are made. In other words, a stopping condition for the algorithm is that the set of centroids does not change from one iteration to the next. A pseudocode of k-means can be seen in the following lines:

```
K-Means(dataPoints, k)
{
cList = InitializeKCentroids()
        clusters = CreateClusters()

while (!stoppingCondition)
{
foreach (pj in dataPoints)
            {
dj = Calculate distance from pj to every centroid cList_j
Assign pj to clusters_jwhose dj is minimum
            }
UpdateCentroids()
}
}
```

The objective function being optimized (minimized in this case) is the *Sum of Squared Errors* (SSE), also known as *Intra-Class distance* or *Compactness*:

$$SSE = \sum_{i=1}^{k} \sum_{x \in C_i} d(x, centroid_i)^2$$

Where k is the number of clusters, C_i is the ith cluster, $centroid_i$ represents the centroid associated with the ith cluster, and $d(a, b)$ is a distance or similarity measure (usually Euclidean distance) between x and $centroid_i$. Thus, another possible stopping condition for k-means is having reached a very small value for SSE.

In Figure 13-4 we can see the first step of the k-means algorithm—choosing k centroids. In this graphic, blue points denote data points and black points denote centroids.

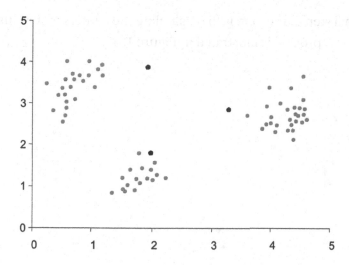

Figure 13-4. *First step of k-means, choosing k = 3 random objects or data points as centroids*

Figure 13-5 shows the $k = 3$ clusters that result from having selected the set of centroids from the first step.

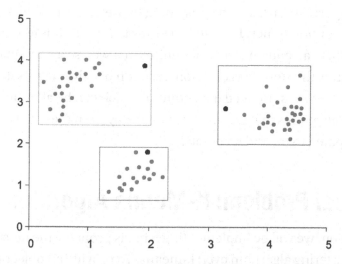

Figure 13-5. *Clustering obtained after choosing the set of centroids in the first step and considering a distance measure to determine similarity between data points*

The final step of the loop is to recalculate the centers of the clusters or centroids; this process is illustrated in Figure 13-6.

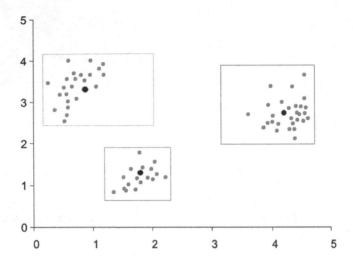

Figure 13-6. *Centroids being recalculated as the average vector of the cluster they represent*

The steps represented in the preceding figures are repeated until a stopping condition is met. To summarize, k-means is a simple, efficient algorithm that can end up at a local minimum if we use a very small value of SSE as the stopping condition. Its main disadvantage is its high sensitivity to outliers (isolated data points), which can be alleviated by removing data points that are much farther away from the set of centroids when compared to other data points.

Practical Problem: K-Means Algorithm

In this section, we will be implementing what is probably the most popular clustering algorithm ever: k-means. To provide an object-oriented approach to our implementation, we will create `Cluster` and `Element` classes that will incorporate all actions and properties related to clusters and objects (data points); the `Cluster` class can be seen in Listing 13-1.

Listing 13-1. Cluster Class

```
public class Cluster
    {
        public List<Element> Objects { get; set; }
        public Element Centroid { get; set; }
        public intClusterNo { get; set; }

        public Cluster()
        {
            Objects = new List<Element>();
            Centroid = new Element();
        }

        public Cluster(IEnumerable<double> centroid, intclusterNo)
        {
            Objects = new List<Element>();
            Centroid = new Element(centroid);
ClusterNo = clusterNo;
        }

        public void Add(Element e)
        {
Objects.Add(e);
e.Cluster = ClusterNo;
        }

        public void Remove(Element e)
        {
Objects.Remove(e);
        }
```

```
        public void CalculateCentroid()
        {
var result = new List<double>();
vartoAvg = new List<Element>(Objects);
var total = Total;
            if (Objects.Count == 0)
            {
toAvg.Add(Centroid);
                total = 1;
            }

var dimension = toAvg.First().Features.Count;

            for (vari = 0; i< dimension; i++)
result.Add(toAvg.Select(o =>o.Features[i]).Sum() / total);

Centroid.Features = new List<double>(result);
        }

        public double AverageLinkageClustering(Cluster c)
        {
var result = 0.0;

            foreach (var c1 in c.Objects)
                result += Objects.Sum(c2 =>Distance.
                Euclidean(c1.Features, c2.Features));

            return result / (Total + c.Total);
        }

        public int Total
        {
            get { return Objects.Count; }
        }
    }
```

The Cluster class contains the following properties:

- Objects: set of objects included in the cluster

- Centroid: centroid of the cluster

- ClusterNo: ID of the cluster to differentiate it from the rest

- Total: number of elements in the group or cluster

The class also contains the following methods:

- Add(): adds an element to the cluster

- Remove(): removes an element from the cluster

- CalculateCentroid(): calculates the centroid of a cluster

- AverageLinkageClustering(): calculates the AverageLinkageClustering similarity measure between clusters, as previously detailed

The Element class representing an object to be clustered is shown on Listing 13-2.

Listing 13-2. Element Class

```
public class Element
{
    public List<double> Features { get; set; }
    public int Cluster { get; set; }

    public Element(int cluster = -1)
    {
        Features = new List<double>();
        Cluster = cluster;
    }
```

```
        public Element(IEnumerable<double> features)
        {
            Features = new List<double>(features);
            Cluster = -1;
        }
    }
```

The class contains a Cluster property that indicates the clusterID of the cluster to which the object belongs; code from both constructors is self-explanatory. The KMeans class, representing the algorithm of the same name, is illustrated in Listing 13-3.

Listing 13-3. KMeans and DataSet Classes

```
public class KMeans
    {
        public int K { get; set; }
        public DataSetDataSet { get; set; }
        public List<Cluster> Clusters { get; set; }
        private static Random _random;
        private constintMaxIterations = 100;

        public KMeans(int k, DataSetdataSet)
        {
            K = k;
DataSet = dataSet;
            Clusters = new List<Cluster>();
            _random = new Random();
        }

        public void Start()
        {
InitializeCentroids();
vari = 0;
```

```
            while (i<MaxIterations)
            {
                foreach (varobj in DataSet.Objects)
                {
varnewCluster = MinDistCentroid(obj);
varoldCluster = obj.Cluster;
                    Clusters[newCluster].Add(obj);
                    if (oldCluster>= 0)
                        Clusters[oldCluster].Remove(obj);
                }
UpdateCentroids();
i++;
            }
        }

        private void InitializeCentroids()
        {
RandomCentroids();
        }

        private void RandomCentroids()
        {
var indices = Enumerable.Range(0, DataSet.Objects.Count).
ToList();
Clusters.Clear();

            for (vari = 0; i< K; i++)
            {
varobjIndex = _random.Next(0, indices.Count);
Clusters.Add(new Cluster(DataSet.Objects[objIndex].Features, i));
indices.RemoveAt(objIndex);
            }
        }
```

```csharp
        private intMinDistCentroid(Element e)
        {
var distances = new List<double>();

            for (vari = 0; i<Clusters.Count; i++)
distances.Add(Distance.Euclidean(Clusters[i].Centroid.Features,
e.Features));

varminDist = distances.Min();
            return distances.FindIndex(0, d => d == minDist);
        }

        private void UpdateCentroids()
        {
            foreach (var cluster in Clusters)
cluster.CalculateCentroid();
        }
    }

public class DataSet
    {
        public List<Element> Objects { get; set; }

        public DataSet()
        {
            Objects = new List<Element>();
        }

        public void Load(List<Element> objects)
        {
            Objects = new List<Element>(objects);
        }
    }
```

The properties or fields are self-explanatory; in this case, we have decided to use a maximum number of iterations as the stopping condition. The methods of the class are described in the following points:

- `InitializeCentroids()`: method created considering the possibility of having different centroid initialization procedures.

- `RandomCentroids()`: centroid initialization procedure where we assign k randomly selected objects as centroids of k clusters

- `MinDistCentroid()`: returns the `clusterID` of the cluster to which the input object is closer; i.e., at minimum distance

- `UpdateCentroids()`: updates the k centroids by calling the CalculateCentroid() method of the `Cluster` class

Now that we have all components in place, let's test our clustering algorithm by creating a test application where we create a data set; Listing 13-4 illustrates this code.

Listing 13-4. Testing the K-Means Algorithm

```
var elements = new List<UnsupervisedLearning.Clustering.
Element>
                              {
                                        new UnsupervisedLearning.
                                        Clustering.Element(new
                                        double[] {1, 2}),
                                        new UnsupervisedLearning.
                                        Clustering.Element(new
                                        double[] {1, 3}),
```

```
                                    new UnsupervisedLearning.
                                    Clustering.Element(new
                                    double[] {3, 3}),
                                    new UnsupervisedLearning.
                                    Clustering.Element(new
                                    double[] {3, 4}),
                                    new UnsupervisedLearning.
                                    Clustering.Element(new
                                    double[] {6, 6}),
                                    new UnsupervisedLearning.
                                    Clustering.Element(new
                                    double[] {6, 7})
                        };

vardataSet = new DataSet();
dataSet.Load(elements);

varkMeans = new KMeans(3, dataSet);
kMeans.Start();

                foreach (var cluster in kMeans.Clusters)
                {
Console.WriteLine("Cluster No {0}", cluster.ClusterNo);
                    foreach (varobj in cluster.Objects)
Console.WriteLine("({0}, {1}) in {2}", obj.Features[0], obj.
Features[1], obj.Cluster);
Console.WriteLine("--------------");
                }
```

The result obtained after executing the code from Listing 13-4 is shown in Figure 13-7. Note that in this case we have three easily distinguished groups, as the figure illustrates.

```
Cluster No 0
<6, 6> in 0
<6, 7> in 0
------------------
Cluster No 1
<1, 2> in 1
<1, 3> in 1
------------------
Cluster No 2
<3, 3> in 2
<3, 4> in 2
------------------
```

Figure 13-7. *Execution of the k-means algorithm with k = 3*

So far, we have examined single-clustering algorithms, or algorithms where we optimize a single objective function. In the case of k-means, it was the Sum of Squared Errors, also known as intra-class distance (minimizes the distance of objects within a group). Another function that we might try to optimize is the inter-class (maximize distance of objects from different groups) function. In the next section we will begin studying multi-objective clustering in which we do not consider only a single function to optimize but rather several functions, and we attempt to optimize them all at once.

Multi-objective Clustering

Nowadays, many real-life problems force us to consider not only the best possible value for a given function but also the value of several functions all related to the problem at hand. For instance, zoning, a technique that belongs to the area of urban studies, appeared for the first time in the nineteenth century to separate residential areas from industrial ones. The main idea with this technique, the most popular in urbanization, is to produce a partition of homogeneous regions according to several variables or criteria. These variables could be demographic—for instance, number of people who are older than twenty, number of people younger than ten, and so on. Finding such a partition is clearly a clustering problem involving the optimization of different functions. Therefore, we might try to find a clustering with the lowest intra-class distance (a.k.a compactness) and at the same time optimize the inter-class distance or any other function, which could very well be demographic in nature. A perfect clustering is that with the minimum intra-class distance and the maximum inter-class distance; hence, one could say that clustering is by nature a multi-objective optimization problem. We will begin this section by examining several relevant concepts or definitions related to multi-objective clustering.

Many optimization problems often involve optimizing multiple objective functions at the same time; such problems are known as a *multi-objective optimization problems* (MOPs). They can be stated as follows:

$$\text{minimize } F(x) = \left(f_1(x), f_2(x), \ldots, f_n(x)\right)$$
$$x \in A$$

In this case, A represents the feasible space of the problem—the set of all feasible solutions, the ones fulfilling every constraint of the problem.

A vector $u = (u_1, u_2, \ldots u_n)$ is said to be *dominated* by another vector, $v = (v_1, v_2, \ldots v_n)$, denoted $u < v$, if and only if for all of index i we can verify that $u_i \leq v_i$. In any other case u is said to be a *non-dominated vector*. Notice that "domination" depends on whether we want to minimize or maximize the objective functions; recall that it's always possible to transform a minimization problem into a maximization problem and the other way around.

Having multiple objectives denotes a significant issue—the improvement of one objective function could lead to the deterioration of another. Thus, a solution that optimizes every objective rarely exists; instead of looking for that solution a trade-off is searched for. *Pareto optimal* solutions represent this trade-off.

A feasible solution x is said to be Pareto optimal if there is no solution y such that $F(x)<F(y)$. In other words, there is no solution vector y whose evaluation vector $(f_1(y), f_2(y), \dots f_n(y))$ would dominate the evaluation vector of x, $(f_1(x), f_2(x), \dots f_n(x))$. The set of all Pareto optimal solutions is known as the *Pareto Set*, and its image is the *Pareto Frontier*. The goal of most MOPs algorithms is to build a Pareto Frontier for a given problem; such methods are typically heuristics or metaheuristics (we shall examine them during the next chapter).

Note   Pareto optimality is a concept named after Vilfredo Pareto (1848–1923), the Italian engineer and economist. Its concept has been applied in academic fields such as economics, engineering, and the life sciences.

Pareto Frontier Builder

Searching through the scientific literature, we can find different methods for discovering the Pareto Frontier. In this book, we will describe one of the author's own creation, named *Pareto Frontier Builder*. It can be applied to bi-objective optimization—the case where you are optimizing two functions. The binary case is ideal for clustering problems since there are two functions (intra- and inter-class) that can provide us with the optimum.

For the binary case, the relation between the two functions and the Pareto Frontier can be represented as illustrated in Figure 13-8.

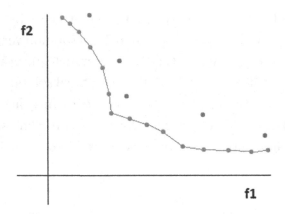

Figure 13-8. *Blue points form the Pareto Frontier and red points are dominated by blue ones; thus, they are not considered as part of the Pareto Frontier. This would be a minimization problem*

The strategy of the Frontier Builder method is divided into different stages. The main idea is to build the Pareto Frontier by areas, as shown in Figure 13-9.

- *Area A*: Points in this area will be obtained by minimizing the second objective function ($f2$); points resulting from this optimization will be the closest to the y-axis.

- *Area B*: Points in this area will be obtained by minimizing the second objective function ($f1$); points resulting from this optimization will be the closest to the x-axis.

- *Area C*: It's intended to act as a linking mechanism, uniting areas A and B and putting together the Pareto Frontier. A procedure known as Pareto Frontier Linkage will find the bridge between areas A and B.

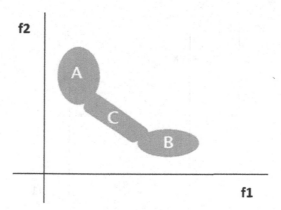

Figure 13-9. *Area A is formed by points obtained after minimizing objective function f2; area B is obtained after minimizing objective function f1, and area C is formed using a linkage mechanism connecting areas A and B*

Seeing the strategy in these steps makes it look very simple. We separate the *f2* optimization from the f1 optimization, build areas A and B, and then link them by finding non-dominated solutions in area C.

Pareto Frontier Linkage is the mechanism applied to construct area C. It requires a step parameter that defines the desired distance between non-dominated solutions in the Pareto Frontier. When a distance between solutions x and y exceeds this step then the linkage mechanism starts a searching machinery to find non-dominated solutions between x and y and build a bridge. This machinery consists of making small variations to the leftmost solution, the one on the left side of the bridge (x, according to Figure 13-10).

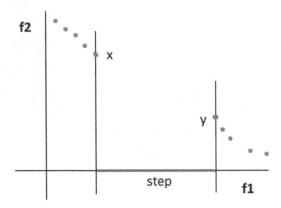

Figure 13-10. *Step to join points x, y*

The variation occurs as follows:

1. Select the leftmost solution.

    •   Modify the current solution. For the clustering
        problem, move an element from its current
        cluster to some other cluster, guaranteeing that $f2$
        increases by currentDistance + k, where k <= step,
        and evaluate and store this new solution.

2. Repeat step 2 and move all elements in the leftmost
    solution to improve clusters' chances of finding
    non-dominated solutions with $f2$ values ranging in
    [currentDistance, currentDistance + step]; this
    strategy slowly builds the bridge and improves the
    Pareto Frontier.

This method was embedded in a Tabu Search metaheuristic (we will discuss them in the next chapter) and applied to a real-world zoning problem. The results obtained after selecting different step values can be seen in Figure 13-11.

After 300 iterations, `step` = 2.0.

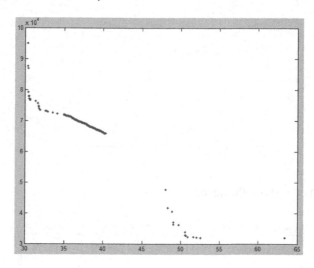

After 500 iterations, `step` = 2.0

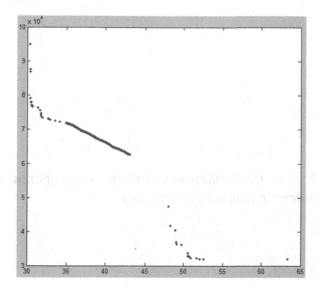

Step = 1.2 after 500 iterations.

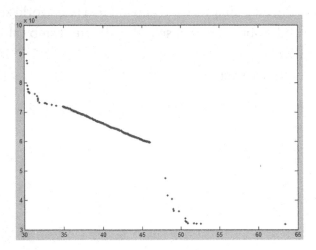

Finally, step = 0.5, 500 iterations.

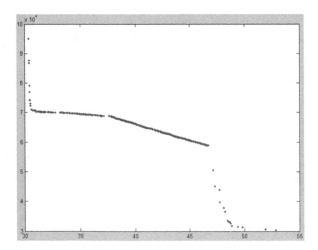

Figure 13-11. *Frontier Builder mechanism using different steps and executing a different number of iterations*

From the set of images forming the previous figure, we can see that the Pareto Frontier is well defined; the smaller the step the better defined it is and the more holes it will fill out of the Pareto Frontier. An interesting enhancement to this strategy would be to apply the `FrontierBuilder` mechanism not only to execute steps along the f2-axis but also along the f1-axis, providing a more accurate approximation to the Pareto Frontier.

Summary

In this chapter, we discussed one of the classic problems of computer science: of clustering. We described it by providing different measures for determining object similarity and cluster similarity. We also introduced the family of clustering methods and presented and developed one of the most popular and reliable algorithms for clustering, which is k-means. Throughout the final sections we examined multi-objective clustering as a particular case of multi-objective optimization problems and detailed a method of the author's own creation for constructing the Pareto Frontier; this method was the Pareto Frontier Builder.

CHAPTER 14

Heuristics & Metaheuristics

So far we have mentioned the word *heuristic* on numerous occasions. We used it in the "Mars Rover" chapter to incorporate a method that seemed logical and simple, used our pragmatic knowledge of reality, and helped us achieve reasonable movements for the robot. This method was based primarily on our experience and not on any scientifically proven procedure.

In computer science we are typically faced with the challenge of designing algorithms that give us both good time complexity and good solutions (optimal if possible) to a given problem. A heuristic is a method that can easily abandon either of the previous premises, or maybe both. For instance, a heuristic can find many solutions for a problem, and some of these solutions may be incorrect or unfeasible, and some might be optimal. Likewise, it could execute in a short time, providing feasible solutions for a problem, and it could happen that none of those solutions would be optimal. This type of algorithm is usually applied to problems that are intrinsically difficult; for instance, NP-Hard problems like the Traveling Salesman, clustering, vehicle routing, and many others. Because of the nature of these problems, their high complexity, we must rely on methods that will output a solution to the problem, or maybe part of a solution, and aid us in ultimately obtaining a definite solution that would be as close as possible to an optimal solution.

© Arnaldo Pérez Castaño 2018
A. Pérez Castaño, *Practical Artificial Intelligence*,
https://doi.org/10.1007/978-1-4842-3357-3_14

A very special type of heuristic is the metaheuristic, a problem-independent iterative process where various heuristics are combined through different strategies or guidelines that try to lead the search toward finding good solutions. Metaheuristics have become very popular; some of them base their functioning on biological or chemical processes and have garnered great interest because of their ability to find good solutions to complicated problems by applying simple algorithms that execute in a decent amount of time.

In this chapter, we'll discuss heuristics, specifically the Hill Climbing heuristic, and we will present two well-known metaheuristics; namely, we will study genetic algorithms and Tabu Search. Practical problems in which we will implement the first two methods will be included.

Note   Multiple algorithms in AI are heuristics by nature or use a heuristic during their execution. An application determining whether a given email is spam uses many heuristics rules to eventually make a decision.

What Is a Heuristic?

A *heuristic* is a method drawn from experience, common sense, or an educated guess that aims at providing or contributing to providing a practical solution to a problem that is usually very difficult to solve (NP-Hard), and consequently an optimal or good, feasible solution is too complicated to obtain. Heuristic methods can be used to speed up the process of finding a good, feasible solution by providing us with a shortcut. This speed-up process is usually carried out via search algorithms where we traverse a tree representing the space of possible solutions. The application of certain problem-specific heuristics can significantly reduce the tree search. Such is the case of the Sliding Tiles Puzzle (shown in Figure 14-1), a popular game whose state game space (all possible game configurations) can be represented by a tree whose nodes indicate different states or configurations of the game. Each parent has up to four children representing the four possible movements of a tile into the empty area.

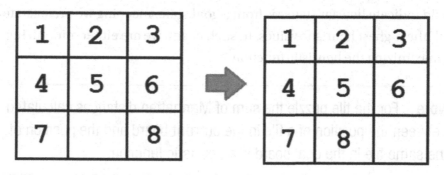

Figure 14-1. *Sliding Tiles Puzzle. The left board shows an unfinished state of the game and the right board the goal state.*

Heuristic methods possess some information about the proximity of every state to the goal state, which allows them to explore the most promising paths first. Summarizing, some of the most general features of heuristic methods are as follows:

- They do not guarantee that a solution will be found, even though it might exist.

- If it finds a solution, it does not guarantee that it will be optimal (minimal or maximal).

- Sometimes (not defined a priori) it will find a good solution in a reasonable time.

We usually work with a heuristic through a *heuristic function*. This function assigns a numeric value to every state of the problem and defines how promising that state is as far as attempting to reach a goal state from a given point (node); it's usually denoted as *H(e)*. The heuristic function can have two interpretations. It could indicate how close state *e* is to the goal state, meaning states with the lowest heuristic value are preferred, or it could indicate how far state *e* is from a goal state, meaning we prefer states with the highest heuristic values. In such cases, we are either minimizing or maximizing the heuristic function.

Note   For the tile puzzle the sum of Manhattan distances calculated between the position of a tile in the current board and the position of the same tile in the goal board is a heuristic function.

Hill Climbing

In the *Hill Climbing* method or heuristic, we begin with an initial random solution and set it up as the current solution. We find the set of neighbors of the current solution and execute a step that defines the current solution as the neighbor providing the maximum decrease (increase) to the function being minimized (maximized). Hill Climbing is an optimization technique that can fall into a local minimum; consequently, it can easily fail to spot the global optimum. Despite its locality issues, it's widely used in AI for problems that have tight time constraints and where one could certainly take advantage of short execution time algorithms.

There exist two types of Hill Climbing approaches:

- *Irreversible*: where we avoid returning to a subset of the set of states if that path happens to be not beneficial

- *Tentative*: where we can go back to an old path if we determine that the chosen path is not appropriate

In this book, we will focus on the first type of method (irreversible), the one that closely resembles the description of Hill Climbing presented at the beginning of this section.

In irreversible Hill Climbing we determine the next step or solution to be processed using two alternatives:

- *Simple climbing*: We choose to process or expand the first solution in the current neighborhood that is more favorable than the current solution. Thus, procedure stops there, and not all neighbors of the current solution are scanned.

- *Maximum slope climbing*: We choose to process or expand the solution from the current neighborhood that is the most favorable of all. Thus, procedure stops when all neighbors of the current solution are scanned.

In both scenarios, if every solution in the current neighborhood turns out to be worse than or equal to the current solution then the procedure ends.

Note   Hill Climbing is an optimization technique of iterative improvement, a variant of the Best First search algorithm, in the family of Greedy algorithms.

Figure 14-2 illustrates how the Hill Climbing algorithm would find the local optimum, denoted by a blue dot.

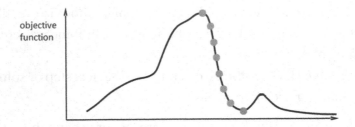

Figure 14-2. *In this case, we minimize the objective function and go "downhill" through a path of orange points until we reach the blue point, a local minimum. We are minimizing, thus the blue point is a local minimum.*

The pseudocode of this algorithm would be as follows:

```
HillClimbing(function F)
{
currentSolution = RandomSolution();
while (No Improvement)
vicinity = Neighbors(currentSolution);
nextEval = -INF;
nextSolution = null;
      for all x in vicinity
     {
 if (Evaluate(x) >nextEval)
            {
nextSolution= x;
nextEval = Evaluate (x);
            }
     }
      if nextEval<= Evaluate (currentSolution)
return currentSolution;
currentNode = nextSolution;
}
```

Hill Climbing is a method that belongs to the family of Local Search (LS) algorithms. In fact, the terms *Hill Climbing* and *Local Search* are sometimes used indistinguishably, meaning they are considered the same algorithm, and they represent a class of metaheuristics known as single solution–based metaheuristics, which includes popular methods such as simulated annealing, Tabu Search, and others that are based on LS.

Note   Local search is a heuristic method for solving computationally hard optimization problems; it moves from solution to solution in the space of candidate solutions (the search space) by applying local changes until a solution deemed optimal has been found, a maximum number of iterations has been reached, or a time limit has elapsed.

Practical Problem: Implementing Hill Climbing

In this section, we will be implementing a Hill Climbing algorithm that optimizes (minimizes) a continuous objective function. The neighborhood in this procedure is calculated by considering the set of points from the n-sphere of radius R surrounding the current solution (Figure 14-3).

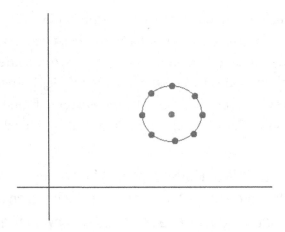

Figure 14-3. *The neighborhood of the current solution (blue point) is formed by all the red points of the n-sphere surrounding it. In this case, n = 1; i.e., the 1-sphere is a circle.*

Coordinates of an n-sphere (generalization of a sphere) can be obtained according to the following formulas:

$$x_1 = r * \cos(\phi_1)$$
$$x_2 = r * \sin(\phi_1) * \cos(\phi_2)$$
$$x_3 = r * \sin(\phi_1) * \sin(\phi_2) * \cos(\phi_3)$$
$$\dots$$
$$x_{n-1} = r * \sin(\phi_1) * \dots * \sin(\phi_{n-2}) * \cos(\phi_{n-1})$$
$$x_n = r * \sin(\phi_1) * \dots * \sin(\phi_{n-2}) * \sin(\phi_{n-1})$$

where r is the radius of the n-sphere and $\phi_1, \phi_2, \dots \phi_{n-1}$ is the set of angular coordinates, which has the first n - 2 in the range $[0; \pi]$ and the last one in the range $[0; 2\pi]$.

To ease our labor with mathematical functions, we will be adding a reference to the *MathParserNuget* package. By using this package we will be able to define functions as strings and have them evaluated at any point we want. Thus, we will have a Function public property in the HillClimbing class as shown in Listing 14-1.

516

Listing 14-1. HillClimbing Class

```
public class HillClimbing
    {
        public Function Function{ get; set; }
        public double Step { get; set; }
        public double Radius { get; set; }
        private static readonly Random Random = new Random();

        public HillClimbing(Function function, double step,
        double radius)
        {
            Function = function;
            Step = step;
            Radius = radius;
        }
}
```

The class contains the following properties or fields:

- Function: function to be optimized

- Step: double value indicating the step or angle to use when computing the neighborhood of a solution

- Radius: double value indicating the radius of the n-sphere surrounding (neighborhood) the current solution

- Random: variable used for computing random values

In Listing 14-2 we can see three methods that are in charge of performing some of the components of the Hill Climbing algorithm.

Listing 14-2. InitialSolution(), Neighborhood(), and
NSpherePoints() Methods of the HillClimbing Class

```
        private List<double>InitialSolution(int dimension)
        {
var result = new List<double>();

            for (vari = 0; i< dimension; i++)
result.Add(Random.NextDouble()*100);

            return result;
        }

        private IEnumerable<List<double>> Neighborhood(List
        <double>currentSolution, int dimension)
        {
var result = new List<List<double>>();

varnewSolutions = NSpherePoints(currentSolution, dimension);
result.AddRange(newSolutions);

            return result;
        }

        private IEnumerable<List<double>>NSpherePoints(List
        <double>currentSolution, int dimension)
        {
var result = new List<List<double>>();
var angles = Enumerable.Repeat(Step, dimension).ToList();

            while (angles.First() < 180)
            {
                for (vari = 0; i< dimension; i++)
                {
varnewSolution = new List<double>(currentSolution);
var prod = 1.0;
```

```
                for (var j = 0; j <i; j++)
                    prod *= Math.Sin(angles[j]);

newSolution[i] = i == dimension - 1 &&i> 0

                                          ?

Radius*(prod)*Math.Sin(angles[i])

                                          :

Radius*(prod)*Math.Cos(angles[i]);

result.Add(newSolution);
            }
                angles = angles.Select(ang => ang + Step).ToList();
        }

        return result;
    }
}
```

In the InitialSolution() method we create a random solution
of n-dimension with random values in the range [0, 100]. In the
Neighborhood() method we make use of the NSpherePoints() method
to calculate the new points that form the neighborhood of the current
solution. The last method is a direct translation of the system of coordinate
equations previously presented. Listing 14-3 illustrates the Execute()
method, which puts all the other components together.

Listing 14-3. Execute() Method of the HillClimbing Class

```
public List<double>Execute()
        {
varcurrentSolution = InitialSolution(Function.
getArgumentsNumber());
varbestEval = double.MaxValue;
```

519

```
            List<double>bestSolution = null;

            while (true)
            {
var neighbors = Neighborhood(currentSolution, Function.
getArgumentsNumber());
varbestCurrentEval = double.MaxValue;
            List<double>bestCurrentSolution = null;

            foreach (var neighbor in neighbors)
            {
vareval = Function.calculate(neighbor.ToArray());
                if (eval<bestCurrentEval)
                {
bestCurrentEval = eval;
bestCurrentSolution = neighbor;
                }
            }

            if (bestCurrentEval == bestEval)
                break;

            if (bestCurrentEval<bestEval)
            {
bestEval = bestCurrentEval;
bestSolution = bestCurrentSolution;
            }
        }

        return bestSolution;
    }
```

We tested the algorithm on a console application by considering the function $f(x) = x^2$, a parabolic function whose graphic can be seen in Figure 14-4.

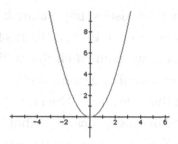

Figure 14-4. *Parabolic function*

Clearly, the minimum value of this function is obtained when $x = 0$. So, let's test our algorithm to see how it goes downhill from a high value that could be 100 to a value very close to 0 (Listing 14-4).

Listing 14-4. Testing the Hill Climbing Algorithm

```
var f = new Function("f", "(x1)^2", "x1");
varhillClimbing = new HillClimbing(f, 5, 4);
var result = hillClimbing.Execute();
Console.WriteLine("Result: {0}", result[0]);
```

After executing this code and setting up a break point to discover the initial solution from which the algorithm begins its processing, we obtain the result seen in Figure 14-5.

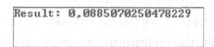

Figure 14-5. *Result obtained after executing Hill Climbing algorithm*

The algorithm started with a value of 95.14 and was able to work its way downhill until it reached a value that is very close to the global optimum (0), which in this case coincides with a local optimum.

In the following sections, we will study S-metaheuristics (single solution based) and P-metaheuristics (population based). The first type is composed of a family where every member inherits from Local Search (LS) or Hill Climbing and tries to overcome their difficulties by creating mechanisms to escape from local optimums and continue the search in other promising areas of the state space. The latter type is a vast group of metaheuristics composed of those procedures that include a population in their execution; their most popular representative without any doubt is the family of genetic algorithms.

Note   Some of the most popular S-metaheuristics include Tabu Search (TS), simulated annealing (SA), iterated local search (ILS), and variable neighborhood search (VNS).

P-Metaheuristics: Genetic Algorithms

Population-based metaheuristics, a.k.a *P-metaheuristics* algorithms, consist of an iterative process of improvement over a set of solutions grouped in a population. In this type of metaheuristics, we usually begin by generating an initial population that is later replaced by another population using some selection criteria. Algorithms such as evolutionary algorithms (EAs), scatter search (SS), Estimation of Distribution algorithms (EDAs), particle swarm optimization (PSO), bee colony (BC), and artificial immune systems (AISs) belong to this class of metaheuristics. In this section, we will focus on a type of evolutive algorithm known as a genetic algorithm (GA).

Genetic algorithms represent a family of metaheuristics inspired by the process of natural selection; they were developed by John Holland in the 1970s and are commonly used to generate high-quality solutions to optimization and search problems by relying on bio-inspired operators, such as mutation, crossover, and selection. Concepts such as chromosomes, genes, and fitness are commonly found in GA literature, and they try to find analogy with their equivalent in areas like biology, chemistry, and so on.

Note   GAs are widely used in the fields of computer science and operations research. In the latter field, GAs deal with the application of advanced analytical methods to help make better decisions.

In GAs we usually need to encode solutions in a "genetic" manner so as to later allow us to efficiently apply mutation and crossover operators. We also need a fitness function that receives as argument an encoded solution and provides us with an assessment or evaluation of the encoded solution. A popular encoding for a solution consists of a binary string; this encoding makes it very easy to apply almost any operator.

Metaheuristics try to optimize on two fronts: by means of the application of intensification and diversification mechanisms. *Intensification* refers to the ability of the algorithm to pursue even further already discovered and promising areas of the state space. It means to exploit those areas of the state space where we have already discovered good solutions.

On the other hand, *diversification* refers to the ability to explore unexplored areas of the state space while trying to discover new, high-quality solutions.

The mutation operator tries to alter a solution by creating a new one that exists in a different area of the state space; thus, it diversifies the search. The crossover operator usually works on two solutions whose fitness values are considered among the best found so far. It then mixes their values on a crossover point; this is an intensification operator, as we try to mix two good solutions in an attempt to find an even better one. Figure 14-6 shows how these operators would function on a binary chromosome (solution).

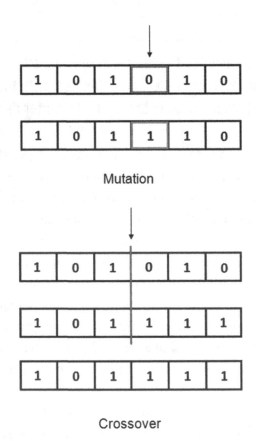

Figure 14-6. *The mutation operator modifies a single bit in the chromosome (solution), and the crossover operator assigns a breaking point on the two parent chromosomes, creating a new solution by taking half the genes from the first chromosome and half the genes from the second part of the second chromosome.*

From Figure 14-6 we can easily deduce that the mutation operator is unary whereas the crossover operator is binary.

Even though the selection, mutation, and crossover methods can change from one specific implementation to another (problem dependent), a generic pseudocode for a genetic algorithm is presented in the following lines:

```
GA ()
{
InitializePopulation();
EvaluatePopulation();

        while(!stopCondition)
        {
                Select the best-fit individuals for reproduction;
                Obtain offsprings through mutation, crossover
                operators on the previously selected individuals;
                Evaluate offsprings;
                Obtain new population by selecting best-fit
                individuals from offsprings and the current
                population;
        }
}
```

From this pseudocode we can see how GAs can be seen as optimization methods based on the biological analogy of "survival of the fittest." Through biological analogies of genetic reproduction, crossover, and mutation the quality of the average population and the individuals is improved over several generations. In principle, the average quality of the population should increase with each generation. However, this strongly depends on some of the parameters (for example, the mutation probability) and the nature of the fitness (quality, probability) function.

In the upcoming section we will implement a GA for a very popular problem in computer science, the Traveling Salesman Problem, also known as TSP. We will tailor our GA (solution encoding, fitness function, and so on) to make it fit into the model of the TSP and provide solutions accordingly.

Practical Problem: Implementing a Genetic Algorithm for the Traveling Salesman Problem

We have already discussed GAs, and we know they are inspired by a biological process that resembles the evolution of a population over time, and that better-fitting individuals represent a better solution for us. GAs alone are merely blueprints waiting to be adapted to a specific problem. In this section we will be adapting a GA to find solutions and optimize a Traveling Salesman Problem (TSP).

The *Traveling Salesman Problem (TSP)* is the problem where we have a salesman who is given the task of going through n cities while seeking to minimize the time spent traveling from one city to another and eventually visiting each and every one of them. Figure 14-7 illustrates a map of the United States where several cities (black points) must be visited by a salesman; purple lines indicate a possible minimum cost path.

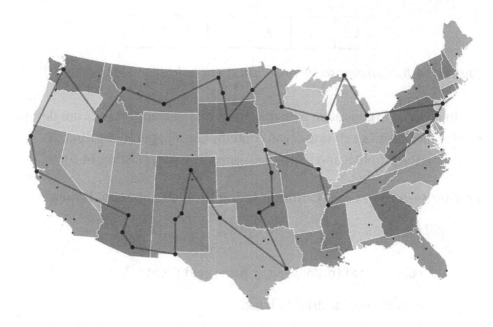

Figure 14-7. *US map showing a possible path to be followed by a salesman through several cities. In this case, the path ends where it started.*

TSP is an NP-Hard problem, meaning we must rely on approximation or heuristic methods to obtain solutions in a practical time. The exact solution would imply developing a combinatorial algorithm that would take $O(n!)$ to execute—i.e., a factorial time on execution—implying for $n = 20$ we would have 2,432,902,008,176,640,000 possible solutions to check.

Because in TSP we try to find the permutation of cities yielding the optimum value for the fitness function, it would seem pretty logical to use this representation as encoding for our GA, and that's the strategy we will follow. Thus, we will have chromosomes as lists of values ranging from $[0, n - 1]$; each value in the list will represent a city, and the order defined on the list is the tour to be followed by the salesman. Figure 14-8 shows an example of a chromosome for our GA oriented toward finding solutions to the TSP.

1	0	2	3	5	4

Figure 14-8. *Chromosome or solution encoding for TSP*

In order to be consistent with the object-oriented approach of our design we will include a Tsp class that will contemplate all operations directly related to the problem and to problem-specific issues (Listing 14-5).

Listing 14-5. Tsp Class Contemplating Problem-Specific Issues

```
public class Tsp
{
    public static double[,] Map { get; set; }

    public Tsp(double [,] map)
    {
        Map = map;
    }

    public static void Evaluate(Solution solution)
    {
var result = 0.0;

        for (vari = 0; i<solution.Ordering.Count - 1; i++)
            result += Map[solution.Ordering[i], solution.
            Ordering[i + 1]];

solution.Fitness = result;
    }
}
```

In this class we store the double [,] matrix Map representing the map of distances; in other words, the matrix storing the distance between any two cities *i, j*. We coded an Evaluate() method where we calculate the fitness value of an input solution. Likewise, we also included a Solution class where all solution-related operations are developed (Listing 14-6).

Listing 14-6. Solution Class

```
public class Solution
{
    public List<int> Ordering { get; set; }
    public double Fitness { get; set; }

    public Solution(IEnumerable<int> ordering)
    {
        Ordering = new List<int>(ordering);
Tsp.Evaluate(this);
    }

    public Solution Mutate(Random random)
    {
vari = random.Next(0, Ordering.Count);
var j = random.Next(0, Ordering.Count);

        if (i == j)
            return this;

varnewOrdering = new List<int>(Ordering);
var temp = newOrdering[i];
newOrdering[i] = newOrdering[j];
newOrdering[j] = temp;

        return new Solution(newOrdering);
    }
```

```
        public Solution CrossOver(Random random, Solution solution)
        {
var ordinal = Ordinal();
varordinalSol = solution.Ordinal();

varparentA = new List<int>(ordinal);
varparentB = new List<int>(ordinalSol);
var cut = parentA.Count/2;

varfirstHalf = parentA.GetRange(0, cut);
varsecondHalf = parentB.GetRange(cut, parentB.Count - cut);

firstHalf.AddRange(secondHalf);
            return DecodeOrdinal(firstHalf);
        }

        public List<int>Ordinal()
        {
var result = new List<int>();
var canonic = new List<int>(Canonic);

            foreach (varcurrentVal in Ordering)
            {
varindexCanonical = canonic.IndexOf(currentVal);
result.Add(indexCanonical);
canonic.RemoveAt(indexCanonical);
            }

            return result;
        }
        public Solution DecodeOrdinal(List<int> ordinal)
        {
var result = new List<int>();
var canonic = new List<int>(Canonic);
```

```
        for (vari = 0; i<ordinal.Count; i++)
        {
varindexCanonical = ordinal[i];
result.Add(canonic[indexCanonical]);
canonic.RemoveAt(indexCanonical);
        }

        return new Solution(result);
    }

    public List<int> Canonic
    {
        get { returnEnumerable.Range(0, Ordering.Count).
ToList(); }
    }
}
```

A solution is composed of two main fields or properties, a list of integers named Ordering, and a double value property Fitness representing the fitness of the solution. It also includes a Canonic property, which outputs a list of integers arranged in increasing order {1, ..., n}, n being the total number of cities. For instance, when $n = 5$ then its canonic form will be {1, 2, 3, 4, 5}. We use the canonic form to calculate the ordinal form of a solution. Why do we need the ordinal form of a solution?

To understand why we transform a solution to its ordinal form consider in Figure 14-9 what might happen if we apply the crossover operator on two solutions.

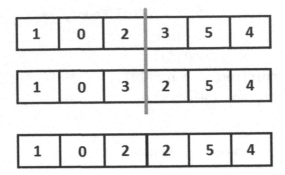

Figure 14-9. *After applying the crossover operator to the parents, the resulting offspring is unfeasible as it represents a tour that passes twice by city number 2*

As we can see from the previous figure, the application of the crossover operator on the parents gives birth to an unfeasible offspring that contains a tour that passes twice by the same city—city number 2. To avoid this issue, we use the ordinal representation of a solution, which can be calculated as described on Figure 14-10.

Current Tour	Canonic Tour	Ordinal
<u>1</u> 2 5 6 4 3 8 7	<u>1</u> 2 3 4 5 6 7 8	1
1 <u>2</u> 5 6 4 3 8 7	<u>2</u> 3 4 5 6 7 8	1 1
1 2 <u>5</u> 6 4 3 8 7	3 4 <u>5</u> 6 7 8	1 1 3
1 2 5 <u>6</u> 4 3 8 7	3 4 <u>6</u> 7 8	1 1 3 3
1 2 5 6 <u>4</u> 3 8 7	3 <u>4</u> 7 8	1 1 3 3 2
1 2 5 6 4 <u>3</u> 8 7	<u>3</u> 7 8	1 1 3 3 2 1
1 2 5 6 4 3 <u>8</u> 7	7 <u>8</u>	1 1 3 3 2 1 2
1 2 5 6 4 3 8 <u>7</u>	<u>7</u>	1 1 3 3 2 1 2 1

Figure 14-10. *To calculate the ordinal form we loop through the canonic form, look for the position of the analyzed value in the current tour, and save that position in the list forming the ordinal representation*

The interesting fact is that while the crossover operator produces unfeasible solutions when applied to regular TSP representations, when we transform these representations to ordinal form, the crossover operator produces a feasible solution (in ordinal form). We would just need to decode that ordinal solution into regular TSP form (permutation of integers in the range 1 ... n) to continue the GA procedure.

The Solution class contains the following methods:

- Mutate(): In this method we mutate a solution by selecting two random index positions in the solution ordering and exchanging their corresponding values.

- CrossOver(): In this method we apply the crossover operator on the ordinal form of the input solutions and eventually decode the obtained ordinal solution into a regular TSP solution. The cut is executed at half the length of the ordering.

- Ordinal(): In this method we transform a regular TSP solution into ordinal form.

- DecodeOrdinal(): In this method we transform an ordinal solution into a regular TSP solution.

Finally, in the GeneticAlgorithmTsp class (Listing 14-7) we incorporated the different phases of the GA. The class includes the following fields or properties:

- Iterations: number of iterations that the algorithm will be executing

- Tsp: instance of the Tsp class previously presented

- Population: set of individuals, each an instance of the Solution class previously described

- Size: size of the population

- Random: random variable

The selection strategy that is coded in the Selection() method shown in Listing 14-8 consists of sorting the population in increasing order of their fitness function and selecting the first Size/2 individuals.

Listing 14-7. GeneticAlgorithmTsp Class

```
public class GeneticAlgorithmTsp
    {
        public int Iterations { get; set; }
        public Tsp Tsp{ get; set; }
        public List<Solution> Population { get; set; }
        public int Size;
        private static readonly Random Random = new Random();

        public GeneticAlgorithmTsp(int iterations, Tsp tsp, int size)
        {
            Iterations = iterations;
            Tsp = tsp;
            Population = new List<Solution>();
            Size = size;
        }
}
```

Listing 14-8 shows the main method of execution of the GA. In the same listing, we can also see the InitialPopulation() method where we create Size random solutions. In the NewPopulation() method we add the newly born offspring to the population and sort them according to the fitness value of individuals, leaving for the next generation the first Size solutions after having ordered the Population list. In the OffSprings() method, we mutate a chromosome (solution) with a probability less than or equal to 0.4 and recombine or apply a crossover operator with a probability of 0.6.

Listing 14-8. GeneticAlgorithmTsp Class

```
        public Solution Execute()
        {
InitialPopulation();
vari = 0;

            while (i< Iterations)
            {
var selected = Selection();
varoffSprings = OffSprings(selected as List<Solution>);

NewPopulation(offSprings);
i++;
            }

            return Population.First();
        }

        private void NewPopulation(IEnumerable<Solution>offSprings)
        {
Population.AddRange(offSprings);
Population.Sort((solutionA, solutionB) =>solutionA.Fitness>=
solutionB.Fitness ?1 : -1);
            Population = Population.GetRange(0, Size);
        }

        private IEnumerable<Solution>OffSprings(List<Solution>
        selected)
        {
var result = new List<Solution>();

            for (vari = 0; i<selected.Count - 1; i++)
            {
```

```
result.Add(Random.NextDouble() <= 0.4
                            ? selected[i].Mutate(Random)
                            : selected[i].CrossOver(Random,
selected[Random.Next(0, selected.Count)]));
        }

        return result;
    }

    private IEnumerable<Solution>Selection()
    {
Population.Sort((solutionA, solutionB) =>solutionA.Fitness>=
solutionB.Fitness ?1 : -1);
        return Population.GetRange(0, Size / 2);
    }

    private void InitialPopulation()
    {
vari = 0;

        while (i< Size)
        {
Population.Add(RandomSolution(Tsp.Map.GetLength(0)));
i++;
        }
    }

    private Solution RandomSolution(int n)
    {
var result = new List<int>();
var range = Enumerable.Range(0, n).ToList();

        while (range.Count> 0)
        {
```

```
var index = Random.Next(0, range.Count);
result.Add(range[index]);
range.RemoveAt(index);
            }

        return new Solution(result);
    }
  }
```

Now that we have all elements of our GA in place we can test it in a console application as we have done with other algorithms.

Listing 14-9. Testing Our GA for Solving the TSP

```
var map = new double[,] {
                {1, 2, 3, 1, 5},
                {5, 1, 1, 1, 8},
                {1, 7, 2, 1, 9},
                {1, 1, 6, 1, 8},
                {1, 1, 4, 1, 2},
        };

varga = new GeneticAlgorithmTsp(100, new Tsp(map), 100);
var best = ga.Execute();

Console.WriteLine("Solution:");
            foreach (var d in best.Ordering)
Console.Write("{0},", d);
Console.WriteLine('\n' + "Fitness: {0}", best.Fitness);
```

In this case, we have chosen to have 100 iterations or evolution cycles, and the map consists of five cities with distances as detailed in the matrix from Listing 14-9. The result obtained can be seen in Figure 14-11.

```
Solution:
4,1,2,0,3,
Fitness: 4
```

Figure 14-11. *Solution outputted by our GA to the previous TSP*

The solution outputted by the algorithm is (4, 1, 2, 0, 3); in other words, first visit city No. 4, then move to cities No. 1, No. 2, No. 0, and finally No. 3. This path has a cost of 4, and since the cost of traveling from one city to the other must be at least 1 we can assert with a high degree of certainty that the path outputted is optimal. Also notice that the solution outputted by the algorithm is the first in the population list, which seems pretty logical as we preserve it sorted in increasing order of the fitness value of individuals.

In the next section we will be examining S-metaheuristics; we already discussed the heuristic from which all S-metaheuristics descend—Hill Climbing, also known as Local Search—and very soon we will address the topic of how a representative of an S-metaheuristic can escape from the local optimum by means of intensification and diversification mechanisms and keep a memory of the search up to a given point.

S-Metaheuristics: Tabu Search

Single solution–based metaheuristics, a.k.a *S-metaheuristics* algorithms, consist of an iterative process where a single solution is improved at each step. They could be viewed as paths created through neighborhoods or search trajectories through the state space of a given problem. The paths or trajectories are built from iterative methods that move from a current solution to another solution in the state space. S-metaheuristics can be very efficient and provide good solutions to multiple optimization problems.

Tabu Search (TS) is a metaheuristic first described by Fred Glover in the 1980s that uses adaptive memory and responsive exploration. It inherits from Hill Climbing (HC), probably the oldest and simplest heuristic method ever created. It could be argued that Tabu Search is just an HC with some considerable improvements or upgrades. Its core functionality is the same as HC; it starts at a given initial solution (usually randomly generated), runs until a stopping rule is reached, and in each iteration the current solution is replaced by another that improves the objective function and is found in the neighborhood of the current solution. The stopping rule for HC is met when no neighbor of the current solution improves the objective function, indicating a local optimum has been found. As we know from previous sections, this is the main disadvantage of HC; it can fall into a local optimum, a disadvantage Tabu Search does not share as it includes mechanisms of diversification that prevent it from getting stuck in a local optimum.

As the name suggests, TS operates by performing a search in areas of the state space that are not marked as "tabu" or forbidden. Such a mark indicates that for some time (iterations) they will not be considered in the search in an attempt to avoid the consequential waste of time and effort of trying to find solutions in the same area in short periods of time.

Adaptive memory is probably the most important characteristic of Tabu Search. It's the ability to remember the evolution of the search and is accomplished through the use of data structures. The *Tabu List* represents one of these data structures. It's traditionally employed to save pairs of data previously swapped, avoiding the possibility of cycling around the same solutions for some time (the length of this list must be finite since memory is finite). The term *intensification* refers to a mechanism that many metaheuristics implement to favor the exploitation of the best solutions found so far; in this case, the more promising regions are explored thoroughly. *Diversification*, on the other hand, refers to the exploration of the search space, trying to visit unexplored solutions.

On top of the HC-related components (initial solution, neighborhood, and so forth), TS also includes the following specific components:

- *Tabu List*: also known as short-term memory, its purpose is to prevent the search from revisiting previously visited solutions, to prevent cycling. As mentioned before, storing the list of all visited solutions is not practical for efficiency issues, thus the Tabu List usually comprehends a maximum size defined a priori, and we store at most the number of solutions defined by that size. Also, we typically don't store an entire solution in the Tabu List, but rather moves or solution attributes, which significantly reduces data storage. A move remains tabu for a number of iterations, known as *Tabu tenure*.

- *Aspiration criterion*: A commonly used aspiration criteria consists of selecting a tabu move if it generates a solution that is better than the best found solution; another aspiration criterion may be a tabu move that yields a better solution from among a set of solutions that include a given attribute.

In order to avoid getting stuck at a local optimum, TS includes intensification and diversification mechanisms; such mechanisms are represented by medium- and long-term memories:

- *Intensification (medium-term memory)*: The medium-term memory stores the elite (e.g., best) solutions found during the search. The idea is to give priority to attributes from the set of elite solutions, usually in a weighted probability manner. The search is biased by these attributes. It's usually represented by a *recency memory* in which one records the number of

consecutive iterations that various solution features
have been present in the current solution without
interruption.

- *Diversification (long-term memory)*: The long-term
  memory stores information on the visited solutions
  along the search. It explores the unvisited areas of the
  solution space. For instance, it will discourage the
  attributes of elite solutions in the generated solutions
  to diversify the search to other areas of the state space.
  It's usually represented by a *frequency memory* that
  memorizes for each component the number of times
  the component is present in all visited solutions.

The pseudocode of the algorithm can be seen in the following lines:

```
TS ()
{
currentSolution = InitialSolution();
                /* TabuList, Medium-Term and Long-Term memories */
InitDataStructures();

                    while (!stopping_criteria_met)
                {
                            neighborhood = GetNeighborhood
                            (currentSolution);
/* Non tabu or aspiration criterion holds */
currentSolution= GetBestNeighbor(neighborhood);
        /* Updatetabu list, aspiration conditions, medium,
        long term memories */
Update();

If (intensificationCriterion)
Intensification();
```

```
If (diversificationCriterion)
Diversification();
                }

        return bestSolutionFound;
}
```

Let's examine a real-life example in order to understand a little bit better the functioning of the TS algorithm. Consider once again the zoning problem from Chapter 13 and a multi-objective optimization problem where we would be minimizing the compactness (intra-class distance) and homogeneity functions. The latter function involves demographic variables; hence, it can tell us how similar two regions are in regards to age, sex, unemployment, or any other demographic variable.

In the zoning problem, a basic geostatical area (BGA) is the manner in which we refer to a basic or primitive region to be clustered. Any BGA consists of a pair (position, variablesValues) where position marks the location of the area in space (usually two coordinates) and variablesValues represents a list of values for each demographic variable in the problem. These are the elements or objects that TS will be clustering in the zoning problem.

In mathematics, homogeneity between elements x, y occurs when $|x - y| = 0$. If one considers the variables list as a vector in space, one could measure how similar regions x, y are by taking into account the EuclideanDistance(x,y) values and how small they are inside a cluster. The closer EuclideanDistance(x,y) is to 0 the closer regions x, y will be to each other. This is the approach we will apply to measure homogeneity, as if variable vectors are vectors in space and their homogeneity is achieved by how close they are. Therefore, the second function to be optimized is similar to the intra-class function, but in this case it considers the homogeneity dissimilarity matrix. Both the compactness and homogeneity functions will be calculated from *dissimilarity matrixes* that determine the level of similarity between any two regions and are associated with any variable.

Since we are dealing with a multi-objective problem we will be using the Pareto Frontier Builder introduced in Chapter 13 to get a decent approximation of the frontier during a diversification phase.

Solutions are encoded as pairs (elements, centers), where elements is an $n-k$ array, n being nthe number of BGAs, k the number of clusters, and x_i indicating that object (region in our case) i is located at cluster x_i. The centers array of length k contains every center. The neighborhood of a given solution x denoted by N(x) is obtained by swapping all pairs of elements (i, j) where i is any center and j any element, so having $s = \left(\left(e_1, e_2, \ldots, e_{n-k} \right), \left(c_1, c_2, \ldots, c_k \right) \right)$ as a solution implies $\left(\left(c_1, e_2, \ldots, e_{n-k} \right), \left(e_1, c_2, \ldots, c_k \right) \right) \in N(s)$. Each element $\left(c_1, e_2, \ldots, e_{n-k} \right)$ in the neighbor solution will be clustered into its closest center or cluster.

The pseudocode of our TS oriented toward the zoning problem (MOP plus clustering problem) is the following:

```
TsZoning()
{
        currentSolution = InitialSolution();

                    while(!stoppingConditionMet)
                    {
neighborhood = GetNeighborhoodSetTabu(currentSolution);
/*Select current solution as the solution with minimum
intra-class value and not tabu in the previously generated
neighborhood set  */
currentSolution = BestFittingNeighbor(neighborhood);
If (intensificationTime){
/*generate neighborhood for current solution, minimizing the
second objective  */
MinimizeSecondObjective();
                    }
```

```
If (diversificationTime) {
FrontierBuilder();
                        }
UpdateParetoFrontier();
                    }
}
```

The initial solution will be generated by taking the first k data-set elements as centers and then clustering the remaining elements around their closest center. Notice how, in general, each new clustering or solution is formed in the neighborhood either by selecting k centers and then clustering the remaining $n - k$ elements to their closest centers or by making step variations to already-formed solutions.

The TS proposed in this book uses a Tabu List data structure in the shape of a hash set list, which stores solution centers as a hash set. If a solution contains centers $c = (1,2,3)$, and another solution contains centers $c'=(3,4,2)$, then the Tabu List will contain $T = ((1,2,3),(3,4,2))$. The list of hash sets allows for easy handling, insertion, and search. Also, one could efficiently check whether a solution with centers $(1,2,3)$ is tabu, and since a set data structure will consider all of these as equals—$(1,2,3)$, $(2,3,1)$, $(1,3,2)$, $(2,1,3)$—it prevents duplication. Our Tabu List will prohibit the use of tuple of centers for some time.

In order to test the algorithm, a real-world problem has been used. It's illustrated as follows: the BGAs of the metropolitan area of Toluca Valley are going to be clustered into five homogeneous groups that only include elements whose variables have values in the ranges indicated here:

- Male Population under 6 years (X001).

- Male population between 6 and 11 years (X003).

- Male population between 15 and 17 (X007).

Homogeneity will be obtained on all three variables. Tabu
Search has run several iterations with `intensificationTime` = 3,
`diversificationTime` = 5. In this example, we have obtained the following
results (for simplicity's sake we have decided not to include the entire
Pareto Frontier found but rather just a subset of it):

```
(50.5901261076844,32885.0892241763)
(50.5758416315104,33770.2868646186)
(52.0662659720778,32047.9735370572)
(52.6236863193259,31963.3459865693)
(50.9352052335638,32227.1149958513)
(51.7073149394271,32224.293243894)
(50.6297645146784,32796.6211680751)
(50.7327985199368,32648.7098303008)
(63.4052030689118,31953.3511763935)
(31.7646782813892,74764.1984211605)
(32.6995744158722,73074.7519844055)
(31.7734798863389,74355.8623848788)
(31.776816796024,73910.6355371396)
(31.9216141687552,73353.8052604555)
(32.6187235737901,73079.8864057969)
(35.171800392375,71677.0312411241)
(35.1767441367242,71676.5767247979)
(35.1343494585806,71697.8434007592)
(35.147462667771,71697.7558703676)
(35.2879720849387,71676.5396553831)
(35.3225361349416,71541.4393240582)
(35.323587070021,71541.1602760788)
```

. . .

(35.5212138666,71384.7335594089)
(35.5222648016794,71384.4545114295)
(35.5310228433471,71384.2874695704)
(35.5614827835752,71363.55569029)
. . .
(40.0890479612853,66076.8575353262)
(40.1225133591276,66076.6462691529)
(40.1281553068144,66056.6499667925)
(40.0820569677191,66076.9379156809)
(40.0951701769095,66076.8503852894)
(40.1358379144876,66056.5493872965)
(40.1373651695288,65921.6511332184)
(40.1384161046082,65921.3720852389)
(40.1471741462759,65921.2050433798)
(40.1806395441182,65920.9937772065)
(40.186281491805,65900.9974748462)
(40.1401831527096,65921.2854237345)
(40.1532963619001,65921.197893343)
(40.21572345198,65900.924086982)
(40.3387179536343,65900.9141882557)

These results match the graphic shown in Figure 14-12.

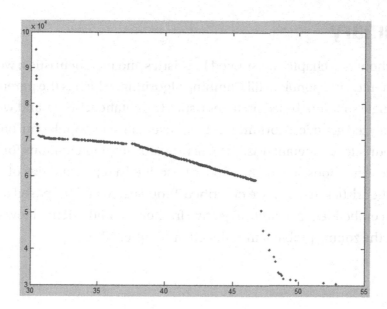

Figure 14-12. *Pareto Frontier outputted by our TS on the zoning problem*

Summarizing, we have applied TS to an interesting clustering-related problem, and by combining it with the Frontier Builder we have obtained a pretty decent approximation of the Pareto Frontier.

The use of metaheuristics to solve the zoning problem, as well as the TSP, quadratic problem, and many others, is mandatory because of their NP-Complete nature. In fact, most of the time we don't find optimal solutions, but rather approximations of these optimal solutions, and sometimes if we are lucky these approximations might equal some optimal solution. Metaheuristics such as genetic algorithms can be combined with other AI methods with the intention of starting some AI procedure with an already optimized solution, thus obtaining better results in the end.

Summary

Throughout this chapter we studied heuristics and metaheuristics; we implemented the popular Hill Climbing algorithm, which is the parent of all single solution–based metaheuristics (S-metaheuristics), and we also analyzed genetic algorithms as a representative of population-based metaheuristics (P-metaheuristics). We provided implementations for both these methods, and at the end we described a representative of S-metaheuristics; namely, we described Tabu Search and proposed a TS method embedded in a multi-objective framework and oriented toward solving the zoning problem introduced in Chapter 13.

CHAPTER 15

Game Programming

Nowadays, the video-game industry is a billion-dollar sector of the U.S. economy. There are thousands of companies developing and publishing games in all fifty states, and each game developed involves dozens of job disciplines, and its component parts employ thousands of people worldwide. It is truly a global and competitive market. The industry typically requires professionals with advanced skills in many different areas. Video-game companies must be leaders in innovation, creativity, ingenuity, and knowledge of the industry, and must be continuously adapting and changing markets. Throughout their short history, video games have seen a tremendous improvement in graphics and realism; accordingly, modern PCs owe many of their advancements and innovations to the game industry: sound cards, graphics cards and 3D graphic accelerators, faster CPUs, and dedicated coprocessors like PhysX are a few of the most notable contributions.

The industry is continuing to grow, and as it does more and more jobs are available. According to *Forbes* magazine, the economic impact of the gaming industry to the US GDP was over $11 billion in 2016, and that number is certain to grow for the foreseeable future. Companies of worldwide reach, like Activision-Blizzard (*Call of Duty*), Take-Two Interactive (*NBA2K* series), Ubisoft (*Assassin's Creed*), and Crytek (*Far Cry*), are shaping and altering our perspective of reality in the digital world with realistic, mind-blowing games that impact our social and economic life.

© Arnaldo Pérez Castaño 2018
A. Pérez Castaño, *Practical Artificial Intelligence*,
https://doi.org/10.1007/978-1-4842-3357-3_15

The game industry employs people experienced in other traditional lines of business, but most people hired have experience tailored to the game industry. Some of the disciplines specific to this industry include game programmer (includes AI), game designer, level designer, game producer, game artist, and game tester. Most of these professionals are employed by video-game developers or video-game publishers. A key element in the video-game development flow is the AI game developer.

The main goal of this chapter is to describe some of the most important game-related AI methods, specifically those that involve searching in a domain space, a basic task that must be tackled in almost every game. We will examine search algorithms such as BFS, DFS, DLS, IDS, bidirectional search, and A*, and we will see how to make use of them when developing an AI for a game. Practical problems where we implement all of the previously detailed algorithms will be included; in case of bidirectional search and A* we will describe them as being oriented toward solving the Sliding Tiles Puzzle.

Note   Companies like Sony, Nintendo, and Microsoft have contributed to keeping gaming fever alive around the globe by improving their consoles almost every year (PlayStation, Nintendo, Xbox).

What Is a Video Game?

As occurs with any other software, a game goes through a process known as *software development* in which it's conceived, specified, designed, coded, documented, tested, and bug-fixed. Thus, a *video game* is a software or computer program (Figure 15-1) that enables one or various people to interact and play a digital, electronic game in the most realistic environment possible, which is perceived through a *display* (screen, lens, etc.), interacted with through a *controller* (joystick, game pad, etc.), and executed by a *platform* (computer, video console, mobile phone, etc.)—the machine in charge of sending images and sound to the displayer and enabling the controller for interaction.

Figure 15-1. *The Halo Series (owned by Microsoft) is one of the most popular "shooters" (first person) and science fiction games ever*

The platform executes the game engine, a compound of graphics and animation, physics, controller interaction, AI, sound, networking, and so forth that follows the logic defined by the video game as coded by its developers.

The design phase of a video game usually includes the participation of a multidisciplinary team of computer scientists, historians, psychologists, musicians, artists, and digital marketers as well as other professionals. They all work together, looking to provide gamers with the most realistic game they can have, assuming the game requires this type of realism.

The AI game developer team would be in charge of creating the AI for the game. What's the AI for a game? The AI of a game defines how smart our opponents are in the game; for instance, in a sports game such as soccer, basketball, or similar, the AI implemented for the computer's side would consist of a set of strategies, plays, behaviors, actions, and so on that ultimately define a level of complexity for the computer player(s) and makes it challenging and entertaining for us to play and enjoy.

One of the main topics in AI game development is that of creating algorithms for searching in games. Search in games will be the focus point of the next section, where we will finally start diving into game-related AI algorithms.

Note   The Electronic Entertainment Expo (a.k.a.f E3) convention is one of the biggest gaming fairs in the world. It's the rendezvous point where leaders of the gaming industry expose their latest creations.

Searching in Games

There are many games that must rely on search procedures to be able to reach a winning state. Board games are probably the best representatives of such a scenario; in a board game like the Sliding Tiles Puzzle (Figure 15-2) we must search in a tree of all possible states for the one that would actually be a winning or goal state. Trees are very common structures used to represent the state space (set of all possible states). How the tree is defined or generated is problem specific; for the Sliding Tiles Puzzle case, each of the four positions to which the blank tile can be swapped represents a child of the current node. Therefore, we would have a tree of all possible states, with subtrees like the one depicted in Figure 15-3.

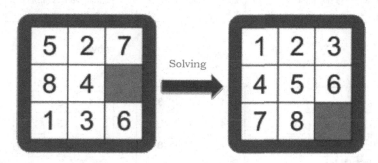

Figure 15-2. *Sliding Tiles Puzzle; a board game that relies on AI search methods*

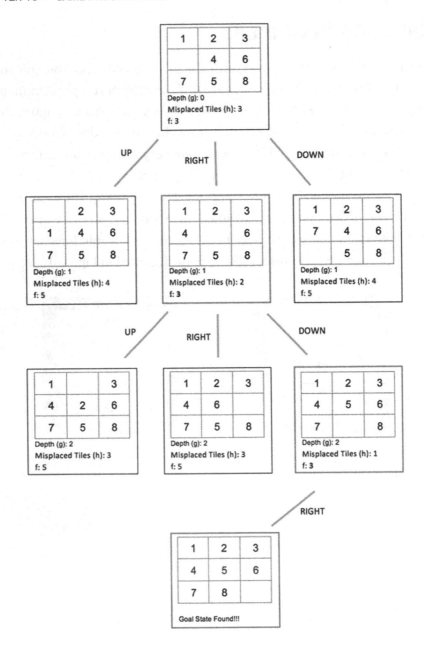

Figure 15-3. *Searching in the Sliding Tiles Puzzle until a goal state is found. In this example we use a heuristics (misplaced tiles) to determine the shortest route (orange boxes) to the goal state.*

The tree generated by the search provides us with a sequence of moves—from the root or start state, all the way down and up to a goal state—thus it provides us with a solution to the game. In Figure 15-3, the solution would be represented by moves {right, down, right}; therefore, a path of length 3 from the root takes us to a goal state. The purpose of combining a search method with a heuristic, as we will see, is to shorten the length of the search path to a goal node.

A *search strategy* can be classified according to the following criteria:

- *Systematicity*: This is a strategy where we structure the state space as a tree; we consider a strategy systematic if and only if
  - the search continues as long as no solution has been found and there are still candidates to examine; and
  - each candidate is examined once.
- *Information Usage*: It refers to whether the search uses domain-specific knowledge; i.e., knowledge of the problem during the search. It can be classified as
  - informed search (Best-First Search, A*); or
  - uninformed or blind search (BFS, DFS, IDS).

In this book, we will focus on systematic strategies, and we will also discuss both informed and uninformed search methods. The following features will be taken into account in future sections when assessing the performance of a search algorithm:

- *b (branch factor)*: maximum number of children of a node
- *d (depth)*: maximum length of all paths from the root to a leaf node
- *m*: minimum length of any path from the root to a goal state

Additionally, we'll assert that a search is *complete* if it's always able to find a solution and *optimal* if it's always able to find the lowest path cost to a goal state.

Note   The oldest type of sliding puzzle is the fifteen puzzle, invented by Noyes Chapman in 1880.

Uninformed Search

In uninformed search methods all non-goal nodes in the frontier look identical to the algorithm; as a result, this type of search is also known as a blind search. The procedure cannot determine whether a path followed from a node X is going to be any better than another path from node Y.

Uninformed search algorithms are essentially graph algorithms; they operate on trees, and trees are a particular kind of graph. Thus, the algorithms herein described are also part of the Graph Theory toolbox.

Breadth-first search (BFS) is one of the most popular graph-based search algorithms. In this method, nodes are discovered by levels; the algorithm discovers all nodes at distance k from the root before discovering any nodes at distance $k + 1$ (Figure 15-4).

BFS is complete when b is finite, both its time and space complexity are $O(b^d)$, and it's optimal if the edge cost equals 1; i.e., if the cost of taking a step in the search equals 1.

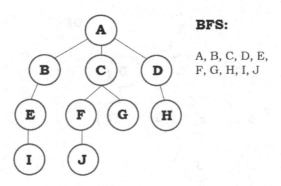

BFS:

A, B, C, D, E,
F, G, H, I, J

Figure 15-4. *Traversing the tree using a BFS procedure; we begin at node A and then discover all nodes from the next level, i.e. nodes B, C, D. We continue like this, discovering nodes at the following level, i.e. nodes E, F, G, H. Finally, we discover nodes I and J at the final level.*

Depth-first search (DFS) is another very popular graph-based search algorithm and is the prototype for many other such search procedures. In DFS, nodes are discovered by their distance downward; the algorithm begins at a root node and follows a path through the leftmost child node until it reaches a leaf, then it "backtracks" to the previously visited node N and continues discovering the next non-visited child of N. Thus, it always goes in depth building a path that looks for the leftmost, non-visited, deepest node and repeats this procedure recursively over the entire tree or graph (Figure 15-5). Notice that in a graph where we can encounter cycles, DFS must guarantee that visited nodes are marked as "visited."

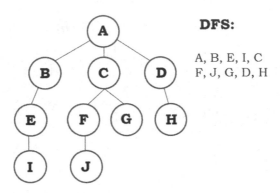

DFS:

A, B, E, I, C
F, J, G, D, H

Figure 15-5. *Traversing the tree using a DFS procedure; we begin at node A and then follow the path leading to the leftmost, non-visited node; therefore, we build the path formed by nodes A, B, E, I, then backtrack all the way up to the root (only node in the built path that has children pending discovery) and move to the leftmost, non-visited child, which would be C. It recursively executes the same procedure on C and eventually on node D, yielding the path seen on the graphic.*

Assuming we implement some sort of control mechanism determining what nodes have been visited along the way, and also assuming we are dealing with a finite space, we can affirm that DFS will be complete; otherwise, it's incomplete because it can fall into infinite loops. Its time complexity is $O(b^m)$, which can be much worse than $O(b^d)$ if m is considerably larger than d. Its space complexity is $O(b*m)$, and it's not an optimal search algorithm.

To compare BFS and DFS, the first method is usually applied in scenarios where we may have possible infinite paths, where solutions can be reached in short paths, or where we can easily discard unsuccessful paths. On the other hand, DFS would be preferred in scenarios where the state space is restricted, where there are many possible solutions with long paths, or where wrong paths are usually terminated quickly and the search can be adjusted accordingly.

BFS and DFS are the main building blocks from which many other search algorithms have been derived. Many of these derivations try to diminish some of the shortcomings of their predecessors; such is the case of depth-limited search and iterative deepening search.

Depth-limited search (DLS) is essentially a DFS where we set a depth limit L (Figure 15-6); i.e., nodes at depth L have no successors, so it's as if we were cutting the tree at depth L, consequently getting rid of the infinite-path problem. If it occurs that $L = d$ then we will obtain an optimal solution; if $L < d$ then we will have an incomplete solution, and when $L > d$ we will have a non-optimal solution.

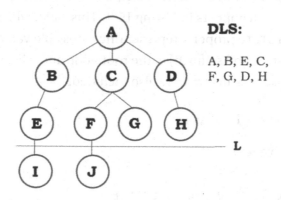

DLS:

A, B, E, C,
F, G, D, H

Figure 15-6.   DLS is a DFS with an imposed depth limit L

Iterative deepening search (IDS) is a strategy to discover the best depth limit L; the main idea is to use DLS as sub-method and gradually increase the depth limit from 1, up to a maximum predefined depth. This algorithm is complete and optimal; it always discovers the shallowest goal node.

Another uninformed search procedure that relies on either BFS or DFS is *bidirectional search (BS)*. In BS we execute two simultaneous searches: one from the initial state to the goal state and another from the goal state backward to the initial state. We hope that these searches will meet at some point. Therefore, in this procedure we must check at each step if the set of nodes expanded forward intersects with the set of nodes expanded backward. The key motivation behind BS is time complexity, since $b^{d/2} + b^{d/2}$ is less than b^d in complexity terms. Thus, this method can provide us with a more efficient, faster way to find a goal state. Furthermore, if both searches (forward, backward) are BFS algorithms, and b is finite, then BS is guaranteed to be both optimal and complete.

Practical Problem: Implementing BFS, DFS, DLS, and IDS

To develop our uninformed search strategies, we will make use of the Tree<T> class, which appears in Listing 15-1. This class, which is a generic class, contains a State property representing a possible value (integer, string, array, matrix, and so forth) of the root node and a list of tree children. Several constructors were also included.

Listing 15-1. Tree<T> Class

```
public class Tree<T>
    {
        public T State { get; set; }
        public List<Tree<T>> Children { get; set; }

        public Tree()
        {
            Children = new List<Tree<T>>();
        }

        public Tree(T state, IEnumerable<Tree<T>> children)
        {
            State = state;
            Children = new List<Tree<T>>(children);
        }
```

```
    public Tree(T state)
    {
        State = state;
        Children = new List<Tree<T>>();
    }

     public bool IsLeaf {
                get {   return Children.Count == 0; }
      }
  }
```

Trying to achieve a fine object-oriented design, we coded the UninformedMethod<T> abstract class (Listing 15-2) as the parent and container of shared fields for all the uninformed search strategies described in this section.

Listing 15-2. UninformedMethod<T> Class

```
public abstract class UninformedMethod<T>
   {
       public Tree<T> Tree { get; set; }

       protected UninformedMethod(Tree<T> tree)
       {
           Tree = tree;
       }

       public abstract List<T>Execute();
   }
```

In the Bfs<T> class (Listing 15-3), we coded the BFS strategy using a Queue data structure. This data structure is used to expand nodes by enqueuing its children and eventually dequeuing the first node enqueued; hence the FIFO (First-In-First-Out) nature of the Queue gives us the effect of traversing the tree by levels.

Listing 15-3. Bfs<T> Class

```
public class Bfs<T>: UninformedMethod<T>
    {
        public Bfs(Tree<T> tree):base(tree)
        { }

        public override List<T>Execute()
        {
var queue = new Queue<Tree<T>>();
queue.Enqueue(Tree);
var path = new List<T>();

            while (queue.Count> 0)
            {
var current = queue.Dequeue();
path.Add(current.State);

                foreach (var c in current.Children)
queue.Enqueue(c);
            }

            return path;
        }
    }
```

The DFS implemented in Listing 15-4 relies on a stack data structure that is used to simulate the intrinsically recursive nature of DFS; thus it helps us avoid having to use function recursion and allows us to reduce the coding to a simple loop. Remember: Stacks are LIFO (Last-In-First-Out) data structures, and therefore we stack children in reverse order, as the following code illustrates.

Listing 15-4. Dfs<T> Class

```
public class Dfs<T> :UninformedMethod<T>
    {
        public Dfs(Tree<T> tree):base(tree)
        {
        }

        public override List<T>Execute()
        {
var path = new List<T>();
var stack = new Stack<Tree<T>>();
stack.Push(Tree);

            while (stack.Count> 0)
            {
var current = stack.Pop();
path.Add(current.State);

                for (vari = current.Children.Count - 1; i>= 0;
                i--)
stack.Push(current.Children[i]);
            }

            return path;
        }
    }
```

Any other uninformed search strategy is basically a variation of the previous ones—DFS and BFS. The depth-limited search class illustrated in Listing 15-5 is a direct descendant of DFS. In this class, we include two properties:

- DepthLimit: defines the maximum depth reached

- Value: determines the value to be found in the tree of states

In this case, we implement the recursive version of the DFS algorithm; it is easier for us to build the path from the root to the Value node if we use recursion. Notice we have three stopping conditions in the algorithm: the Value node has been found, we have reached the depth limit, or we have reached a leaf.

Listing 15-5. Dls<T> Class

```
public class Dls<T>: UninformedMethod<T>
    {
        public intDepthLimit{ get; set; }
        public T Value { get; set; }

        public Dls(Tree<T> tree, intdepthLimit, T value) :
        base(tree)
        {
DepthLimit = depthLimit;
            Value = value;
        }

        public override List<T>Execute()
        {
var path = new List<T>();
            if (RecursiveDfs(Tree, 0, path))
                return path;
            return null;
        }

        private bool RecursiveDfs(Tree<T> tree, int depth,
        ICollection<T> path)
        {
            if (tree.State.Equals(Value))
                return true;
```

```
            if (depth == DepthLimit || tree.IsLeaf)
                return false;

path.Add(tree.State);

            if (tree.Children.Any(child =>RecursiveDfs(child,
            depth + 1, path)))
                return true;

path.Remove(tree.State);
            return false;
        }
    }
```

Finally, iterative deepening search, as previously described, uses depth-limit search as a submethod to find the shallowest depth to a goal state (Listing 15-6).

Listing 15-6. Ids<T> Class

```
public class Ids<T> :UninformedMethod<T>
    {
        public Dls<T>Dls{ get; set; }
        public intMaxDepthSearch{ get; set; }
        public intDepthGoalReached{ get; set; }
        public T Value { get; set; }

        public Ids(Tree<T> tree, intmaxDepthSearch, T value)
            : base(tree)
        {
MaxDepthSearch = maxDepthSearch;
            Value = value;
        }
```

```
        public override List<T>Execute()
        {
            for (var depth = 1; depth <MaxDepthSearch; depth++)
            {
Dls = new Dls<T>(Tree, depth, Value);
DepthGoalReached = depth;
var path = Dls.Execute();
                if (path != null)
                    return path;
            }
DepthGoalReached = -1;
            return null;
        }
    }
```

The Ids<T> generic class includes properties that correspond to the Value searched for in the tree as well as properties for determining the depth of the goal node found (DepthGoalReached) and the maximum depth the search will get to (MaxDepthSearch). From the Execute() method we can see the algorithm consists of a loop that applies DLS on depths 0, 1, …, MaxDepthSearch.

Let's test our algorithms in a console application and declare a tree, like the one illustrated in Listing 15-7.

Listing 15-7. Testing Uninformed Search Algorithms

```
var tree = new Tree<string>{ State = "A" };
tree.Children.Add(new Tree<string> { State = "B",
            Children = new List<Tree<string>>
                          {
                              new Tree<string>("E")
                          } });
tree.Children.Add(new Tree<string> { State = "C",
          Children = new List<Tree<string>>
                          {
                              new Tree<string>("F")
                          }
          });
tree.Children.Add(new Tree<string> { State = "D" });

varbfs = new Bfs<string>(tree);
vardfs = new Dfs<string>(tree);
vardls = new Dls<string>(tree, 21, "E");
var ids = new Ids<string>(tree, 10, "F");

var path = bfs.Execute();
        //var path = dfs.Execute();
       // var path = dls.Execute();
        //var path = ids.Execute();

foreach (var e in path)
Console.Write(e + ", ");
```

Uncommenting the Execute() lines for each method, we would get the results seen in Figure 15-7, shown in the order BFS, DFS, DLS, IDS.

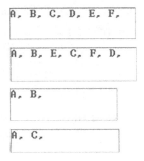

Figure 15-7. *Results obtained after executing BFS, DFS, DLS, and IDS*

Notice that in this case, and as it was implemented, both BFS and DFS traverse the tree in their defined order while DLS and IDS perform searches on the tree by looking for a specific value.

Practical Problem: Implementing Bidirectional Search on the Sliding Tiles Puzzle

We have mentioned several times the Sliding Tiles Puzzle as an example of a board game that can be solved using search strategies like the ones discussed thus far, and in this section we will implement a bidirectional search to solve the 8-puzzle (3 x 3 grid). The positive aspect of applying bidirectional search to the Sliding Tiles Puzzle is that it's very easy to calculate the reverse of the swap operation; in other words, it's very easy to calculate the predecessors of a goal state. We would just need to move the blank tile in every possible direction. Thus, in order to move from the goal state backward, we wouldn't need to implement any extra features, but rather slightly adapt the same expansion procedure we use for the forward search.

First of all, let's examine the `SlidingTilesPuzzle` and `Board` classes we will be using to deal with node expansion and game-related logic (Listing 15-8). The `SlidingTilesPuzzle` class is very simple, and its only purpose is to provide a meaningful way to refer to a "game" and organize the logic of the program. The key support class for developing the AI is `Board<T>`.

Listing 15-8. Sliding Tiles Puzzle and Board Classes

```
public class SlidingTilesPuzzle<T>
    {
        public Board<T> Board { get; set; }
        public Board<T> Goal { get; set; }

        public SlidingTilesPuzzle(Board<T> initial, Board<T> goal)
        {
            Board = initial;
            Goal = goal;
        }
    }

public class Board<T> :IEqualityComparer<Board<T>>
    {
        public T[,] State { get; set; }
        public T Blank { get; set; }
        public string Path { get; set; }
        private readonly Tuple<int, int> _blankPos;
        private readonlyint _n;

        public Board() {}

        public Board(T[,] state, T blank, Tuple<int,
        int>blankPos, string path)
        {
```

```
            State = state;
            Blank = blank;
            _n = State.GetLength(0);
            _blankPos = blankPos;
            Path = path;
        }

        public List<Board<T>>Expand(bool backwards = false)
        {
var result = new List<Board<T>>();

var up = Move(GameProgramming.Move.Up, backwards);
var down = Move(GameProgramming.Move.Down, backwards);
varlft = Move(GameProgramming.Move.Left, backwards);
varrgt = Move(GameProgramming.Move.Right, backwards);

            if (up._blankPos.Item1 >= 0 && (string.IsNullOrEmpty
            (Path) || Path.Last() != (backwards ? 'U' : 'D')))
            result.Add(up);
            if (down._blankPos.Item1 >= 0 && (string.IsNullOrEmpty
            (Path) || Path.Last() != (backwards ? 'D' : 'U')))
            result.Add(down);
            if (lft._blankPos.Item1 >= 0 && (string.IsNullOrEmpty
            (Path) || Path.Last() != (backwards ? 'L' : 'R')))
            result.Add(lft);
            if (rgt._blankPos.Item1 >= 0 && (string.IsNullOrEmpty
            (Path) || Path.Last() != (backwards ? 'R' : 'L')))
            result.Add(rgt);

            return result;
        }
```

```
        public Board<T>Move(Move move, bool backwards = false)
        {
varnewState = new T[_n, _n];
Array.Copy(State, newState, State.GetLength(0) * State.
GetLength(1));
varnewBlankPos = new Tuple<int, int>(-1, -1);
var path = "";

            switch (move)
            {
                case GameProgramming.Move.Up:
                    if (_blankPos.Item1 - 1 >= 0)
                    {
                        // Swap positions of blank tile and x tile
var temp = newState[_blankPos.Item1 - 1, _blankPos.Item2];
newState[_blankPos.Item1 - 1, _blankPos.Item2] = Blank;
newState[_blankPos.Item1, _blankPos.Item2] = temp;
newBlankPos = new Tuple<int, int>(_blankPos.Item1 - 1,
_blankPos.Item2);
                        path = backwards ? "D" : "U";
                    }
                    break;
                case GameProgramming.Move.Down:
                    if (_blankPos.Item1 + 1 < _n)
                    {
var temp = newState[_blankPos.Item1 + 1, _blankPos.Item2];
newState[_blankPos.Item1 + 1, _blankPos.Item2] = Blank;
newState[_blankPos.Item1, _blankPos.Item2] = temp;
newBlankPos = new Tuple<int, int>(_blankPos.Item1 + 1,
_blankPos.Item2);
                        path = backwards ? "U" : "D";
                    }
                    break;
```

```
                    case GameProgramming.Move.Left:
                        if (_blankPos.Item2 - 1 >= 0)
                        {
var temp = newState[_blankPos.Item1, _blankPos.Item2 - 1];
newState[_blankPos.Item1, _blankPos.Item2 - 1] = Blank;
newState[_blankPos.Item1, _blankPos.Item2] = temp;
newBlankPos = new Tuple<int, int>(_blankPos.Item1,
_blankPos.Item2 - 1);
                            path = backwards ? "R" : "L";
                        }
                        break;
                    case GameProgramming.Move.Right:
                        if (_blankPos.Item2 + 1 < _n)
                        {
var temp = newState[_blankPos.Item1, _blankPos.Item2 + 1];
newState[_blankPos.Item1, _blankPos.Item2 + 1] = Blank;
newState[_blankPos.Item1, _blankPos.Item2] = temp;
newBlankPos = new Tuple<int, int>(_blankPos.Item1,
_blankPos.Item2 + 1);
                            path = backwards ? "L" : "R";
                        }
                        break;
                }

            return new Board<T>(newState, Blank, newBlankPos,
            Path + path);
        }

        public bool Equals(Board<T> x, Board<T> y)
        {
            if (x.State.GetLength(0) != y.State.GetLength(0) ||
x.State.GetLength(1) != y.State.GetLength(1))
                return false;
```

```
            for (vari = 0; i<x.State.GetLength(0); i++)
            {
                    for (var j = 0; j <x.State.GetLength(1); j++)
                    {
if (!x.State[i, j].Equals(y.State[i, j]))
return false;
                    }
            }

            return true;
        }

        public intGetHashCode(Board<T>obj)
        {
            return 0;
        }
    }

    public enum Move
    {
        Up, Down, Left, Right
    }
```

The Board<T> class contains the following properties and variables:

- State: matrix of T values; recall T is generic and as a result it can be of any type, e.g., integer, string, or any other

- Blank: determines the blank element to be used in the board

- Path: path built from the root up to the node representing this board

- `_blankPos`: integer tuple determining the position of the blank tile on the board

- `_n`: number of rows (columns) of the board

In the `Expand()` method we generate the neighborhood of the current node; in other words, we generate the set of neighbor boards (obtained by moving the blank tile in every possible direction). Because we can generate a move in either the forward or the backward search, we define the `Boolean` variable backward to identify whether the generated move is forward or backward. Using this variable, we control several aspects of node generation and contemplate the cases where we execute a search from the root to the goal node (forward) or from the goal node to the root node. This is actually the intention of bidirectional search—to execute two searches and have them meet at some point along the way. This meeting point determines the path or sequence of moves needed to solve the puzzle. The statement `Path.Last() != (backwards ? 'U' : 'D')` guarantees that, in either the forward or the backward search, we avoid repeating states on consecutive moves. For instance, if we are moving forward in the search, we would not want to move the blank tile to the right and then, when expanding that same node, move it back to the left, because that would leave us in the same state, thus causing the algorithm to consume more computational time.

In the `Move()` method, we make use of the `Move` enum shown in Listing 15-8 to develop the logic behind blank tile moves and to determine whether certain moves are possible given the boundaries of the board. Again, the statement `path = backwards ? "R" : "L"` has the purpose of deciding the type of move executed at the current step and determining whether we are searching backward or not; this decision is then added to the `Path` variable of the generated node as an extension of the path "walked" so far. Remember that when going backward, right means left, left means right, up means down, and down means up from the forward perspective. Because, eventually, we want to concatenate this backward path with the forward path, we decided to transform it into its "forward" version from the beginning. To achieve this transformation, we have the previous statement (path = backwards ? "R" : "L").

Because we need to compare different boards to determine whether the forward and backward searches have met, we implement the IEqualityComparer<Board<T>> interface on the Board<T> class, which forces us to implement the Equals() and GetHashCode() methods. The last one will be left to the reader as an exercise, and in this book we simply leave it to return 0. The first one compares the State matrixes of each board, and if each cell coincides it outputs true; otherwise, it outputs false.

The bidirectional search class is illustrated in Listing 15-9.

Listing 15-9. Bs<T> Class

```
public class Bs<T>
{
        public SlidingTilesPuzzle<T> Game { get; set; }

        public Bs(SlidingTilesPuzzle<T> game)
        {
            Game = game;
        }

        public string BidirectionalBfs()
        {
varqueueForward = new Queue<Board<T>>();
queueForward.Enqueue(Game.Board);

varqueueBackward = new Queue<Board<T>>();
queueBackward.Enqueue(Game.Goal);

            while (queueForward.Count> 0 &&queueBackward.Count> 0)
            {
varcurrentForward = queueForward.Dequeue();
```

```
varcurrentBackward = queueBackward.Dequeue();

varexpansionForward = currentForward.Expand();
varexpansionBackward = currentBackward.Expand(true);

            foreach (var c in expansionForward)
            {
if (c.Path.Length == 1 &&c.Equals(c, Game.Goal))
                    return c.Path;
queueForward.Enqueue(c);
            }

            foreach (var c in expansionBackward)
queueBackward.Enqueue(c);

var path = SolutionMet(queueForward, expansionBackward);

            if (path != null)
                return path;
        }

        return null;
    }

    private string SolutionMet(Queue<Board<T>>expansion
    Forward, List<Board<T>>expansionBackward)
    {
        for (vari = 0; i<expansionBackward.Count; i++)
        {
            if (expansionForward.Contains
            (expansionBackward[i], new Board<T>()))
            {
var first = expansionForward.First(b =>b.Equals(b,
expansionBackward[i]));
```

```
return first.Path + new string(expansionBackward[i].Path.
Reverse().ToArray());
            }
        }

        return null;
    }
}
```

Our BS algorithm will perform two searches, each consisting of a BFS procedure that uses a queue to traverse the state tree through levels. We implement a BFS to search forward and another to search backward, and the point where these two searches meet is iteratively checked by the SolutionMet() method. The loop examining whether every expanded node with Path length 1 matches the goal state acts as a base case for the scenario where the goal state is a step away from the initial board. Figure 15-8 graphically depicts the functioning of the bidirectional search algorithm.

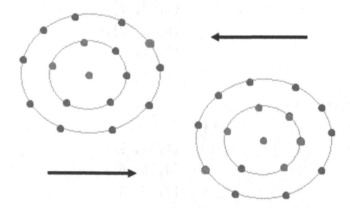

Figure 15-8. *The forward search (on the left) and the backward search (on the right).The point in the middle indicates the current node being processed in the BFS, and the circles around it represent different levels of the tree. Blue points indicate nodes that have been discovered and processed during the search, and gray ones indicate queued nodes. The green points indicate the node where both searches would meet.*

Both searches meet at the green point. To find this link or relationship between the forward and backward searches we checked the set of expanded nodes (gray points in the figure) using the SolutionMet() method. The purpose of this method is to check all enqueued points from the forward search against all expanded nodes (points in the nearest circle to the middle processed node) from the backward search and look for matches in their state or board. If a full match is found then we output the path that results from adding the subpaths of the node, forward and backward, where both searches met.

In order to test our BS we will create the experiment shown in Listing 15-10.

Listing 15-10. Testing Our Bidirectional Search Algorithm on the Hardest 8-Puzzle Configuration

```
var state = new[,]
                        {
                            {6, 4, 7},
                            {8, 5, 0},
                            {3, 2, 1}
                        };

vargoalState = new[,]
                        {
                            {1, 2, 3},
                            {4, 5, 6},
                            {7, 8, 0}
                        };

var board = new Board<int>(state, 0, new Tuple<int, int>(1, 2), "");
var goal = new Board<int>(goalState, 0, new Tuple<int, int>
(2, 2), "");
```

```
varslidingTilesPuzzle = new SlidingTilesPuzzle<int>(board,
goal);
varbidirectionalSearch = new Bs<int>(slidingTilesPuzzle);
varstopWatch = new Stopwatch();
stopWatch.Start();
var path = bidirectionalSearch.BidirectionalBfs();
stopWatch.Stop();

        foreach (var e in path)
Console.Write(e + ", ");
Console.WriteLine('\n' + "Total steps: " + path.Length);
Console.WriteLine("Elapsed Time: " + stopWatch.
ElapsedMilliseconds / 1000 + " segs");
```

In this experiment, we are using one of the hardest 8-puzzle configurations; it requires 31 steps to be solved in the optimal case. We are also using an object of type Stopwatch to measure the time consumed by the algorithm while finding a solution. The result after executing the previous code can be seen in Figure 15-9.

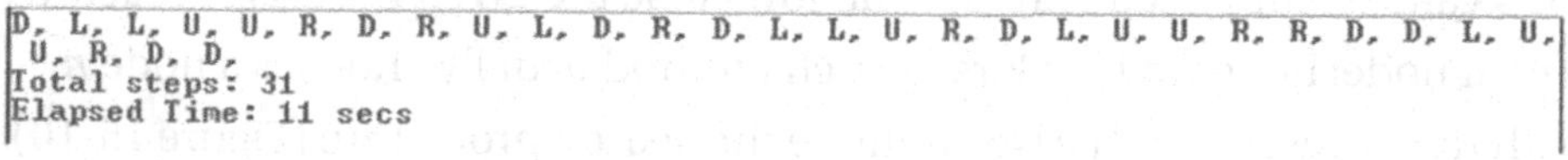

```
D, L, L, U, U, R, D, R, U, L, D, R, D, L, L, U, R, D, L, U, U, R, R, D, D, L, U,
U, R, D, D,
Total steps: 31
Elapsed Time: 11 secs
```

Figure 15-9. Solution obtained in 11 seconds

To verify the correctness of the solution we can simply loop through the path or list of moves obtained and execute the equivalent moves from the initial board, checking that the last board obtained matches the goal state.

> **Note**   Before outputting the sequence of moves of the BS algorithm
> we must reverse the path string obtained in the backward search.
> Remember that this path was built by adding moves to the end, not
> the beginning, of the string; therefore, we must reverse it in order to
> get the correct path to the goal node.

Informed Search

In an informed search we use knowledge of the problem apart from
its own definition with the intention of using it in solving a problem as
efficiently as possible. Thus, in an informed search algorithm we try to be
smart about what paths to explore. The general approach for informed
search methods is represented by a family of algorithms known as *Best
First Search*.

A Best First Search type of method always relies on an evaluation
function $F(n)$ that associates a value with every node n of the state tree.
This value is supposed to represent how close the given node is to reaching
a goal node; hence, a Best First Search method usually chooses a node n
with the lowest value $F(n)$ to continue the search procedure (Figure 15-10).
Even though we refer to this family of algorithms as "Best First," in reality
there's no certain way to determine the lowest-cost path to a goal node.
If that were possible then we would always be able to obtain an optimal
solution without the need to put in any extra effort (heuristics and so
forth).

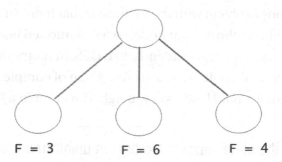

F = 3   F = 6   F = 4

Figure 15-10. *In a Best First Search method we always pick a node n with the lowest possible F(n) value to continue the search. In this case, F = 3, so the search continues from that node.*

Because informed search strategies search the most promising branches of the state space first, they are capable of

- finding a solution more quickly;

- finding solutions even when there is limited time available; and

- finding a better solution, since the more profitable parts of the state space can be examined while ignoring the unprofitable parts.

Best First Search is a search strategy and, as mentioned before, a family of algorithms whose main representatives are Greedy Best First Search and the A* search.

A *Greedy Best First Search* is basically a Best First Search in which the evaluation function $F(n)$ is a heuristic function; i.e., $F(n) = H(n)$. Examples of heuristic functions for different problems include straight distance on a map between two points, number of misplaced elements, and so on. They represent an approach for embedding additional knowledge in the solution process of a problem. When $H(n) = 0$ it implies we have reached a goal node. Greedy Best First Search expands the node that appears to be closest to goal but is neither optimal nor complete (can fall into infinite loops). An obvious problem with the method is that it doesn't take into account the cost up to the current node, so as mentioned before it isn't optimal and can wander into deadends, like DFS. In methods where we use heuristics we could obtain a drastic reduction of complexity if we use a smart heuristic that would lead us in the right direction in a few steps.

Note   When the state space is too big, an uninformed blind search can simply take too long to be practical, or can significantly limit how deep we're able to look into the space. Thus, we must look for methods that reduce the area of the state space by making smart decisions along the way; i.e., we must look for informed methods.

A* search (Hart, Nilsson, and Raphael, 1968) is a very popular method and is the best-known member of the Best First Search family of algorithms. The main idea behind this method is to avoid expanding paths that are already expensive (considering the cost of traversing through the root to the current node) and always expanding the most promising first. The evaluation function in this method is the sum of two functions; i.e., $F(n) = G(n) + H(n)$, where

- $G(n)$ is the cost (so far) of reaching node n; and

- $H(n)$ is a heuristic to estimate the cost of reaching a goal state from node n.

Because we're actually looking for the optimal path between the initial state and some goal state, a better measure of how promising a state is would be the sum of the cost-so-far and our best estimate of the cost from that node to the nearest goal state (Figure 15-11).

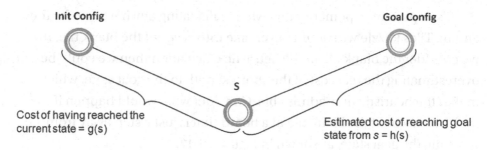

Figure 15-11. *Diagram showing the relation between G(s) and H(s)*

To guide the search through the immense space state, we use
heuristics. The information provided by the heuristic is supposed to help
us find a feasible, short path to the goal state or configuration.

When developing a heuristic it's important to make sure that it holds
the admissibility criteria. A heuristic is considered *admissible* if it doesn't
overestimate the minimum cost of reaching the goal state from the current
state, and if admissible then the A* search algorithm will always find an
optimal solution.

A* for the Sliding Tiles Puzzle

The tree structure representing the state space for the Sliding Tiles Puzzle
will be the same as was developed for the bidirectional search. The
neighborhood of the current node will consist of boards that have their
blank tile swapped into all possible positions.

The most common heuristic for the Sliding Tiles Puzzle is Misplaced
Tiles, and it is probably also the simplest heuristic for this puzzle. The
Misplaced Tiles heuristic, as the name suggests, returns the number of tiles
that are misplaced—whose position in the current board does not match
their position in the goal state or board. It's admissible since the number
returned does not overestimate the minimum number of moves required
to get to the goal state. At the very least you have to move every misplaced
tile once to swap them to their goal position; hence, it is admissible.

It's important to point out that when calculating any heuristic for the Sliding Tiles Puzzle we should never take into account the blank tile. If we consider the blank tile in the heuristic calculation then we could be overestimating the real cost of the shortest path to the goal state, which makes the heuristic non-admissible. Consider what would happen if we took into account the blank tile in a board that is just a step away from reaching the goal state, as shown in Figure 15-12.

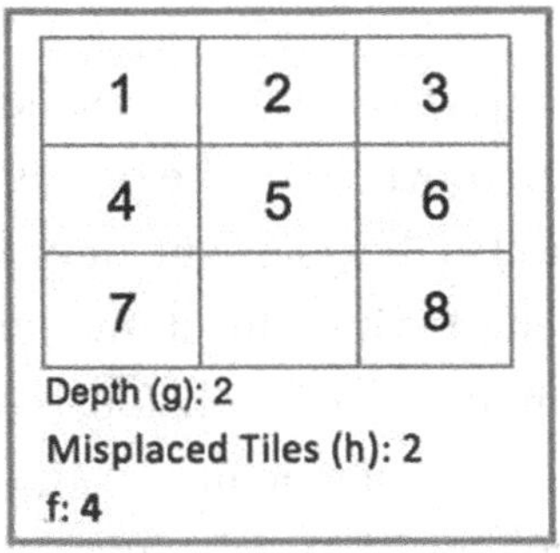

1	2	3
4	5	6
7		8

Depth (g): 2
Misplaced Tiles (h): 2
f: 4

Figure 15-12. *If we consider the blank tile, our path to a goal state would be 2, but in reality it is 1; thus, we are overestimating the real cost of a shortest path toward a goal state*

The A* algorithm with the Misplaced Tiles heuristic takes about 2.5 seconds to find the goal state. In reality, we can do much better than that, so let's try to find a more clever heuristic that will lower the timeframe and the number of nodes visited.

Note   For a full code in C# of this problem, refer to the following article by the author: `https://visualstudiomagazine.com/Articles/2015/10/30/Sliding-Tiles-C-Sharp-AI.aspx`.

The *Manhattan Distance*, or *Block Distance*, heuristic between points
$A=(x1, y1)$ and $B=(x2, y2)$ is defined as the sum of the absolute difference
of their corresponding coordinates:

$$MD = |x_1 - x_2| + |y_1 - y_2|$$

Manhattan Distance is admissible because for each tile it returns the
minimum number of steps required to move that tile to its goal position.
Manhattan Distance is a more accurate heuristic than Misplaced Tiles;
therefore, the reduction in time complexity and nodes visited will be
substantial. We are providing better information to guide the search and
so the goal is found much more quickly. Using this heuristic, we get an
optimal solution in 172 milliseconds (refer to the previously detailed
article for the complete code in C#).

The *Linear Conflict* heuristic provides information on necessary moves
that are not counted by the Manhattan Distance. Two tiles *tj* and *tk* are said
to be in a linear conflict if *tj* and *tk* are in the same line, the goal positions
of *tj* and *tk* are both in that line, *tj* is to the right of *tk*, and the goal position
of *tj* is to the left of the goal position of *tk*.

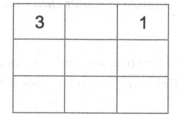 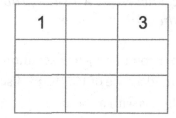

Figure 15-13. *Tiles 3 and 1 are in the correct row but in the wrong*
column

To get them to their goal positions we must move one of them down
and then up again; these moves are not considered in the Manhattan
Distance. A tile cannot appear related in more than one conflict, as solving

a determined conflict might imply the resolution of other conflicts in the same row or column. Hence, if tile 1 is related to tile 3 in a conflict then it cannot be related to a conflict with tile 2, as this may become an overestimation of the shortest path to a goal state and could turn our heuristic into a non-admissible one.

To test the Linear Conflict + Manhattan Distance heuristic combination, we'll use the 4×4 board seen in Figure 15-14; this board requires 55 moves to reach the goal state. The value of a node n will be given by $F(n) = Depth(n) + MD(n) + LC(n)$. It's possible to combine these heuristics as the moves they represent do not intersect, and consequently we will not be overestimating the cost of the shortest path to a goal state.

5	10	14	7
8	3	6	1
15		12	9
2	11	4	13

Figure 15-14. 4×4 board for testing Manhattan Distance + Linear Conflict heuristic. A 15-tile problem has a much broader state space than the 8-tile problem.

After completing an execution that traversed over a million nodes and consumed a time of 124199 milliseconds (little over 2 mins), the algorithm provided us with a solution.

The *pattern database* heuristic is defined by a database containing different states of the game. Each state is associated with the minimum number of moves required to take a pattern (subset of tiles) to its goal position. In this case, we built a small pattern database by making a BFS backward, starting at the 8-tile goal state. The results were saved in a

.txt file of merely 60,000 entries. The pattern chosen for the database is typically known as the *fringe*, and in this case it contains tiles from the top row and the leftmost column.

1	2	3
4	?	?
7	?	?

Figure 15-15. *Pattern used in 3 × 3 board*

The pattern database heuristic function is computed by a table look-up function. In this case, it's a dictionary lookup that has 60,000 stored patterns. It philosophically resembles those of the Divide and Conquer and Dynamic Programming techniques.

Using the pattern database technique, we can obtain a time of 50 milliseconds for solving the hardest 8-tile problem or configuration.

The more entries we add to the database the lower the time consumed by the algorithm in finding a goal state. In this case, the trade-off between memory and time favors the former and helps us obtain a good running time. This is how it usually works; you use more memory in order to reduce the execution time of your algorithms. The pattern database heuristic represents the definitive alternative when you want to solve 4 x 4 puzzles or *m* x *n* puzzles where *n* and *m* are greater than 3. A final suggestion to the reader would be to combine the A* search and heuristics presented in this section with a bidirectional search and compare results.

Summary

In this chapter we introduced game programming and, more specifically, searching in games. We analyzed the fundamental methods for searching in state space, including those that classify as uninformed search—BFS, DFS, DLS, IDS, and BS—and those that classify as informed search: Best-First Search and A*. We implemented a bidirectional search tailored to the Sliding Tiles Puzzle and using BFS as a sub-procedure. Ultimately, we showed how to develop an A* search for the Sliding Tiles Puzzle using different heuristics, combining some of those heuristics, and assessing their performance in regards to time complexity through the use of the C# Stopwatch class.

CHAPTER 16

Game Theory: Adversarial Search & Othello Game

The most relevant figure associated with game theory is, without any doubt, John von Neumann, the Hungarian-American mathematician—one of the greatest of the twentieth century. Although others preceded him in formulating concepts connected to game theory (notably Emile Borel), it was von Neumann who in 1928 published the paper that laid the foundation for the theory of *two-person zero-sum* games. His work culminated in an essential book on game theory written in collaboration with Oskar Morgenstern and titled *Theory of Games and Economic Behavior* (1944).

The theory developed by von Neumann and Morgenstern is highly associated with a class of games called two-person zero-sum games, or games where there are only two players and in which one player wins what the other player loses. Their mathematical framework initially made the theory applicable only under special and limited conditions. Over the past six decades this situation has dramatically changed, and the framework has been strengthened and generalized. Since the late 1970s it has been possible to assert that game theory is one of the most important and useful

© Arnaldo Pérez Castaño 2018
A. Pérez Castaño, *Practical Artificial Intelligence*,
https://doi.org/10.1007/978-1-4842-3357-3_16

tools in many fields of science, particularly in economics. In the 1950s and 1960s, game theory was broadened theoretically and applied to problems of war and politics. Additionally, it has found applications in sociology and psychology and established links with evolution and biology. Game theory received special attention in 1994 with the awarding of the Nobel Prize in Economics to John Nash, John Harsanyi, and Reinhard Selten.

John Nash, the subject of the 2001 Oscar-winning movie *A Beautiful Mind*, transformed game theory into a more general tool that enabled the analysis of win-win and lose-lose scenarios, as well as win-lose situations. Nash enabled game theory to address a central question: should we compete or cooperate?

In this chapter, we will discuss various concepts and ideas drawn from game theory. We will address a sub-branch of game theory known as adversarial search, and we will describe the Minimax algorithm, which is typically applied in two-player zero-sum games of perfect information in a deterministic environment.

Note   In 1950, John Nash demonstrated that finite games always have an equilibrium point at which all players choose actions that are best for them given their opponents' choices. The Nash equilibrium, also called strategic equilibrium, is a list of strategies, one for each player, that has the property that no player can unilaterally change his strategy and get a better payoff.

What Is Game Theory?

A *game* is a structured set of tasks defined in an entertaining environment and manner so as to attract players (1 or more) to comply with logical rules that if properly fulfilled result in the game's being completed.

Game theory is the mathematical theory of how to analyze games and how to play them optimally; it's also a way of looking at multiple human behaviors as if they were part of a game. Some of the most popular games that can be analyzed in game theory are Othello, blackjack, poker, chess, tic-tac-toe, backgammon, and so on. In reality, not only games as we know them or think about them are the topic of analysis in game theory. Rather, there are many other situations that can be formulated as games. Whenever rational people must make decisions within a framework of strict and known rules, and when each player gets a payoff based on the decisions of other players, we have a game. Examples include auctions, negotiations, military tactics, and more. The theory was initiated by mathematicians in the first half of the last century, but since then much research in game theory has been done outside of the mathematics area.

The key aspects of game theory revolve around the identification of process participants and their various quantifiable options (choices), as well as the consideration of their preferences and subsequent reactions. If all these factors are carefully thought of, then the task of modeling the problem by game theory—along with the identification of all possible situations—becomes easier.

One of the classic examples presented in the scientific literature to describe how games are analyzed in game theory is the *Prisoner's Dilemma (PD)*. The name of the game derives from the following situation, typically used to exemplify it.

Suppose the police have arrested two people they know have committed an armed robbery together. Unfortunately, they lack enough admissible evidence to get a jury to convict them. They do, however, have enough evidence to send each prisoner away for two years for theft of the getaway car. The police chief now makes the following offer to each prisoner: If you will confess to the robbery, implicating your partner, and he does not also confess, then you'll go free and he'll get ten years. If you both confess, you'll each get five years. If neither of you confesses, then you'll each get two years for the auto theft. Table 16-1 illustrates the payoff or benefit matrix in this problem.

Table 16-1. *Prisoner's Dilemma Payoff Matrix*

	Prisoner B, stays silent	Prisoner B, betrays
Prisoner A, stays silent	2, 2	0, 10
Prisoner A, betrays	10, 0	5, 5

The cells of the matrix define payoffs for both players and for each combination of actions. In every pair (a, b), player A's payoff equals a and player B's payoff equals b.

- If both players stay silent then they each get a payoff of 2. This appears in the upper-left cell.

- If neither of them stays silent, they each get a payoff of 5; this appears as the lower-right cell.

- If player A betrays and player B remains silent then player A gets a payoff of 10 (going free) and player B gets a payoff of 0 (ten years in prison); this appears in the lower-left cell.

- If player B betrays and player A stays silent then player B gets a payoff of 10 and player A gets 0; this appears in the upper-right cell.

Each player evaluates his or her two possible actions here by comparing their personal payoffs in each column, since this shows which of their actions is preferable, just to themselves, for each possible action by their partner. Therefore, if player B betrays then player A gets a payoff of 5 by also betraying and a payoff of 0 by staying silent. If player B stays silent then player A gets a payoff of 2 by also staying silent or a payoff of 10 by betraying player B. Consequently, player A is better off betraying regardless of what player B does. Player B, on the other hand, evaluates his actions by comparing his payoffs down each row, and he comes to exactly the same conclusion that player A does. Whenever an action for a player is superior when compared to each possible action by an opponent we say that the first action strictly dominates the second one (recall terms such as Pareto set and Pareto optimality from Chapter 13). In the PD, confessing strictly dominates refusing for both players. Both players know this about each other, entirely eliminating any temptation to depart from the strictly dominated path. Hence, both players will betray, and both will go to prison for five years.

These days, AIs capable of defeating human champions for games such as chess, checkers, and backgammon have been created. Most recently (March 2016), the Google DeepMind's AlphaGo program, using a self-learning algorithm (we'll look into this in Chapter 17, "Reinforcement Learning"), was able to defeat the world champion of Go, Lee Sedol (Figure 16-1).

Adversarial Search

In this book, we will focus on a sub-branch of game theory known as *adversarial search*, which is usually applied to board games. In adversarial search, we examine problems that arise when we try to plan ahead or look into the future of a world where other agents are planning against us. Thus, adversarial search becomes necessary in competitive environments where there are conflicting goals and more than one agent.

Board-game analysis is one of the oldest branches of AI (Shannon, Turing, Wiener, and Shanon 1950). Such games present a very abstract and pure form of competition between two opponents and clearly require a form of "intelligence." The states of a game are easy to represent, and the possible actions of the players are well defined. The world states are fully accessible even though it's a contingency problem, because the characteristics of the opponent are not known in advance. Board games are not only difficult because of their contingency, but also because the search trees can become astronomically large.

Figure 16-1. *Lee Sedol vs AlphaGo, March 2016*

Concepts from the area of game theory for which we will need to find a common ground of understanding are presented in the following points:

- *Deterministic Game Environment*: A game is said to be deterministic if it does not involve any random process like the throwing of a dice; i.e., a player's actions lead to completely predictable outcomes. Games such as checkers, chess, and Othello are deterministic.

- *Stochastic Game Environment*: A game is said to be stochastic if it involves some random process like the throwing of a dice. Games such as backgammon and dominoes are stochastic.

- *Utility Function*: is a mapping from states of the world to real numbers. These numbers are interpreted as measures of an agent's level of happiness in the given states.

- *Constant-Sum Game*: A two-player game is constant-sum if there exists a constant c such that for each strategy $s \in A1 \times A2$ it is the case that $u1(s) + u2(s) = c$ being A1 is the set of actions of one of the players and A2 the set of actions of the other player.

- *Zero-Sum Game*: a constant-sum game where $c = 0$; i.e., utility values at the end of the game are always equal in absolute value and opposite in sign.

- *Imperfect Information Game*: a game where the players do not have all information regarding the state of other players. Games such as poker, Scrabble, and bridge are imperfect in their information.

- *Perfect Information Game*: a game whose environment is fully observable by all players; i.e., every player is aware of other players' state. Games such as Othello, checkers, and chess are of perfect Information.

Considering previously detailed concepts, we can create Table 16-2, which details by row and column headers what method would be required to solve a game that depends on conditions defined.

Table 16-2. *Methods for Solving Different Types of Games*

	Zero-Sum	Non-Zero Sum
Perfect Information	Minimax, Alpha-Beta	Backward induction, retrograde analysis
Imperfect Information	Probabilistic Minimax	Nash equilibrium

In this book, we will focus on two-player zero-sum games—games where the value achieved by a player is lost, in the same quantity, by the other. Thus, from the next section onward, we'll be discussing the most relevant algorithm that is applied to this type of game.

Note   An international program known as "Prism" run by the US Secret Service agencies uses a software model based on game theory to determine the predictability of terrorist activities, identities, and possible locations.

Minimax Search Algorithm

Minimax search is an algorithm applied in two-player, zero-sum, deterministic, perfect information games to determine the optimal strategy for a player (MAX) at a given stage of the game and assuming the other player will also make optimal plays (MIN). It's applied in games such as chess, Othello, tic-tac-toe, and more. When executing this algorithm, we traverse the state space tree and represent each move in terms of losses or gains for one of the players. Therefore, this method can only be used to make decisions in zero-sum games, where one player's loss is the other player's gain. Theoretically, this search algorithm is based on *Von Neumann's Minimax* theorem, which states that in these types of games (zero-sum, deterministic, perfect information) there is always a set of strategies that leads to both players' gaining the same value, and that seeing as this is the best possible value one can expect to gain, one should employ this set of strategies.

Note   A Minimax player (MAX) is a player that plays optimally, assuming its opponent (MIN) is also playing optimally but in a different direction; i.e., one maximizes and the other minimizes results.

Hence, in the Minimax algorithm we assume there are two players; namely, MAX and MIN. A search tree is generated in a depth-first style, starting with the current game position and going all the way up to an end-game position. An end-game position could be reached when we get to either a leaf node (node representing an actual end of the game) or a node at MaxDepth, the maximum depth the search will go to. Because most games possess a gigantic state search, we typically cannot make it to a leaf node. Thus, it is usually the node at MaxDepth where the DFS stops and starts backtracking. Before backtracking, the procedure gets a utility value from the end-game position node. This value is obtained from a heuristic that tells us how close we are to winning from that point onward.

Afterward, the utility value is backtracked, and, depending on whether the parent node N belongs to a tree level or a depth corresponding to a MAX player or a MIN player, the utility value of N is obtained from its children $c1, c2, ... ,cm$ as $Max(c1, c2, ..., cm)$, where $Max()$ is a function returning the maximum value of its arguments, or as $Min(c1, c2, ..., cm)$, where $Min()$ is a function returning the minimum value of its arguments. Figure 16-2 illustrates the functioning of the algorithm.

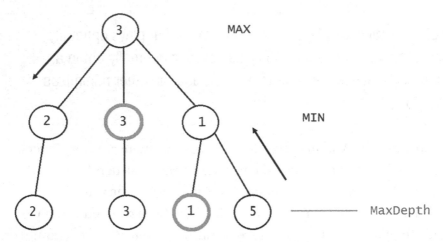

Figure 16-2. *Execution of a Minimax algorithm where MaxDepth = 2.*
The method first calculates the values of nodes at MaxDepth and then
moves those values up according to whether a node is a Max node or
a Min node. Nodes denoted in orange are the ones selected to have
their values elevated in the tree.

A pseudocode of the algorithm would be the following:

```
Minimax(Node n): output Real-Value
{
    if (IsLeaf(n)) then return Evaluate(n);
    if (MaxDepth) then return Heuristics(n);

    if (n is a MAX node) {
          v = NegativeInfinity
    foreach (child of n)
          {
      v' = Minimax (child)
     if (v' > v) v= v'
          }
return v
    }
```

```
  if (n is a MINnode)  {
     v = PositiveInfinity
     foreach (child of n)
     {
          v' = Minimax (child)
 if (v' < v)  v= v'
     }
   · return v
  }
}
```

Notice in the pseudocode that we distinguish two methods for evaluating end-game nodes (leaf or MaxDepth reached). If we reached a leaf node, the evaluation procedure would output H or L depending on whether the root player is MAX or MIN. These values correspond to the range $[L; H]$ of possible values a node can take. H indicates a win for MAX and L a win for MIN; because this is a zero-sum game we know that $L + H = 0$; i.e., $L = -H$. If we reach a node at MaxDepth then we output a value in the range $[L; H]$ indicating how good that path would be from that point onward.

Note   Every single-agent problem can be considered as a special case of a two-player game by making the environment one of the players, with a constant utility function; e.g., always 0.

Alpha-Beta Pruning

A Minimax algorithm can potentially explore many nodes of the generated tree whose paths would eventually be dismissed by the algorithm as they would be overtaken (in terms of higher or lower values) by the value of other nodes. Let's consider this scenario in the Minimax tree shown in Figure 16-3.

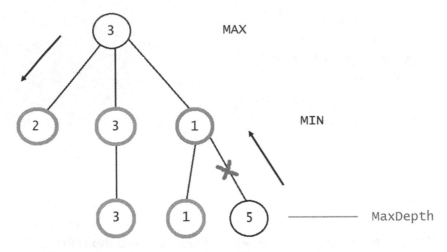

Figure 16-3. *Pruning child nodes of MIN node with utility value 1*

In this Minimax tree we have a subtree that can be pruned. Remember: Minimax executes a DFS for traversing the tree; therefore, at some point it will backtrack to the MIN node colored green—let it be *G* from now on. Once at *G*, it would have already discovered and updated values for MIN nodes 2 and 3. All discovered nodes whose values would have been updated at the moment of updating *G* are colored orange. Because when updating *G* the algorithm would already be aware of sibling nodes and their corresponding utility values 2 and 3, and considering that it already knows that because *G* is a MIN node its value will be always lower than the value it already discovered (1), then by simple logic facts, it must be that the final value of the root at MAX node must be 3. Thus, any further exploration of children of *G* would be in vain, and those branches can be dismissed, pruned in the search.

For determining which branches or subtrees can be pruned, the Minimax algorithm suffers a slight modification where two values are added; namely, Alpha and Beta. The first will continuously update the highest value found on a level of the tree, while the latter will continuously update the lowest value. Using these values as reference, we will be able to decide whether a subtree should be pruned. A pseudocode of the algorithm can be seen in the next lines:

MinimaxAlphaBetaPruning(Node n, Real beta, Real alpha): output
Real-Value

```
{
if (IsLeaf(n)) then return Evaluate(n);
if (MaxDepth) then return Heuristics(n);

 if (n is a max node) {
v = beta
        foreach (child of n) {
v' = minimax (child,v, alpha)
if (v' > v) v = v'
if (v >alpha) return alpha
}
return v
      }
if (n is a min node) {
v = alpha
foreach (child of n) {
v' = minimax (child,beta, v)
if (v' < v) v = v'
if (v <beta) return beta
}
return v
}}
```

How can Alpha-Beta pruning influence our Minimax search? That
depends on the order in which children are visited. If children are
visited in the worst possible order, then it could occur that no pruning
is ever done. For Max nodes, we want to visit the best child first. For Min
nodes, we want to visit the worst child first (from our perspective, not the
opponent's).

When the optimal child is selected at every opportunity, Alpha-Beta pruning causes the rest of children to be pruned away at every other level of the tree; only that child is explored. This means that on average the tree can be searched twice as deeply as before, which represents a very significant increase in searching performance.

Othello Game

Othello (a.k.a. Reversi, Yang) is a board game created in London during the late nineteenth century and modified in 1971 by Japanese inventor Goro Hasegawa (Figure 16-4), who registered the game as Othello (for Shakespeare's play of the same name), changing several rules in the process.

Figure 16-4. *Goro Hasegawa, creator of Othello as we know it today*

Othello is played on an 8 x 8 board (Figure 16-5), and there are two players. One controls the set of white pieces, and the other controls the set of black pieces. The total number of pieces is 64, and once the game has ended, the player with the higher number of pieces of its color on the board wins the game. This is a strategic, abstract game, as is the case with other board games such as Go.

Figure 16-5. *Othello board*

The initial configuration of the board is depicted in Figure 16-6.

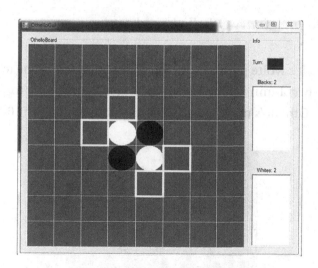

Figure 16-6. *Initial configuration of Othello board and GUI of the Windows Forms application we'll be developing throughout this chapter*

The player controlling the black pieces starts the game by making the first move. Available moves for this player are denoted in Figure 16-6 as yellow squares on the board. A move in Othello consists of setting a piece on the board in a cell where it would flank the opponent's pieces in a horizontal, vertical, or diagonal direction. In Figure 16-7, we can see an imaginary arrangement of pieces on the board.

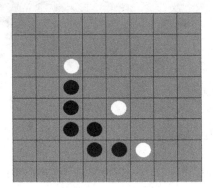

Figure 16-7. *Imaginary Othello board setting*

Assuming it's white pieces' turn, a possible play would be to set a piece on row 6, column 2, numbered starting at 0 and going top-to-bottom (according to Othello's move rules); it is illustrated in Figure 16-8.

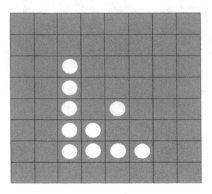

Figure 16-8. *Resulting board after setting a white piece on (6, 2)*

After setting a white piece on (6, 2), all black pieces will be flanked in all directions (horizontal, vertical, diagonal); thus, these pieces are flipped and become white pieces.

If a player cannot move any of their pieces (cannot flank any of the opponent's pieces), their turn passes to the other player. If neither of the players has a move available, then it" game over, and the winner is the player with the highest number of pieces on the board; likewise for the case where all 64 pieces are on the board. This is clearly a deterministic, perfect information, zero-sum game. Therefore, one can develop an AI under a Minimax search.

Heuristics applied to this game seek to improve the performance of the search (Minimax); some of these heuristics are as follows:

- *Piece Difference*: A basic feature to analyze and build a heuristic from in Othello is piece difference; i.e., the difference between black and white pieces. Ultimately, the value obtained is the percentage of black (B) or white (W) pieces on the board, except when $W = B$. The calculation goes as follows:

  - $(B > W)$: $100 * B / (W + B)$
  - $(B < W)$: $100 * W / (W + B)$
  - $(B = W)$: 0

- *Corner Occupancy*: Corners are key positions in an Othello game; the player controlling corners controls a big part of the game. Corner occupancy measures how many corners are owned by each player. To compute the corner occupancy, we count the number of black pieces in corners, B, and the number of white pieces in corners, W. We then let the corner occupancy score be:

  - $25B - 25W$

- *Corner Closeness*: Squares contiguous to corners can be deadly if the corner is empty; they can create an opportunity for the opponent to capture the corner. Therefore, corner closeness measures those "deadly" pieces adjacent to empty corners. To compute the corner closeness score, we count the number of black pieces adjacent to corners and the number of white pieces adjacent to corners. The final score would be:

  - $-12.5B + 12.5W$

- *Mobility*: One of the worst scenarios in Othello occurs when a player is out of moves and misses their turn; thus, this heuristic measures how many moves a player has. As with the Piece Difference heuristic, it's calculated as a percentage, as follows:

  - $(B > W)$: $100 * B / (W + B)$

  - $(B < W)$: $100 * W / (W + B)$

  - $(B = W, W = 0, B = 0)$: 0

There are other heuristics, but we'll settle for the ones just described in this book. Notice all of them output a value in the range [-100; 100]. This is the range of values we'll contemplate for our Othello implementation, so a leaf node (assuming we can reach it at some point) with $B > W$ will be rewarded with a value of 100, and a leaf node with $W > B$ will be rewarded with a value of -100; a draw will return a value of 0.

To combine the previous heuristics, we can formulate a weighted sum that has weights in the range [0, 1], as if they would represent a percentage of priority given to every heuristic. The final utility value of a node would be

$$\text{UtilityValue} = \frac{1}{n}\sum_{i=1}^{n} h_i * w_i$$

where n is the number of heuristics combined, w_i is the weight associated with the ith heuristic, and h_i is the value of the ith heuristic. Notice we guarantee with the previous formulation that the utility value of a node will always be in the range [-100, 100]. In the following section, we will begin coding the Othello game in Windows Forms as well as the Minimax algorithm representing its AI component.

Practical Problem: Implementing the Othello Game in Windows Forms

In this section, we will implement the Othello game in Windows Forms. We'll boost this program later with a Minimax AI that follows the ideas described thus far and that should make it easy for us to test and improve the code. First, we'll examine the OthelloBoard class shown in Listing 16-1.

Listing 16-1. OthelloBoard Class, Properties, and Constructors

```
public class OthelloBoard
    {
        public int[,] Board { get; set; }
        public int N { get; set; }
        public int M { get; set; }
        public int Turn { get; set; }
        public List<Tuple<int, int>> Player1Pos { get; set; }
        public List<Tuple<int, int>> Player2Pos { get; set; }
        public Tuple<int, int>MoveFrom{ get; set; }
        internal double UtilityValue{ get; set; }
        internal readonly Dictionary<Tuple<int, int>,
List<Tuple<int, int>>> Flips;
```

```
public OthelloBoard(int n, int m)
{
    Board = new int[n, m];
    Turn = 1;
    Flips = new Dictionary<Tuple<int, int>, List<Tuple
    <int, int>>>();
    Player1Pos = new List<Tuple<int, int>>
                    {
                        new Tuple<int, int>(n / 2 - 1,
                        m / 2),
                        new Tuple<int, int>(n / 2,
                        m / 2 - 1)
                    };
    Player2Pos = new List<Tuple<int, int>>
                    {
                        new Tuple<int, int>(n / 2 - 1,
                        m / 2 - 1),
                        new Tuple<int, int>(n / 2,
                        m / 2)
                    };

    // Initial Positions
Board[n / 2 - 1, m / 2 - 1] = 2;
Board[n / 2, m / 2] = 2;
Board[n / 2 - 1, m / 2] = 1;
Board[n / 2, m / 2 - 1] = 1;
    N = n;
    M = m;
}

private OthelloBoard(OthelloBoardothelloBoard)
{
```

```
        Board = new int[othelloBoard.N, othelloBoard.M];
        M = othelloBoard.M;
        N = othelloBoard.N;
        Turn = othelloBoard.Turn;
        Flips = new Dictionary<Tuple<int, int>,
List<Tuple<int, int>>>(othelloBoard.Flips);
Array.Copy(othelloBoard.Board, Board, othelloBoard.N *
othelloBoard.M);
        Player1Pos = new List<Tuple<int, int>>
        (othelloBoard.Player1Pos);
        Player2Pos = new List<Tuple<int, int>>
        (othelloBoard.Player2Pos);
    }
}
```

In the OthelloBoard class we included two constructors; one is intended to act as an initialization of the game and the other as a way to clone an Othello game received as argument. The class contains the following properties:

- Board: represents the Othello board

- N: number of rows

- M: number of columns

- Turn: player who should make the next move on the board; black player equals 1, white player equals 2

- Player1Pos: list of black pieces' positions on the board detailed as pairs (x, y)

- Player2Pos: list of white pieces' positions on the board detailed as pairs (x, y)

- MoveFrom: represents the move that generated the current board. It can serve as a way to build the entire path from the root up to the current node.

- UtilityValue: represents the utility value of the board on a Minimax tree. Recall that this value is updated as the algorithm backtracks and has values calculated at lower levels of the tree.

- Flips: dictionary containing as key a pair (x, y) representing a position on the board where the player in turn can set one of their pieces and a value $(f1, f2, .., fm)$ of the pieces that will have to be flipped after setting a piece at (x, y)

The class also includes the methods seen in Listing 16-2.

Listing 16-2. Methods EmptyCell(), Expand(), AvailableMoves(), and IsLegalMove()

```
public bool EmptyCell(inti, int j)
{
return Board[i, j] == 0;
}

public List<OthelloBoard>Expand(int player)
{
var result = new List<OthelloBoard>();
var moves = AvailableMoves(player);

    foreach (var m in moves)
    {
varnewBoard = SetPieceCreatedBoard(m.Item1, m.Item2, player);
newBoard.MoveFrom = m;
result.Add(newBoard);
```

```
        }

        return result;
    }

    public List<Tuple<int, int>>AvailableMoves(int player)
    {
var result = new List<Tuple<int, int>>();
varoppPlayerPositions = player == 1 ? Player2Pos : Player1Pos;

        foreach (varoppPlayerPos in oppPlayerPositions)
result.AddRange(AvailableMovesAroundPiece(oppPlayerPos, player));

        return result;
    }

    private bool IsLegalMove(inti, int j)
    {
        return i>= 0 &&i< N && j >= 0 && j < M &&EmptyCell
        (i, j);
    }
```

A description of the previous methods is given in the following points:

- EmptyCell(): determines whether a cell on the board is empty

- Expand(): this method is mainly used in the Minimax algorithm. It expands the current board, returning a list of boards representing the execution of every possible move for the player in turn.

- AvailableMoves(): outputs a list of available moves for the player in turn

- IsLegalMove(): returns true if a move to cell (i, j) is valid according to board specifications

Both Expand() and AvailableMoves() rely in their implementations on other methods; these methods are described in Listing 16-3.

Listing 16-3. Methods AvailableMovesAroundPiece() and SetPieceCreatedBoard()

```
        private IEnumerable<Tuple<int, int>>AvailableMovesAroun
        dPiece(Tuple<int, int>oppPlayerPos, int player)
        {
var result = new List<Tuple<int, int>>();
vartempFlips = new List<Tuple<int, int>>();

        // Check Down
        if (IsLegalMove(oppPlayerPos.Item1 + 1,
        oppPlayerPos.Item2))
        {
var up = CheckUpDown(oppPlayerPos, player, (i =>i>= 0), -1,
tempFlips);
            if (up)
            {
UpdateFlips(new Tuple<int, int>(oppPlayerPos.Item1 + 1,
oppPlayerPos.Item2), tempFlips);
result.Add(new Tuple<int, int>(oppPlayerPos.Item1 + 1,
oppPlayerPos.Item2));
            }
        }

        // Check Up
        if (IsLegalMove(oppPlayerPos.Item1 - 1,
        oppPlayerPos.Item2))
```

```
                {
tempFlips.Clear();
var down = CheckUpDown(oppPlayerPos, player, (i =>i< N), 1,
tempFlips);
                if (down)
                {
UpdateFlips(new Tuple<int, int>(oppPlayerPos.Item1 - 1,
oppPlayerPos.Item2), tempFlips);
result.Add(new Tuple<int, int>(oppPlayerPos.Item1 - 1,
oppPlayerPos.Item2));
                }
            }

            // Check Left
            if (IsLegalMove(oppPlayerPos.Item1, oppPlayerPos.
            Item2 - 1))
            {
tempFlips.Clear();
varrgt = CheckLftRgt(oppPlayerPos, player, (i =>i< M), 1,
tempFlips);
                if (rgt)
                {
UpdateFlips(new Tuple<int, int>(oppPlayerPos.Item1,
oppPlayerPos.Item2 - 1), tempFlips);
result.Add(new Tuple<int, int>(oppPlayerPos.Item1,
oppPlayerPos.Item2 - 1));
                }
            }

            // Check Right
            if (IsLegalMove(oppPlayerPos.Item1, oppPlayerPos.
            Item2 + 1))
```

```
                {
tempFlips.Clear();
varlft = CheckLftRgt(oppPlayerPos, player, (i =>i>= 0), -1,
tempFlips);
                if (lft)
                {
UpdateFlips(new Tuple<int, int>(oppPlayerPos.Item1,
oppPlayerPos.Item2 + 1), tempFlips);
result.Add(new Tuple<int, int>(oppPlayerPos.Item1,
oppPlayerPos.Item2 + 1));
                }
            }

            // Check Up Lft
            if (IsLegalMove(oppPlayerPos.Item1 - 1,
            oppPlayerPos.Item2 - 1))
            {
tempFlips.Clear();
vardownRgt = CheckDiagonal(oppPlayerPos, player, (i =>i< N),
(i =>i< M), 1, 1, tempFlips);
                if (downRgt)
                {
UpdateFlips(new Tuple<int, int>(oppPlayerPos.Item1 - 1,
oppPlayerPos.Item2 - 1), tempFlips);
result.Add(new Tuple<int, int>(oppPlayerPos.Item1 - 1,
oppPlayerPos.Item2 - 1));
                }
            }

            // Check Down Lft
            if (IsLegalMove(oppPlayerPos.Item1 + 1,
            oppPlayerPos.Item2 - 1))
```

```
                    {
tempFlips.Clear();
varupRgt = CheckDiagonal(oppPlayerPos, player, (i =>i>= 0),
(i =>i< M), -1, 1, tempFlips);
                    if (upRgt)
                    {
UpdateFlips(new Tuple<int, int>(oppPlayerPos.Item1 + 1,
oppPlayerPos.Item2 - 1), tempFlips);
result.Add(new Tuple<int, int>(oppPlayerPos.Item1 + 1,
oppPlayerPos.Item2 - 1));
                        }
                }

                // Check Up Rgt
                if (IsLegalMove(oppPlayerPos.Item1 - 1,
                oppPlayerPos.Item2 + 1))
                    {
tempFlips.Clear();
vardownLft = CheckDiagonal(oppPlayerPos, player, (i =>i< N),
(i =>i>= 0), 1, -1, tempFlips);
                    if (downLft)
                    {
UpdateFlips(new Tuple<int, int>(oppPlayerPos.Item1 - 1,
oppPlayerPos.Item2 + 1), tempFlips);
result.Add(new Tuple<int, int>(oppPlayerPos.Item1 - 1,
oppPlayerPos.Item2 + 1));
                        }
                }

                // Check Down Rgt
                if (IsLegalMove(oppPlayerPos.Item1 + 1,
                oppPlayerPos.Item2 + 1))
```

```
            {
tempFlips.Clear();
varupLft = CheckDiagonal(oppPlayerPos, player, (i =>i>= 0),
(i =>i>= 0), -1, -1, tempFlips);
                if (upLft)
                {
UpdateFlips(new Tuple<int, int>(oppPlayerPos.Item1 + 1,
oppPlayerPos.Item2 + 1), tempFlips);
result.Add(new Tuple<int, int>(oppPlayerPos.Item1 + 1,
oppPlayerPos.Item2 + 1));
                }
            }

        return result;
    }

    public OthelloBoardSetPieceCreatedBoard(inti, int j,
    int player)
    {
varnewOthello = new OthelloBoard(this);
newOthello.Board[i, j] = player;
FlipPieces(i, j, player, newOthello);

newOthello.Flips.Clear();
        return newOthello;
    }
```

As has been the model so far, we describe the set of methods from Listing 16-3 in the following points:

- `AvailableMovesAroundPiece()`: This method starts at the position of an opponent's piece and checks all of its adjacent cells, seeking to set a piece that would flank various opponent pieces.

- `SetPieceCreatedBoard()`: sets a piece on the board and flips all opponent's pieces that are flanked by the new piece

To process and analyze every possible direction from an opponent's piece, we have included methods `CheckUpDown()`, `CheckLftRgt()`, and `CheckDiagonal()`. To avoid or minimize any duplicated code, we have condensed searches up and down in a single method. These searches are very similar in their coding; their only difference lies in the condition and direction of the loop (increase or decrease). Therefore, we coded the `CheckUpDown()` method using anonymous functions and a "direction" integer defining the direction the loop will take. Similar approaches were applied for `CheckLftRgt()` and `CheckDiagonal()`, as shown in Listing 16-4. You can check the conditions set for these methods in Listing 16-3.

Listing 16-4. Methods CheckUpDown(), CheckLftRgt(), CheckDiagonal(), UpdateFlips(), SetPiece(), FlipPieces(), and UpdatePiecePos()

```
private bool CheckUpDown(Tuple<int, int>oppPlayerPos,
int player, Func<int, bool> condition, int direction,
List<Tuple<int, int>>tempFlips)
{
    for (vari = oppPlayerPos.Item1; condition(i);
    i+=direction)
    {
```

```
            if (Board[i, oppPlayerPos.Item2] == player)
            {
UpdateFlips(oppPlayerPos, tempFlips);
                return true;
            }
            if (EmptyCell(i, oppPlayerPos.Item2))
            {
tempFlips.Clear();
                break;
            }
tempFlips.Add(new Tuple<int, int>(i, oppPlayerPos.Item2));
        }

        return false;
    }

    private void UpdateFlips(Tuple<int, int>oppPlayerPos,
    IEnumerable<Tuple<int, int>>tempFlips)
    {
        if (!Flips.ContainsKey(oppPlayerPos))
Flips.Add(oppPlayerPos, new List<Tuple<int, int>>(tempFlips));
        else
            Flips[oppPlayerPos].AddRange(tempFlips);
    }

    private bool CheckLftRgt(Tuple<int, int>oppPlayerPos,
    int player, Func<int, bool> condition, int direction,
    List<Tuple<int, int>>tempFlips)
    {
        for (vari = oppPlayerPos.Item2; condition(i);
        i+= direction)
        {
            if (Board[oppPlayerPos.Item1, i] == player)
```

```
                {
UpdateFlips(oppPlayerPos, tempFlips);
                return true;
                }
                if (EmptyCell(oppPlayerPos.Item1, i))
                {
tempFlips.Clear();
                break;
                }
tempFlips.Add(new Tuple<int, int>(oppPlayerPos.Item1, i));
            }

        return false;
    }

    private bool CheckDiagonal(Tuple<int, int>oppPlayerPos,
    int player, Func<int, bool>conditionRow, Func<int,
    bool>conditionCol, intdirectionRow, intdirectionCol,
    List<Tuple<int, int>>tempFlips)
    {
vari = oppPlayerPos.Item1;
var j = oppPlayerPos.Item2;

        while(conditionRow(i) &&conditionCol(j))
        {
            if (Board[i, j] == player)
            {
UpdateFlips(oppPlayerPos, tempFlips);
                return true;
            }

            if (EmptyCell(i, j))
            {
```

```
tempFlips.Clear();
                    break;
                }
tempFlips.Add(new Tuple<int, int>(i, j));
i += directionRow;
                j += directionCol;
            }

            return false;
        }

        public void SetPiece(inti, int j, int player)
        {
Board[i, j] = player;
FlipPieces(i, j, player, this);
        }

        private void FlipPieces(inti, int j, int player,
        OthelloBoardothello)
        {
varpiecesToFlip = Flips[new Tuple<int, int>(i, j)];
UpdatePiecePos(new Tuple<int, int>(i, j), player, othello);

            foreach (var pair in piecesToFlip)
            {
othello.Board[pair.Item1, pair.Item2] = player;
UpdatePiecePos(pair, player, othello);
            }
        }
```

```
        private void UpdatePiecePos(Tuple<int, int> pair, int
        player, OthelloBoardothello)
        {
varremoveFrom = player == 1 ? othello.Player2Pos : othello.
Player1Pos;
varaddTo = player == 1 ? othello.Player1Pos : othello.
Player2Pos;

            if (!addTo.Contains(pair))
addTo.Add(pair);
removeFrom.Remove(pair);
        }
```

Some of the methods just listed have not been discussed thus far; therefore, they are described in the following points:

- UpdateFlips(): adds the coordinate of an opponent's piece that must be flipped after a piece of the opposite color has been set on the board

- SetPiece(): sets a piece on the board and flips all opponent's pieces that are flanked by the new piece

- FlipPieces(): flips the set of opponent pieces using the Flips dictionary previously described and considering the coordinate of the new piece set on the board

- UpdatePiecePos(): updates properties Player1Pos and Player2Pos as pieces are flipped or added to the board

Finally, to assign a `UtilityValue` to every node in the Minimax tree, we will be relying on the set of methods illustrated in Listing 16-5.

Listing 16-5. Methods for Obtaining a Utility Value for a Game-End Node (Either a Leaf or a Maximum Depth Reached)

```
internal double HeuristicUtility()
{
    return PieceDifference();
}

private intPieceDifference()
{
    if (Player1Pos.Count == Player2Pos.Count)
        return 0;
    if (Player1Pos.Count > Player2Pos.Count)
        return 100 * Player1Pos.Count / (Player1Pos.
        Count + Player2Pos.Count);
    return -100 * Player2Pos.Count / (Player1Pos.Count
    + Player2Pos.Count);
}

internal double LeafNodeValue()
{
    if (Player1Pos.Count > Player2Pos.Count)
        return 100;
    if (Player1Pos.Count < Player2Pos.Count)
        return -100;
    return 0;
}
```

HeuristicUtility() is the method we call when we want to calculate a heuristic for a given board. Other methods are representatives of the heuristics explained before (in this case we will include onlyPieceDifference) and the leaf-node evaluation, which was also detailed before.

The OthelloBoard class assumes much of the lifting regarding game functionality, but we are still missing a component—the GUI (graphical user interface) that Othello requires to make it easier and more enjoyable for users to play. As mentioned before, this GUI will be coded in a Windows Forms application whose main class can be seen in Listing 16-6. The GUI will include controls such as turnBoxColor, a picture box whose background will be set to black or white depending on the current turn; board, a picture box representing the Othello board; aiPlayTimer, a timer used for the AI to check whether its turn is up; blackCountLabel and whiteCountLabel, two labels showing the number of pieces on the Othello board for the black and white players, respectively; and blacksList and whiteList, which are rich-text boxes displaying the cells occupied by each player. All these controls will be seen in future listings.

Listing 16-6. OthelloGui Class Representing the Visual Application of the Othello Game

```
public partial class OthelloGui : Form
    {
        private readonlyint _n;
        private readonlyint _m;
        private readonlyOthelloBoard _othelloBoard;
        private List<Tuple<int, int>> _availableMoves;
        private int _cellWidth;
        private int _cellHeight;
        private Minimax _minimax;
```

```
        public OthelloGui(OthelloBoardothelloBoard)
        {
InitializeComponent();
            _othelloBoard = othelloBoard;
            _n = _othelloBoard.N;
            _m = _othelloBoard.M;
            _availableMoves = _othelloBoard.AvailableMoves
            (_othelloBoard.Turn);
turnBox.BackColor = _othelloBoard.Turn == 1 ?Color.Black
:Color.White;
            _minimax = new Minimax(3, false);
aiPlayTimer.Enabled = true;
        }
}
```

The constructor of the class receives the OthelloBoard instance to be visualized using Windows Forms facilities. Its fields are also initialized in the constructor; these fields are as follows:

- _n: number of rows of the board

- _m: number of columns of the board

- _othelloBoard: instance of the OthelloBoard class

- _availableMoves: list of pairs (x, y) representing the available moves of the player in turn

- _cellWidth: cell width of the board as it will be represented graphically

- _cellHeight: cell height of the board as it will be represented graphically

- _minimax: instance of the Minimax class (to be described in the next section)

In this class we also implemented methods for handling paint and mouse-click events (Listing 16-7); the first draws all graphical elements (lines defining board, black and white pieces) and the second allows users to interact with the board by putting a piece of their color on the cell where the click occurred and assuming that cell matches an available move.

Listing 16-7. Methods for Handling Paint and Mouse-Click Events

```
        private void BoardPaint(object sender, PaintEventArgs e)
        {
var pen = new Pen(Color.Wheat);
            _cellWidth = board.Width / _n;
            _cellHeight = board.Height / _m;

            for (vari = 0; i< _n; i++)
e.Graphics.DrawLine(pen, new Point(i * _cellWidth, 0),
new Point(i * _cellWidth, i * _cellWidth + board.Height));

            for (vari = 0; i< _m; i++)
e.Graphics.DrawLine(pen, new Point(0, i * _cellHeight), new
Point(i * _cellHeight + board.Width, i * _cellHeight));

            for (vari = 0; i< _n; i++)
            {
                for (var j = 0; j < _m; j++)
                {
                    if (_othelloBoard.Board[i, j] == 1)
e.Graphics.FillEllipse(new SolidBrush(Color.Black), j *
_cellWidth, i * _cellHeight, _cellWidth, _cellHeight);
                    if (_othelloBoard.Board[i, j] == 2)
e.Graphics.FillEllipse(new SolidBrush(Color.White), j *
_cellWidth, i * _cellHeight, _cellWidth, _cellHeight);
                }
            }
```

```
            foreach (varavailableMove in _availableMoves)
e.Graphics.DrawRectangle(new Pen(Color.Yellow, 5),
availableMove.Item2 * _cellWidth, availableMove.Item1 *
_cellHeight, _cellWidth, _cellHeight);

        }

        private void BoardMouseClick(object sender, MouseEventArgs e)
        {
            if (e.Button == MouseButtons.Left)
            {
var click = new Tuple<int, int>(e.Y / _cellWidth, e.X / _cellHeight);
                if (_availableMoves.Contains(click))
                {
                    _othelloBoard.SetPiece(click.Item1, click.
                    Item2, _othelloBoard.Turn);
UpdateBoardGui();
                }
            }
        }
```

Notice that cells matching available moves are denoted on the board as yellow squares. The UpdateBoardGui() method (Listing 16-8), which is called in the mouse-click event, takes care of updating different GUI and game elements; for example, changing a label's text, modifying a rich-text box to show position of black and white pieces, changing the turn back to the other player, clearing the flips dictionary for a new play, calculating new available moves, and checking whether is empty. If there are no moves available for the player who just received the turn, then its turn is passed to the other player. If no player has any available move then the game has ended; determining that scenario is the goal of the final loop of length 2.

Listing 16-8. UpdateBoardGui() Method and AiPlayTimerTick()
Method for Handling the Timer Tick Event

```
        private void UpdateBoardGui()
        {
blackCountLabel.Text = "Blacks: " + _othelloBoard.Player1Pos.Count;
whiteCountLabel.Text = "Whites: " + _othelloBoard.Player2Pos.Count;

var blacks = "";
var whites = "";

            foreach (var black in _othelloBoard.Player1Pos)
                blacks += "(" + black.Item1 + "," + black.Item2
                + ")" + '\n';

            foreach (var white in _othelloBoard.Player2Pos)
                whites += "(" + white.Item1 + "," + white.Item2
                + ")" + '\n';

whitesList.Text = whites;
blacksList.Text = blacks;

board.Invalidate();

            for (vari = 0; i< 2; i++)
            {
                _othelloBoard.Turn = _othelloBoard.Turn ==
                1 ?2 : 1;
                _othelloBoard.Flips.Clear();
                _availableMoves = _othelloBoard.
AvailableMoves(_othelloBoard.Turn);
turnBox.BackColor = _othelloBoard.Turn == 1 ?Color.Black
:Color.White;
```

```
                   if (_availableMoves.Count> 0)
                       return;
               }
MessageBox.Show("Game Ended", "Result");
           }

       private void AiPlayTimerTick(object sender, EventArgs e)
       {
           if (_othelloBoard.Turn == 2)
           {
var move = _minimax.GetOptimalMove(_othelloBoard, false);
               _othelloBoard.SetPiece(move.Item1, move.Item2,
_othelloBoard.Turn);
UpdateBoardGui();
           }
       }
}
```

In order to allow the AI to play, we use a timer that checks every 1.5 secs if it's the AI's turn; if it is then we execute the Minimax algorithm, which will be coded in the following section, set the outputted move on the board, and update the game components as just detailed using the UpdateBoardGui() method.

Practical Problem: Implementing the Othello Game AI Using Minimax

At this point we have a complete, functional Othello game like the one depicted in Figure 16-9.

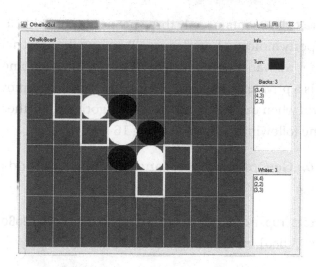

Figure 16-9. *Othello game developed using Windows Forms*

We are missing a fundamental component: the AI of the game. As mentioned before, our AI will consist of a Minimax player—a player that tries to play optimally assuming the other player is also playing optimally. The Minimax class, along with its properties, fields, and constructor, is shown in Listing 16-9.

Listing 16-9. Minimax Class, Properties, and Fields

```
public class Minimax
{
        public intMaxDepth{ get; set; }
        public bool Max { get; set; }
        private Tuple<int, int> _resultMove;

        public Minimax(intmaxDepth, bool max)
        {
MaxDepth = maxDepth;
            Max = max;
        }
}
```

The Minimax class contains only three properties or fields. The MaxDepth property indicates how deep we'll go into the search tree, Max defines whether we want to maximize or minimize the outcome, and _resultMove is a private variable we use for storing the first move of the best path found when executing the Minimax algorithm. Furthermore, we will include the following methods (Listing 16-10).

Listing 16-10. GetOptimalMove() and Execute() Methods of the Minimax Class

```
        public Tuple<int, int>GetOptimalMove(OthelloBoard
        board, bool max)
        {
Execute(board, max, 0);
            return _resultMove;
        }
private double Execute (OthelloBoard board, bool max, int depth)
        {
            if (depth == MaxDepth)
                return board.HeuristicUtility();
var children = board.Expand(max ? 1 : 2);
            if (children.Count == 0)
                return board.LeafNodeValue();
var result = !max ? double.MaxValue : double.MinValue;
            foreach (varothelloBoard in children)
            {
var value = Execute(othelloBoard, !max, depth + 1);
othelloBoard.UtilityValue = value;
                result = max ?Math.Max(value, result) :Math.
                Min(value, result);
            }
```

```
if (depth == 0)
    _resultMove = children.First(c =>c.UtilityValue
    == result).MoveFrom;

return result;
}
```

The Minimax algorithm is coded in the Execute() method. The GetOptimalMove() method is the simplified, public face of the algorithm used in the GUI. It is a simple design issue as it saves us from having to include the initial depth as well as other arguments in the public method; these arguments are unnecessary information for the GUI component.

It's now up to the reader to complement the code herein provided. You can add more heuristics, combine them in a weighted sum, experiment with weight values, optimize the Minimax algorithm (by means of an Alpha-Beta pruning technique), and create the strongest AI for the Othello game—the foundations have already been created throughout this chapter.

Summary

In this chapter, we briefly mentioned and studied some of the basic elements and problems of game theory. We ultimately submerged ourselves in a sub-branch of game theory known as adversarial search and examined one of its most popular representatives: the Minimax algorithm. We described an optimization technique for the algorithm—the Alpha-Beta pruning technique. Then, we introduced the famous Othello game and presented multiple heuristics for it. A full implementation of the Othello game in Windows Forms was also included, and the implementation of a very simple AI for this game using a single heuristic (PieceDifference) was included as well.

CHAPTER 17

Reinforcement Learning

So far in this book we have examined both supervised and unsupervised learning algorithms. In this chapter, we will discuss reinforcement learning algorithms. Remember: In *supervised learning* we had a dataset composed of samples (x, y) where x was usually a vector of features of some object (house, plane, person, city, and so on) and y was the correct classification of x. Thus, supervised learning was the process of learning or approximating a function from tabular data. This approach more closely resembles the way computers analyze data than the way humans do. Supervised learning simulates the process where you teach someone about different kinds of objects available in the world; for instance, you could show someone the image of an object with all its properties (color, size, etc.) and assign a name to it (y), so something like (yellow, 10cm, eatable, fruit) is a banana.

In *unsupervised learning* we don't have labeled data as we do in supervised learning. In this case, we don't use any external information (correct label of data). In unsupervised learning our goal is to learn the structure of data using the information that the data itself provides or intrinsically possesses, without the use of any external help as we did in supervised learning. In this sense, one could say that unsupervised learning is more independent of external entities or information and

© Arnaldo Pérez Castaño 2018
A. Pérez Castaño, *Practical Artificial Intelligence*,
https://doi.org/10.1007/978-1-4842-3357-3_17

more attached to data structure or data relations. Clustering, which was discussed in Chapter 13, is a clear example of unsupervised learning algorithms.

In this chapter we will study *reinforcement learning*, the machine learning paradigm that is considered the best approximation of the human way of thinking. This paradigm allows us to create AIs that evolve over time; this evolution of the "mind" is accomplished by means of penalties and rewards given to the agent for executing incorrect or correct actions. Thus, during this chapter, we will describe Markov decision processes (MDP), describe reinforcement learning methods such as Q learning and temporal difference (TD), and provide a coding example of a situation where RL allows us to design an agent that improves its performance over time and learns how to solve a maze in the shortest number of steps.

Note   AlphaGo, the AI created by Google's Deep Mind that defeated the world champion of the complex game of GO, Lee Sedol, in March 2016, learned the game through a reinforcement learning algorithm.

What Is Reinforcement Learning?

Reinforcement learning (RL), as with supervised learning and unsupervised learning, is not a method or algorithm but rather a broad family of algorithms that follow a common idea or paradigm. In reality, the three just mentioned represent paradigms for building AI methods; they represent the blueprint, and algorithms represent the realization of a procedure that resembles what the blueprint detailed.

In the RL paradigm, learning occurs by *trial-and-error*, having as the outcome either a reward or a punishment (negative reward), and the goal is to achieve the highest reward in the long term. One could say that RL is a continuous evolution or optimization over time. Figure 17-1 illustrates the basic flow of an RL algorithm. The agent interacts with the environment *acting* over it, then the environment updates the state of the agent and assigns a *reward* (which could be negative) to the agent for having moved to this new state.

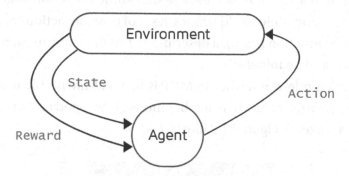

Figure 17-1. *Basic flow of a RL algorithm. The agent observes the environment, executes an action to interact with the environment, and receives positive, negative, or zero reward.*

It's important to consider that rewards do not have to always be immediate; there might be states with reward 0, which is the same as saying no reward. When developing an RL method, we model the environment, states, agent actions, and rewards; hence, the entire problem is a Markov decision process (we'll soon discuss this topic).

RL is based on the *Reward Hypothesis*, which states that all goals can be described by the maximization of expected cumulative reward.

A RL agent may implement different components—a policy that defines an agent's behavior, a value function defining how good each state and/or action is, and a model as a representation of the environment.

Note   Like a human, RL agents can construct and learn their own knowledge directly from raw inputs, such as vision, without any hardwired features or domain-specific heuristics.

Markov Decision Process

Markov decision processes (MDPs) are the most common approach to formally describing an environment in RL, and many problems can be modeled as MDPs. An MDP is a discrete state–time transition system that includes a set of possible world states *s*, a set of possible actions *a*, a real valued reward function *R(s, a)*, a description *T* of the effect of each action in each state, and an initial state s_0.

In order to understand what an MDP is in a real-life problem, let's consider an environment where a robot mouse is trapped and must find its way out of a maze, as Figure 17-2 illustrates.

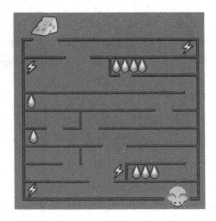

Figure 17-2. *The robot mouse must find a way out of the maze. Finding a water location rewards him with +100, finding the cheese has a reward of +10000, and electricty spots result in a punishment or negative reward of -1000.*

Assume the robot mouse is trying to reach the ultimate reward of cheese at the end of the maze (+10000 points) or the less significant reward of water along the way (+100 points), and at the same time it wants to avoid locations that deliver an electric shock (-1000 points). The mouse's wandering through the maze can be formalized as an MDP, which is a process with specified transition probabilities from state to state. An MDP for this problem could be modeled as follows:

- *Finite set of states*: possible positions of the mouse within the maze

- *Set of actions available in each state*: all possible moves of the mouse at each state, i.e., {up, down, left, right}, and when available; e.g., if on a corner it would have only two moves available

- *Transitions between states*: combination of a current state (given cell on the maze) and some action (move left) that leaves the mouse robot in a new position (state). Transitions can be associated with a set of probabilities that relate to more than one possible state.

- *Rewards associated with transitions*: in the maze scenario and for the mouse robot; most of the rewards are 0, but they're positive if you reach a point that has water or cheese and negative if you reach a cell with electricity

- *Discount factor γ in the range [0, 1]*: quantifies the difference in importance between immediate rewards and future rewards. For instance, when γ equals .7, and there's a reward of 5 after three steps, the present value of that reward is $.7^3 * 5$.

- *Memorylessness or Markov Property*: Once the current state is known, the history of the mouse's travels through the maze can be erased because the current Markov state contains all useful information from the history. In other words, "the future is independent of the past given the present." This is also known as the *Markov Property*.

Now, our goal in RL is to *maximize the sum of rewards in the long term,* which is given by the following formula:

$$\sum_{t=0}^{t=\infty} \gamma^t * r\big(x(t), a(t)\big)$$

where *t* is a time step, *r(x, a)* is the reward function, *x(t)* represents the state of the agent at time *t*, and *a(t)* the action executed when at that state and also at time *t*. This is the main problem RL algorithms try to solve, and it's basically an optimization problem where we optimize time. The sooner we get a reward, the more it will mean to us, because the discount factor will decrease the value of rewards over time. We use a discount factor for several reasons:

- To prefer earlier rewards

- To represent the uncertainty of the future

- Animal/human behavior shows preference for immediate reward

- Avoids infinite returns (we will soon define what a *return* is) in cyclic Markov processes

- When dealing with financial rewards an immediate reward may earn more interest than a delayed reward.

Other types of rewards we might find in different textbooks could be the following:

- *Total Reward:*

$$\sum_{t=1}^{\infty} r_t$$

- *Average Reward:*

$$\lim_{n \to \infty} \frac{r_1 + r_2 + \ldots + r_n}{n}$$

We could also see an MDP as a combination of a Markov reward process (MRP) and decisions. A *Markov reward process* consists of a set of states S, a state transition matrix T (as earlier), a reward function R, and a discount factor γ.

At the same time, an MRP) can be seen as a Markov chain with values. A *Markov chain* (a.k.a. Markov process) consists of a set of states S and a state transition matrix T. Figure 17-3 illustrates an MRP where we briefly model the working day of an android (it checks Facebook). Real numbers in the range [0.0; 1.0] indicate the probabilities of having a transition from one state to the other; circles indicate states, and rows indicate the transition from one state to the other. In this case, the leftmost state is the initial state.

In this figure, all actions are either stochastic— i.e., $T : S \, x \, A -> Prob(S)$ where $Prob(S)$ is a probability distribution—or deterministic, where $T : S \, x \, A -> S$.

Note   Both planning and MDPs are considered search problems, with the difference being that in the first we deal with explicit actions and subgoals and in the latter we deal with uncertainty and utilities.

In MDPs, a *horizon* determines whether our decision-making process will have an infinite time, a finite time, or an indefinite time (until some criteria is met). MDPs with infinite horizons are easier to solve as they do not have a deadline; furthermore, because in many cases it's not clear how long a process will execute, it's popular to consider infinite-horizon models of optimality.

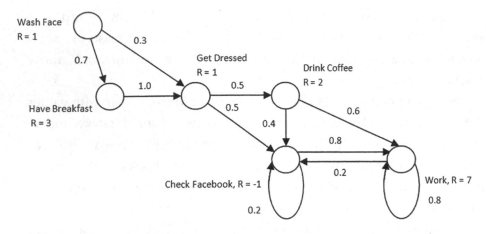

Figure 17-3. *MRP modeling the working day of an android*

An *infinite-horizon return* v_t is the total discounted reward from time step t up to infinity:

$$v_t = r_{t+1} + \gamma * r_{t+2} + \ldots = \sum_{k=0}^{\infty} \gamma^k * r_{t+k+1}$$

Notice again the convenience of the discount factor. If we were to add up all the rewards out into infinity, the sums would be infinite in general. To keep the math nice, and to put some pressure on the agent to get rewards sooner rather than later, we use a discount factor.

Value/Action–Value Functions & Policies

Having rewards in MRPs and MDPs permits us to define values for states depending on the associated rewards. These tabular values are part of the *value function, state–value function,* or simply *value of a state in an MRP*. It's the expected return starting from state s:

$$V(s) = R(s) + \gamma * \sum_{s' \in N(s)}^{|N(s)|} T[s, s'] * V(s')$$

In the preceding formula, we compute the expected long-term value of the next state by summing over all possible next states or neighbor states, s', the product of the probability of making a transition from s to s', and the infinite horizon expected discounted reward; i.e., value of s. This formulation is based on Bellman's Equation (1957), a.k.a. the Dynamic Programming Equation, and its Principle of Optimality, which states that an optimal policy has the property that whatever the initial state and initial decision are, the remaining decisions must constitute an optimal policy with regard to the state resulting from the first decision. In this case, the value function can be decomposed into an immediate reward R and a discounted value of a successor, neighbor state s'; i.e., $\gamma * V(s')$.

Note   In computer science, a problem that can be divided into subproblems that produce an overall optimal solution (such as using Bellman's Principle) is said to have optimal substructure.

To see how to calculate this equation, let's assume a discount factor $\gamma = 0.9$ and the MDP shown on a prior figure; we can calculate the value of the leftmost state (Wash Face) as follows:

$$V('Wash\ Face') = 1 + 0.9 * (0.7 * V('Have\ Breakfast') +$$
$$0.3 * V('Get\ Dressed'))$$

Notice that if we were to set $\gamma = 0$ then the values associated with each state would match its reward. To fully compute $V(s)$, for all s, we would need to solve n equations in n unknowns, considering n is the number of states in the MRP.

In classical planning, we created a plan that was either an ordered list of actions or a partially ordered set of actions (we discussed it in prior chapters) meant to be executed without reference to the state of the environment. In an MDP, the assumption is that you could potentially go from any state to any other state in one step. And so, to be prepared, it is typical to compute a whole policy rather than a simple plan.

A *policy* is a mapping from states to actions that defines a course of action or sequence of actions that the agent will follow in the environment. It's usually denoted by the Greek letter pi: $\pi(s)$. Because of the Markov property, we'll find that the choice of action only needs to be dependent on the current state (and possibly the current time) and not on any of the previous states. We'll try to find the policy that maximizes, for each state, the expected reward of executing the policy in that state. We will call such a policy an *optimal policy* and denote it as $\pi^*(s)$.

A policy can be deterministic and output a single action for each state or stochastic and output an action dependent on various probabilities.

Note   Since a policy is a sequence of actions, when you take an MDP and fix a policy then all actions have been chosen and what you have left is a Markov chain.

The *state-value function* V. at follows policy π in an MDP is the expected return starting from state s and then following policy π:

$$V_\pi(s) = R_\pi(s) + \gamma * \sum_{s' \in N(s)}^{|N(s)|} T_\pi[s, s'] * V_\pi(s')$$

An *optimal state-value function* is the maximum value function over all policies, as follows:

$$V_\pi^*(s) = \max_\pi V_\pi(s)$$

The *action-value function* Q(s, a), or simply *Q-function*, is the expected return starting from state s, taking action a, and then following policy π, as follows:

$$Q_\pi(s, a) = R(s, a) + \gamma * \sum_{s' \in N(s)}^{|N(s)|} T_\pi^a[s, s'] * V_\pi(s')$$

Note that $Q(s, a)$ can be expressed in terms of $V(s)$ and that it considers not only states but also actions leading to states.

Note   The Q-function represents the quality of a certain action given a state.

An *optimal action–value function* is the maximum action–value function over all policies, as follows:

$$Q_\pi^* (s, a) = \max_\pi Q_\pi (s, a)$$

What would be the goal of an RL agent? Its goal should be to learn an optimal policy by optimizing either $V(s)$ or $Q(s, a)$; it has been proven that all optimal policies achieve the optimal state–value and action–value functions, as follows:

$$V_\pi^* (s) = Q_\pi^* (s, \pi(s)) = V^* = Q^*$$

where V*, Q* represent the optimal values of $V(s)$ and $Q(s, a)$ respectively. Thus, it would seem logical to try to optimize one of these functions to obtain an optimal policy for the agent. Remember that this is our main goal in MDP and specifically in RL.

If the reward and transition values are known to the agent, then he can use a *model-based* algorithm known as *value iteration* to calculate V* and obtain an optimal policy.

Another approach for obtaining an optimal policy and solving MDPs is the *policy iteration* algorithm. This is also a model-based method that manipulates the policy directly rather than finding it indirectly via the optimal value function. As occurs with the value iteration method, it assumes the agent is aware of the reward and transition functions.

Later, we will discuss *Q-learning*, a *model-free* learning method that can be used in situations where the agent initially knows only that certain states and actions are possible but is unaware of the transition and reward probability functions. In Q-learning the agent improves its behavior by learning from the history of interactions with the environment. It only discovers that there is a reward for going from one state to another via a given action when it does so and receives a reward. Similarly, it only figures out what transitions are available from a given state by ending up in that state and looking at its options. If state transitions are stochastic, it learns the probability of transitioning between states by observing how frequently different transitions occur.

Note   In a model-based method, the agent has a built-in model (reward and transition functions) of the environment and therefore can simulate it so as to find the right decision. In a model-free method, the agent knows how to act, but doesn't explicitly know anything about the environment.

Value Iteration Algorithm

In *value iteration* we will compute V*(s) for all states *s* by applying an iterative procedure in which our current approximation for $V^*(s)$ gets closer to the optimal value over time. We start by initializing $V(s)$ to 0 for all states. We could actually initialize to any values we want, but it's easiest to just start at 0. This algorithm uses the updating rule for $V(s)$; a pseudocode of the method is shown in the following lines:

```
ValueIteration(R, T, S, A, γ, ε)
{
        V(s) = InitializeZero();
        V'(s) = InitializeZero();
        δ = MinValue;

        do
        {
                foreach (state s in S)
                {
```

$$V'(s) = R(s) + \gamma * max_a \sum_{s' \in N(s)}^{|N(s)|} T[s, a, s'] * V'(s');$$

```
                        if (|V(s)-V'(s)| > δ ) {
                                δ=|V(s)-V'(s)|;
                        }
                }
        }
        while (δ < ε * (1−γ)/γ)

        return V(s);
}
```

A common stopping condition for this problem is having a change in value from step t to step $t + 1$ less than or equal to a predefined epsilon multiplied by a discount factor variable, as shown in the previous pseudocode. In this case, δ represents the maximum change of $V(s)$ in some iteration. V and V' represent utility vectors and ε the maximum error allowed in the utility of a state. This algorithm converges to the correct utilities over time.

Policy Iteration Algorithm

In the *policy iteration* algorithm we search for optimal policy and utility values at the same time; thus, we manipulate the policy directly rather than finding it indirectly via the optimal value function. A pseudocode of the algorithm is shown in the following lines:

```
PolicyIteration(R, T, S, A)
{
        π = Random();

        do
        {
                V  = PolicyEvaluation(π);
                unchanged = true;
                foreach (state s in S)
                {
                        if (maxₐ Σ ... T[s,a,s'] * V(s') >
```

$$\text{if } (max_a \sum_{s' \in N(s)}^{|N(s)|} T[s, a, s'] * V(s') >$$

$$\sum_{s' \in N(s)}^{|N(s)|} T[s, \pi(s), s'] * V(s')) \ \{$$

$$\pi(s) = max_a \sum_{s' \in N(s)}^{|N(s)|} T[s, a, s'] *$$

$$V(s');$$

```
                        }
                        unchanged = false;

                }
        }
        while (unchanged )

        return π;
}
```

where V is the utility vector and π. presents the policy outputted by the algorithm, initialized with random values. The `PolicyEvaluation()` subroutine solves the following:

system of linear equations:

$$R(s_i) + \gamma * max_a \sum_{s' \in N(s_i)}^{|N(s_i)|} T[s_i, \pi(s_i), s'] * V'(s')$$

PI picks an initial policy, usually just by taking rewards on states as their utilities and computing a policy according to the maximum expected utility principle. Then, it iteratively performs two steps: value determination, which calculates the utility of each state given the current policy, and policy improvement, which updates the current policy if any improvement is possible. The algorithm terminates when the policy stabilizes. Policy iteration often converges in a few iterations, but each iteration is expensive; recall the method has to solve large systems of linear equations.

Q-Learning & Temporal Difference

The value iteration and policy iteration algorithms work perfectly for determining an optimal policy, but they assume our agent has a great deal of problem-specific knowledge. Specifically, they assume the agent accurately knows the transition function and the reward for all states in the environment. This is actually quite a bit of information; in many cases, our agent may not have access to this.

Fortunately, there is a way to learn this information. In essence, we can trade learning time for a priori knowledge. One way to do this is through a form of reinforcement learning known as Q-learning. *Q-learning* is a form of model-free learning, meaning that an agent does not need to have any model of the environment; it only needs to know what states exist and what actions are possible in each state. The way this works is as follows: we assign each state an estimated value, called a Q value. When we visit a state and receive a reward, we use this to update our estimate of the value of that state. (Since our rewards might be stochastic, we may need to visit a state many times.)

Considering that $V^*(s) = \max\limits_{a'} Q(s,a')$, we can rewrite the previously detailed formula for $Q(s, a)$ only in terms of the Q function.

$$Q_\pi\left(s,a\right) = R\left(s,a\right) + \gamma * \sum_{s' \in N(s)}^{|N(s)|} T_\pi^a\left[s,s'\right] * Q_\pi\left(s',a\right)$$

The previous formula is the update rule used in the Q-learning algorithm, described in the following lines:

```
QLearning(R,T,S,A)
{
        Q = InitQTableZeros();

        do
        {
                a  = SelectAction();
                s' = NewState();
                r = ReceiveReward();

                Q(s, a) = r + γ * maxₐ, Q(s',a')
        }
        while (conditionNotMet)
}
```

For Q-learning to converge we must guarantee that every state is visited infinitely often; one cannot learn from that which it does not experience, and therefore it must infinitely visit every state in order to guarantee convergence and find an optimal policy.

Q-learning belongs to a class of methods known as temporal difference algorithms. In a *temporal difference algorithm (TDA)* we learn by reducing the difference between estimates at different time frames (t, t'). Q-learning is a particular case of TDA where we reduce the estimate of Q for a state and its consecutive states, also known as neighbors or successors. We could just as well design an algorithm that reduces discrepancies between this state and more distant descendants or ancestors.

The most popular TD algorithm is probably TD(λ) (Sutton 1988), a general version of TDA that relies on the idea that we can calculate Q as follows:

$$Q^n\left(s_t, a_t\right) = r_t + \gamma * r_{t+1} + \ldots + \gamma^{n-1} * r_{t+n-1} + \gamma^n * \max_a Q\left(s_{t+n}, a\right)$$

Notice in the previous formulation that we do not only include a one-step lookahead as we did in Q-learning, but rather we are considering n steps into the future. TD(λ) mixes various lookahead distances using a $0 \le \lambda \le 1$ parameter in the following manner:

$$Q^\lambda\left(s_t, a_t\right) = (1-\lambda) * \left[Q^1\left(s_t, a_t\right) + \lambda * Q^2\left(s_t, a_t\right) + \lambda^2 * Q^3\left(s_t, a_t\right) + \ldots\right]$$

When considering $\lambda = 0$ we end up with the Q-learning rule, the one where we simply look one step ahead. As we increase λ, he algorithm places more emphasis on discrepancies based on more-distant lookaheads. When we reach the value $\lambda = 1$, only the observed r_{t+i} values are considered, with no contribution from the current Q estimate value. The motivation for the TD(λ) method is that in some settings training will be more efficient if more-distant lookaheads are considered.

Practical Problem: Solving a Maze Using Q-Learning

In this practical problem we will demonstrate the application of the Q-learning method through a very simple and intuitive situation: solving a maze. In the maze, the agent starts at cell (0, 0) and must find a way out at cell (n - 1, m - 1) where n represents the number of rows and m the number of columns in a zero index–based matrix. Figure 17-4 illustrates the maze to be solved in this chapter.

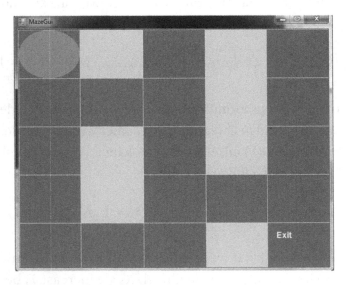

Figure 17-4. *Maze to be solved*

Notice how in the previous maze there are several policies the agent can follow to reach the exit cell, but there's only one optimal policy (Figure 17-5).

Because learning will occur over time (as occurs in real life) we must guarantee a continuous visit of every state (cell) in each episode; this is the necessary condition for Q-learning to converge. An *episode* is how we'll refer to an agent's completing the maze, and whenever the maze is completed we'll say that the agent will move from episode E to episode E + 1.

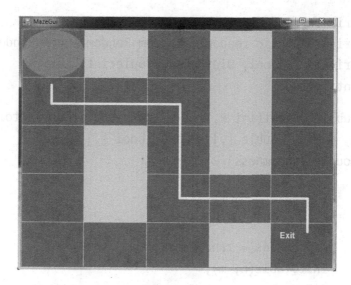

Figure 17-5. *Optimal policy followed by the agent to solve the maze*

The Q-learning agent, which we will call *Qagent*, is represented by the class shown in Listing 17-1.

Listing 17-1. Properties, Fields, and Constructor of the QAgent Class

```
public class QAgent
{
        public int X { get; set; }
        public int Y { get; set; }
        public Dictionary<Tuple<int, int>, List<double>>
        QTable { get; set; }
        public double Randomness { get; set; }
        public double[,] Reward { get; set; }
        private readonly bool[,] _map;
        private readonly int _n;
        private readonly int _m;
```

```
private readonly double _discountFactor;
private static readonly Random Random = new Random();
private readonly Dictionary<Tuple<int, int>,
int> _freq;

public QAgent(int x, int y, double discountFactor, int
n, int m, double [,] reward, bool [,] map,
double randomness)
{
    X = x;
    Y = y;
    Randomness = randomness;
    InitQTable(n, m);
    _n = n;
    _m = m;
    Reward = reward;
    _map = map;
    _discountFactor = discountFactor;
    _freq = new Dictionary<Tuple<int, int>, int>
    {{new Tuple<int, int>(0, 0), 1}};
}
}
```

This class contains the following properties or fields:

- X: represents the row of the agent's position on the board

- Y: represents the column of the agent's position on the board

- QTable: matrix representing the Q function in tabular form, i.e., the $Q(s, a)$ function where rows indicate states and columns indicate actions. It's coded as a dictionary of Tuple<int, int> (states) and a list of four (actions up, down, left, right) double values for each tuple.

- Randomness: Because from time to time we need to wander around to try to get the agent to visit every state, we use the Randomness variable to indicate a value in the range [0; 1] corresponding to the chance of generating a random action.

- Reward: represents the reward matrix for every state

- _ map: variable that represents the map of the environment (maze)

- _n: number of rows in the environment

- _m: number of columns in the environment

- _discountFactor: discount factor as previously detailed and used in the Q-learning update rule

- _freq: dictionary detailing the frequency of visit of every state; it will be used in the strategy applied to guarantee the agent visits every state infinitely often and seeking to obtain an optimal policy

The InitQTable() method (Listing 17-2) included in the class constructor was created with the purpose of initializing the QTable; i.e., the dictionary of (state, {actionUp, actionDown, actionLeft, actionRight}) entries. At the beginning it will be that $Q(s, a) = 0$ for every possible action a.

Listing 17-2. InitQTable() Method

```
private void InitQTable(int n, int m)
{
    QTable = new Dictionary<Tuple<int, int>, List<double>>();

    for (var i = 0; i < n; i++)
    {
        for (var j = 0; j < m; j++)
            QTable.Add(new Tuple<int, int>(i, j), new
            List<double> { 0, 0, 0, 0});
    }
}
```

The Q-learning process occurs in the following method (Listing 17-3); the `actionByFreq` parameter will determine if we use the strategy of visiting states by *frequency + randomness* or if we will rely only on Q values to complete the maze. Since every learning process requires some time, we will need to rely merely on the frequency + randomness strategy to try to "learn"—i.e., visit every state frequently enough to learn from these experiences and be able to learn in the end an optimal policy that would lead us to the exit of the maze in the shortest time and in the shortest number of steps.

Listing 17-3. InitQTable() Method

```
public void QLearning(bool actionByFreq = false)
{
    var currentState = new Tuple<int, int>(X, Y);
    var action = SelectAction(actionByFreq);

    if (!_freq.ContainsKey(ActionToTuple(action)))
        _freq.Add(ActionToTuple(action), 1);
```

```
    else
        _freq[ActionToTuple(action)]++;
    ActionToTuple(action, true);

    var reward = Reward[currentState.Item1,
    currentState.Item2];

    QTable[currentState][(int) action] = reward +
    _discountFactor * QTable[new Tuple<int, int>(X, Y)].Max();
}
```

The very important action-selection strategy that will lead the agent into learning an optimal policy is coded in the SelectAction() method shown in Listing 17-4. In case the actionByFreq variable has been activated (set to True), the agent will perform an action according to a frequency + randomness strategy; otherwise, it will always choose the $Q(s', a)$ with the highest value.

Listing 17-4. SelectAction() Method

```
private QAgentAction SelectAction(bool actionByFreq)
{
    var bestValue = double.MinValue;
    var bestAction = QAgentAction.None;
    var availableActions = AvailableActions();

    if (actionByFreq)
        return FreqStrategy(availableActions);

    for (var i = 0; i < 4; i++)
    {
        if (!availableActions.Contains(Action
        Selector(i)))
            continue;
```

```
        var value = QTable[new Tuple<int, int>(X, Y)][i];
        if (value > bestValue)
        {
            bestAction = ActionSelector(i);
            bestValue = value;
        }
    }

    return bestAction;
}
```

The previous method uses the FreqStrategy() method seen in Listing 17-5. In this method, we apply a random action with probability 0.5 or a frequency-based visit; i.e., visit the adjacent state least visited according to the _freq dictionary.

Listing 17-5. FreqStrategy() Method

```
private QAgentAction FreqStrategy(List<QAgentAction>
availableActions)
{
    var newPos = availableActions.Select(availableAction =>
    ActionToTuple(availableAction)).ToList();
    var lowest = double.MaxValue;
    var i = 0;
    var bestIndex = 0;

    if (Random.NextDouble() <= Randomness)
        return availableActions[Random.Next
        (availableActions.Count)];

    foreach (var tuple in newPos)
    {
```

```
    if (!_freq.ContainsKey(tuple))
    {
        bestIndex = i;
        break;
    }

    if (_freq[tuple] <= lowest)
    {
        lowest = _freq[tuple];
        bestIndex = i;
    }

    i++;
}

return availableActions[bestIndex];
}
```

To determine the set of available actions for the agent (the one that does not make the agent stumble against a wall) we included in the *QAgent* class the *AvailableActions()* method, as Listing 17-6 illustrates.

Listing 17-6. AvailableActions() Method

```
private List<QAgentAction> AvailableActions()
{
    var result = new List<QAgentAction>();

    if (X - 1 >= 0 && _map[X - 1, Y])
        result.Add(QAgentAction.Up);

    if (X + 1 < _n && _map[X + 1, Y])
        result.Add(QAgentAction.Down);

    if (Y - 1 >= 0 && _map[X, Y - 1])
        result.Add(QAgentAction.Left);
```

657

```
    if (Y + 1 < _m && _map[X, Y + 1])
        result.Add(QAgentAction.Right);

    return result;
}
```

We adopted the convention of matching actions in the order
{up, down, left, right} with integers starting from 0; hence, up = 0,
down = 1, left = 2, right = 3. The ActionSelector() method shown in
Listing 17-7 mutates an integer into its equivalent action (we'll soon see
the QAgentAction enum).

In Listing 17-7 we can also see the ActionToTuple() method, which
converts a QAgentAction into a Tuple<int,int> representing the resulting
state after executing that action.

Listing 17-7. ActionSelector() and ActionToTuple() Methods

```
public QAgentAction ActionSelector(int action)
{
    switch (action)
    {
        case 0:
            return QAgentAction.Up;
        case 1:
            return QAgentAction.Down;
        case 2:
            return QAgentAction.Left;
        case 3:
            return QAgentAction.Right;
        default:
            return QAgentAction.None;
    }
}
```

```
public Tuple<int, int> ActionToTuple(QAgentAction action,
bool execute = false)
{
    switch (action)
    {
        case QAgentAction.Up:
            if (execute) X--;
            return new Tuple<int, int>(X - 1, Y);
        case QAgentAction.Down:
            if (execute) X++;
            return new Tuple<int, int>(X + 1, Y);
        case QAgentAction.Left:
            if (execute) Y--;
            return new Tuple<int, int>(X, Y - 1);
        case QAgentAction.Right:
            if (execute) Y++;
            return new Tuple<int, int>(X, Y + 1);
        default:
            return new Tuple<int, int>(-1, -1);
    }
}
```

To conclude the QAgent class, we add the Reset() method (Listing 17-8), which resets or prepares the agent for a new episode by setting it to the start position and cleaning the _frequency dictionary. The QAgentAction enum describing possible agent actions is shown in Listing 17-8.

Listing 17-8. Reset() Method and QAgentAction Enum

```
public void Reset()
{
    X = 0;
    Y = 0;
```

```
        _freq.Clear();
    }

public enum QAgentAction
{
    Up, Down, Left, Right, None
}
```

We already presented the machine learning code of the program, but we are missing a component: the GUI on Windows Forms.

The inheritor of the Form class that will visually represent the maze is MazeGui, illustrated in Listing 17-9. Remember that we are coding a Windows Forms application.

Listing 17-9. Fields and Constructor from MazeGui Class

```
public partial class MazeGui : Form
    {
        private readonly int _n;
        private readonly int _m;
        private readonly bool[,] _map;
        private readonly QAgent _agent;
        private Stopwatch _stopWatch;
        private int _episode;

        public MazeGui(int n, int m, bool [,] map, double [,]
        reward)
        {
            InitializeComponent();
            timer.Interval = 100;
            _n = n;
            _m = m;
            _map = map;
            _agent = new QAgent(0, 0, 0.9, _n, _m, reward,
            map, .5);
```

```
        _stopWatch = new Stopwatch();
    }
}
```

The class contains the following properties or fields:

- _n: number of rows in the maze

- _m: number of columns in the maze

- _map: matrix with Boolean values indicating whether a cell is a wall or not

- _agent: instance of the QAgent class

- _stopWatch: stopwatch used to measure the time taken in every episode of the Q-learning process

- _episode: number of episodes carried out so far in the Q-learning process

To draw all elements on the maze, we implement the Paint event for the drawing control (Picture Box) as shown in Listing 17-10.

Listing 17-10. Paint Event of the Picture Box Representing the Maze

```
private void MazeBoardPaint(object sender, PaintEventArgs e)
{
    var pen = new Pen(Color.Wheat);

    var cellWidth = mazeBoard.Width / _n;
    var cellHeight = mazeBoard.Height / _m;

    for (var i = 0; i < _n; i++)
        e.Graphics.DrawLine(pen, new Point(i * cellWidth, 0),
        new Point(i * cellWidth, i * cellWidth +
        mazeBoard.Height));
```

```
for (var i = 0; i < _m; i++)
    e.Graphics.DrawLine(pen, new Point(0, i * cell
    Height), new Point(i * cellHeight + mazeBoard.Width,
    i * cellHeight));

for (var i = 0; i < _map.GetLength(0); i++)
{
    for (var j = 0; j < _map.GetLength(1); j++)
    {
        if (!_map[i, j])
            e.Graphics.FillRectangle(new Solid
            Brush(Color.LightGray), j * cellWidth,
            i * cellHeight, cellWidth, cellHeight);
    }
}

for (var i = 0; i < _map.GetLength(0); i++)
{
    for (var j = 0; j < _map.GetLength(1); j++)
    {
        if (_map[i, j])
            e.Graphics.DrawString(String.Format("{0:0.00}",
            _agent.QTable[new Tuple<int, int>(i, j)][0].
            ToString(CultureInfo.GetCultureInfo
            ("en-US"))) + "," +
            String.Format("{0:0.00}", _agent.QTable[new
            Tuple<int, int>(i, j)][1].ToString(CultureInfo.
            GetCultureInfo("en-US"))) + "," +
            String.Format("{0:0.00}", _agent.QTable[new
            Tuple<int, int>(i, j)][2].ToString
            (CultureInfo.GetCultureInfo("en-US"))) + "," +
```

```
            String.Format("{0:0.00}", _agent.QTable[new
            Tuple<int, int>(i, j)][3].ToString(CultureInfo.
            GetCultureInfo("en-US")))
        ,new Font("Arial", 8, FontStyle.Bold),
        new SolidBrush(Color.White), j * cellWidth,
        i * cellHeight);
    }
}

    e.Graphics.FillEllipse(new SolidBrush(Color.
    Tomato), _agent.Y * cellWidth, _agent.X *
    cellHeight, cellWidth, cellHeight);
    e.Graphics.DrawString("Exit", new Font("Arial", 12,
    FontStyle.Bold), new SolidBrush(Color.Yellow),
    (_m - 1) * cellWidth + 15, (_n - 1) * cellHeight + 15);
}
```

We will draw the agent as an ellipse and the walls as gray cells; we will also draw four values on each walkable cell: the values $Q(s, a)$ for state s and all possible actions.

To get and execute an action from the agent we included a timer that triggers every second and calls upon the QLearning() method of the agent using the frequency + randomness strategy while the current episode is less than 20. It's also in the method that handles the tick event (Listing 17-11) that we reset the stopWatch and the agent's state and write the episode elapsed time in a file.

Note   When in a goal state *s*, we do not apply the Q-learning rule to update *Q(s, a)*; on the contrary, we take the reward value of the goal state and assign it directly to *Q(s, a)*.

Finally, we refresh the mazeBoard to show the new set of changes to the GUI.

Listing 17-11. Method Handling the Tick Event

```
private void TimerTick(object sender, EventArgs e)
{
    if (!_stopWatch.IsRunning)
        _stopWatch.Start();
    if (_agent.X != _n - 1 || _agent.Y != _m - 1)
        _agent.QLearning(_episode < 20);
    else
    {
        _agent.QTable[new Tuple<int, int>
        (_n - 1, _m - 1)] = new List<double>
                                        {
                                        _agent.Reward
                                        [_n - 1, _m - 1],
                                        _agent.Reward
                                        [_n - 1, _m - 1],
                                        _agent.Reward
                                        [_n - 1, _m - 1],
                                        _agent.Reward
                                        [_n - 1, _m - 1]
                                        };
        _stopWatch.Stop();
        _agent.Reset();

        var file = new StreamWriter("E:/time_difference.txt",
        true);
        file.WriteLine(_stopWatch.ElapsedMilliseconds);
        file.Close();
```

```
        _stopWatch.Reset();
        _episode++;
    }

    mazeBoard.Refresh();
  }
}
```

Now that we have all components in place, let's try to test the application and run it, as we have done throughout this book, in a console application, creating the necessary map and reward matrixes (Listing 17-12).

Listing 17-12. Testing the MazeGui Application

```
var map = new [,]
            {
                {true, false, true, false, true},
                {true, true, true, false, true},
                {true, false, true, false, true},
                {true, false, true, true, true},
                {true, true, true, false, true}
            };
var reward = new [,]
            {
                {-0.01, -0.01, -0.01, -0.01, -0.01},
                {-0.01, -0.01, -0.01, -0.01, -0.01},
                {-0.01, -0.01, -0.01, -0.01, -0.01},
                {-0.01, -0.01, -0.01, -0.01, -0.01},
                {-0.01, -0.01, -0.01, -0.01, 1},
            };

Application.EnableVisualStyles();
Application.SetCompatibleTextRenderingDefault(false);
Application.Run(new MazeGui(5, 5, map, reward));
```

The result obtained after executing the code from Listing 17-12 would be an instance of the Windows Forms application developed throughout this chapter (Figure 17-6). The reward function contains a reward of 1 for the goal state and -0.01 for any other state. Once the agent has completed the first episode the goal state (Exit) will contain reward 1 for every action; i.e., Q('Exit', {up, down, left, right}) = 1.

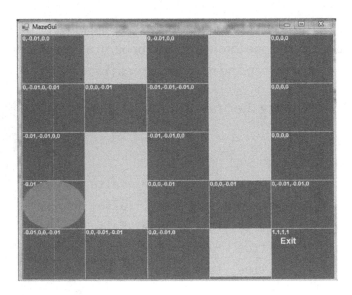

Figure 17-6.   *Episode 2, the QAgent is learning and updating Q values, which are shown in the upper-left corner of every cell*

Using the exploration strategy previously described (the one where we mix frequency of visited cells and randomness for executing actions), we continuously visit each state in each episode. After 20 episodes have been completed, the agent starts taking actions that rely only on the Q values learned and always executing the action that corresponds to *Q(s', a)* with the highest value. In this case, we were able to find the optimal policy, which was detailed in Figure 17-5.

Figure 17-7 illustrates the values ultimately calculated for *Q(s, a)* and after 20 episodes have passed. The reader can check that a path starting at cell (0, 0) and choosing always the action (remember they appeared in the order up, down, left, right) with the highest Q value will lead it to the optimal policy—the one leading to the Exit (goal state) in the least number of steps.

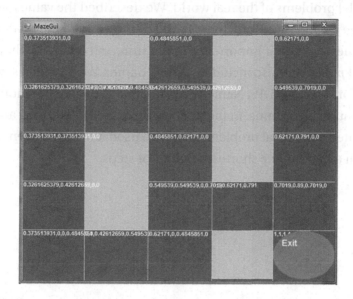

Figure 17-7. *Optimal policy found and executed by the agent*

Recall that our goal in Q-learning is to actually learn the Q function, *Q(s, a)*. In this case, we learn the function in its tabular form, which has states as rows and actions as columns of a table or matrix. In some scenarios it might be intractable to do it this way, given the fact that we may have a large state space. In such a scenario, we can rely on a function approximator such as neural networks to approximate the Q function. This is actually the approach used by Tesauro in its popular backgammon agent, capable of defeating the backgammon world champion of its time.

Summary

In this chapter, we described the interesting topic of reinforcement learning (RL), one of the most important machine learning paradigms along supervised and unsupervised Learning. We began by defining Markov decision processes (MDPs), the mathematical framework used in RL to model problems of the real world. We described the value function (V) and the action–value function (Q) and demonstrated the relationship between these and their importance in obtaining an optimal policy. The concept of *policy* was also included in the chapter. We provided several methods for solving MDPs. Namely, we detailed the value iteration and policy iteration algorithms. In the end, we discussed Q-learning and implemented a practical problem where we used it to get an agent to learn how to exit a maze in the shortest number of steps.

Index

A

A Beautiful Mind, 590
Activision-Blizzard
      (Call of Duty), 549
Adversarial search
  agents, 593
  board-games analysis, 593
  constant-sum game, 595
  deterministic game
     environment, 594
  imperfect information
     game, 595
  Lee Sedol *vs.* AlphaGo, 594
  methods, game types, 595
  Minimax search algorithm (*see*
     Minimax search algorithm)
  perfect information game, 595
  stochastic game
     environment, 594
  utility function, 594
  zero-sum game, 595
Agent architectures
  deliberative architecture
    alternatives generation, 122
    BDI architecture (*see* Beliefs,
     Desires, and Intentions
     (BDI) architecture)
    diagram, 120
    filtering, 122
    goal-based behavior, 119
    logical reasoning, 119
    means-end reasoning, 121
    planning component,
     121–122
    practical reasoning, 121
    problems, 119
  hybrid architecture
    goal-based component, 127
    horizontal and vertical
     layering, 128–130
    mediator function, 130
    reactive and deliberative
     components, 128
  InteRRaP, 133–134
  properties, 113
  reactive architecture
    (subsumption)
    behavior-based, 115
    Brooks' architecture, 115
    characteristics, 116
    cleaning agent, 115–118
    diagram, 114
    principle, 116
    reactive agent, 114
  touring machines, 131–132

© Arnaldo Pérez Castaño 2018
A. Pérez Castaño, *Practical Artificial Intelligence*,
https://doi.org/10.1007/978-1-4842-3357-3

K

L

Printed in the United States
By Bookmasters